£50.85

The State of the Environment of England and Wales: Coasts

March 1999

London: The Stationery Office Ltd

Commissioning organisation
Environment Agency
Rio House
Waterside Drive
Aztec West
Almondsbury
Bristol BS32 4UD

Tel 01454 624400
Fax 01454 624409

ISBN 011 310 162 7

Acknowledgements
Several organisations have helped identify relevant information sources for this report. Particular
thanks are due to the Centre for Coastal and Marine Sciences, Plymouth; CSERGE, University of East
Anglia; Department of Marine Sciences and Coastal Management, University of Newcastle upon
Tyne.

Data from the Wetland Bird Survey were kindly provided by the British Trust for Ornithology. The
Wetland Bird Survey (WeBS) indices are collated by a partnership between the British Trust for
Ornithology, The Wildfowl & Wetlands Trust, Royal Society for the Protection of Birds and the Joint
Nature Conservation Committee (the last on behalf of English Nature, Scottish Natural Heritage and
the Countryside Council for Wales and the Environment and Heritage Service in Northern Ireland)

Cover photographs: top   Three Cliffs Bay, Gower, Wales (Environment Agency)
                       bottom   Torquay Marina, Devon, England (Environment Agency)

Foreword

Following on from an evaluation of the state of the freshwater environment of England and Wales, we have now examined the state of the coastal environment. There could be no better time to do it. Globally, we are threatened with the uncertainties brought about by the recent evidence of an increase in the warming of the Earth's atmosphere. The greatest threats are to the coastal environment.

Expected sea level rises, exacerbated in places by the sinking of the land, will place increasing strains on our coastal defences. This is not simply a problem for the coast itself, because some 2,200 square kilometres of land - primarily in eastern England - are below sea level. And on top of this, there is likely to be an increase in storm intensity which can have very serious consequences for many coastal areas. Increased temperatures will also encourage increased algal growth in shallow coastal waters, which will probably be to the detriment of inshore fisheries, wildlife and amenities. It is therefore important to establish, now, the state of the coastal environment and the pressures placed upon it - both by human activities and by nature.

The coastline of England and Wales has a remarkable history. It has been shaped by many processes since the last ice age, and has been subject to the complete range of pressures which the human population is capable of bringing to bear upon it. Our coastline has been heavily occupied, modified and, in places, abused. Materials have been extracted from it, both animate and inanimate, and unwanted materials have been deposited onto beaches and disposed of into neighbouring coastal waters. Such practices are now carefully controlled under a range of environmental licences, but still present an increasingly complex set of stresses and strains upon the sustained use of our coasts and coastal waters.

In addition to the early industrial use of the coastal margin, the seaside and coastal areas in general have for a long time been a focal point of leisure and recreation. Indeed, with the exception of the exploitation of oil and gas, leisure activities constitute by far the largest commercial value of our coastal areas. These combined uses of the coasts - which in themselves are usually in conflict - have to be reconciled with the incalculable value of this nation's rich and varied wildlife which depends upon a clean and undisturbed range of unique habitats.

The problems confronting the coastal environment are complex and increasing, partly exacerbated by the effects of climate change. The current means of integrating all of these problems into a comprehensive management strategy is also likely to come under increasing pressure. There is clearly a need to develop better and more accurate means of monitoring changes to the coastal environment. And there is little doubt that integrated management plans will need to be developed further, if the coastline of England and Wales is to be sustained in a manner which will satisfy the many demands being placed upon it. It is not the purpose of this report - nor the Agency's remit - to set out what future coastline management strategies should be. But it is hoped that the contents of this report will both inform and accelerate their development.

Dr R J Pentreath
Chief Scientist and Director of Environmental Strategy

Contents

List of figures

Section 4

Section 5

List of tables

Symbols

Bq/kg	becquerels per kilogramme (radiation activity per unit mass)
Bq/l	becquerels per litre (radiation activity per unit volume)
cm	centimetre (unit distance)
°C	degrees Celsius (standard temperature scale)
d	day
ha	hectare (unit area)
km	kilometre (unit distance)
m	metre (unit distance)
m^2	square metre (unit area)
m^3	cubic metre (unit volume)
m^3/d	cubic metres per day
m^3/s	cubic metres per second
mg/l	milligrammes per litre (level of concentration)
mg Pt/l	milligrammes of platinum per litre
mm	millimetre
mm/yr	millimetres per year (distance in relation to time)
Mm^3	megacubic metre, one million cubic metres (unit volume)
Ml/d	megalitres per day, that is one million litres per day (unit volume in relation to time)
‰	parts per thousand
pH	measure of acidity/alkalinity (for example pH7 = neutral)
μg/l	microgrammes per litre, one millionth of a gramme per litre (level of concentration)
μmol/l	micromoles per litre, one millionth of a mole per litre (level of concentration)

Abbreviations

BOD	Biochemical oxygen demand
CASI	Compact Airborne Spectrographic Imager
CEFAS	Centre for Environment, Fisheries and Aquaculture Science
CSO	Combined sewer overflow
CSTT	Comprehensive Studies Task Team
DDT	Dichlorodiphenyltrichloroethane
DETR	Department of the Environment, Transport and the Regions
DO	Dissolved oxygen
DoE	Department of the Environment
DTI	Department of Trade and Industry
EC	European Commission
E.coli	*Escherichia coli*
EDMAR	Endocrine Disruption in the Marine Environment
EMP	Estuary Management Plan
EQS	Environmental quality standard
HCH	Hexachlorocyclohexane
HMS	Harmonised Monitoring Scheme
JNCC	Joint Nature Conservation Committee
LEAP	Local Environment Agency Plan
LIDAR	Light Detection and Ranging
MAFF	Ministry of Agriculture, Fisheries and Food
MPMMG	Marine Pollution Monitoring Management Group
NALG	National Aquatic Litter Group
NMP	National Monitoring Programme
NRA	National Rivers Authority
OECD	Organisation for Economic Co-operation and Development
OFWAT	Office of Water Services
OSPAR	Oslo and Paris Commission
PAH	Polycyclic aromatic hydrocarbon
PARCOM	Paris Commission
PCB	Polychlorinated biphenyls
SAC	Special Area of Conservation
SEPA	Scottish Environment Protection Agency
SMP	Shoreline Management Plan
SNIFFER	Scotland and Northern Ireland Forum for Environmental Research
SSSI	Site of Special Scientific Interest
STW	Sewage treatment works
TBT	Tributyl tin
UNEP	United Nations Environment Programme
UWWTD	Urban Waste Water Treatment Directive (91/271/EEC)

Executive Summary

Introduction

This report provides a detailed assessment of the state of coasts and estuaries in England and Wales. It brings together and examines information on the various stresses placed upon them and their consequent state as looked at from different points of view. In the light of this information, the report considers how well the coastal environment is being managed to meet the needs of future generations. The report concludes with an overall view of the state of the coastal environment and identifies a set of priority issues that require further action to move towards a more sustainable management of it.

Stresses on the coastal environment

Since 1988 the UK has experienced exceptional climatic extremes, including an increased frequency of severe storms which, together with tide surges and waves, batter the coast. Globally, average temperatures have risen during the past century and are predicted to rise further. One effect of this may be an acceleration of sea level rise, a process that has been taking place over the past 10,000 years. Other effects may be reduced freshwater flows to estuaries in parts of the country, causing siltation and changes to sediment processes, including erosion and deposition around the coast. These changes could have significant implications for different uses of some estuaries and coastal zones, and for some habitats and wildlife, but could lead to benefits elsewhere. Climate change predictions surrounding storms are very uncertain but if the severity of storms increases, the effects may include increased coastal damage from storms, flooding and erosion.

There has been a continuing increase in the number of households across England and Wales and about one-third of the total population lives in the coastal zone, although the resident numbers may increase by as much as one half in the summer months, because of the influx of tourists. Development of coastal urban areas including residential areas, industrial and commercial developments, roads, ports, marinas, and other leisure facilities compete for the limited land in the coastal zone, with the danger of squeezing natural habitats and spoiling the aesthetic appeal of the area. Runoff from urban surfaces, including roads, and emissions from ships, can have a significant local impact on the water and air quality respectively. Changing lifestyles are placing new demands on coasts; increases in leisure time and rapidly developing forms of recreation such as jet-skiing have to be carefully managed to avoid conflicts with other uses and the environment.

As much as 40 per cent of large-scale industry, including power generation, steel manufacturing, chemical production and oil refining is sited in the coastal zone in England and Wales. Cooling water for industrial uses and power generation accounts for almost all of the water abstracted from estuaries and coasts. The sea bed provides about 27 million tonnes of aggregates each year, equivalent to between one and two tonnes per household, for use in the construction industry and in coastal protection schemes. Aggregate removals are forecast to increase by 63 per cent in order to reduce the amount taken from land sources. There is a presumption against extraction unless the environmental and coastal impact issues are satisfactorily resolved. But understanding about the interaction between offshore extraction and coastal erosion is incomplete so this projected increase is of real concern.

The fishing industry has changed over the past 20 years; there has been a decline in fish landings and a steady rise in shellfish landings since the 1960s. A greater range of species is exploited than in the past. Shellfish farms around the south east and south west of England, in Wales and Morecambe Bay produce over 5,000 tonnes of mussels a year amongst other species. These may cause localised impacts but one of the greatest risks to the environment comes from non-native species introduced with imported stock.

There have been significant reductions in the amounts of contaminants discharged, both directly to coastal waters from sewage treatment works and industrial discharges, indirectly from rivers draining into estuaries and from airborne sources. This has been the result of increased investment, effective regulation and changes in the nature of industries. Although pollution from point sources has declined, that from intermittent combined sewer overflows and from diffuse sources continues to be of concern. Localised water quality problems associated with pesticides, polycyclic aromatic hydrocarbons, nutrients, and abandoned mines persist and require further action. Land-based discharges to the North Sea may provide as much as 40 per cent of the total oil input to the sea; the sources of this need to be tackled.

Disposal of sewage sludge and industrial wastes at sea have been banned; only dredgings are now regularly dumped at sea. In general, the number of pollution incidents caused by accidents or illegal practices has fallen. Oil spills and illegal discharges from ships are a significant source of pollution in the coastal zone. The number of spills has declined and less oil has been spilt but occasional catastrophic tanker accidents can cause severe impacts locally.

Viewpoints on the coastal environment

England and Wales has one of the longest coastlines in Europe. Human uses, including developments, agriculture and forestry, take up four-fifths of the available land within 10km of the coast and the proportion of natural habitats remaining is small. Over the centuries the amount of intertidal areas, including saltmarshes, has declined substantially, affecting the wildlife that depends on these habitats and also reducing these natural defences against the sea. The history of defending lives and property against storms, erosion and sea flooding is long. In total, a third of the coastline has some form of artificial protection. Repairs are needed to over a tenth of the length of coastal defence structures if they are to remain effective. The coastal environment provides some significant energy resources, with oil being produced in Dorset, and the potential for wind and wave generation elsewhere yet to be fully exploited.

Coastal habitats are varied and 21 habitat types are recognised nationally as being important for UK biodiversity but are of concern because of their vulnerability to change. Some of the wildlife living in coastal environments is thriving, such as some seabirds and waders, but other components of the wildlife, particularly fish, are in decline. Salmon have returned to many estuaries only in the last decade or so, after the clean-up of pollution. So it is of serious concern that other factors appear to be affecting populations now. About one-fifth of priority species identified in the UK Biodiversity Action Plan are found in coastal zones, including the natterjack toad and the harbour porpoise, and action is therefore needed to secure their protection.

An assessment of the water quality of estuaries in 1995 suggested that over 90 per cent of estuaries are of good or fair quality. Compliance with the statutory water quality standards arising from European legislation is high but needs to be further improved. Of particular concern is the continuing failure of several bathing waters to meet the standards set, despite an overall total of £1.5 billion being spent by the water companies to meet these requirements. Further investment is planned.

More direct measurements of the health of the environment are urgently needed. There is increasing concern over the possible ecological and human health effects of exposure to chemicals present in the environment at low concentrations, such as those which can cause hormone disruption in wildlife. Further investigation into the effects of nutrient enrichment of coastal waters is also needed because, although the available evidence suggests that nutrient inputs to coastal waters are stable or declining in some areas, long-term plankton records show that algae numbers have been increasing in the North Sea since 1960. Novel airborne remote sensing techniques have recorded unusual algal blooms in coastal and estuarine waters although the extent of natural blooms of algae is unknown. These can affect shellfish, making them unfit for human consumption, and result in the closing of fisheries for temporary periods.

Sediments in saltmarshes and estuaries have provided a long-term record of the overall trends in contamination of the coastal environment. These generally show that pollution from metals was most severe in the early part of this century and that substantial reductions in pollution have taken place since the 1970s. But not all substances accumulate in sediments and there is very little information on the presence of many of the thousands of chemicals in use today.

The aesthetic quality of the coastal environment is perhaps the most important viewpoint to the many people who visit the coast every year. There is no national scheme for measuring this as yet, but surveys have found litter ranging from plastics to sewage-derived debris with the main sources being tourists, shipping and fishing. Attitude surveys show that this is a concern to many people.

The Environment Agency's response

This analysis of available information on the stresses and strains on the coastal environment and its consequent state shows the varied nature of the many issues that require active collaborative management. The report also shows how between £490 and £650 million is invested in capital schemes every year to improve coastal defences and the quality of discharges and emissions by industry (including the water industry) to the coastal environment. Based upon this analysis, concerted action is required to address:

- sea level change and increased storminess;

- the quality of bathing waters and beaches;

- loss of habitats and the implications for biodiversity;

- decline in fisheries;

- pollution by hazardous substances;

- development pressures on the coast;

- understanding of the coastal environment.

The Agency's *Environmental Strategy for the Millennium and Beyond* addresses a range of specific issues to be progressively addressed across its environmental management functions. Further action in the coastal zone will be tackled as part of this overall strategy by:

- addressing some of the causes of, and helping to ameliorate the effects of, climate change;

- ensuring that the industrial impact on the coastal environment is progressively reduced, both for the benefit of industry itself and for the enjoyment of coastal areas by everyone;

- improving air quality and thus a specific source of pollutant loads to the coast;

- managing wastes so that they do not add to the polluting pressures on coasts;

- ensuring long-term and integrated approaches to the management of water resources which will have an impact on residual flows to estuaries;

- delivering an integrated approach to the management of river basins, which naturally impinge on the coastal environment;

- conserving the land, which includes working with nature to reduce coastal flooding and reporting regularly on the state of flood defences;

- managing our freshwater fisheries (many fish migrate through estuaries) in a sustainable way;

- improving the biodiversity of coastal habitats.

The Agency cannot bring about all the necessary changes on its own. An important element of our environmental strategy is developing working relationships with others to ensure that their actions contribute to the achievement of agreed environmental goals. This is particularly important in the coastal zone where so many organisations are involved in developing plans for different purposes. To succeed, integrated coastal zone management is essential and the role of existing voluntary coastal groups needs to be promoted further. It will become increasingly important with the formation of the Regional Development Agencies. Another important aspect is to ensure that the investment on the coast is properly targeted to maximise environmental benefits and, in the case of coastal defence, is working with, and not against, nature. The water industry has an important role to play in improving the quality of bathing waters by bringing about further improvements to sewerage systems and sewage treatment. Much more investment has been planned, although in some areas more investigation of diffuse sources of pollution is needed.

New, and changes to existing, European Directives could also require further investment in the next millennium which should allow even greater environmental benefits. International action is needed to tackle some issues, particularly the decline in fisheries and also pollution from offshore sources. There has been much debate on these and further progress is needed. The extent to which the goals of sustainable development can be achieved ultimately depends upon the willingness of all sectors, including the public, to take responsibility. This is certainly true in the case of the coastal environment which continues to be under significant strain in meeting society's needs. The Agency therefore attaches great importance to the role of education in improving general awareness and in influencing behaviours where necessary.

Section 1 Introduction

This is the second of a series of Agency reports which analyse the state of the environment of England and Wales, sector by sector, in order to provide a basis for more sustainable management into the new millennium.

The report is timely for many reasons. There is mounting concern about climate change and the impact of sea level rise and storminess which pose threats to low-lying coastlands, with the risk of loss of life and land. Last year was the UN International Year of the Oceans which raised the profile of marine issues, and 8 June 1998 was World Ocean Day. 'The Oceans' was the theme of the international trade fair, EXPO '98, in Portugal, and the Oslo and Paris Commission also met in Portugal and reached new agreements on measures to protect our seas. In 1998 the UK Government identified seven specific threats to seas - shipping operations, overfishing, discharges from the land, dumping of waste at sea, exploitation of oil, gas and other sea bed minerals, coastal zone development and climate change.

There are developments at a European level which are seeking to improve the coastal environment as well - proposals to change the Bathing Water Directive, a proposed Framework Directive on water, the phasing out of sewage sludge disposal at sea and other requirements to meet the Urban Waste Water Treatment Directive. The first European assessment on the state of the European environment concluded that *"for many coasts, the scale of environmental problems has not been fully quantified or understood"* and that there is a need for detailed quality and status reports (Stanners and Bourdeau, 1995). It is therefore a good time to take stock and to assess what has been achieved so far through vast investment programmes, and to identify what still remains to be done.

At a national level, the Director General of the Office of Water Services is currently carrying out a periodic review of water prices. This sets levels of investment for the water companies into the next millennium and could have significant potential for coastal improvement schemes. Reviews of abstraction licensing and fisheries legislation are ongoing and the Agriculture Select Committee has recently reported on *Flood and Coastal Defence* (House of Commons, 1998).

This report aims to provide clear, integrated and sound scientific information to help these public debates so that decisions can be made with a full understanding of available knowledge. It examines the state of the coastal environment of England and Wales by addressing the following questions.

- What is the state of the coastal environment and how has it improved or deteriorated over time?

- Why is the coastal environment like this and how much are human activities influencing it?

- How much money has been invested in tackling the impact of human activities on coasts and has this money been well spent?

- Are there any causes for concern in the state of coasts and estuaries and what problems are predicted in the near future?

- What are the priorities for action and investment in the future?

An estimated 200 million (31 per cent) of the European population live within 50km of coastal waters (Stanners and Bourdeau, 1995), but defining the extent of the coastal environment is difficult - where does it begin and end? A general workable definition is:

"the part of the land affected by its proximity to the sea, and that part of the sea affected by its proximity to the land as the extent to which man's land-based activities have a measurable influence on water chemistry and marine ecology" (US Commission on Marine Science, Engineering and Resources, 1969).

In this report we have considered all factors which impinge on the coastal environment and generally assumed an inland limit of 10km unless other reasons suggest a need for a different limit. The report looks at the coast and estuaries up to their tidal limits and extends to about 5km offshore, the limit to which the Agency's pollution control functions extend, although again anything outside this limit that impinges on the coast has been considered. This approach has its limitations; in theory, any part of England and Wales could be considered within the coastal zone, as many events which occur well inland have a major impact on coastal ecosystems. Setting boundaries is a complex issue and biogeochemical and socio-political boundaries may not be coincident. Thus, change is intimately linked to many different boundaries and the report adopts a flexible approach, depending on the information presented.

Section 2 of the report provides a general background to the coastal environment including a historical perspective on the dependence that society has placed on coasts. It also gives an overview of the formation of the coast and estuaries and how the evolution of the coast continues today. It outlines the role of the many organisations and bodies that are involved in managing the coastal environment.

Subsequent sections of the report have organised available information into the pressures on coasts, the state of coasts, and how society has responded to these pressures and states.

Section 3 looks at the pressures caused by natural processes and human activities in more depth, and how these have changed over time and are predicted to change in the future. The information has been organised into a framework of 'stresses and strains' which cover:

- natural forces;

- societal influences;

- removals and abstractions;

- discharges and releases;

- waste arisings and disposals;

- illegal practices.

Section 4 provides information on the state of coasts and estuaries. It is organised into six viewpoints which the Agency has adopted in order to examine the state of the environment generally; and which recognise the role of many organisations in providing information on the state of the environment. These are:

- land use and environmental resources;

- the status of key biological populations and communities, and of biodiversity;

- the quality of the environment as determined by assessing compliance with standards and targets;

- the 'health' of environmental resources;

- environmental changes at long-term reference sites;

- the aesthetic quality of the environment.

Section 5 builds on Sections 3 and 4 by attempting to explain why coasts are in their current state. Human activities in one form or another can explain many of the changes and the present state; many of these being regulated. To identify how much effort has been put into trying to minimise the impact of human activities on the coastal environment, this section presents the amount of investment by industry, coastal defence authorities and others, together with planned investment where known. It also considers the value placed by our society on coasts and how much people are willing to pay for investment in the coastal environment.

Having looked at the information contained in this 'pressures, states, response' framework, Section 6 pulls it together to present the Agency's overview on the state of coasts. This identifies the key successes and key areas where further effort is needed.

The information contained in this report has been acquired from as many sources as possible and, unless otherwise stated, refers to the coastal area and estuaries of England and Wales. Regional data presented from Agency sources relate to the river catchments managed by each Agency Region (shown inside the back cover). Most of the raw datasets owned by the Agency are available on the public registers held in the Agency's regional offices, and summary data are available on the World Wide Web which can be found at http://www.environment-agency.gov.uk.

Section 2 Background to the coastal environment

This section gives a general background to the geological and geomorphic processes that have shaped our coasts, the historical development and the importance of the coastal environment to our economy. Many of the subjects covered are addressed in greater depth later in the report and some readers may be able to bypass this section altogether. The final part of this section gives an overview of who does what in regulating coastal activities.

2.1 The formation of the coastal landscape

The coastline of Britain, as recognised today, began to be defined as the sea level rose at the end of the last ice age about 10,000 years ago. The action of waves, tides, currents and winds in sculpting the geological landscape, created over some 500 million years, has led to the distinctive features of cliffs, bays, sand dunes, beaches, salt marshes, spits, bars, estuaries and their associated habitats.

The coastal scenery of Britain reflects four stages of evolution:

- pre-glacial landforms;

- erosion and deposition during the ice ages;

- changes of sea level during and since the last ice age;

- processes of coastal erosion and deposition operating since the last ice age.

The great variety of coastline reflects the geological diversity of Britain. Hard granitic and volcanic rocks, mainly on the western coast give rise to cliffs or rocky shores, while rocks less resistant to erosion - shales and chalk - outcropping on the south coast appear as cliffs and bays, and soft clays and loose superficial deposits, exemplified on the east coast, appear as coastal lowlands.

Erosion and deposition during the ice ages greatly affected the nature and variety of the coast. In some places, for example Holderness, Lincoln Marsh and much of East Anglia, the coastline would be several kilometres inland of its present position if there were no glacial deposits. These deposits are eroding quickly under wave attack.

During glacial periods, the sea levels were much lower than at present because vast amounts of water were locked up in the ice sheets. Where rivers flowed in areas south of the ice sheet, the valleys cut down to this low sea level. When the ice age ended, sea levels rose again, flooding these valleys and forming estuaries including rias, as found at Dartmouth in south west England and Milford Haven in Wales. In the soft clays of lowland England the drowned estuaries are not bound with valley sides but are surrounded with a maze of winding shallow creeks, mudflats and broad tracts of tidal marsh. With certain exceptions, these are the coasts of deposition, where off-shore

bars, spits and forelands help to straighten out many of the indentations caused by the submergence of the coast. For example, the marshy backwaters of Poole, Portsmouth and Chichester are almost closed off from the Channel but are kept open by creeks flowing into inlets and tidal scour. Similar coastal scenery occurs around the Isle of Sheppey in Kent, in the great Essex marshes and further north in Suffolk's Deben, Orwell and Stour.

Along with the rise in sea level, there has been an 'isostatic re-adjustment' (vertical movements) due to the removal of the weight of the ice sheets from the last ice age. The centre of the ice loading was in Scotland and consequently this area together with much of western England has experienced crustal rebound, while most of southern England has experienced subsidence. This has lead to a net rise in sea levels in the south and east of England which continues today, although the rates of sea level rise have varied over this time period from 100cm per century initially to 20cm per century 5,000 years ago.

Since the retreat of the ice, life forms on the coast have been evolving too, so that today coastal environments provide a wide variety of habitats for both aquatic and terrestrial plants and animals, reflecting the diverse physical conditions. They provide some of the most productive ecosystems, particularly in the areas below tide level (for example seaweeds and seagrasses) and inter-tidal areas (for example saltmarshes). These ecosystems support a variety of life essential to many animals, including humans, and enhance our quality of life, and in many places now require protection so that they are sustained for future generations.

The coastline is evolving continuously. It is an extremely dynamic environment which has altered significantly in the last 10,000 years and continues to be shaped as a result of natural processes as well as human intervention. The timescales can be quite different. Many natural processes have taken place at a slow rate over the centuries since the last ice age, with occasional catastrophic events, whereas human interventions have been largely restricted to the last 1,000 to 2,000 years with much more significant interventions in recent decades. But the coast is a fundamental part of a functioning landform which adjusts to environmental inputs and thus protects society from the sea. Human intervention can have unforeseen effects on this natural balance. These processes need to be understood in order to know how to manage the coast effectively and to understand the coastal environment.

Waves, tides and currents are all factors in shaping the coastline because they contribute most of the energy that erodes, transports and deposits sediment. These factors are now described briefly.

Waves are caused by wind blowing across the surface of the open sea. The height of a wave and the distance between waves, together with the wave energy, are largely determined by the

17

wind speed, the time that the wind has been blowing and the distance (fetch) the wave has travelled over the surface of the water. The fetch can extend for many thousands of kilometres. For example, the waves that affect the west coast of England and Wales are generated by weather systems over the west Atlantic. A coastline exposed to an ocean or large sea can experience large waves even at times when there are no local winds. Because the predominant direction of winds across Britain is from the west-south west, particularly that of storm winds, wave conditions on the Atlantic margin tend to be more severe.

The way in which waves arrive at a coast can be described in terms of how often a wave of a certain height is expected to occur, or be exceeded. On the south coast, the massive waves from the Atlantic and their associated energy are quickly attenuated due to reducing depth. For example, at Lyme Bay in Dorset waves of 20m occur with a 50-year return period, but by the time the wave reaches the Isle of Wight this reduces to 15m and at Dover to 10m. A similar pattern occurs towards north Wales and the Cumbrian coast and down the North Sea.

As waves move onshore into shallower water, they lose their energy and 'break' and water rushes onshore as swash. The process of wave breaking involves the release of the energy carried in the wave, which can then perform work in terms of the erosion of cliffs or the transport of beach material, although this occurs in conjunction with longshore currents which occur seawards of the breakpoint. On a sloping beach the water returns to the sea under the effect of gravity as backwash, in some circumstances this can become concentrated as 'rip' currents, which are particularly erosive.

Waves are also important in the movement of sediment along, up and down beaches. Beaches adjust to increasing wave energy by changing their dissipative surface area. Flat beaches with nearshore bars are a natural response to higher energy waves.

Tides are a response to the gravitational attraction of the moon and to a lesser extent the sun. The tidal range (the difference in the depth of water between high and low tide) has a major

Figure 2.1 *Tidal ranges*

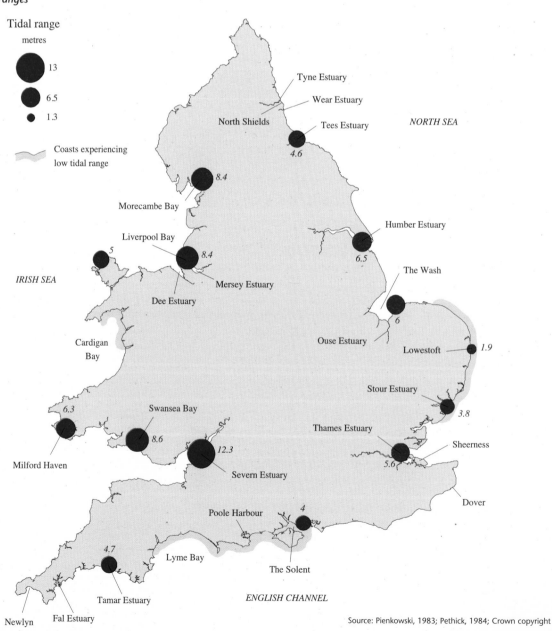

Source: Pienkowski, 1983; Pethick, 1984; Crown copyright

influence on the coastal environment. The Earth's rotation and the constrictions imposed by the coastline contribute to the range of the tide. The biggest tides occur in narrowing inlets such as estuaries and bays, and vary from place to place around England and Wales (Figure 2.1). The tidal range of the Severn Estuary, at over 12m on an average spring tide, is one of the largest in the world. A small tidal range concentrates the power of the sea onto a narrow band of shore line, while a large tidal range results in the shore being in a constantly changing state. 'Spring tides', with a large tidal range, occur when the moon and the sun are directly in line with the Earth, their gravitational fields reinforcing each other. When they are 90 degrees out of alignment, each partially offsets each other's gravitational force and the smallest tidal range is observed - called neap tides. There are two spring tides and two neap tide cycles during each lunar month. In addition to this lunar cycle, there are other cycles which influence tidal range. The very largest spring tides of the year occur on a regular cycle, one in autumn and another in spring. Tides control estuary morphology and estuary morphology controls tides: a complex interdependence. Spring tides are particularly important in this; furthermore, they resuspend greater volumes of sediment from the bed than smaller tides, which can cause deterioration in water quality. The heights of tides are measured by 28 gauges around England and Wales in the National Tide Gauge Network, operated by many organisations and collated by the Centre for Coastal and Marine Sciences' Proudman Oceanographic Laboratory (part of the Natural Environment Research Council) and funded by the Ministry of Agriculture, Fisheries and Food (MAFF).

Storm surges occur in our coastal waters as a result of storms, which usually cross the Atlantic and pass to the north of Britain, but track farther south across the country in the winter. This affects sea levels through atmospheric pressure changes and strong winds. As these weather systems are mainly depressions (areas of low pressure), rises in the height of the sea's surface of up to 50cm may result. The wind fields around a depression have an even more pronounced effect on sea levels. The wind drags the surface of the water along with it. The surge height may remain the same as it travels along a coast or may be amplified or attenuated, according to the direction of the existing wind and the aspect of estuaries. Storm surges can force water into estuaries such that the height exceeds that of the highest astronomical tides, even when low tide water levels are predicted.

Currents may be set up in various ways. Wave currents can help generate rip and longshore currents. Tidal currents and tidal residual currents are important in moving sediment on continental shelves and in shallow coastal waters, although they are usually only strong enough to move silt sized particles except when larger particles are stirred up by waves. The formation of coastal features in sheltered coastlines, bays and estuaries are often due to tidal residual currents (the net effect of tidal currents when averaged over many tidal cycles). All natural coastal change is the result of currents.

These forces lead to erosion of parts of the coast and deposition elsewhere, depending on the geography and geology. Erosional features include cliffs and wave cut platforms; depositional features include dunes and beaches. Coastal landforms have an important role in protecting the coastline from erosion and flooding. Saltmarshes, for example, absorb wave energy arriving at the coast and provide a defence against sea flooding. Beaches, spits and bars perform a similar function and can protect the open coast from erosion. The sediment supplied by erosion of cliffs is vital in sustaining these landforms and, hence, natural coastal defences (Rendel Geotechnics, 1993). The forces of erosion and deposition are described in more depth in Section 3.1.

Figure 2.2   *Coastal cells around England and Wales*

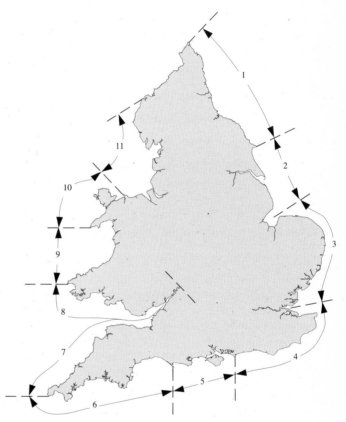

Source: Ministry of Agriculture, Fisheries and Food, 1993a; Crown copyright

An understanding of coastal processes is required in the planning of coastal defences and allows the definition of the 'coastal cell'. A coastal cell is a stretch of coastline in which the amount of sediment is more or less stable and self-contained. The cell concept is employed in the management of coastlines in much the same way as the drainage basin is used in river management, because any human-induced changes within the cell may affect other parts of the cell. For example, Hallsands in south Devon is a village that suffered disastrous damage earlier this century when off-shore dredging for aggregates effectively lowered the natural beach levels, leaving the village unprotected from the sea, showing the knock-on effect of change at a local level. Houses fell into the sea and the village had to be evacuated. Coastal cells around England and Wales are shown in Figure 2.2 (MAFF, 1993a).

Estuaries

A typical estuary is the tidal mouth of a river, although in many cases the river may be almost non-existent. It is a partially enclosed area, open to saline waters from the sea and receiving fresh water from rivers, land runoff or seepage. Estuaries are characterised by the interaction of fresh water from river flow and saline water as a result of the twice-daily intrusion of the tide. The variation in salinity is influenced by the strength of the river flow, which is in turn affected by rainfall, evaporation and abstraction higher up the catchment.

A significant proportion of the sediment load carried by rivers is deposited within the estuary, as the fresh water mixes with salt, but most estuarine sediment in the UK is from marine sources. Where the sediment load carried by the estuary flow is heavy and sustained this can lead to the formation of tidal mudflats in the estuary and outside the river mouth on the coast. The tidal mudflats have in the past been reclaimed for agriculture, such as around the margins of the Wash and Romney Marsh. Fine sediment deposition, for example on mudflats and saltmarshes, is critically important in terms of flood defences and ecological productivity.

Most estuaries are in, or close to, some form of dynamic equilibrium between sediment deposition and erosion where the balance occurs over a number of cyclic periods such as tidal cycles. Over longer periods (for example decades), estuaries may alter their morphology significantly with movement of flood channels and changes to sand and mud banks, but they still tend to be in equilibrium with neither a gain nor a loss of material within the estuary.

Estuaries generally contain a wide range of sediments ranging from granular materials (sand and gravel) to cohesive sediments (silts and muds). The latter show intricate behaviour depending on their physical and chemical properties, the properties of the water, and on ecological processes. All these factors vary spatially and over time, leading to complex patterns of sediment transport and deposition (Hydraulics Research Wallingford, 1997).

Ecological activity also influences the evolution of estuaries by affecting the stability of sediments and chemical processes within the water column. Marshes and mudflats are typical estuarine features which play an important physical role in defending the coast and are important and productive habitats. Biological activity is often linked to temperature and daylight cycles so that seasonal differences are an important feature.

An understanding of the physical characteristics of estuaries is important for understanding the differences within and between them and in order to manage problems that have arisen from the high demands placed on them in terms of human occupation. A contaminant discharged to the estuary may not be rapidly dispersed to the sea. It may remain in the estuary for many days oscillating to and fro with the tide, slowly mixing with estuary water and moving down the estuary until it eventually reaches the sea. The rate at which this happens, the flushing or retention time of the estuary, depends on the flow of fresh water to the head of the estuary, the tidal

range and on the volume of the estuary. A typical flushing time for the Mersey has been calculated as 30 days but it can be as low as 20 days or as high as 50 days depending on river flow (NRA, 1995). Similarly, understanding sediment movement is essential before engineering works are undertaken in estuaries. For example, a port expansion or barrage could alter the morphology of an estuary leading to increased flood risks elsewhere.

2.2 Historical setting

In contrast to most geomorphic processes, human activities on the coastline have taken place over a much shorter timescale. This broad overview gives some background to the development of human activities on the coast, and the dependence of our social and economic wellbeing on the coast.

Defence from invasion

The history of England and Wales has been heavily influenced by its island status. It was the need to trade and to defend the island from invasion that was responsible for the first human influences on the coastal environment. Forts, castles and early warning systems have been built on the coast to defend against attackers for at least the last 2,500 years.

During the Iron Age many forts were built, like that on the cliff top at Berry Head, Devon, and then the Romans built their own fortifications and signal stations, making use of existing sites. In the late 3rd century, fortifications were built along the coast of north west England and Wales to guard against raiders from Ireland, and 'the Saxon shore forts' were constructed along the south and east coast of England to defend against Saxon attack. The threat of Viking invasion in the 9th century led to more Anglo-Saxon towns being established and the revival of many abandoned Roman towns including Sandwich, Dover, Portchester and Southampton.

Following the Norman conquest in 1066, a major programme of defence construction was begun. These fortifications often supported large garrisons that led to the development of the surrounding villages which became locally important trading centres, such as Dover. Edward I built a series of castles in Wales in the 13th and 14th centuries, many of which were located on the coast so that they could be provisioned by sea, and which still stand today, for example Caernarfon. Fortifications were added to various sites over the following centuries and augmented by innumerable gun implacements in the two world wars. Although many of these sites are now derelict, military use of the coast has continued in some places, such as on the Pembrokeshire coast and at Lulworth in Dorset.

In addition to land-based defensive measures, the growth of the navy influenced the development of the coast. The knowledge of the sea and crews for the navy often came from merchants and fishermen. The south eastern ports of Dover, Hastings, Hythe, Romney and Sandwich formed the 'Cinque Ports' in the Middle Ages and enjoyed trading privileges in return for their contribution to naval defence. It was the demand for substantial war ships during the reign of the Tudor monarchs which led to the expansion of the ports of Greenwich, Chatham and Portsmouth. The need for a western naval base during the war with Spain led to the development of Plymouth as a naval base. It was from Plymouth that Sir Francis Drake went out against the Armada, and many other Devon and Cornish seafarers played an important role in the wars with France and in the voyages of discovery.

History of ports

Over the last 2,000 years it is trade that has largely determined the growth or decline of ports around the coast. The success of a port has been influenced by many factors, including the nature of the goods to be traded, the countries traded with and ease of access to the ports and from the ports to the markets. Trade has generated substantial wealth and there has been considerable rivalry between ports.

In the late Iron Age, Cornwall (then known as Belerian) traded minerals such as tin with Armorica, Spain and the Romans. This industry was largely a domestic affair with a small number of conspicuous defended settlements commanding river crossings and coastal harbours. The south east had links with Belgic Gaul, eastern France and Italy.

The Romans established many coastal ports along the south east coast such as Dover and Lympne, trading with Gaul and the Roman Empire. Dover is still a thriving port but Lympne, along with other ports on this coast that were important up until medieval times, is now situated some way inland on the inner margins of Romney Marsh as a result of material accumulating naturally on the coast and the silting-up of estuaries. Chester was also a Roman port, before the head of the Dee Estuary filled with silt.

Kent retained the monopoly on trade to the continent until the 7th century when the Suffolk coast started to grow in importance and the West Saxons established Southampton as a trading post. Viking dominance of the Irish Sea led to a lucrative trade between Dublin and the shores of the Bristol Channel. Scandinavian place names are evident on the Welsh shores of the Channel where staging posts were established on the run to Bristol, Cardiff and Newport. The 12th century saw the building of more substantial quays in the important ports of London, Bristol, Newcastle, Shoreham, Exeter and Kings Lynn.

By the later part of the 12th century London, Southampton and Bristol were among the major ports of north west Europe. These ports were open to the new large ships, which contributed to the general economic growth of the time. Coastal trade was of prime importance, the sea around England being described as 'merely a river round England'. London, in particular, benefited greatly from its ideal location for waterborne trade. Its ready and continually growing market for food and fuel meant a constant flow of grain and dairy produce from East Anglia and Kentish ports and, later, raw materials and coal from the north east.

In the 16th century coastal trade continued to develop to supply London with coal, corn and building materials. East coast ports such as East Lynn, Hull and Newcastle grew to satisfy this need. As southern and western coasts were brought into the system the range of goods traded became more varied, although corn and coal remained the most important. Hull flourished on the whaling and fishing industry and on its importance as a chief garrison town of northern England. Plymouth, like Bristol and Liverpool, benefited from the growing trade with Britain's transatlantic colonies but also through its own importance as the western base of the navy.

As the size and importance of the navy increased during the 17th century so the naval bases of Chatham, Portsmouth and Devonport (Plymouth) developed. Long-distance voyages for trading and exploration necessitated more elaborate docks where ships could be fitted out, repaired, loaded and unloaded. The first wet docks in Britain were built at Blackwell and Rotherhithe on the Thames. The first docks in Liverpool were built in 1720, and further docks were built in London, Liverpool and Southampton in the 1800s as well as the breakwater at Plymouth, which gave better protection from the westerly winds. The development of the Welsh ports began to cater for the expansion of the coal and steel industries. Swansea's first dock was opened in 1855, in the same year as West Bute Dock in Cardiff.

In the 1830s London was the premier centre for British and world trade. Newcastle held the next greatest tonnage of ships and Liverpool was the third, largely for the American trade. By 1913, around one half of the sea-borne trade of the world was carried in British vessels and, in the 25 years prior to the First World War, about two-thirds of new ships launched were made in Britain. Tyneside led the world in the building of oil tankers.

Since the end of the Second World War many ports have suffered a spectacular decline but some have survived through development for specialist functions - Dover, Ramsgate, Fishguard and Folkestone have become ferry and hovercraft terminals. Many small harbours, once important for trade or fishing, have benefited from the growth in tourism and sailing as a recreational sport leading to the development of marinas. The redundant sites of the major docks of Liverpool, London, Bristol and Newcastle have been revitalised by new housing, refurbishment of old buildings and the conversion of warehouses to new uses.

Economic development

Salt used to be vital for the preservation of food and the process of making salt by evaporation of sea water has been known since the Bronze Age. The industry is documented from the 8th century, when the Saxon kings granted monastic houses land to develop salt working and cut peat for fuel. The presence of salt production is indicated by place names such as Salcombe in Devon and Salcot in Essex. In Lincolnshire, East Anglia, Essex and Sussex the coastal levels comprised inundated saltmarshes and salterns, which were abundant until medieval times when pressure grew to convert these areas into agricultural land. In the 11th century Salthouse was the site for a salt warehouse, collecting salt made all round the Wash and along the coast. By the 16th century salt production was largely confined to northern England and Scotland. Competition from inland sources in Cheshire meant that the coastal production of salt had all but disappeared at the end of the 18th century. Maldon in Essex continues the tradition of salt making as it has done for 2,000 years.

The pressure for agricultural land for food production over the years has led to the building of banks out in the fens and marshes in order to bring in new land. Around the Lincolnshire and Norfolk Marshland of the Wash there is substantial evidence of construction of banks and ditches. A pre-Norman conquest sea bank called the Roman Bank is thought to have been built around the 6th or 7th century. Between about 1150 and 1300 historical documents tell of the fen drying up at this period which made the reclamation easier. To the south of the Wash between 1160 and 1241, the settlements of Holbeach, Whaplode and Fleet added 130km² to their arable and pasture land. Reclamation was carried out during the medieval period in the Somerset levels, the Kentish marshes and in Holderness. The reclamation of marsh and fen brought hundreds of square kilometres into cultivation and produced a characteristic landscape of willow-lined drainage ditches, rich green pasture that carried sheep and scattered farmsteads. Reclamation has continued through the ages, and coastal defences still protect much agricultural land.

Most early settlements were located to farm the surrounding area and there is little to suggest that fishing was any more than a supplementary activity. It was the arrival of the Normans and the later revival in religious devotion whereby the church insisted on a meatless Friday that brought a growth in the demand for fish.

The monasteries became the earliest proprietors of fisheries, especially in coastal waters. Fish weirs, used to divert the fish into an opening where they could be caught by net or wicker basket, were most common in muddy estuaries with wide intertidal areas, for example on the Severn and the Blackwater estuaries. Until the late 1700s fishing was predominantly an inshore, coastal industry, carried out in small boats, by hand line and seine net, catching the fish that were locally in season.

Most catches were landed on beaches but from the 15th century more harbours were built, for example Staithes in North Yorkshire and Mevagissey and Bude in Cornwall. The nature of the industry led to local areas of the country largely specialising - Hull and the north east coast were involved in whaling, Yarmouth became prosperous due to the herring and the extreme south west's fishing industry rapidly developed based on the pilchard.

It was the fishermen of the south west with their larger, faster and safer boats who led to the opening up of new deep sea fishing grounds in the North Sea and the north Atlantic. Trawl fishing is considered to have begun in Brixham. Fishing grew in importance with the use of steam trawlers which enabled fishing further afield and the development of the railway which meant the fish could be transported more efficiently. Fleetwood, Grimsby and Lowestoft all developed very important fishing industries in the 1800s, with new docks and housing being built to cater for this growth.

Quarrying was an important coastal industry, and the sea provided easier transportation of stone such as Portland stone from Dorset and Delabole slate from Cornwall. In the north east coal was extracted from levels driven into the steep banks of the Tyne until around 1600 when coal fields further from the river began to be exploited. Most of the coal was shipped down the coast or across the North Sea. There were many tin mines on the coast of Cornwall, such as Botallack Mine perched

Figure 2.3 *The total annual turnover by the marine-related sector in 1994/95*

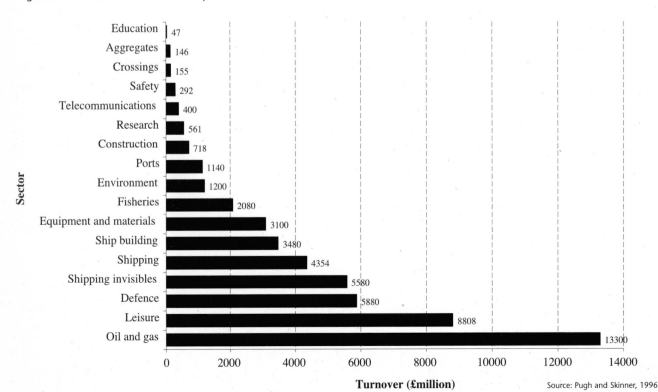

Turnover (£million)

Source: Pugh and Skinner, 1996

right over the Atlantic, producing tin and copper as far back as 1721. The shafts of some of these coastal mines extended out under the Atlantic Ocean, but none operate today and they have left a legacy of environmental impacts.

The importance of these coastal industries and of the ports led to the development of many coastal settlements. The importance of ports, particularly London and Liverpool, in world trade led to massive development of the Thames, Mersey and other estuaries. Material could be imported, processed and exported without additional transport costs. Estuaries provided the water for powering mills, steam engines, processing and cooling. Paper, car manufacture, food processing, oil refining and power stations were among the many industries to develop along these and other estuaries. The estuaries also provided the means of disposing of the effluent to the sea which led to chronic pollution problems in the 19th and 20th centuries. The development of an understanding of pollution and the legislation to deal with it has led to the subsequent cleaning-up of the estuaries (NRA, 1995; Environment Agency, 1997a).

In 1994/95 the contribution to gross domestic product from UK marine-related activities was about five per cent, roughly £51 billion per annum. Oil and gas and leisure were by far the two most important sectors, together accounting for 43 per cent of all marine-related turnover in that year (Figure 2.3) (Pugh and Skinner, 1996). Breaking down these figures further suggests that 50 per cent can be attributed to estuaries alone, particularly those activities associated with shipping and the ports. The issue of the value of coasts to society is returned to in Section 5.7.

Seaside development

Some seaside resorts have developed from earlier fishing villages, but most were newly laid out on virgin sites, often reflecting the vision of a single landowner or a group of individuals. Prior to the 17th century neither the sea nor the coastline was of significant interest for visitors. However in 1626 a medicinal spring was discovered in the cliffs at Scarborough which developed as a spa town to rival inland Harrogate and Bath, rather than as a seaside resort. It was only in the early 18th century, when sea bathing and 'taking in the sea air' had been established, that Scarborough's history as a seaside resort began.

Brighton, which had been a small fishing village, was to become the Scarborough of the south. A Dr Russell settled there in 1753 and encouraged 'the use of sea water in the diseases of the glands'. This immediately brought in visitors. The town became the most fashionable place in England when George, Prince of Wales, started visiting in 1783. Brighton's greatest period of development came in the 1820s with the building of what was, at the time, the finest sea front in the country. There were almost 11km of promenades in the combined townships of Brighton and Hove, all of which still exist today.

As an interest in the seaside began to grow the development of Brighton was mirrored elsewhere on a smaller scale, for

example at Teignmouth and Torquay in Devon. But it was the spread of the railways across England and Wales that started a great development of new and existing towns as seaside resorts, for example at Llandudno, Skegness and Blackpool, which gave the people of the industrial towns access to the coast.

With the widespread development of resort towns a new feature of the coastline appeared. Piers had originally been designed to facilitate passengers embarking and disembarking from shipping in the early 1800s, but by the last quarter of the century almost every major resort town boasted at least one pier, some as long as 400m and of very grand design, and some even including rail access. However, because of their situation and size piers are vulnerable to the ravages of the sea and collisions from shipping and are prone to fire, so few have survived intact. Among the most famous existing ones are Southend, Brighton and Blackpool piers.

The coast became very popular in the late 19th and early 20th centuries with many people taking their annual holiday at the seaside. This resulted in the continued expansion in guest houses, hotels and, later, holiday camps and caravan sites, which spread out from around the most popular resorts. Since the 1950s the growth of the cheap overseas holiday has led to a decline in the popularity of the UK seaside resorts, but in 1996 there were still an estimated 170 million day trips to the coast. Increased interest in other leisure activities - such as walking and water sports - has maintained the popularity of the coast.

2.3 Regulation

The regulation of the coastal environment must encompass and balance all the different pressures upon it. These range from the development needs of industry and commerce and the growth in leisure activity to the need to conserve natural coastal features. This has resulted in many organisations having obligations or interests in the regulation and management of the coastal zone. Some of these overlap and as a consequence co-ordination, planning and management in coastal zones can be complicated.

Planning

Overall responsibility for development and land use lies with the Secretary of State for the Environment or the Secretary of State for Wales, with local planning authorities responsible for development plans and for deciding the majority of planning applications under the town and country planning system. There are a number of planning policy guidance notes issued from the Department of the Environment, Transport and the Regions (DETR) and the Welsh Office, covering the key development issues for coastal planning. In particular, Planning Policy Guidance Note 20, issued in September 1992, relates to Coastal Planning. This covers planning policy for the coastal areas of England. It sets the general context for policy and identifies policies which cover conservation, economic and social development, risks, environmental assessment and quality and improving the environment. Guidance is given on how these policies should be reflected in the development plans of local authorities. There are also relevant Planning Guidance

Papers for Wales on policy and advice, for example Advice Note 14 covers coastal planning. The secretaries of state and their inspectors must have regard to the guidance in dealing with appeals and called-in planning applications, and expect local planning authorities to have regard to it in the exercise of their planning functions (DoE and Welsh Office, 1992).

Resource exploitation

Mineral dredging in territorial waters and on the sea bed can only be carried out with the consent of the owner of the mineral rights. The Crown Estate owns some 55 per cent of the foreshore and virtually all the sea bed within the territorial limits and the continental shelf. It is therefore responsible for licensing most seabed extraction and issues licences for both prospecting and production. Under current procedures, production licences are only given if there has been a favourable 'government view' which is administered by DETR and the Welsh Office. Following the report of the Environment Select Committee on Coastal Zone Protection and Planning in 1992, the non-statutory system was reviewed (House of Commons Environment Committee, 1992). In November 1995 the Government announced proposals for a new statutory licensing arrangement governing the extraction of marine sand and gravel in which all sea bed below the low water mark will be covered regardless of ownership.

Draft Environmental Assessment and Habitats (Extraction of Minerals by Marine Dredging) Regulations were issued for comment in October 1998. These are designed to implement the requirements of relevant EC Directives in so far as they affect marine dredging within British waters, specifically Directive 97/11/EC which amends Directive 85/337/EEC on Environmental Impact Assessment and Directive 92/43/EEC on the conservation of natural habitats and of wild fauna and flora. To comply with EC Directive 97/11/EC, the Government has decided to introduce statutory procedures for the control of marine dredging. Draft Guidance on Marine Dredging Procedures accompanied the draft regulations. The powers and duties of the Secretary of State for Wales under these draft Regulations will be transferred to the Welsh Assembly.

Licences for exploration and development and consents for oil and gas production are awarded by the Department of Trade and Industry (DTI) with DETR and the Welsh Office giving consents for the location of offshore installations. The statutory conservation agencies advise DTI as appropriate. For example, the Joint Nature Conservation Committee advises on the terms and conditions in marine areas of environmental sensitivity. Development of fields within 25 miles (40km) of the coast or in other marine areas of environmental sensitivity requires a full environmental assessment. This must be drawn up in conjunction with advisory bodies and local authorities. Where licences are granted in sensitive areas, strict conditions will apply to protect the environmental resources concerned, including fisheries.

Coastal defence

MAFF has responsibility for setting policy relating to flood defence and coast protection in England while in Wales the responsibility rests with the Welsh Office. The Agency, under the Water Resources Act 1991 has powers to carry out work both above and below the low-water mark for the purpose of reducing risk to low-lying coastal or estuarine land from tidal flooding. The flood defence functions of the Agency are controlled by regional flood defence committees, each of which is chaired by a ministerial appointee, with the majority of members being local council nominees. Flood defence work may also be undertaken under the Land Drainage Act 1991 by other organisations including local authorities, internal drainage boards and private land owners.

Coast protection is the protection of land from erosion and encroachment by the sea. This is the primary responsibility of the maritime district or unitary councils, under the provision of the Coast Protection Act 1949 and within the policy set by MAFF and the Welsh Office. The Agency and the internal drainage boards are statutory consultees in respect of proposals to carry out coast protection work. Councils may also have to apply for a licence for coastal works under the Food and Environment Protection Act 1985. All schemes require ministerial approval and relevant government departments, the Crown Estate Commissioners, the Countryside Commission and English Nature or the Countryside Council for Wales are consulted before MAFF or the Welsh Office can give formal approval.

In carrying out flood defence duties, the internal drainage boards and the Agency must adhere to certain conservation duties imposed upon them by Part IVA of the Land Drainage Act of 1991, the Land Drainage Act of 1994 and the Environment Act 1995. These duties ensure that conservation and enhancement of natural beauty, flora and fauna and geological or physiographical features of special interest are taken into account in formulating or considering any proposals relating to any functions of the board or Agency so far as may be consistent with these functions. They must also have regard to the desirability of protecting and conserving buildings, features and sites of archaeological, architectural or historical interest and must take account of any effect which the proposals would have on the beauty or amenity of any rural or urban area or on those flora, fauna, features, buildings, sites or objects. They also have a duty to have regard to the desirability of preserving public access to places of natural beauty and to ensure that the water or land is made available for recreational purposes. In addition, the Agency is required to have regard to any effects which proposals would have on the economic and social well-being of rural communities. These duties need to be considered in conjunction with those in the Environment Act 1995 which establish the principal aim of the Agency: to protect the environment taken as a whole, so as to make such contribution towards attaining the objective of achieving sustainable development, as the ministers consider appropriate.

Fisheries

MAFF has the responsibility for setting policy and the regulatory framework within which fisheries are managed. Sea fisheries committees can regulate coastal fisheries out to six nautical miles (about 11km) through their bylaws. They are constituted as committees or joint committees of local government with representatives of local authorities, ministerial appointees and a representative of the Agency. The Agency is responsible for regulating salmon and sea trout fisheries out to six nautical miles. Fishing activities within six nautical miles of the coast must comply with common fisheries policy regulation, national legislation and bylaws or other controls introduced by the sea fisheries committees and the Agency. The Environment Act 1995 amended fisheries legislation to give fisheries regulators, that is the sea fisheries committees and the Agency, new powers to control sea fisheries for environmental purposes.

Navigation and shipping

DETR has a general duty to regulate construction and other such operations in tidal waters which might obstruct, endanger or interfere with navigation. It also administers applications for orders under the Transport and Works Act 1992 relating to works in the sea. The most commonly used procedure for controlling effects on navigation is the consent procedure in Section 34 of the Coast Protection Act 1949. A licence under the Food and Environment Protection Act 1985 is normally required from MAFF for works which involve materials or articles placed in the sea (such as during construction), or for the deposit of dredged material at sea.

DETR is the regulatory department for commercial harbours and MAFF has a similar role in relation to fisheries harbours as listed in Schedule IV of the Sea Fishery Industry Act 1951. Almost all port undertakings are administered by statutory harbour authorities whose powers and functions relate to the safety of navigation and the public right of access to port facilities. Harbour authorities are each governed by their own local legislation tailored to meet the needs of each port.

DETR has responsibility for the safety of shipping and the control of pollution from ships, for taking steps to minimise the threat of pollution from ships and for the National Contingency Plan. Pollution control measures are the responsibility of the Maritime and Coastguard Agency (an executive agency of DETR). Local authorities have accepted the non-statutory responsibility of dealing with pollution that impacts on the coast and harbour authorities for the clean-up within ports or harbours. In the event of major incidents involving oil and chemical spills from ships, the Maritime and Coastguard Agency directs offshore operations and assists onshore, setting up command and control arrangements where necessary to co-ordinate activities of all responsible bodies involved in shoreline cleaning operations. The Agency's role is to advise the Maritime and Coastguard Agency on risks to controlled waters and to ensure that environmental considerations are given appropriate and timely consideration in any decision-making. The Agency takes lead responsibility for incidents with a land-based source, including pipelines. The

Agency and the Maritime and Coastguard Agency have agreed a *Memorandum of Understanding* which clearly defines their respective roles and responsibilities relating to oil and chemical pollution events in coastal waters, although this document is currently under review.

Shipping regulation is largely derived from the requirements of various international conventions adopted through the International Maritime Organisation, such as the International Convention for the Prevention of Pollution from Ships (MARPOL). A series of Merchant Shipping Acts implement the conventions in UK law. The Merchant Shipping and Maritime Security Act 1997 implements some of the recommendations of the Donaldson report on the *Braer* spill of 1993. It gives the Secretary of State powers to intervene when a spill threatens large-scale oil pollution in UK waters up to the 200-mile (320km) limit. It also enables regulations to be made for the provision of a ship's waste reception facilities and pollution cost recovery (Department of Transport, 1994).

Pollution control

DETR in England and the Welsh Office in Wales are responsible for formulating policy and providing the legislative framework on water quality issues. Legislation to control the discharge of sewage and trade effluent to coastal waters and estuaries was established later than for inland waters. The Clean Rivers (Estuaries and Tidal Waters) Act 1960 extended the requirement of the 1951 Rivers (Prevention of Pollution) Act for consent, to cover new discharges to specified tidal and estuarine waters. Those discharges made before 1960 still escaped regulation. It was not until the Control of Pollution Act 1974 that all existing and new discharges to tidal or coastal waters out to the three-mile limit (5km) were covered. The legislation allowed consent limits to be applied to the sewage or trade effluent, which are monitored to ensure compliance. Subsequent legislation including EC Directives such as the Dangerous Substances Directive and the Urban Waste Water Treatment Directive have further tightened the control of discharges.

The Agency is responsible for consenting to any proposed discharge of trade or sewage effluent into coastal waters of England and Wales, for monitoring water quality for compliance with the relevant standards and for dealing with pollution incidents (illegal discharges). The Agency is required to consult MAFF (in England) and the Welsh Office (in Wales) about applications for consents to discharge to coastal waters, and copies of applications may also be sent to the relevant sea fisheries committee.

The Environment Protection Act 1990 introduced the concept of integrated pollution control. Its principal objective is to prevent the release to the environment of any prescribed substance using the principle of 'best available technique not entailing excessive cost' and to ensure the 'best practicable environmental option' is taken to ensure the effect of any release on the environment is minimised. The Agency is responsible for authorising Part A processes, the large industrial processes such as oil refineries and power stations, which are frequently situated on estuaries and coasts. The smaller Part B processes are regulated by the local authorities. Together with the local authorities, the Agency will be responsible for implementing the EC Directive on Integrated Pollution, Prevention and Control (96/61/EEC) from October 1999. The Agency is also responsible for issuing abstraction licences. Under the definition for 'Inland Waters' in the Water Resources Act 1991 (S221) the Agency interpretation is that most abstractions from the sea are not licensable unless they are clearly in a dock, channel, creek, bay, estuary or arm of the sea.

The UK Government is a signatory of the 1992 Oslo and Paris Convention for the Protection of the Marine Environment of the North East Atlantic. The work of that convention includes considerations of pollution from land-based sources and the reduction of discharges of the most toxic substances (Annex 1A, the Hague Declaration). The UK Government also co-operates with other states within the North Sea Conference, which agrees strategies for the protection of the North Sea, including actions with regard to coastal waters. The aims of the regulations are to protect, maintain and improve the quality of coastal waters. Consents to discharge must take into account relevant water quality standards or other requirements of national, European or international law. The European Directives which relate to coastal water quality are listed in Appendix 1. A proposed Directive - the water framework - is not yet in place but is likely to have a significant impact on the coastal environment in the next millennium.

Waste disposal

Disposal of material in the sea, for example dredgings, requires a licence from MAFF under the Food and Environment Protection Act 1985. With the coming into force of the 1992 OSPAR Convention on the Protection of the Marine Environment of the North East Atlantic there is a general ban on sea dumping with a limited number of exceptions that may be considered such as fish waste, inert materials of natural origin and vessels and aircraft (the latter only up until 2004). Currently, only dredged material and small quantities of fish waste are licensed for disposal at sea by the UK subject to rigorous assessment of the potential environmental impact. Where waste derives from dredging operations MAFF will consider whether there are appropriate beneficial uses, for example beach replenishment or coastal defence works.

Dumping of sewage sludge stopped at the end of 1998 in line with the OSPAR Convention and European requirements. *"The Urban Waste Water Treatment Directive requires that the dumping of sewage sludge at sea should cease by the end of 1998 and sludge be re-used whenever appropriate. Alternative disposal routes include incineration, an increase in beneficial recycling to land, use as a composting agent, and energy generation. The Government is encouraging the development of beneficial uses wherever possible"* (DETR, 1998a). The Agency is responsible for enforcing the Sludge (Use in Agriculture) Regulation 1989. The Government has expressed its intention that by the year 2002 all sewage sludge that is disposed of to land should be subject to stabilisation and pasteurisation and is in the process of drawing up new regulations on the disposal of sewage sludge to land.

The disposal of minestone at sea ceased in 1993 and disposal on the foreshore ceased at the end of 1995. In one area however, it continues to be deposited on the foreshore as an interim coastal defence measure.

Dredged material is now the main waste routinely licensed for sea disposal. An assessment of the potential impact on the marine environment is made before any licence is granted. The licensing authority also has a duty to consider what practical alternative disposal options are available before granting a licence. The options for disposal will depend on several factors including type of material, quantities for disposal, geographical location, chemical composition and access to the site to be dredged. Beneficial uses for dredged spoils are always sought, if possible. These include coastal defence, habitat creation and land reclamation.

Under the Agency's statutory function to regulate the treatment, keeping, movement and disposal of controlled waste so as to prevent pollution of the environment or harm to human health, landfill sites must be licensed and conditions may be imposed to meet these aims. The draft European Directive on landfill prohibits co-disposal of hazardous and non-hazardous waste as well as the landfill of certain wastes such as tyres and liquid waste. With the cessation of dumping of sewage sludge at sea and the increasing control of waste to landfill, alternative methods of dealing with sewage sludge which deliver environmental benefits, such as composting or incineration with energy recovery, are likely to become important. Both composting and incineration are regulated by the Agency.

Radioactive substances

DETR and the Welsh Office are responsible for formulating national policy and providing the legislative framework for controlling radioactive substances, including radioactive waste. Under the Radioactive Substances Act 1993, the Agency regulates the use of radioactive materials and the storage and disposal of radioactive waste. On nuclear licensed sites, it is responsible for authorising the disposal of radioactive waste, including discharges of effluent into the environment. In determining applications for authorisations it consults many organisations including MAFF/Welsh Office, the Health and Safety Executive, English Nature, the Countryside Council for Wales, local authorities and sewage and water undertakers.

In exercising its duties the Agency undertakes an extensive monitoring programme for radioactivity in the coastal environment. Monitoring programmes for radioactivity cover beaches, estuaries and inter-tidal areas. The Agency also liaises with MAFF which has a long-standing aquatic monitoring programme for radioactivity in foodstuffs. The Agency has agreed a *Memorandum of Understanding* with MAFF and the Welsh Office which sets out the respective responsibilities.

Conservation

DETR is responsible for fulfilling the Government's objectives and policies for nature conservation and for ensuring that its obligations under international conventions and European and national law are met in England; the Welsh Office carries this responsibility in Wales although DETR takes the UK lead on European and international matters. The Government's statutory advisers are English Nature, the Countryside Council for Wales and the Joint Nature Conservation Committee. Local authorities play an important role through statutory development plans, development control, management plans and management of some local nature reserves. Guidance is given under Planning Policy Guidance Note 9, *Nature Conservation*. The Wildlife and Countryside Act 1981 lists animals and plant species which are strictly protected as well as sites notified as Sites of Special Scientific Interest and Marine Nature Reserves. The Convention on Wetlands of International Importance Especially as Waterfowl Habitat (the 'Ramsar' Convention) requires contracting parties to list appropriate wetlands on account of their international significance and to promote the wise use of wetlands generally. Some 50 per cent of the UK sites listed under the convention have a coastal element. Special consideration applies to areas protected under EC Directives. Marine sites are under consideration for designation as Special Areas of Conservation under the Conservation of Natural Habitats and of Wild Flora and Fauna Directive and many estuaries and coasts qualify for designation as Special Protection Areas under the Conservation of Wild Birds Directive (Appendix 1).

Recreation

The Department of National Heritage is responsible for sponsorship of the tourism industry and has policy responsibility for active recreation. The Agency has a duty to promote the use of inland and coastal waters and land associated with such waters for recreational purposes (without prejudice to the conservation and enhancement of natural beauty and the conservation of flora, fauna and geological or physiographical features of special interest). Under the Government's code of practice on *Conservation, Access and Recreation*, issued under the Water Act 1989, the Agency must secure the best recreational use of suitable existing and new resources, catering fairly for as broad a range of interest groups as is practicable, and ensure the recreational needs of the surrounding area are taken fully into account. Public use of recreational facilities should be subject to suitable terms and conditions. The Sports Council promotes appropriate sport and active recreation in coastal areas and the Countryside Commission promotes opportunities for people to enjoy and appreciate the landward coast for informal recreation. Local authorities also take actions to promote sport, recreation and tourism in their areas.

Section 3 Stresses and strains on the coastal environment

The pressures on the coastal environment can be thought of as different sets of stresses, and the manner in which they affect the state of the environment as causing different strains upon it. The pressures themselves arise from what are sometimes referred to as different drivers, which are essentially sociological and economic: they include the need for improved standards of living, wealth creation, and improved quality of life as expressed by improved health, happiness and a clean and varied environment. For the purposes of the Agency, however, although an appreciation and understanding of these factors is extremely important, the success of its own actions in this area are judged primarily on how it has been able to reduce or alleviate the pressures themselves - for example, in terms of the quantities of substances abstracted and discharged into the environment - plus other measures of events (for example, pollution incidents) which place a direct strain upon, and ultimately change, the state of the environment itself.

There are obviously many ways in which data and information on the pressures upon the environment could be categorised. One is that of looking at them in a hierarchical context: thus the environment of England and Wales is affected by events which occur at global and European levels, as well as regionally and locally. Another way of categorising them is in terms of their sociological context, encompassing different modes of living, including the use of industrial processes and practices, and their impact on the environment. Yet another way is to examine pressures in terms of whether they are historic, current or have yet to arise.

But in view of the Agency's own direct responsibilities, as reflected in its regulation of a wide range of environmental licences and operational activities, the framework it uses is centred on these particular aspects and is therefore based upon the following six categories.

- Natural forces - including climate variations, the extent and rate of change in sea level, erosion rates, changes in weather and rainfall patterns, temperature extremes and so on.

- Societal influences - these, together with natural forces, are perhaps the greatest and all-embracing pressures placed upon the coast and range from the size and distribution of the population and the development of ports and transport to planned changes in land use, and recreational practices and activities.

- Abstractions and removals - these include the removal of water, aggregates and fish where the quantities, the processes involved, the timing or the rate of removal are of sufficient concern to require some form of regulatory control.

- Usage, releases and discharges - these include emissions from point sources to the environment, for example from sewage treatment works and industry, and the cumulative input from diffuse sources (such as fertilisers and pesticides).

- Waste arisings and disposals - these include the by-products of industry and society in general which, by their very presence, in one way or another can either directly increase pressures on the coast or, by the manner in which they are handled, alleviate pressures on the environment.

- Illegal practices - these include pollution incidents, accidents such as tankers causing oil spills, and fly-tipping.

3.1 Natural forces

Climate change

The climate of Britain and the level of the surrounding seas and the shape of its coastline have varied considerably over time due to natural events and processes. But there is now evidence that human activities have also been influencing the world's climate, by raising levels of greenhouse gases in the atmosphere, primarily through the burning of fossil fuels.

In the 20th century global surface air temperatures have risen by 0.3°C to 0.6°C (Figure 3.1). In the UK they are predicted to continue to rise by between 0.1°C and 0.3°C per decade, but by slightly less in the north west, and by slightly more in the south east. In general, the warming is expected to be slightly greater in winter than in summer. Extremely warm seasons and years are also expected to occur more frequently. By the 2020s the UK may be on average 1°C warmer than at present and by the 2050s it is predicted to be on average 1.5°C warmer (UK Climate Impacts Programme, 1998). This rise in temperature could have many effects, some of which may increase pressures on the coast directly, and some indirectly. The major impacts of increased air temperatures are predicted to be as follows.

- A northward shift of natural habitats by 50km to 80km per decade may occur. This could affect both terrestrial and marine coastal habitats and may stress even further species that are threatened or under severe pressure. The potential effects of climate change on ocean circulation, fish populations, spawning and growth could also cause fundamental shifts in the distribution and abundance of different fish stocks (UNEP, 1994). It may also encourage more non-native species to become established in UK coastal waters.

- An increase in demands for fresh water by the public and farmers is expected. If these demands are met by further abstraction from rivers then any reduction in river flows could have important consequences for estuarine ecosystems (CCIRG, 1996).

Figure 3.1 *Annual average global temperature anomalies (relative to 1961-1990), 1856 to 1996*

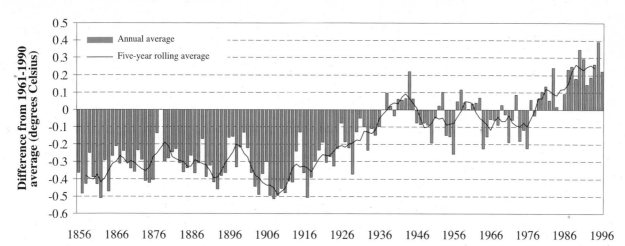

Source: University of East Anglia, Norwich and the Hadley Centre

- An enhanced potential for tourism and recreation is expected, especially in the south, where it is predicted that it will be warmer and where a large proportion of the population lives. Pressures on the coast from recreation have grown steadily in the 1980s and 1990s and climate change could increase this further.

Another important facet of climate change is how rainfall patterns may change with time. There has been a tendency for warmer, wetter winters and hotter, drier summers in the last two to three decades. Annual precipitation is expected to increase overall by between two and five per cent by the 2050s. In general, increases in winter precipitation are predicted to be larger than in summer, and summer precipitation may decrease in the south east. The number of rain days and the average intensity of precipitation are expected to increase over the north of the UK all year round, whereas in the south precipitation intensities are expected to increase in winter only.

There is potential for drought in the south east in summer, and for floods in the north west to become more common. It is expected that there will also be more intense precipitation. This may in turn lead to more flash flooding and increased soil erosion, although there are considerable uncertainties in any predictions of climate change and its effects (Hulme and Jenkins, 1998).

Significant changes in flow patterns in rivers, especially reduced flows in summer, which may occur from low summer rainfall and increased demand for fresh water, will impact considerably upon estuarine ecosystems, as they are adapted to certain hydrographic regimes. Changes might include altering flushing times for nutrients and other substances, changing sedimentation patterns and stressing plants and animals that are not tolerant of large salinity or temperature ranges.

In some coastal locations there has already been a foretaste of the likely impacts of climate change. For example, the relatively dry summers in the late 1980s and the early 1990s led to the tidal River Ouse, which runs into the Wash, silting up and affecting navigation. This occurred because the reduced

flow of fresh water into the estuary was not strong enough to balance the landward transport of sediments from the action of the tides. In 1997 the Agency had to spend an extra £170,000 on dredging specific locations in the Ouse in order to fulfill its statutory obligations with respect to navigation.

One of the largest uncertainties in future climate prediction surrounds storms. Ten of the 47 most severe storms recorded in the UK in the period 1920 to 1990 occurred between 1981 and 1990, with the severest storm occurring on 25 January 1990. It appears that storms over the British Isles have increased in severity and frequency in recent years (Hulme and Barrow, 1997). There were an average of 12 severe gales per year over the period 1961 to 1990, mostly in the period November to March. The middle decades of this century were rather less prone to severe gales than the early and later decades, while the most recent decade - 1988 to 1997 - has recorded the highest frequency of severe gales (15.4 per year) since records began in 1881 (Hulme and Jenkins, 1998).

Winter gale frequencies are expected to decline in the future although very severe gales may increase in number. By the 2080s a 10 per cent increase in summer gales is forecast (Hulme and Jenkins, 1998). If storms are more severe the effects may include increased coastal damage, flooding and erosion. Increased damage from storms, especially with rising sea levels, may change the geomorphology of significant stretches of coastline by altering sediment erosion and accretion patterns and could also increase the need to maintain adequate flood and coastal defences and for sound planning in low-lying coastal areas. With an increase in potential evaporation over most of the UK (due to higher air temperatures), there may be additional stresses on freshwater resources and hence changes to the freshwater flow into estuaries and the flushing of estuaries.

The 'best' estimate describes only one possible evolution of climate and sea level in the UK and implies a linear response of the climate system to increasing greenhouse gas concentrations in the atmosphere. Other responses are also possible and some may involve more abrupt changes in climate related to, for example, changes in the circulation of the North Atlantic. A change in the path of the Gulf Stream, which provides the UK with a relatively warm year-round climate, might mean that we experience climatic conditions more like those of other places at the same latitude, for example, eastern Canada has much colder winters and snow and ice are commonplace.

Sea level change

The coastline of Britain is fairly young in geological terms - 20,000 years ago sea level was thought to be about 100-150m below its present level. It was only after the most recent ice age about 8,000 to 15,000 years ago that sea level rose, initially at a rate of 1cm per year, and inundated low-lying land forming the North Sea and English Channel. After this inundation the rise slowed down and sea level has remained relatively constant (geologically speaking) for the last 3,000 years (Figure 3.2). The extent of recent sea level rise is shown in Figure 3.3 and the rise for selected sites over the past two centuries is shown in Figure 3.4.

Figure 3.2 *The variation in sea level over time (relative to present sea level)*

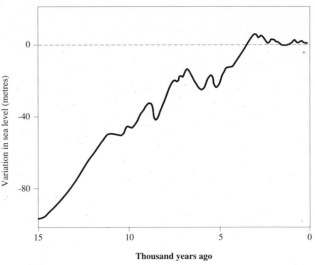

Source: Carter, 1988 Academic Press

Figure 3.3 *Recent mean sea level changes around England and Wales*

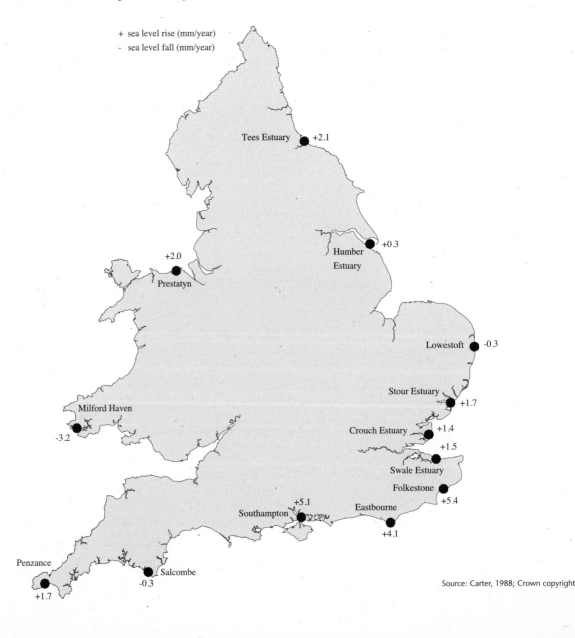

Source: Carter, 1988; Crown copyright

Figure 3.4 *Relative sea-level rise at long-term observation sites*

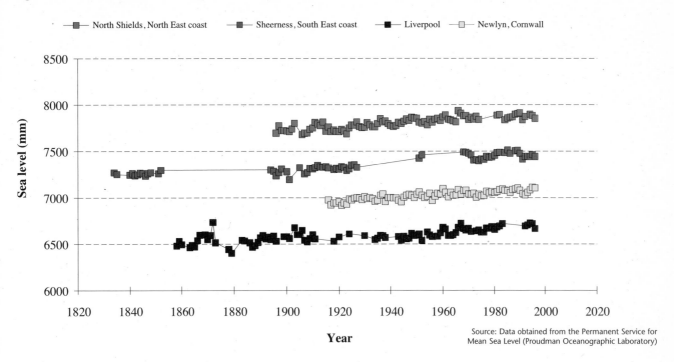

Source: Data obtained from the Permanent Service for Mean Sea Level (Proudman Oceanographic Laboratory)

Sea level rises and falls in response to several factors, which act over different time scales. 'Eustatic' change in sea level is due to long-term fluctuations in ocean circulation or ocean volume. These fluctuations can be brought about by warming or cooling of the oceans, or by the addition or subtraction of water previously locked up in other forms, for example ice. 'Steric' change in sea level is due to changes in regional water properties, like salinity or temperature. Meteorological factors such as storm surges, runoff in rivers and waves reflecting in bays and harbours cause very localised, but often quite large, sea level changes in time and space.

In addition to the sea's surface rising and falling the land can also undergo vertical movements, called 'isostatic' changes (see Section 2.1). Consequently, any rises in sea level around the UK will be felt differentially along the coast because of these vertical land movements (Figure 3.3) (Woodworth *et al.*, 1998). Changes in mean sea-level around the UK coast due to climate change are predicted to be similar to the global-mean, that is a rise of between 12cm and 67cm by the 2050s. There will also be regional differences, and the overall rise in sea level will depend on natural land movement which can exacerbate or reduce the estimated climate-induced change in sea level (Hulme and Jenkins, 1998).

A rising sea level puts low-lying land at greater risk of inundation. This may happen simply by the sea covering the land if it has no defences, but also by storms acting together with higher sea levels to overtop sea defences if they are not adapted. The overtopping of sea defences, during storm surges, is likely to occur more frequently if mean sea levels rise. For example, floods which currently occur on the east coast of England once in 100 years could have a return period of 50 years by 2050, and on the west coast (for example at Avonmouth) the return period for a 100-year flood could reduce to 1.5 years (Graff, 1981).

Sea level rise has not always led to coastal loss. The impact of local factors such as movement and build-up of sediment or tidal range or both have limited or even reversed the effect. During the Holocene Period (10,000 to 7,000 years ago), when sea level rose rather rapidly (perhaps at more than 2m per century), there was sufficient sediment available to allow coastal habitats to form. The situation today may be somewhat different.

'Coastal squeeze' occurs when sea level rises along a shore protected by a hard barrier such as a sea defence or rocky cliff constraining it from moving inland. The extent of coastal squeeze is likely to be exacerbated with further rises. If there are intertidal areas of mud or marshes they will be effectively squeezed out of existence as sea level rises and meets the barrier. Three-quarters of eroding saltmarshes are backed by a sea wall or embankment. This may lead to the loss of certain coastal species, communities or habitats such as saltmarshes. In some places accretion has kept pace with sea level rises of 8mm per year and saltmarshes have extended inland. Sea level rise could also change sedimentation patterns in estuaries and inlets and may mean that in some locations more dredging will be required to maintain harbours and ports. Furthermore, sea level rise could cause the loss of four per cent of coastal shingle and two per cent of dunes by 2012 (Pye and French, 1993a).

Monitoring the extent and rates of erosion and the extent of coastal squeeze requires accurate measurements of topography, land cover and sediment movement. Two relatively new technologies are used by the Agency to help provide these measurements on a large scale and at low cost. The Compact Airborne Spectrographic Imager (CASI) and the Light Detection and Ranging (LIDAR) systems are deployed in light aircraft to measure the colour and height of underlying features. The terrain maps produced using LIDAR have a typical height accuracy of 10-15cm, and a horizontal resolution of 1-4m. This is at least an order of magnitude better than conventional

Figure 3.5 *CASI and LIDAR image of the Arun Estuary, taken in July 1997*

Perspective view of the Arun catchment generated by draping a high resolution CASI image over a LIDAR digital elevation model. The viewing position looks north towards Arundel. The CASI image is true colour and is therefore providing a picture of the ground cover as an aerial photograph would.

Source: Environment Agency

surveying techniques and, together with CASI, allows very detailed mapping and categorisation of features like saltmarshes, dunes or intertidal areas (Figure 3.5). These maps can be combined with other geographical information systems or models to provide, for example, maps of areas at risk from inundation given specified sea levels.

There is a need to investigate the potential consequences of climate change in more depth, for example the loss of habitats and species, changes in water quality, increased erosion from storms and invasion by non-native species. This should be achieved by appropriate monitoring and modelling work so that a strategy based on priorities can be determined.

Flooding

Areas which are less than 5m above Ordnance datum are at greatest potential risk of flooding from the sea. Some five per cent of the population and 1.5 per cent (2,200km²) of the land lie below this level but sea defences have reduced the risk in many places. Furthermore, over 50 per cent of all grade 1 agricultural land in England and Wales lies below this level.

The east coast of England, particularly the area between the Humber and the Thames, is at the greatest risk from flooding from the sea (DoE, 1995a). This is due to a range of factors:

Figure 3.6 *Extremely low-lying land in England and Wales*

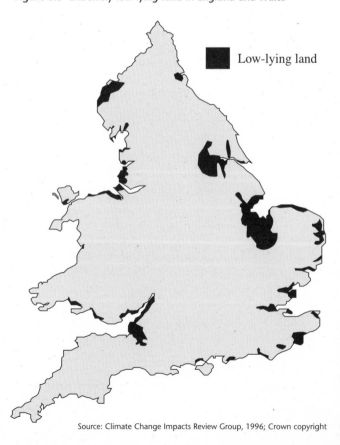

■ Low-lying land

Source: Climate Change Impacts Review Group, 1996; Crown copyright

- much of the land along the east coast is flat and low-lying (Figure 3.6);

- a history of land reclamation has resulted in a substantial proportion of the coastal strip and some inland areas lying below the high tide level and reclamation has interfered with the natural process of deposition;

- the relatively shallow waters of the North Sea result in the tide forming a special sort of wave which causes complex tidal patterns;

- storm surges may coincide with high tides to cause abnormally high water levels in the North Sea.

But other coasts are at risk of flooding too. It is the interaction of the tide and storm surges that is the crucial factor in determining extreme water levels and the potential for flooding. Surges that occur at or near a neap tide are unlikely to cause dangerously high sea levels, but at or near a high spring tide even a modest surge can cause flooding. The greatest danger is when a large storm surge coincides with the time of high water during an abnormally high tide, although there is a tendency for the maximum surge to occur about four hours after high water. The east coast of England experiences an average of 19 storm surges over 0.6m above 'normal' tide height each winter. The west coast has a similar frequency of surges and the south coast fewer (DoE, 1995a).

Severe wave action can add considerable height to water levels and can also contribute to the damage through battering. It can be a crucial factor in the breaching or overtopping of sea defences. Table 3.1 shows the history of major floods.

Table 3.1 *Major floods since the start of historical records*

Year	Estimated effects of flooding
1362	Up to 30,000 people lost their lives across northern Europe and many parishes disappeared
1570	Up to 400,000 lost their lives across Europe
1634	Up to 6,000 people lost their lives and land loss was similar to 1362
1703	About 8,000 people died across Britain and the storm surge caused extensive flooding
1717	Up to 11,000 people lost their lives across Europe
1953	In eastern England 300 people drowned, 65,000ha of farming land were flooded, 24,000 houses were flooded and 200 major industrial premises were inundated, costing about £900m
1990	In north Wales 2,800 homes were inundated and 5,000 people were evacuated

Source: DoE, 1995a Crown copyright

The 1953 flood was the most devastating flood of recent times. Although the tide of 31 January 1953 was only a moderate spring tide, a large surge had been generated which was amplified by winds as it progressed southwards along the east coast. Sea levels in the North Sea rose over two metres higher than tidal predictions. The severity of the disaster was certainly increased because it all happened in darkness. There has been a series of less destructive floods since 1953 (DoE, 1995a).

Table 3.2 *Less destructive floods since 1953*

Date	Effects of flooding
January 1976	Port of Hull flooded, tides and waves breached sea defences at a number of points along the east coast of England, with large areas of Norfolk under water
January 1978	Still water levels higher than in 1953, some areas suffered worst floods in 25 years
February 1983	Hull dry docks gates collapsed under the weight of water. Walcott, Scarborough, Filey and Whitby suffered flooding
October 1996	Tide levels rose to the highest in a decade, the closing of the Thames Barrier prevented flooding in London

Source: DoE, 1995a; Environment Agency Crown copyright

Flooding is a natural pressure on coasts, and nature has its own defences - mudflats and saltmarshes - which protect against flooding by absorbing tidal energy and reducing wave height (Figure 3.7). But since Roman times these natural defences have been thought insufficient and further defences have been constructed for protection and to gain much better agricultural land.

After the flood defences failed in the 1953 storm, many of them were rebuilt and improved using the 1953 levels as a maximum. The Thames Barrier was built as recommended in the Government's report on the 1953 flood, although not completed until 1982. The design recognised that sea level was rising by 0.8cm per year and allows for the rise to continue to 2030. The barrier, which will cope with events up to a return frequency of one in 1,000 years, was designed to protect London and upper parts of the Thames Estuary from storm surges. It protects up to £200 billion worth of property and over a million housing equivalents in London. As well as tidal defences, about 126,500 domestic and commercial properties in England rely on sea defences for their protection and some 366,000 people live in houses liable to flooding from the sea. For Wales the figures are 33,000 properties and 84,000 people (House of Commons Committee of Public Accounts, 1992).

Constructed defences including barriers may increase the risk of flooding elsewhere because they interrupt sediment transport - the movement of shingle, sand and mud. For example, defences can interrupt sediment movement and reduce accretion of mudflats and saltmarshes which are natural

Figure 3.7 *Wave attenuation by saltmarsh*

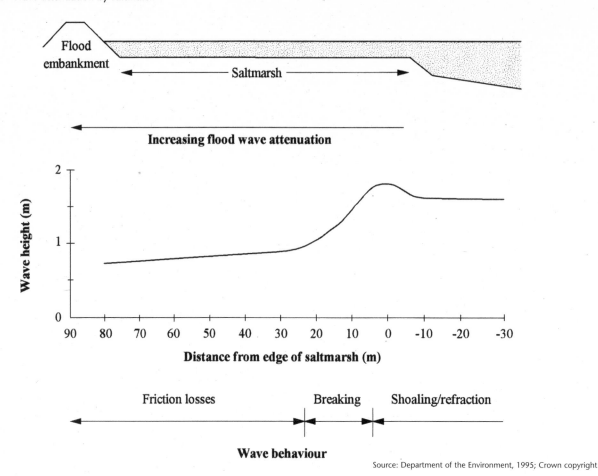

Source: Department of the Environment, 1995; Crown copyright

defences. Some of these effects may occur some distance away depending on the size of the coastal cell (Figure 2.2). Sea Palling on the east Norfolk coast is an example. Coastal protection works here caused a decrease in sediment availability to the sea, making further defences necessary. Constructing defences along one part of the coast can have serious consequences locally and further away. The three main types of hard engineering defence are:

● breakwaters and sea walls which oppose wave energy;

● groynes designed to increase sediment storage on the shore;

● flood embankments and barrages which are watertight barriers (MAFF, 1993a).

In addition to constraining habitat and sediment movement, hard defences have impacts associated with development including use of land, disturbance and visual intrusion. Some 85 per cent of estuaries have some form of artificial embankment which restricts the tide and hence the natural development and movement of intertidal sediments (Davidson *et al.*, 1991). The energy assault on hard defences is high and frequent maintenance is required. Some 90 per cent of sea walls require maintenance within 10 years of construction and nearly all are damaged over 30 years which requires expenditure, although this must be balanced against the benefits they provide.

Increasing recognition of the problems of hard defences has led to a movement towards 'soft engineering' which aims to work with natural systems. These approaches include:

● stable bays which reduce shoreline erosion and tidal flooding by acting as discrete cells which trap sediment and reduce wave energy;

● beach recharge, usually using material from offshore dredging. For example, this takes place along 24km of shoreline between Mablethorpe and Skegness;

● managed retreat where there is a controlled move back from the present defences which allows new landforms to develop naturally and provide natural defences;

● dune management where sand storage is enhanced by fencing and planning, and recreation and grazing is controlled;

● cliff management where protection at the bottom, drainage and slope reprofiling can reduce instability (MAFF, 1993a).

Soft defences also require maintenance on a regular basis.

On the whole there are large uncertainties regarding the long-term impact of defences and natural variations in estuarine and coastal form, and more research is needed. This has been

Figure 3.8 *Characteristic eroding cliff types*

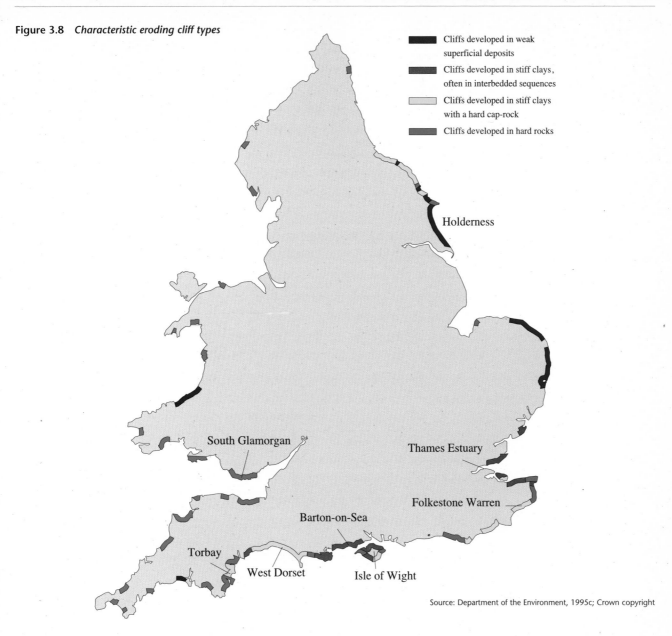

Cliffs developed in weak superficial deposits

Cliffs developed in stiff clays, often in interbedded sequences

Cliffs developed in stiff clays with a hard cap-rock

Cliffs developed in hard rocks

Source: Department of the Environment, 1995c; Crown copyright

recognised and a large research and development programme, amounting to some £15 million, is about to commence based on a scoping study funded by a large group of regulators and other organisations (Hydraulics Research Wallingford, 1997). More details on the response to flooding in terms of coastal protection and sea defences are given in Section 5.4.

Erosion and deposition

Cliffs act as a natural defence to the sea. They erode constantly, supplying material to maintain beaches, dunes, marshes and mudflats elsewhere on the coast. These features also act as flood defences for low-lying areas. Erosion of the sea bed and rock platforms are also important sources of sediment and may be considerably more important sources than cliff erosion. The natural forces which drive erosion include wave energy, sea level rise, tidal currents and the percolation of rain water through rocks. Heavy rain may trigger high water pressure in rock pores which reduces cliff stability.

The areas in England and Wales which are most vulnerable to coastal erosion include:

● the weak deposits of glacial drift on the east coast of England, as at Holderness, which are highly unstable and subject to slumping and collapse;

● the clays of southern and eastern England, for example on the Isle of Wight, Christchurch Bay at Barton-on-Sea, and the south shore of the Thames Estuary which is retreating at up to 2m per year;

● the unstable combinations of rock over clay on the Isle of Wight, west Dorset and at Folkestone Warren in Kent, which are vulnerable to landslides;

● hard rock undermined by the sea, including the chalks of the south coast of England which retreat at about 1m per year, the interbedded limestone and mudstone cliffs of south Glamorgan, and the impure limestones in Torbay (Figure 3.8).

Unstable cliffs have had substantial impacts on human communities at Sandgate, Ventnor on the Isle of Wight, Barton-on-Sea, Swanage, Charmouth, Lyme Regis, Torbay, Downderry and Fairlight in East Sussex. At Ventnor, 50 properties have been demolished over 100 years and repeated road repairs are necessary. Contributory factors include development itself, which can increase pore water pressure by causing the rapid discharge of surface runoff, and leakage from mains and sewers. Excavations for housing can cause slopes to fail, as at Marine Parade in Lyme Regis in 1962. The expansion of Folkestone Harbour in the 19th century disrupted sediment drift, causing beach shrinkage at the foot of Folkestone Warren which is now protected by major erosion control structures (DoE, 1995a).

The Holderness coast, with a 40km line of cliffs, has been retreating at an average rate of 1.8m per year and has lost about 2km and at least 26 villages over the past 1,000 years. This erosion provides an important supply of some one million cubic metres of sediment to the Humber Estuary and the surrounding coastline, including the beaches of Lincolnshire, and the North Sea. These rates of erosion are some of the highest recorded in Europe. Erosion on the south coast is about 0.6m to 1m per year and on the coast of East Anglia between 0.4m and 0.96m per year (Goudie and Brunsden, 1994). Erosion is steepening the intertidal profile in East Anglia and the low water mark is moving landward at 0.5m to 1m per year, and in some places 2m per year.

Rates of sedimentation (or deposition) vary enormously. In the sub-tidal channels of estuaries they may be as high as 15-25cm per week, as in the Heysham channel. On tidal mudflats average sedimentation rates lie between 1cm and 10cm per year (DoE, 1995b). The supply of sediment to an estuary over time can vary and lead to significant changes in character. By analysing navigation charts, a change in sedimentation rates from seven million cubic metres per year between 1900 and 1920 to 1.5 million cubic metres per year by 1970 has been shown in the Humber Estuary (Pethick, 1993). The decline in sedimentation is attributed to reduced sediment supply by reduced erosion rates on the Holderness cliffs due to coastal protection works, and possibly the removal of sediment by dredging at the estuary mouth.

On hard rock coasts marine erosion proceeds more slowly. Rocks of greater resistance may be less subject to collapse from above, but yield to wave attack at the base of cliffs leading to near-vertical cliffs, such as those at Beachy Head in Sussex and Bempton Cliffs in Yorkshire. The different rates and magnitude of cliff erosion depend not only on the hardness of the rock but also on the joint pattern, the direction of the rock strata and on the occurrence of structural weaknesses, such as faults. Where these occur, or where relatively weak rock layers alternate with more resistant rock layers, waves are often able to etch out a complex mosaic of caves, arches and stacks, such as those found in the Stack Rocks area of the Pembrokeshire Coast National Park.

A factor in recent coastal erosion has been an increase in wave heights since 1960, especially an increase in the most extreme wave heights (Figure 3.9). This increase in extreme waves is likely to cause significant increases in erosion which is dominated by storm events (Carpenter and Pye, 1996). The balance between erosion and deposition is also affected by tidal flows. For example, in estuaries a shift to ebb dominant tides in the south and south east has tended to accelerate erosion

while flood-dominant tides to the north favour sediment deposition (Pye and French, 1993b).

Erosion supplies the sediment essential for the development of beaches, dunes, mudflats, saltmarshes and other such features. Beaches may be composed of a number of sediment sizes, ranging from fine sand particles to boulders. The composition of a beach depends on the materials which have moved from adjacent areas (through the coastal cell), materials moving in from offshore, and riverine inputs. The form and composition of beaches and mudflats are functions of both source material and wave energy. Where sandstone, or sand from glacial deposits, predominate then sandy beaches may occur and where clay, or clay and silt-rich river sediments are deposited then mudbanks are more likely. All beaches are in a constant state of flux and are continually responding to wave events. For example, at Torcross in Devon the beach was lowered by a storm leaving little protection for the properties behind, which consequently suffered significant damage during a storm in January 1979. In areas of soft cliff retreat (Holderness and, in the past, the London clay of south east England) eroding sediments provide an important contribution to the local sediment budget. In other areas, such as the coastline bordering the Irish Sea or north east England, landward movement of sediments is the dominant source of material infilling coastal embayments.

At points where the coastline abruptly changes direction, as at river and estuary mouths and bays, spits and bars may form, for example at Spurn Head, at the mouth of the Humber Estuary and Hurst Spit in Hampshire. These form important natural coastal defences, protecting the coastline from wave attack.

Dunes develop when an onshore wind blowing over a dry beach transports sand-sized particles in a landward direction. Any obstruction on the upper beach will slow the wind down and cause it to deposit some of the sand. Small mounds develop and, once they have grown above the level of most high tides, are colonised by salt-tolerant plants. The plants act as an efficient sediment trap and the embryo dunes grow rapidly, coalescing to form low, narrow ridges on the upper beach. With further accretion tough, salt-resistant grasses such as marram (Ammophila arenaria) are able to grow, promoting yet further build-up until a large dune ridge develops running parallel to the shoreline. The troughs between the ridges, known as dune slacks, are quite damp environments and often support a wide diversity of plant species. If the vegetation cover of the dune ridge is broken, sand movement can be reactivated and a large hollow or blow-out may develop.

Most large dunes are found in areas subjected to westerly winds such as at Perranporth in Cornwall and Swansea Bay in Wales. Occasionally the mobility of the sand has led to the burial of coastal settlements. For example, St Piran's oratory (close to Perranporth), built in the 6th century, was buried by sand in about 1608, exhumed in 1835, and exhumed again in 1910.

Erosion and deposition are important natural processes acting on the coast. They have been taking place for millions of years and have shaped our present coastline. Development on the coast, land reclamation, dredging and the engineering

Figure 3.9 *Changes in wave heights around England and Wales, 1960 to 1990*

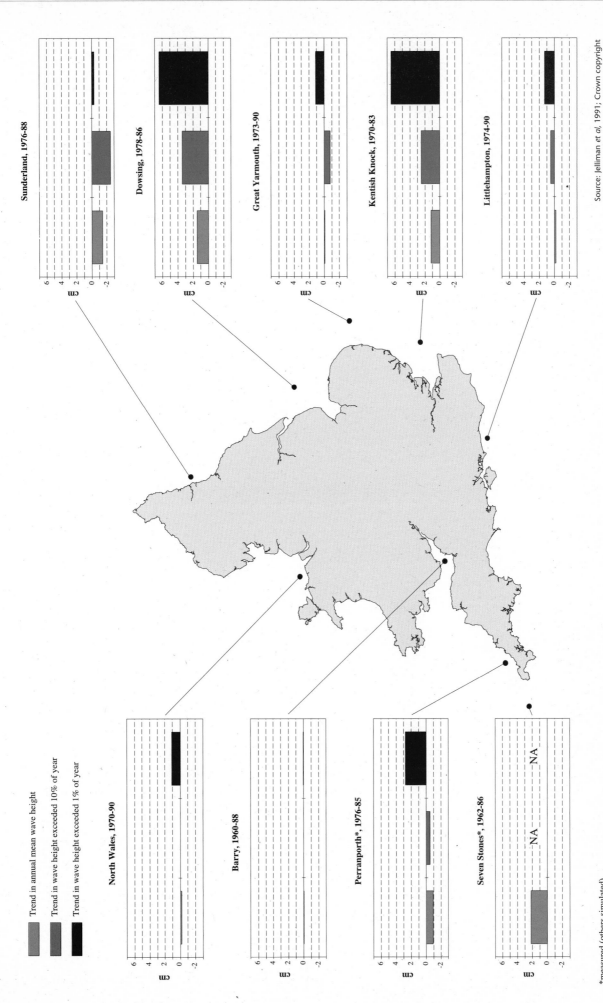

Trend in annual mean wave height

Trend in wave height exceeded 10% of year

Trend in wave height exceeded 1% of year

Sunderland, 1976-88

Dowsing, 1978-86

Great Yarmouth, 1973-90

Kentish Knock, 1970-83

Littlehampton, 1974-90

North Wales, 1970-90

Barry, 1960-88

Perranporth*, 1976-85

Seven Stones*, 1962-86

NA

NA

*measured (others simulated)

Source: Jelliman *et al*, 1991; Crown copyright

structures which protect the coast from flooding and erosion have altered the natural processes in many areas. This can lead to the insufficient supply of sediment to maintain beaches, mudflats and saltmarshes which may then be degraded or washed away. Understanding of the natural processes acting over a large scale is essential but often, in the past, coastal defences and developments have been on a local scale without knowledge of potential consequences elsewhere. There is now an awareness of the need to work with natural forces, not against them, and this is discussed further in Section 5.4.

3.2 Societal influences

Population and development

In 1995 the population of England and Wales was 51.8 million and it is projected to grow by five per cent over the 40-year period to 2031 (DETR, 1997a). Most people in this country live in the cities and major towns, many of which are located by estuaries or on the open coast. They have for the most part grown up around fishing or trading ports, fortifications or industries. Some small towns have developed in remote coastal locations to serve recreational needs because they are in areas of outstanding natural beauty or have other features that people enjoy.

The number of people living within 10km of the coast in England and Wales is about 16.9 million or about a third of the population (based on the Agency's analysis of the 1991 census data). This 10km coastal strip is 23 per cent of the total land area of England and Wales. Seven per cent of the population (about 3.6 million) live within 10km of the Thames Estuary in London alone. The immediate coastal zone is a particularly densely populated part of the country (Figure 3.10). Roughly 11.5 million people are estimated to live within one kilometre of an estuary in Great Britain.

Figure 3.10 *Population by census enumeration district in the 10km coastal zone, 1991*

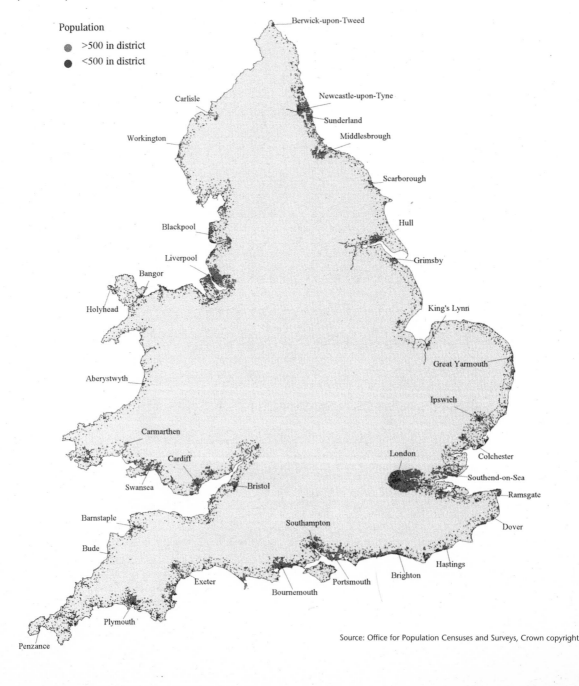

Source: Office for Population Censuses and Surveys, Crown copyright

In England and Wales the point furthest from any coastline is about 110km (about 70 miles) inland. If a settlement is 50km from the coast it is likely to be considered 'inland', somewhere in the heart of the country, whereas some countries would use 50km from the coast to define their onshore coastal zone boundary. If that definition was used in the UK, nearly 75 per cent of the population would be coastal, one of the highest proportions in Europe. In Germany, only 11 per cent of the population live within 50km of the sea, and corresponding figures for other countries are France 24 per cent, Spain 54 per cent, Netherlands 75 per cent and Denmark 100 per cent (Brady Shipman Martin, 1997).

Coastal resorts experience a large influx of visitors in summer. In Torbay for example, the resident population in the tourist season may increase by 50 per cent and this does not include day visitors. Some rural communities, which are host to caravan and camping sites or holiday camps, may be very small in winter but have a substantial summer population. For example, in Devon there is a caravan and camping site at Berry Narbor which raises the population from 700 in winter to 4,500 in summer (Devon County Council, 1998). These additional people are often extremely important for the local economy and may even determine the continued existence of some communities. However, without adequate development planning and suitable management they may introduce an uncontrolled pressure on the environment.

The number of retired people is very significant in some coastal areas and is often due to migration on retirement. Some 36 per cent of the coastal population of Devon are over 60 years of age (Barne et al., 1996a). This seawards migration sometimes leads to pressure for new residential accommodation and other amenities. Also, the retired population is growing. The proportion of people aged 65 and over rose from 12 per cent in 1961 to 16 per cent in 1995, and is predicted to grow to 24 per cent by 2031. In 2016 the proportion of people aged 65 and over is forecast to exceed those aged under 16 for the first time (Office for National Statistics, 1997).

Other demographic changes may also cause pressures on the coast. There has been a steady increase in the number of households in England and Wales since the 1970s, reflecting the increase in population and a move to more people living alone. The number of households is projected to grow at a faster rate than the population in the next 20 years. Over the 25 years from 1991 to 2016, there is a projected increase in the number of households by about 4.4 million to 23.6 million (a 23 per cent increase) in England (DoE, 1995b; DoE, 1996a), and by 223,000 in Wales. Because a substantial proportion of the present UK population is situated near the coast, it is not unreasonable to assume that further growth will occur there, imposing greater pressure on the environment.

A significant percentage of the coastline is already developed in industrial, commercial, residential and recreational terms. Around 31 per cent of the coastal frontage of England and Wales is occupied by buildings, roads and recreation facilities such as caravan parks, camping sites, car parks and golf courses. Economic pressure for further expansion of these facilities is likely to increase in the future.

Coastal development has always required land and since Roman times one-quarter to one-third of intertidal estuarine areas, affecting nearly 90 per cent of British estuaries, are thought to have been reclaimed, primarily for stock grazing. For example, in the Wash an estimated 47,000ha of intertidal area have been reclaimed since the Romans and since the early 1700s, about 27 per cent (6,000 ha) of the Dee Estuary and 86 per cent (3,300 ha) of the Tees Estuary have been reclaimed. Subsequently reclaimed land has been used for arable farming, housing, industry, rubbish tipping and disposal of power station fuel ash (Davidson et al., 1991). By reclaiming land, many of the natural processes at work evolving the coast and maintaining dynamic equilibrium have been affected. This can lead to a significant pressure on the coast.

Barrages

Weirs, barriers and barrages have been built in England and Wales since early times. Altering the location of the tidal limit on estuaries has been carried out for a variety of reasons in the past, including to make pools of fresh water for drinking, industry or agriculture, to power water mills, to make new land available, to alleviate flooding and to make fishing or navigation easier. Developments of this kind usually involved some loss of intertidal area, and modifying tidal currents, sedimentation and ecosystems. Shoreline development was also often drawn to the areas around these structures. Nowadays, very few estuaries in England and Wales have natural tidal limits.

In the last two decades the building, or planning, of large barrages has developed (Figure 3.11). This section looks at these in some detail because they present a significant potential pressure on coasts and estuaries. They have been built for a number of reasons: for surge protection, for example, on the Thames and the Essex Colne; and for amenity and economic regeneration, for example on the Wansbeck, the Tawe, the Tees and Cardiff Bay. They have also been proposed for power generation on the Severn and the Mersey.

Barrage development needs to be managed to minimise environmental impacts, and to take account of the impacts on tidal range elsewhere. Typical impacts may be seen at the barrage completed on the Wansbeck Estuary in Northumberland in 1975. The objective was to create an amenity lake and a riverside park and to cover up 'unsightly' saltmarshes. The barrage has not met this objective completely, although the impounded waters do have some amenity use. The environmental problems that have emerged in the two decades since impoundment include:

- an ecosystem which has been severely restricted by the unnatural salinity regime, with a habitat dominated by a few opportunistic species;

- impounded waters which are stratified with respect to salinity and which are poorly oxygenated along the bed;

- sediment deposition which is silting up the impounded embayment and acting to recreate saltmarshes flooded as part of the original barrage scheme (Worrall and McIntyre, 1998).

Figure 3.11 *Major coastal barrages and barriers*

Principal purpose

▲ Abstraction
★ Amenity
■ Flood defence

Source: Environment Agency

There have been mixed results in achieving economic regeneration from some barrage projects. For example, urban regeneration around the Tawe Barrage has not yet reached the level that was expected before its construction, although it is still early days. The Tawe Barrage was completed in 1992 and has 22ha of impounded surface water. Water quality in the impoundment has been an intermittent problem, with a low oxygen, high salinity layer of water sometimes forming at the bed. A fish pass was built into the barrage, but current evidence shows it has been extremely difficult for migratory fish to pass through it. Estuarine barrages pose a threat to migrating fish as the design of fish passes cannot ensure that upstream passage is not impeded to some extent. In the case of the Tees, economic and physical regeneration are both occurring, aided by the presence of the barrage. The Tees Barrage was completed in 1995 and the impoundment covers 40ha. The Tees Estuary has a legacy of industrial contamination, and poor sediment and water quality meant that migratory fish could not get inland to fresh water (Burt and Watts, 1996).

In 1999, a barrage across Cardiff Bay should be finished and 200ha of intertidal mudflats will be covered permanently with a freshwater amenity lake. The rivers Taff and Ely will flow into this lake, whose waters and shoreline are intended to be a catalyst for urban regeneration. The barrage will also reduce the risk of flooding from extreme or surge tides in Cardiff (Burt and Watts, 1996). Water quality and fisheries in the bay and its two rivers have recovered since the early 1980s, after 200 years of industrial pollution. After impoundment, re-oxygenation of the lake is planned for dry weather or low wind conditions. Due to the loss of the mudflats in the bay, Cardiff Bay Development Corporation has agreed to attempt to recreate alternative habitats elsewhere in the Severn Estuary. Cardiff Bay is being rapidly developed, but it is too early to tell whether the final economic regeneration will match the expectations.

Proposals have been considered for barrages for power generation on the Severn and Mersey estuaries, but neither proposal has progressed very far due to the huge financial investment required and the complex environmental investigations necessary. The consequences of a Severn Barrage have already been subject to expensive environmental investigations in the early 1970s (Energy Technology Support Unit, 1989).

Figure 3.12 *Domestic tourism in England and Wales and overseas visitors to the UK*

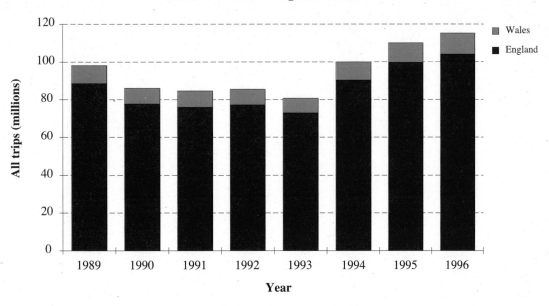

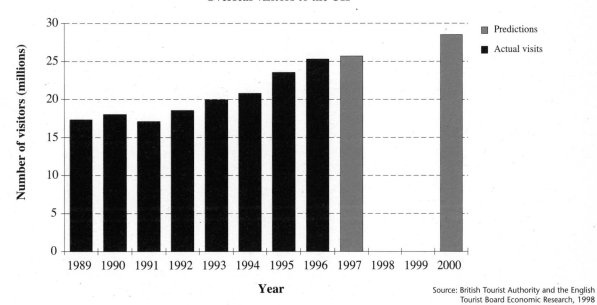

Source: British Tourist Authority and the English
Tourist Board Economic Research, 1998

Recreation

Household expenditure on recreation, entertainment and education has increased substantially over the past 30 years, reflecting a rise in real household disposable income. Part of this increase in recreational expenditure relates to time spent at the coast. There has also been dramatic growth in outdoor pursuits, including those which impact on or make use of coastal amenities (Sports Council, 1991):

● walking club membership increased by 138 per cent from 1980 to 1990;

● in 1990 there were 10,000 regular surfers and the same number of seasonal surfers (a 69 per cent increase on 1980) and one-third of a million water skiers (a 35 per cent increase on 1980);

● in 1991 there were over half a million windsurfers, 3,000 jet skis and 5,000 participants;

● yacht club membership increased by 64 per cent from 1980 to 1990.

In addition to sport, coastal locations are also very popular for other activities such as sightseeing, shopping and eating out. Over 50 per cent of people in England and Wales took a day trip to the coast in 1996. In total there were about 170 million day trips to the coast in 1996, with about £2 billion spent on those trips. There was a 10 per cent increase in the number of day trips from 1994 to 1996 and cars were the main form of transport for visitors (Social and Community Planning Research, 1997). Table 3.3 shows the number of visitors to some of the coast's most popular tourist attractions with free admission.

Table 3.3 *Visits to the most popular coastal tourist attractions in 1995*

Destination	Visitors in 1995 (millions)
Blackpool Pleasure Beach	7.3
Palace Pier, Brighton	3.8
Eastbourne Pier	2.3
Pleasure Beach, Great Yarmouth	2.0
Pleasureland, Southport	2.0

Source: Office for National Statistics, 1997 Crown copyright

About 115 million tourist trips (a stay of one or more nights away from home for holidays, visits to friends or relatives, and business trips) are taken in England and Wales by British residents in the UK each year (Figure 3.12). This is over 90 per cent of all the tourist trips taken in the UK by residents of the UK. Domestic tourism in the UK is predicted to grow annually by an average of seven per cent between 1996 and 2000 (BTA and ETB, 1998). Over the whole of the UK, 45 per cent (£6.2 billion of £14.5 billion) of the total amount spent by residents on tourism in 1994 was on seaside holidays. About 245,000 people are employed in the industry. The principal items of expenditure are accommodation (30 per cent), leisure

attractions (11 per cent), catering (nine per cent) and retail and non-foods (23 per cent) (Pugh and Skinner, 1996).

There are over 25 million overseas visitors to the UK every year (Figure 3.12). The majority are holiday makers, many of whom will visit the coast during their stay. Tourism from overseas is predicted to grow annually by an average of four per cent between 1996 and 2000 (BTA and ETB, 1998). Tourism from overseas has a share of five per cent of the total value of UK exports, and there are an estimated 245,000 jobs in seaside-related tourism in the UK (Pugh and Skinner, 1996).

Leisure activities are important to the economy and provide immense enjoyment, contributing to the quality of life, and the coast is home to a wide range of leisure facilities (Figure 3.13). However, if not properly controlled these activities can create pressures on the coastal environment and there are often conflicts between different activities. Table 3.4 summarises the potential impacts of specific leisure activities on sensitive habitats and species. Land-based amenities (for example golf courses, holiday camps, campsites) which are not developed sensitively may have an aesthetic impact by altering the landscape or encroaching upon or destroying fragile habitats. Even low impact activities (for example, bathing, walking, birdwatching) can cause litter, soil erosion and trampling of

Figure 3.13 *Tourist and leisure facilities along the south coast of England*

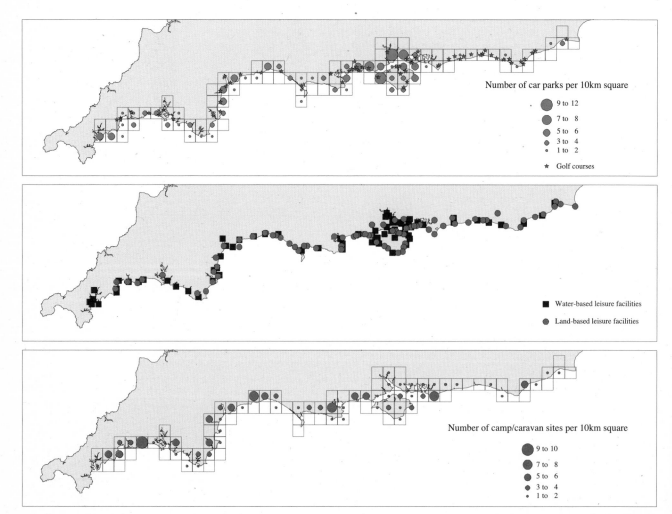

Source: Joint Nature Conservation Committee

vegetation and conflict between users when in overcrowded or sensitive areas. Motorised activities and boating (for example four-by-four vehicles, power boats, jet skis, yachts) need marinas, roads, car parks and slipways which can result in severe soil erosion and vegetation loss, disturbance to wildlife, conflict with other users, oil pollution, contamination from antifoulant paints and habitat loss (House of Commons Environment Committee, 1995).

Sea angling is increasing as a major recreational use of coastal foreshores and inshore areas. Locally, there may be threats to wildlife from bait collection and discarded tackle, as well as the subsequent aesthetic nuisance of discarded items. Angling, for

bass in particular, but also for some off-shore wreck-dwelling species (for example conger, pollack and ling), is carried out under the guise of recreation but is often commercial and has raised concerns about overfishing.

The building of groynes on beaches to protect them from movement and the artificial replenishment of beaches are often for recreational purposes. These works can create pressures on other parts of the coast by interfering with the natural processes at work. Furthermore, marinas have the potential to interfere with coastal currents, sediment budgets and waves unless well planned and designed.

Table 3.4 *Summary of the potential impacts from specific leisure activities*

Activity	Habitat or species	Potential impact
Aircraft (helicopters, microlights and light aircraft)	Coastal birds in breeding season.	a) Increased risk of abandoning/predation of eggs/chicks. Abandoning of breeding sites. b) Reduction in feeding and roosting time. Energy reserves depleted in search for alternative sites.
Climbing	Geological and geomorphological formations; cliff nesting birds.	Removal of vegetation; disturbance to nesting birds.
Golf	Lowland grassland/heathland.	Demand for water abstraction; habitat modification; fertiliser use; herbicide use; cutting management; ancillary development.
Fishing and angling	Coastal birds, coastal fish, benthic organisms.	Ensnarement in 'lost' fishing line; disruption from bait digging; pressure on some fish stocks.
Off-road vehicles (4x4 and trail bikes)	Effects on coastal birds during breeding season, wintering and passage. 1. Shingle. 2. Sand dunes. 3. Saltmarshes. 4. Maritime grassland and heath, beaches.	See (a) and (b) above, but more localised. 1. Destruction of shingle vegetation and of geomorphological structure. 2. Destruction of dune vegetation and initiation of erosion. 3. Localised destruction of vegetation; and in some cases, erosion. 4. As for 3 (but less significant or widespread).
Walking and dogs	1. Effects on coastal birds during breeding season, wintering and passage. 2. Any habitat on seawalls. 3. Sand dune communities.	1. See (a) and (b) above, but more localised. 2. Damage to seawall vegetation.
Small, power craft: jet ski, power-boats, water skiing, sailboarding.	Coastal birds.	Disturbance to feeding and roosting birds and to seal colonies.
Wildfowling (coastal)	Passage and wintering birds.	Localised disturbance to feeding and roosting birds. Death of quarry species.
General beach recreation.	Beaches, cliff tops, shingle, sand dunes.	Public use of beaches in breeding season (April to July) limits sites available to some birds, for example terns, little ringed plover, oyster catcher. Localised erosion leading to: 1. Destabilisation of dunes. 2. Loss or modification of cliff top grasslands through trampling, leading to erosion. 3. Preventing shingle plants completing life cycle, for example shore dock, sea pea. Trampling limits the distribution of shingle vegetation, not the geomorphological structure.

Source: House of Commons Environment Committee, 1995 Crown copyright

Transport

Ports are strategically located in estuaries, bays and inlets to make use of deep, natural harbours or calm sheltered waters. They provide access to rivers and seas and are at the head of trade routes into the hinterland. Ports are now part of a large, international network of transport links between our cities and industrial centres and those of other nations. In many cases they are also sites of industrial or commercial activity with large populations of their own, and the type of goods moved through ports reflects these industrial needs (Figure 3.14).

The major ports in terms of volume include London, Southampton, Milford Haven, Liverpool, Grimsby and Immingham, Hartlepool and Felixstowe. In addition, some ports specialise in certain types of traffic. Unitised traffic (for example containers) is concentrated in Felixstowe, Dover, London, Grimsby and Immingham, Liverpool and Southampton, although other ports also handle unitised goods. Dover and Portsmouth are important ports for passengers and vehicles. Oil and gas terminals and refineries are found at many ports including Milford Haven, Hartlepool, Grimsby and Immingham, Southampton and London. Hartlepool, Grimsby and Immingham, Manchester and Hull are important for handling large volumes of chemicals (DETR, 1997b).

There has been a steady increase in the overall traffic of goods into and out of UK ports over the last 30 years, from 294 million tonnes in 1965 to 406 million tonnes in 1996 (Figure 3.15). This represents a growth rate of about one per cent per year for goods traffic into and out of English and Welsh ports. Cargoes in which traffic has increased in the UK in the last few

Figure 3.14 *All foreign and domestic traffic through English and Welsh ports, 1996*

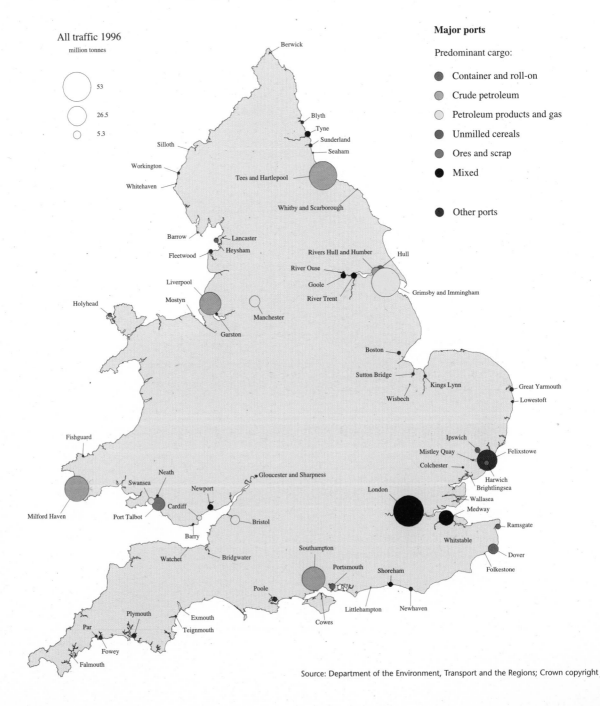

Source: Department of the Environment, Transport and the Regions; Crown copyright

Figure 3.15 *All UK ports traffic, 1965 to 1996*

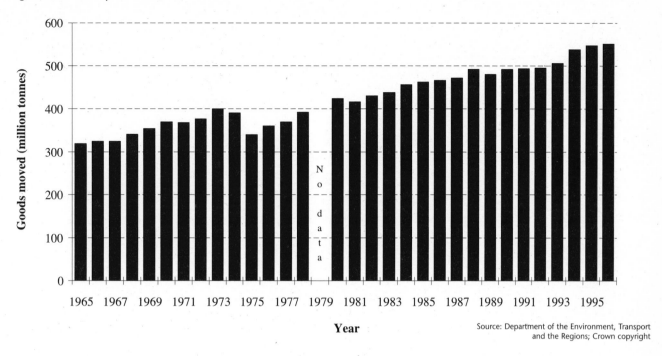

Source: Department of the Environment, Transport
and the Regions; Crown copyright

Figure 3.16 *Accompanied passenger vehicles through UK ports, 1987 to 1996*

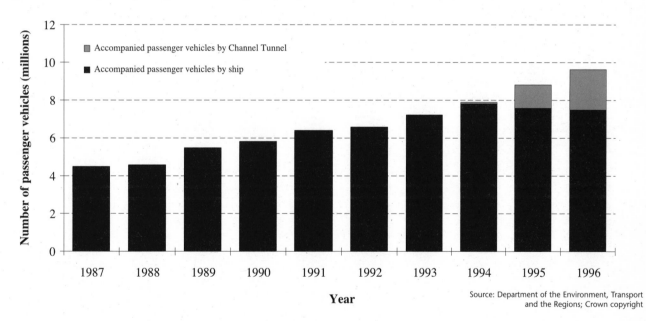

Source: Department of the Environment, Transport
and the Regions; Crown copyright

years include crude petroleum, bulk fuels, containers and roll-on-roll-off cargoes, passengers and vehicles (Figure 3.16). The growth in traffic has not been evenly distributed among the ports. Some ports have grown much faster than others, for example the traffic of goods through Felixstowe increased from 0.8 million tonnes in 1966 to about 26 million tonnes in 1996, and some ports have even seen a decline, for example Bristol and London (DETR, 1997b).

In addition to the benefits that ports bring, they also exert pressures on the environment. Many harbours and ports require artificial structures such as breakwaters and coastal defences to protect them, and dredging in order to maintain navigable channels and free access. These alter the natural erosion and deposition of sediments, create potentially polluted dredging spoils which must be disposed of and, together with the need for large areas of land, contribute to pressures on habitats.

Shipping

Ships in ports can create pressures on the environment. Accidental leakage of hydrocarbons to the atmosphere and oil spills from ships can be a significant pressure. These can occur during the purging of tanks and during the storage, loading and unloading of petroleum products. Most aerial emissions from crude oil distribution occur during loading and unloading of tankers, contributing about four per cent of the UK's total emissions of volatile organic compounds in 1988.

Aerial emissions from ships' exhausts may disperse over a large area when ships are underway but can impact directly on the air quality of ports when ships are at berth. Oil tankers, for example, may spend several days in port, discharging their cargoes with their engines running. Ships' fuel (often called 'bunker fuel') typically contains three per cent sulphur. An estimated four million tonnes of bunker fuel are used in the English Channel and southern North Sea each year and about 29 per cent of this fuel is consumed in ports (about 26 per cent of the sulphur). Exhaust gases contribute a significant amount to sulphur dioxide concentrations in major ports. From modeling of local air quality in ports, the contributions to annual mean sulphur dioxide concentrations from ships are predicted to be in the range 4 to 8μg/m³ in Dover, Felixstowe, Portsmouth and Southampton (the World Health Organisation's annual mean criteria for sulphur dioxide is 50μg/m³ for human health, 30μg/m³ for crops and 20μg/m³ for natural vegetation). So, although ships on their own may not pose a serious threat to air quality, in ports where air quality is already badly affected by other factors, like road traffic, ships' exhaust

gases may exacerbate the problem. Ships may be a significant source of ground level nitrous oxides in ports as well (CONCAWE, 1994).

Shipping in the north east Atlantic emits an amount of sulphur dioxide equivalent to 60 per cent of the UK's emissions and nitrous oxides equivalent to 84 per cent of the UK's emissions. These estimates do not include emissions from ships at anchor or in berth, which can be significant and can also have a pronounced effect on local air quality (Lloyd's Register, 1995).

Sulphur deposition from ships' exhaust gases are thought to contribute up to eight per cent of the total deposition over land predicted by United Nations Economic Commission for Europe and up to 20 per cent of its target loads. In terms of critical loads exceedance over the whole of the UK, the Institute for Terrestrial Ecology calculated that ships were responsible for less than 10 per cent of the critical load, but in some sensitive areas it could be as much as 25 per cent (CONCAWE, 1994).

Figure 3.17   *Road traffic on coastal roads, 1982 to 1996*

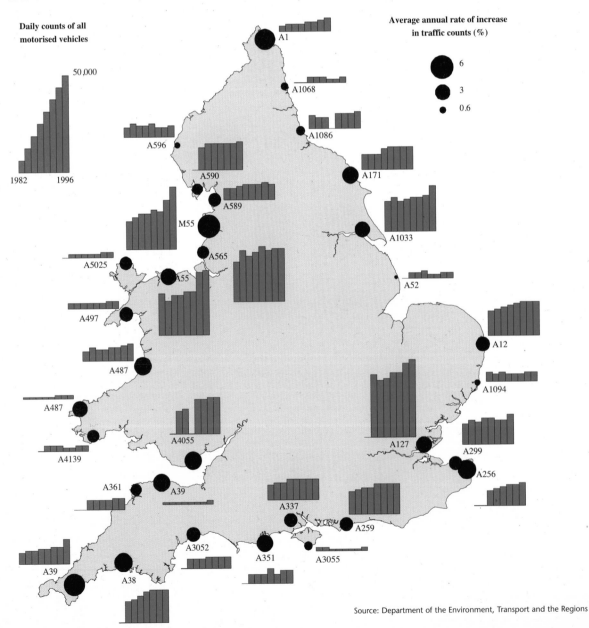

Source: Department of the Environment, Transport and the Regions

Fouling of ships' hulls by algae, mussels, barnacles and other invertebrates causes an increase in water resistance, resulting in an increase in fuel use and possibly lowering the ship's performance. To overcome this, paints containing biocides are applied to ships' hulls (and other underwater structures) to prevent or reduce fouling. In addition to entering the environment through leaching from painted surfaces, biocides can be released during paint stripping, boat maintenance and paint application. As biocides are by their very nature toxic to aquatic organisms, there is a potential for antifouling paints to have an effect on non-target organisms. The problems associated with the biocide tributyl tin (or TBT) are well known and it has been banned from use on small vessels (under 25m in length) since 1987. However, there are only limited data on the potential for other approved biocides to enter the environment and the effects that these might have. Antifouling paints are a diffuse source of pollution associated with ships, boats and ports. Controls on pollution from shipping are discussed in Section 5.2.

Roads

Road traffic generates polluted runoff from the emissions from vehicles, and from abrasion and corrosion of the vehicles and the road surface. The runoff is likely to contain metals, PAHs and oil. Pollutants from roads can be washed into groundwaters and rivers, and eventually end up in estuarine sediments and the sea. The quantities of pollutants in runoff are highly variable. Road runoff is thought to be a significant source of contaminants to estuaries directly and via rivers. But at the moment not enough data exist to allow a proper assessment of the magnitude of this pressure on coastal waters.

Road vehicle traffic in Britain has grown almost tenfold since the Second World War and in the period from 1985 to 1995 grew from 310 billion vehicle kilometres to 431 billion vehicle kilometres (a 39 per cent increase overall and about a three per cent year-on-year increase). Road traffic is forecast to grow at a rate of between 17 and 39 per cent from 1997 to 2011, and 29 to 63 per cent by the year 2021 (DETR, 1997c).

Average daily motor vehicle flows on all classes of road (motorways, major roads and minor roads) increased by 33 per cent overall between 1985 and 1995 and is increasing by about three per cent year-on-year (DoT, 1996a; DoT, 1996b).

Most coastal roads have experienced similar growths in traffic volume and flows. Daily counts of all motorised vehicles from DETR's National Road Traffic Survey have been analysed for 32 randomly selected coastal roads. These data indicate an average annual increase in vehicle flows of about 2.7 per cent (and a range of 0.5 per cent to six per cent) from the mid 1980s to the mid 1990s (Figure 3.17). For each of the road types the average annual rates of increase in vehicle flows are broadly similar to those for Britain as a whole (six per cent for the one motorway in the sample, 2.4 per cent for the nine built-up major roads and 2.6 per cent for the 22 non built-up major roads). There are coastal roads where the rate of increase in vehicle traffic (however it is measured) is much faster than the average (for example the A39 near Falmouth) and in these

places there may be unplanned and localised pressures. For example, there is evidence from a study of the Tamar Estuary that the increased traffic, resulting from the new bridge in 1961, resulted in an increase in the volume of oil related contaminants entering the estuary (Section 4.3). Otherwise, from this limited sample of vehicle flows, coastal road traffic seems to show the same trend of steady growth as in the country as a whole. Roads cause diffuse pollution of estuaries and coastal water. More details are given in Section 3.4.

3.3 Abstractions and removals

Water resources

In England and Wales an estimated 23,600 Ml/d of tidal water was abstracted in 1996 for various uses, although cooling water is dominant. Regional variations in the total volumes abstracted largely reflect the distribution of power generating capacity around the country (Figure 3.18). Over 99.9 per cent of abstracted tidal water is used for cooling water in industry and electrical power generation. Most (over 80 per cent) of this is for once through-cooling, where the cooling water is returned to the estuary or coast after use. About 20 per cent of cooling water is used in evaporative cooling processes, where the water is released to the atmosphere as vapour. About 93 per cent of cooling water is used by the electricity supply industry. Other uses of abstracted water are minimal because it is saline and unfit for most other purposes.

Fish entrainment into industrial cooling water intakes can reduce plant efficiency or cause damage to equipment, as well as being lethal to the fish themselves, unless protecting measures are taken. It is not known exactly how or why fish are entrained into cooling water abstraction intakes, but it is believed that fish may be drawn into water intakes whose suction overcomes their swimming speeds, or alternatively that they swim randomly into intakes, or that they are attracted by the change in water velocity near the intakes. Mostly it is the smaller, juvenile seafish which are affected, either because they can pass through protective gratings or because they have lower swimming speeds, and therefore nursery areas can be particularly vulnerable. Migratory fish passing between fresh water and the sea, and vice versa, are also potentially at risk (Solomon, 1992).

On occasions, power stations are forced to cease operation temporarily when vast quantities of sprats block intake screens. Although large numbers of fish can become entrained in intakes, calculations have been unable to show that losses are significant compared with the total population from which the fish are drawn. Even for species suspected of forming local sub-populations, which might be expected to suffer to a proportionately greater extent, no impact has been demonstrated (Solomon, 1992). An assessment of the impact of fish impingement and entrainment made for the proposed development of Pembroke Power Station found that, without additional protective measures, fewer than five per cent of locally landed commercial stocks (by value) would be affected (Bamber, 1995). Although fish entrainment is a real cause for concern at some installations it is generally considered not to be

Figure 3.18 *Estimated abstractions of coastal and estuarine waters by industry, 1980 to 1996*

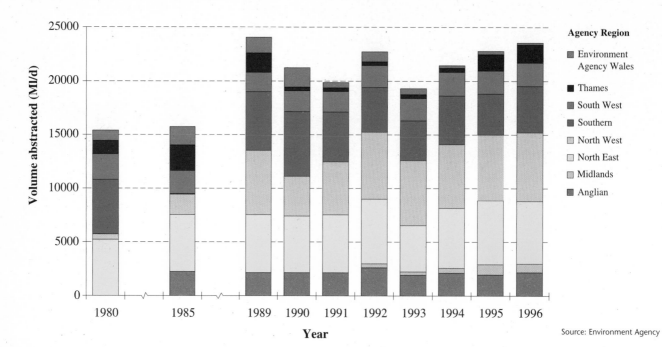

a widespread problem for sea fisheries, but sensitive design of intakes can help to further minimise their impact and ensure the safe operation of industrial plants.

Freshwater abstractions

Our coasts and estuaries are modified by activities in catchments above the freshwater limit. The sediment and pollution loads to the sea are largely delivered by rivers. A freshwater flow into estuaries is required to protect water quality, ecology and fisheries, prevent saline intrusion and balance the landward transport of sediments by tidal currents. Water abstracted from the freshwater environment will necessarily cause a reduction in flow to estuaries and coastal waters. This is unavoidable and there is a need to know how much can be abstracted without causing unacceptable change. It is also important to consider the whole flow regime and not just the minimum acceptable flows. Managing the pattern of river flows to estuaries is just as important as ensuring that they are held above some lower limit. For example, variations in river flows determine the position, size and motion of salt/freshwater boundaries, sedimentation patterns and cues for the movement of migratory fish. Reducing freshwater flows may even lead to a dearth of nutrients in coastal waters (Wade, 1996). So integrated river basin management is an essential tool in maintaining the estuary environment.

There are also boreholes close to the coast in parts of the country where saline water does not intrude into groundwater. In some places, evidence of a link between these abstraction licences and dune-slack wildlife is relatively strong. The Sefton Coast in the North West Region is an example; an area that has been designated as a Special Area of Conservation under the Habitats Directive (92/43/EEC). There is increasing pressure on the groundwater resources for use on golf courses along this coastline. This has prompted intensive study of the effects of existing and proposed increases in abstractions upon the designated habitats. This work is being carried out by the Agency in collaboration with English Nature, the Countryside Council for Wales, local environmental organisations and the golf clubs. The studies will ensure that these highly valued habitats are not adversely affected by the licensed abstractions.

In other areas some aquifers that occur at the coast are in direct contact with either the sea or estuarine waters, or both. Under these conditions groundwater commonly flows toward the coast and discharges via seepages or submarine springs directly into the sea or estuary. In many such cases there are licensed abstractions from the groundwater in these coastal aquifers. One such example is the Denge Gravel Aquifer at Dungeness where the water is abstracted both for power generation and for public water supply. Other examples include use of the chalk aquifer along the southern English coastline for public water supplies for Brighton, Eastbourne and Dover. Where these abstractions occur they are subject to licence conditions and operating rules to ensure that any resulting encroachment of saline water into the aquifer and associated habitat features do not have an adverse impact. However, historic over-abstractions have in some coastal areas resulted in a legacy of undesirable saline intrusion. An example is the Triassic Sandstone of the Mersey Estuary which is now subject to strict licensing control and is the subject of intensive study.

Desalination

In the UK the use of desalination to provide fresh water is minimal. Users include oil rigs (for potable supply), Jersey (for potable supply in dry summers), British Steel in Lincolnshire (for industrial use) and the Channel Tunnel during construction (temporarily for industrial use). A few water companies have plans to develop desalination plants, but none of these has reached an advanced stage (for example Mid-Kent Water Company at Reculver on the north Kent coast and Southern Water Plc near Brighton).

A more concerted move towards desalination by water companies could lead to demands for large plots of land and planning permission for development of plants by the coast. Desalination uses relatively large amounts of energy and produces very saline effluents, which have to be treated or dispersed in coastal waters in an environmentally protective way.

Dredging and mineral extraction

Dredging of the sea bed takes place to create and maintain channels for navigation and to extract minerals, mainly sand and gravel, from the marine environment. Dredging is a major expense in the maintenance of port and harbour facilities and has led to the relocation of many port facilities seawards, closer to the mouths of estuaries, where the channels are deeper and dredging requirements are less. Major capital expenditure is required to provide new access facilities (DoE, 1995a).

Ports and harbours ideally require deep channels and narrow intertidal areas, which sometimes conflicts with the natural wide cross-sections of estuaries with extensive mudflats and saltmarshes. Dredging new or deeper channels in estuaries can disrupt the natural sedimentation patterns, leading to possible erosion of surrounding saltmarshes and mudflats and in turn to an increase in the risk of flooding. Dredging can result in an asymmetry in tidal flows in some estuaries whereby they become ebb-dominant and erode intertidal areas. The effect of sea level rise in some estuaries could be to produce deeper

Figure 3.19 *Demand and resource estimates for sand and shingle in coastal cells, and licensed dredging areas*

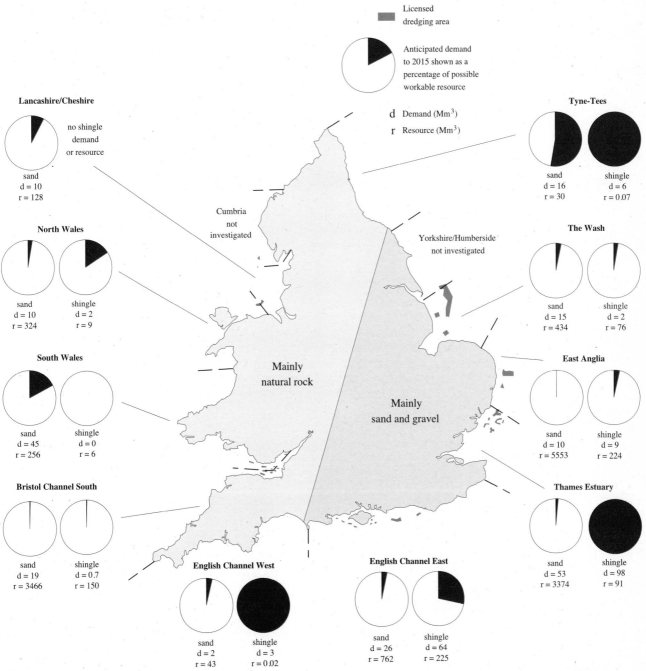

Source: British Marine Aggregate Producers Association, 1995;
Construction Industry Research and Information Association, 1996

channels and larger tidal ranges, with heightened flood risk. Estuaries may then naturally accumulate sediment at an enhanced rate, minimising these effects (DoE, 1995a). But there could be obvious conflicts with port and harbour interests.

Some dredged materials are used for coastal defence (for example beach nourishment), habitat creation, material for land reclamation and retention within the coastal system to maintain the sediment budget, but most is dumped at sea - quantities are given in Section 3.5. Matching needs for materials and availability can be difficult; sand beaches cannot be nourished with mud, and habitat recreation by dumping is not appropriate when winter migrant birds are present.

Demand for aggregates is high. On average 4.3 tonnes of aggregates per person per year are used and each new home requires 50 to 60 tonnes. A mile of motorway may use up to 200,000 tonnes and a mile of new railway line will use 70,000 tonnes of aggregate (British Marine Aggregate Producers Association, 1995). Licensed dredging areas currently cover 1,652km² of the sea bed, mainly off the south east coast, the Humber, the Bristol Channel and the Irish Sea (Figure 3.19). The possible workable resources of marine aggregate are about 16,000Mm³, 95 per cent of which is sand and gravel, and the remainder is shingle. In 1996, 26.6 million tonnes of aggregates were dredged from the sea, with 7.2 million tonnes (27 per cent) of this specifically for beach nourishment, 11.5 million tonnes (13 per cent) for use in the construction industry, and 6.7 million tonnes (25 per cent) for export.

The total amount of marine sand and gravel removed appears to be related to the strength of the economy. Quantities removed for construction have fallen from a high of 131 million tonnes in the late 1980s, but extraction for beach nourishment has increased (Figure 3.20) (Crown Estate, 1990 to 1997 and Central Statistical Office, 1996).

Between 1996 and 2015 the demand for marine aggregate is expected to be about 765 million tonnes (including export) (Construction Industry Research and Information Association, 1996). This is an average of 38.3 million tonnes per year, which is a 63 per cent increase on the average extracted per year from 1989 to 1996. The Government wants to reduce the proportion of aggregates supplied from land sources in England from 83 per cent in 1989 to 68 per cent by 2006 (DoE, 1994a). The alternative sources promoted are marine-based sources, coastal superquarries, secondary aggregates and recycled aggregates. Coastal superquarries are those capable of producing at least five million tonnes per year and with reserves of at least 150 million tonnes. In Britain, only Scotland may offer potential locations for such quarries. It is expected that as the onshore supply becomes increasingly more difficult to extract (due to other land uses and conservation pressures), the marine market (as well as the recycling of construction materials and other alternative sources) may be further developed to fill the gap. However, marine dredging has potentially damaging effects and like land-based sand and gravel, marine aggregates are a finite resource, which should only be exploited after rigorous assessment to ensure there is no significant environmental effect. The areas of greatest anticipated demand are the Thames Estuary and the eastern English Channel.

The current use of marine aggregates instead of land-based sources means that about 400ha of land are not being used for sand and gravel extraction (British Marine Aggregate Producers Association, 1995). Marine aggregate extraction can also reduce road transportation needs because they can often be brought ashore close to the demand. For example, over 25 per cent of the sand and gravel supplied to the south east of England is marine dredged and landed at ports close to its final destination.

Figure 3.20 *Marine sand and gravel removal in the UK, 1989 to 1996*

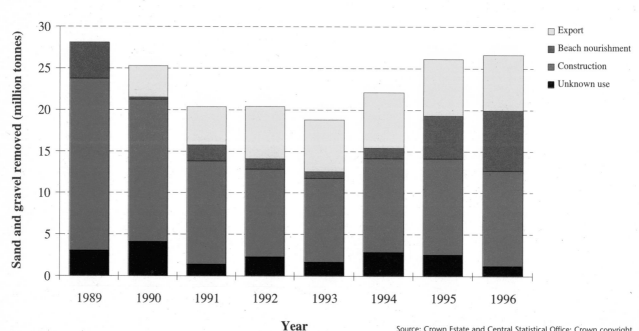

Source: Crown Estate and Central Statistical Office; Crown copyright

The UK Government acknowledges that dredging may cause disturbance to fisheries and damage to the marine environment, particularly where there is a concentration of licences. Alterations to the longshore transport of beach material will affect shoreline stability. In addition, dredging offshore bars may alter the protection they afford from wave attack and steps should be taken to ensure that sediment transport pathways are not disrupted. It is also essential that areas are dredged far enough offshore, in deep enough water, so that material is not drawn down the beach into the deepened area and that changes in the wave refraction pattern do not take place.

The ecological impacts of marine aggregate extraction are due to possible changes in sediment topography and type through removal of material and resettlement of fine particles. There will also be secondary biological effects as a consequence of seabed alteration and disturbance, resulting in modification of benthic community structures, with consequent effects upon food supply for higher organisms including commercial fish and shellfish species. These effects are thought to be highly localised and not widespread, although there is a continuing

need for research fully to assess these potential problems, especially if exploitation of marine aggregates increases in future (Nunny and Chillingworth, 1986).

The 'Government View Procedure' co-ordinated by DETR in England contributes to the current non-statutory system of licensing administered by the Crown Estate Commissioners (although these arrangements are shortly to be replaced by statutory licensing controls). The MAFF input to this procedure aims to protect against these effects. In Wales, the Government View procedure is administered by the Welsh Office. There is a presumption against the licensing of marine dredging unless the environmental and coastal impact issues are satisfactorily resolved (DoE, 1994a).

Commercial fishing and aquaculture

Britain has historically been a major sea fishing nation though our dependence on fish protein is declining. Since 1948 weekly personal consumption of fish has more than halved and we now eat about seven times as much meat as fish. In 1995,

Figure 3.21 *Fish landings by the UK fleet, 1995*

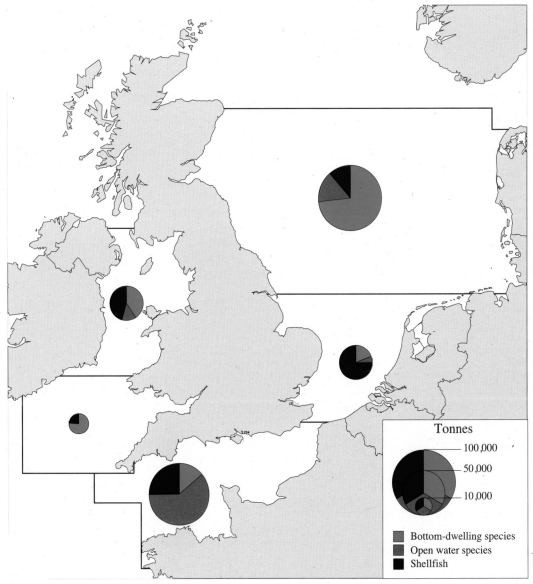

Tonnes
— 100,000
— 50,000
— 10,000

■ Bottom-dwelling species
■ Open water species
■ Shellfish

Source: Ministry of Agriculture, Fisheries and Food; Crown copyright

household consumption of fish and shellfish was 438,000 tonnes, about 140 grammes (5 ounces) per person per week. Some 400,000 tonnes of fish products were made, including 50,000 tonnes for animal feeds. Some 726,000 tonnes of fish were landed in the UK by UK vessels in 1995, of which less than one-third were landed in England and Wales. The UK is now a net importer of fish products. It exported 360,000 tonnes in 1995 while importing 484,000 tonnes, of which one-third were tuna (MAFF, 1996). The UK fishing industry employed about 20,000 fishermen in 1995, down only slightly since 1970 but half the number of 1950. Although the bulk of the catch is taken in the North Sea, coastal fisheries are distributed all around England and Wales (Figure 3.21).

Salmon and sea trout are netted along the coast and around estuaries on their return to rivers to spawn. The number of netting licences has decreased substantially in recent years; currently there are about 700 licences issued annually. The single largest fishery, lying off the north east coast of England, takes about 70 per cent of the total net catch. The remaining

fisheries, utilising a wide variety of fishing methods, some with heritage value, are mainly confined to estuaries and coastal foreshores. Poaching of migratory salmonids by inshore fishermen, ostensibly fishing for bass and flounder, for example, is a continuing issue for the Agency, requiring substantial enforcement resources to control. Fyke nets and traps are set to catch eels on their spawning migration down rivers and hand-held dip nets are used to collect elvers on the return migration up estuaries and rivers. Some 2,500 fishermen are licensed to take eels.

Bottom-dwelling ('demersal') species including plaice, sole and cod form about 60 per cent of the fish catch and upper water ('pelagic') species the rest (Figure 3.21). Of the demersal species, cod is landed in the highest quantities at around 30,000 tonnes in England and Wales, followed by plaice, haddock, whiting, skates and rays, monk or angler fish, and sole. The pelagic species are dominated by mackerel at 34,000 tonnes and horse mackerel at 25,000 tonnes, with herring currently at only 5,000 tonnes (MAFF, 1996).

Figure 3.22 *The major molluscan fisheries of England and Wales*

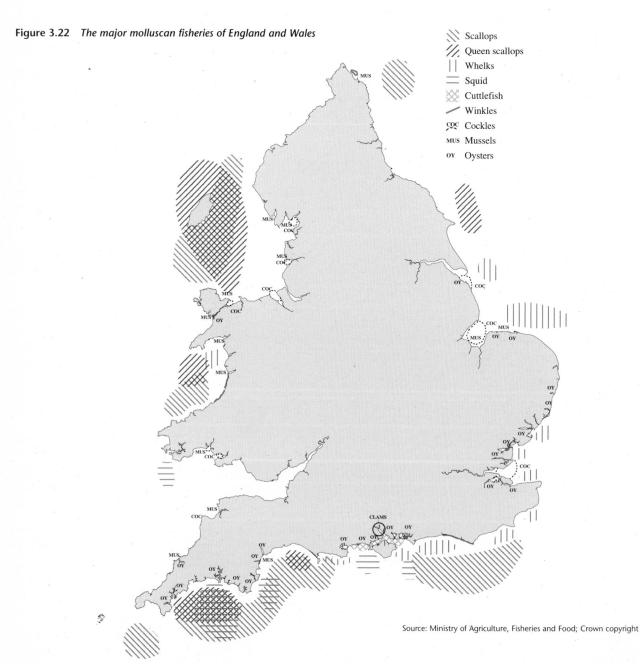

Source: Ministry of Agriculture, Fisheries and Food; Crown copyright

Shellfish form nearly one-third of the total catch in England and Wales and are led by 25,000 tonnes of cockles which are dredged or collected by hand from a few major inshore beds (Figure 3.22). Major mussel beds occur on the west coast and in the Wash. Scallops are found a few kilometres offshore mainly off the south coast, in Cardigan Bay and the Irish Sea (Gray, 1995). Brown crabs are taken from all round the coast while the Dublin Bay prawn (*Nephrops*) has its major grounds off the north east and north west coasts (Figure 3.23).

The UK fishing fleet is some 9,000 vessels out of a European Union fleet of 100,000. Over the past 20 years the trend has been for a reduction in large, long-distance trawlers towards smaller coastal vessels, and about 70 per cent of the fleet is

Figure 3.23 *The major crustacean fisheries of England and Wales*

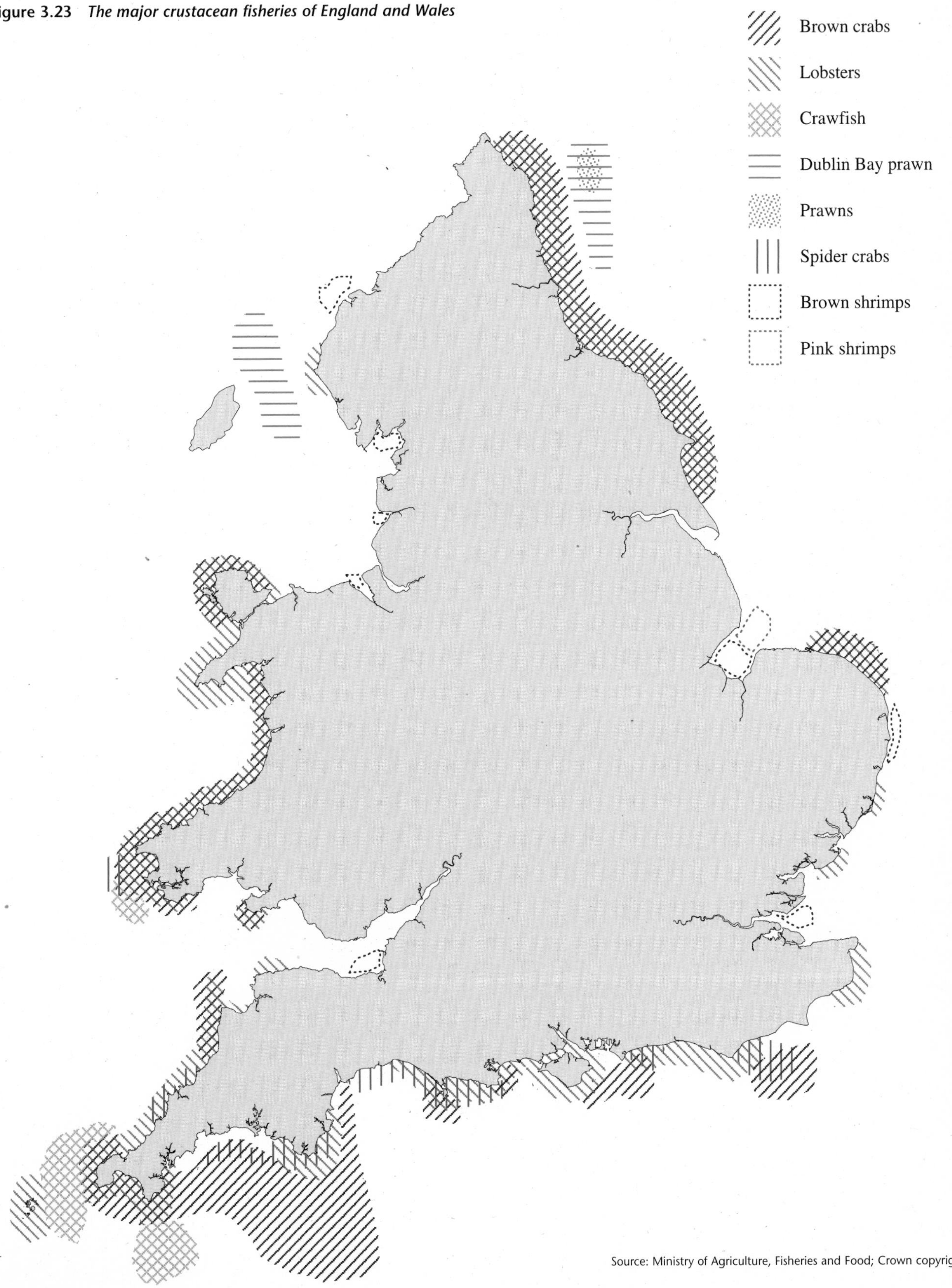

Legend:
- Brown crabs
- Lobsters
- Crawfish
- Dublin Bay prawn
- Prawns
- Spider crabs
- Brown shrimps
- Pink shrimps

Source: Ministry of Agriculture, Fisheries and Food; Crown copyright

Figure 3.24 *Fish and shellfish landings into the UK by UK vessels, 1946 to 1995*

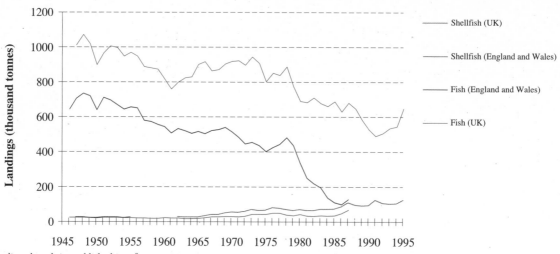

From 1998 landings have been published in a form incompatible with pre-1988 data, except for UK totals

Source: Ministry of Agriculture, Fisheries and Food; Crown copyright

under 10m in length. The development of synthetic monofilament nets which are cheap and durable has greatly increased the capacity of inshore boats over this period (Gray, 1995). A greater range of species is exploited and there has been a steady rise in shellfish landings since the 1960s and a decline in the landings of fish since the 1940s (Figure 3.24), although fish catches have been increasing during the 1990s (MAFF, 1996).

The impacts of fishing on the main commercial stocks are discussed in Section 4.2. There are also significant effects on other organisms which are captured incidentally (the 'by-

Figure 3.25 *Distribution of cultivated molluscs in England and Wales*

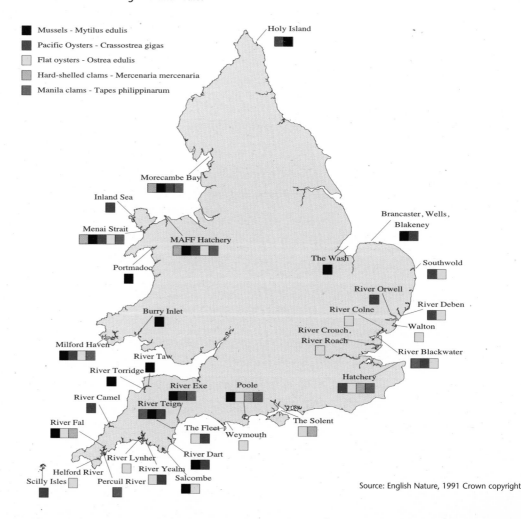

Source: English Nature, 1991 Crown copyright

catch') or damaged by fishing gear. Data on by-catches are poor, although up to half of the initial catch may be discarded at sea because it is undersize, over-quota, or an unwanted species (North Sea Task Force, 1993). Seabirds, seals, dolphins and porpoises are also caught in working and discarded nets. Trawls, tangle nets, shellfish dredges and pots can impact the bottom fauna by damaging fragile organisms or by disturbing the sea bed. The increasing scale and mechanisation of dredging and potting is likely to increase this risk. Fishing restrictions to prevent such impacts are imposed occasionally, for example at Skomer off west Wales, but the effects are potentially extensive. Scallop dredges can penetrate up to 4cm into the sea bed and beam trawls up to 6cm. In an area of 44,000km^2 along the English east coast in 1989, beam trawls swept up to 54 per cent of the total area while otter trawls swept a further 26 per cent though with lesser impact (ICES, 1992). In the Irish Sea about 25 per cent was swept by otter trawls, 22 per cent by beam trawls and eight per cent by shellfish dredging in 1994 (Kaiser *et al.*, 1996). The actual areas affected will be lower because activity is concentrated in certain areas which are swept several times a year.

There are over two million sea anglers, and recreational sea fishing may have minor effects on some shoreline habitats. Bait collecting of crabs from rocky shores, and lugworm and ragworm dug from sandy shores, may cause disturbance and depletion of these and other species in intensively searched areas. There are over 100 bait diggers active around Swansea bay at certain times, and around 150 tonnes of king ragworm (*Nereis virens*) were sold in England and Wales in 1985/86, in addition to those collected privately. A study at Mumbles Head near Swansea found that around 90 per cent of boulders were turned within a two week period by anglers looking for crabs for bait, and seaweeds and other animals such as sponges may be damaged incidentally. Bait digging by anglers has been linked to a reduction of species diversity in the Menai Straits, a decline in the population of heart urchins in Northumberland and reduced macroinvertebrate numbers at Budle Bay, Lindisfarne. Most populations do not appear to be threatened by this activity and any depletion is likely to be made up by recolonisation and annual recruitment. Spearfishing is also a possible concern because the selective elimination of large conspicuous fish may deplete their numbers locally and spoil the enjoyment of other divers (Fowler, 1989; Fowler, 1992).

Salmon farming is rare in England and Wales but there are about 130 shellfish farms in estuaries around the south east and south west of England, in Wales, and Morecambe Bay (Figure 3.25) (English Nature, 1991). Cultivated native species include mussels, European oysters and palourde (a native clam), while

Figure 3.26   Location of large* coastal sewage works, 1998

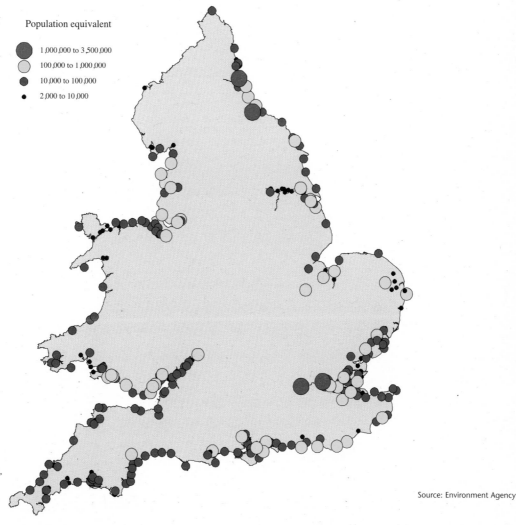

Population equivalent

- 1,000,000 to 3,500,000
- 100,000 to 1,000,000
- 10,000 to 100,000
- 2,000 to 10,000

*Coastal works greater than 10,000 population equivalent, estuarine works greater than 2,000 population equivalent

Source: Environment Agency

Figure 3.27 *Consented discharges* to estuaries and coasts by region*

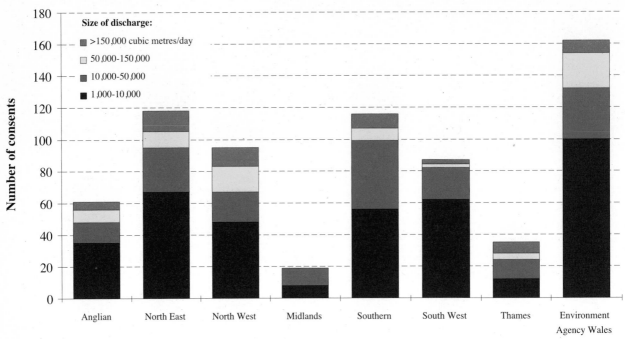

*Greater than 1,000 cubic meters per day

Region

Source: Environment Agency

Pacific oysters, hard-shelled clams and Manila clams have been introduced. In 1995 production in England and Wales was dominated by mussels at over 5,000 tonnes, followed by about 300 tonnes of Pacific oysters and 100 tonnes of native oysters (Howard, 1996). There are many physical and chemical effects in the vicinity of farms which may include smothering of the sea bed, deoxygenation and disturbance of the habitat. A greater risk may arise from the introduction of non-native species with imported stock. This could have brought at least 15 non-native marine species into British waters, some of which have become pests and may spread further if temperatures increase with climate change (Eno *et al.*, 1997).

3.4   Usage, releases and discharges

Point discharges from sewerage system

There were more than 5,000 consented discharges to the coast in 1997. Of these 74 per cent were from the sewerage systems, including treated sewage effluents and storm overflows as well as surface water sewers in some regions, and 17 per cent were for trade or industrial discharges. Although the coast receives the effluent from only seven per cent by number of all consented discharges these are generally much larger than inland discharges and constitute over one-third of the total volume of effluent. Only 0.1 per cent of discharges to fresh water are over 150,000m³/day, compared with one per cent of coastal discharges. About five per cent of inland discharges are of more than 1,000m³/day, compared with 14 per cent of coastal discharges (Figures 3.26 and 3.27). The five largest sewage treatment works in England and Wales discharging to estuaries are Mogden (420,000m³/day), Crossness (550,000m³/day) and Beckton (1,000,000m³/day), all of which serve London and discharge to the Thames Estuary, Howdon (250,000m³/day) which serves the whole of Tyneside and discharges to the Tyne Estuary, and Sandon (950,000m³/day) which serves Liverpool and discharges into the Mersey Estuary. Table 3.5 shows how many sewage treatment works serve inland, estuarine and coastal populations in England and Wales and the average quality of their effluents.

Table 3.5 *Number and effluent quality of significant water company-owned sewage treatment works in England and Wales*

Media	Number of STWs	Population equivalent served (millions)	Estimated total flow (million m³/day)[1]	Estimated average size (thousand m³/day)[1]	Population weighted mean biochemical oxygen demand in effluent (mg/l)[2]		Population weighted mean ammonia in effluent (mg/l)[2]	
					1990	1995	1990	1995
Inland [3]	3,700	45	9	2.4	12	9	5.5	3.7
Estuarine [4]	232	22.8	4.55	19.6	33	28	10.2	11.5
Coastal [5]	71	4.3	0.86	12.1	213	190	31	29

[1] assumes water usage of 200 litres/person/day
[2] effluents with numeric consents
[3] works with numeric consents
[4] works greater than 2,000 population equivalent
[5] works greater than 10,000 population equivalent

Figure 3.28 *Polluting loads discharged to the Thames Estuary, 1950 to 1990*

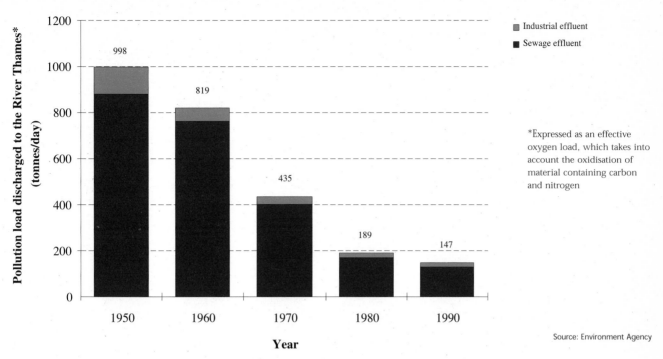

■ Industrial effluent
■ Sewage effluent

*Expressed as an effective
oxygen load, which takes into
account the oxidisation of
material containing carbon
and nitrogen

Source: Environment Agency

Significant sewage treatment works which discharge to estuaries alone serve about one-third of the population and yet are just a few per cent of all works. On average, estuarine works are eight times bigger than inland works.

Historically, sewage discharges to rivers have received a much higher level of treatment than coastal or estuarine discharges.

In rivers, dilution can be limited and there are often downstream uses which need to be protected, such as fisheries and abstraction points for potable water. Coastal waters on the other hand have a much larger capacity for diluting and dispersing effluents and so discharges to these waters have received far less treatment, which is reflected in effluent quality. Estuaries are in some cases much more sensitive ecologically

Figure 3.29 *Dissolved oxygen levels in the tidal Thames between 1950 and 1995, April to September mean*

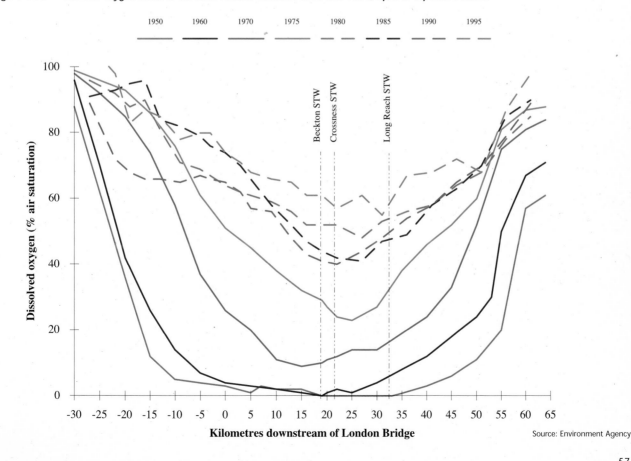

Source: Environment Agency

57

Figure 3.30 *Water quality at Howley Weir (the tidal limit of the Mersey Estuary), 1962 to 1997*

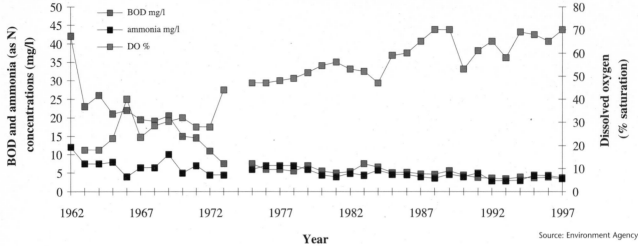

Source: Environment Agency

than coastal waters. Dilution and dispersion in estuaries relies mostly on freshwater flows from rivers and exchanges of water with the open sea. Because estuaries are areas of great biological productivity, spawning grounds for some marine fish and, in some cases, host shellfisheries and populations of migratory freshwater fish, effluents that discharge to them require higher levels of treatment than for coastal waters. For example, many coastal discharges have, until recently, only treated effluents at a primary level (screening and settling) whereas some estuarine discharges, for example Beckton on the Thames, achieves one of the most stringent ammonia standards in the country during the summer months, requiring full nitrification (Environment Agency, 1997a). This is reflected in the mean quality figures shown in Table 3.5.

Discharges of sewage and industrial effluents to coastal waters are subject to consents which are issued by the Agency. These consents dictate the volume and quality of effluents that may be legally discharged to estuaries and coasts and take into account the requirements of various European Directives and national regulations. In particular, improvements have been necessary at many coastal works in order to meet fully the Urban Waste Water Treatment Directive (91/271/EEC) by 2005 (some aspects were met by 1998). Appendix 1 gives an overview of requirements for this Directive. The quality of sewage effluents is monitored by the Agency to ensure they comply with the conditions of their consents. The overall level of consent compliance is an indirect measure of improvements in effluent quality. In 1964/65, nearly 60 per cent of sewage works (discharging to fresh and saline waters) failed their consents, mainly due to lack of adequate available treatment capacity. Compliance levels for sewage treatment works improved steadily in the late 1980s and 1990s, largely as a result of increased investment following water privatisation, so that in 1995 fewer

Figure 3.31 *Population weighted mean concentrations of ammonia and BOD in sewage-treatment works effluents discharged to estuaries, North East Region, 1990 to 1995*

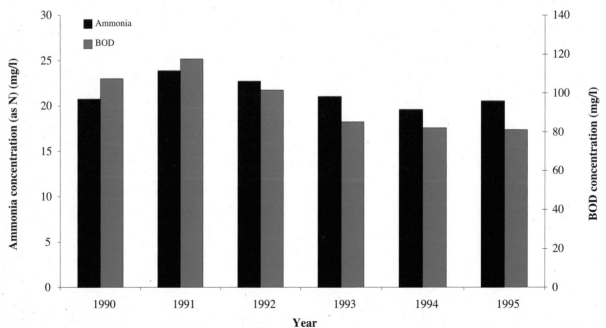

Population weighted mean concentration is calculated by multiplying the mean effluent concentration by the population served at each works, summing over all works and then dividing this sum by the total population served at all works

Source: Environment Agency

Figure 3.32 *Long sea outfalls, 1998*

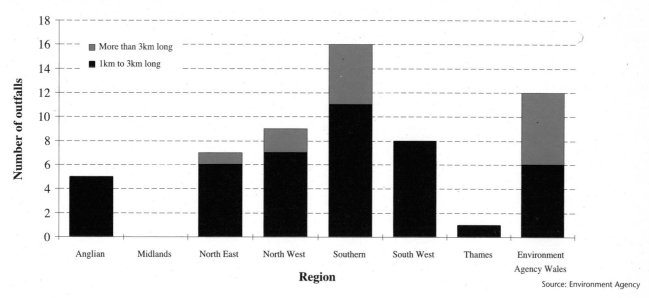

Source: Environment Agency

than four per cent failed to meet the standard set (Environment Agency, 1998a). Because consent conditions may change in time, and usually to a more stringent set of conditions governing effluent quality, improvements in effluent quality may not be evident by examining compliance levels alone.

Since the 1970s there have been huge efforts to reduce the polluting loads to estuaries and coasts from sewage treatment works and industrial effluents. These load reductions have had a demonstrable effect on water quality in many estuaries, for example the Thames and Mersey (Figures 3.28, 3.29 and 3.30), and on improvements in bathing water quality (Section 4.3). In the period 1990 to 1995 progress was made in improving the quality of sewage treatment works' discharges to estuaries and coasts, as demonstrated by population weighted mean biochemical oxygen demand and ammonia in effluents (Figure 3.31). Further improvements are expected as planned improvements to meet the Urban Waste Water Treatment Directive come on line by 2005.

The location of outfalls determines the degree of dilution and subsequent dispersion of discharged effluents. Before the 1980s many coastal outfalls discharged effluents close to the shoreline, sometimes above the water level at low tide. Without adequate treatment such effluents posed a threat to water quality and provided an aesthetic nuisance. In the 1980s long sea outfalls were built in some locations to move discharges further from the shore into deeper water to gain better initial dilution, or into stronger currents which would disperse effluents more effectively. They were also the most cost-effective or technically simple disposal method available. Since then sewage treatment levels have improved in many places.

Long sea outfall construction has varied considerably between different Agency regions, reflecting local oceanographic conditions (Figure 3.32). In Southern Region, where the majority of coastal discharges receive only preliminary or primary treatment, 16 outfalls over 1km have been constructed to ensure that effluent is discharged away from the shallow waters and slow currents close to shore.

Figure 3.33 *Indicative condition of combined storm overflows*, 1998*

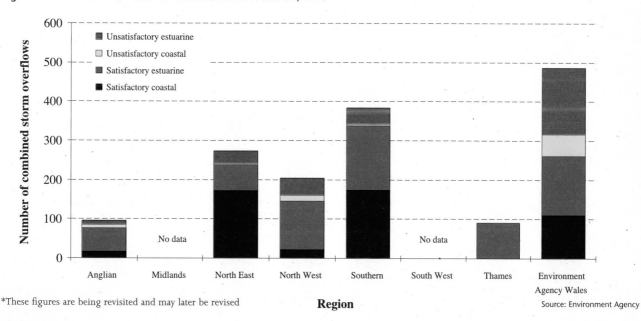

*These figures are being revisited and may later be revised

Source: Environment Agency

Figure 3.34 *Dissolved oxygen profiles in the Thames Estuary before, during and after the August storm, 1977*

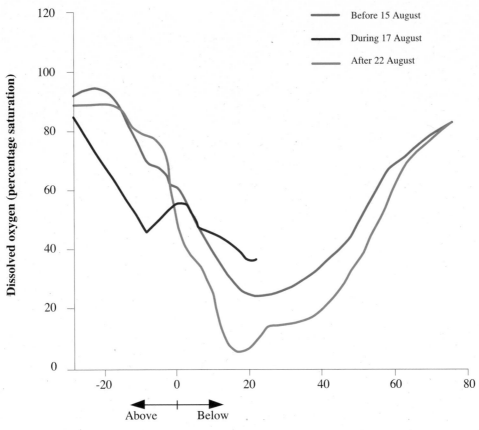

Sewers and sewage works are designed to accommodate a certain amount of flow. It would be uneconomic to size sewers and treatment works to be capable of dealing with all the flows that are ever likely to occur, so they are designed to deal with flows that occur for most of the time. While the main component of sewer flow is domestic and industrial waste, many sewers were built at a time when drains from roads and other areas were also connected to the sewers. In these areas of 'combined' sewers, storm water from rainfall can lead to the capacity of the sewers being exceeded and overflows discharging directly from the sewers to watercourses, including estuaries and coastal waters. Furthermore, in the major urban areas many sewers date back to Victorian times and their capacity is insufficient to cope with the large volumes of wastewater generated now. As a consequence of this, storm sewer overflows which were designed only to deal with storm flows sometimes operate in dry weather conditions resulting in water quality problems. The number of combined storm overflows discharging to coasts and estuaries in each region are shown in Figure 3.33.

Overall, the polluting load from storm overflows is generally much less than that from treated sewage because most of the flow is rainwater. It is, however, contamination with sewage which can cause extremely high loads of pollution for a short period of time, especially during the 'first flush' of rain. Problems arise in some receiving waters due to the consumption of oxygen by bacteria decomposing sewage-derived material. This is shown by measurements of dissolved oxygen in the Thames Estuary before, during, and after a storm (Figure 3.34). Episodes of low dissolved oxygen can lead to fish kills; the situation on the Thames Estuary being managed by using a 'Bubbler' which adds oxygen from a boat (Environment Agency, 1997a), but in other cases improvements are still needed and are due to be addressed by investment for the Urban Waste Water Treatment Directive. Sewage-contaminated rainwater entering coastal waters near bathing beaches can be a health hazard, although most of these problems have been addressed through investment since privatisation of the water companies. Storm overflows can also cause aesthetic problems if the discharges are not screened, allowing litter in the form of rags, plastics and sanitary products to be discharged, but these should also be addressed in the investment programmes of the water companies.

The magnitude of the problem varies from place to place depending on how the sewerage network was designed in the past, the age of the system, recent investment programmes and the geography of the area. New towns, for example, have separate systems for rainwater and so there should be no problems. Past designs reflected regional needs, but there has always been a great reliance on the sea for dispersing sewage and stormwaters.

Further improvements to coastal discharges - both storm overflows and treated sewage effluents - are expected by 2005 in order to meet the Bathing Waters Directive and the Urban Waste Water Treatment Directive. One aspect of particular note is the changing view on 'high natural dispersion areas'. These

Figure 3.35 *EC Urban Waste Water Treatment Directive designated areas in England and Wales*

● High natural dispersion area

◆ Eutrophic sensitive area

Key to Humber Estuary sites

1	Howdendyke
2	Gilberdyke
3	Ellerker
4	Winteringham
5	Brough
6	North Ferriby
7	Barton-on-Humber
8	Hull
9	Hedon
10	Immingham
11	Pyewipe

Source: Environment Agency

were zones in which, due to high dilution, sewage works exceeding 15,000 population equivalents could meet less stringent treatment standards. In 1994, 58 high natural dispersion areas were designated, although 18 of these were recommended for status removal in 1998. The Government has also announced its intention to remove the high natural dispersion area status from the remaining areas (DETR and Welsh Office, 1998). There are 91 'significant' sewage discharges into the original 58 areas (Figure 3.35). So we will now expect improvements at these works.

Regulated releases and discharges from industry

All the major estuaries of England and Wales are home to large expanses of industrial and urban development (the Mersey, Dee, Milford Haven, Severn, Southampton Water, Thames, Humber, Tees and the Tyne) and many smaller estuaries also host industrial activities. About 40 per cent of UK manufacturing industry is situated on or near the coast (CCIRG, 1996). Because of this and the clustering of industries on estuaries there is a continuing need for adequate, co-ordinated regulation

Figure 3.36 *Estimated emissions of aerial pollutants by industry, 1970 to 1996*

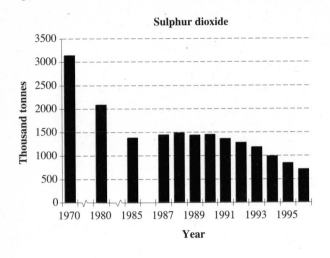

Sulphur dioxide

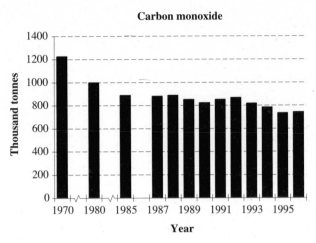

Carbon monoxide

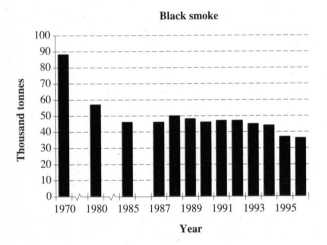

Black smoke

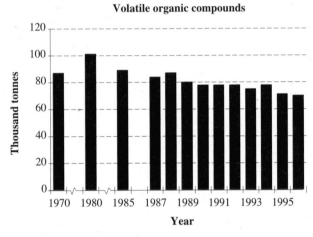

Volatile organic compounds

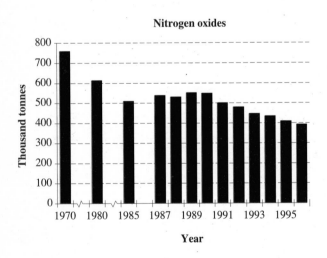

Nitrogen oxides

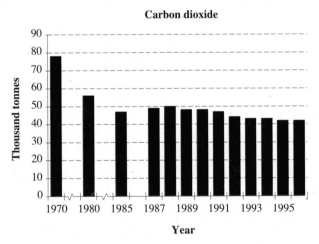

Carbon dioxide

Source: Department of the Environment, Transport and the Regions; Crown copyright

to protect the coastal environment. The Chemical Release Inventory, which is maintained by the Agency, contains information on the loads of potentially polluting substances from major industrial activities. This database is currently being improved to map all of these release sites. Large reductions in the loads of dangerous substances emitted from direct industrial discharges to coastal waters and estuaries have already been secured, for example mercury from the chlor-alkali industry on the Mersey.

Many large combustion plants - most power stations, all oil refineries and a proportion of iron and steel and other combustion and non-combustion processes - are situated on the coast. The aerial emissions generated by these mean that the coastal zone is a significant source of atmospheric pollutants. Due to tighter regulation, investment by industry and structural changes in the economy, estimated aerial emissions of the major polluting substances from industry have been falling over the last 25 years (Figure 3.36) (DTI, 1997a). From 1970 to 1995:

- sulphur dioxide emissions from all large combustion plants fell by 60 per cent and from industry by 63 per cent;

- nitrous oxides emissions from all large combustion plants fell by 49 per cent and from industry by 48 per cent;

- black smoke emissions from industry fell by 58 per cent;

- carbon monoxide emissions from industry fell by 41 per cent;

- volatile organic compounds from industry fell by 23 per cent;

- carbon dioxide emissions from industry fell by 47 per cent.

These figures are UK averages, and the assumption is that the reductions in aerial emissions achieved will apply equally well to coastal industries, refineries, combustion plants and power stations.

Electricity generation is an activity which relies heavily on the coast. Seventy per cent of the UK's fossil fuel-powered generating capacity is coastal. Section 3.3 explains that the electricity supply industry is by far the largest user of tidal water for cooling. Cooling water is, by necessity, heated in use and returned to the environment warmer than when abstracted, often in the same body of water as the abstraction point. The temperature difference between the cooling water discharge and the receiving water is typically 10°C and the flow rate of the discharge can be substantial (30m³/s per 1,000MW for fossil fuel stations or 45m³/s per 1,000MW for nuclear stations) (English Nature, 1991; Whitehouse et al., 1985). This may result in the returned water forming thermal plumes in the receiving water body. Thermal plumes can present a barrier for migratory fish to pass through estuaries if they are large in extent, poorly mixed with seawater or are sufficiently warmer than their surroundings. Raising the local water temperature may also modify the structure of marine ecosystems in the vicinity of an outfall, and there is also some evidence that

thermal planes benefit some fisheries by boosting productivity. Outfalls are designed, monitored and regulated to minimise adverse impacts.

Apart from temperature the water quality of the returned cooling water is not usually very different from that abstracted, but this depends largely on where and when the water is abstracted, what it is used for and how quickly the water is returned. In some power stations and industrial plants biocides must be added to cooling water to prevent organisms growing in pipes and vessels, where they could create a hazard or reduce plant efficiency. Integrated pollution control is implemented by the Agency to ensure that returned cooling water quality has no unacceptable effects on environmental water quality or on marine and estuarine ecosystems.

In 1998 there were nine oil refineries in England and Wales, with a total crude distillation capacity amounting to some 92,700 kilotonnes per year, nearly a quarter of the capacity of the OSPAR member states (OSPAR, 1997). Refineries and crude oil terminals potentially impact on coasts through the discharge of waste water, emissions to air as a result of combustion, flaring and 'fugitive' losses or leaks, and leakage of hydrocarbons during storage, loading and unloading at the terminal or refinery, although the processes are regulated through IPC authorisations. UK refinery emissions of volatile organic compounds were 78 kilotonnes in 1996, about three per cent of the UK total. Refineries emit sulphur dioxide from processes and combustion plant. These emissions have fallen by 18 per cent between 1970 and 1995, contributing eight per cent of UK sulphur emissions in 1995 (Environment Agency, 1998b).

The amount of oil discharged in refinery waste water has been progressively reduced over the past 25 years (Figure 3.37). This has been achieved because of improvements in effluent treatment even though the amount of oil processed has increased. The most recent review of North Sea countries in 1993 showed that UK refineries discharged 9.6 tonnes of oil for every million tonnes processed, more than twice the OSPAR average (OSPAR, 1997).

Figure 3.37 *Oil discharged from UK refineries, 1970 to 1997*

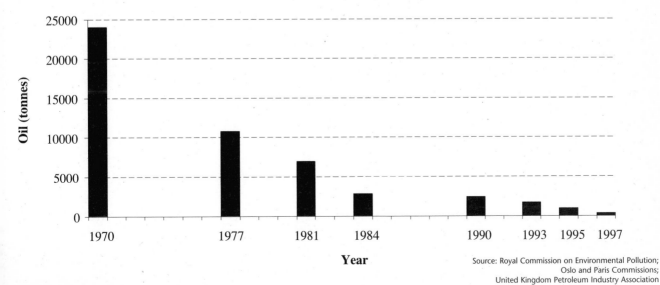

Source: Royal Commission on Environmental Pollution; Oslo and Paris Commissions; United Kingdom Petroleum Industry Association

The British marine industry is extremely diverse in nature and consists almost entirely of small and medium-sized enterprises. Approximately 90 per cent of these businesses employ fewer than 50 people, with many employing fewer than 10. The businesses range from craft manufacturers, using a multitude of materials, through engine and equipment manufacturers to marina developers and managers, credit and insurance brokers, retail and wholesale distributors and boat hire companies, contributing to a total industry turnover for 1991 of approximately £11.2 billion. Total employment in the industry was 18,947 in 1991, with a further 1,772 part-time employees and 1,332 seasonal employees. While these industries have few significant direct discharges, the demand for land for work premises, diffuse inputs from sites and, for example, boats using antifouling paints, all create some pressure on the coastal environment (UK Centre for Economic and Environmental Development, 1993).

Diffuse discharges

As reserves of oil and gas are exhausted in the North Sea, the search for oil has moved into new areas, including coastal waters to the west of England and Wales. Pressures from exploration and drilling that are acceptable within the deep waters of the North Sea pose different risks in shallow coastal waters. For example, discharges and spills from production platforms off western coasts may be subject to westerly winds and currents bringing the pollutants into shallow coastal waters or onshore. There will need to be proper assessment, as elsewhere, to determine the potential environmental impacts of oil exploitation and the Agency needs to be consulted early in the planning process (Environment Agency, 1998b).

Diffuse and point discharges from abandoned metal and coal mines can also have a significant, if localised, impact on the environment. Throughout England and Wales there are many hundreds of discharges from abandoned mines, some of which affect coastal water quality. They are, in the majority, a legacy of the past but mines abandoned in the last 10 to 20 years may present problems for the future. As mining operations are curtailed and pumping ceases, groundwaters return to original levels. The water becomes contaminated as it rises through the previously mined strata, often resulting in new, and difficult to predict, outbreaks of mine drainage. These discharges can be extremely variable but normally have significant metal concentrations. Staining of stream beds and the sea bed by reddish-brown deposits of oxidised iron may also occur.

The best known example of minewaters impacting on the coast occurred at Wheal Jane, an abandoned tin mine in the Carnon Valley, near Truro in Cornwall. Pumping of minewater stopped when the mine was closed in 1991, and the uncontrolled release of acidic metal-laden minewater followed in January 1992 when water levels in the mine rose. The release created significantly elevated levels of metals and widespread discolouration in the Carnon River, Restronguet Creek, Carrick Roads, and the Fal Estuary. The Agency operates a minewater treatment plant and pumps within the mine to maintain water levels below an overflow threshold. This has significantly reduced pollution of the Carnon River and Fal Estuary, holding

water quality within the catchment to at least pre-incident (background) levels.

Atmospheric deposition and diffuse sources of nitrate and phosphorus pollution from agriculture also contribute nutrient loads to fresh and saline waters.

Contaminant loads from land to sea

The total contaminant load discharged by rivers to the sea has been estimated using data from the Harmonised Monitoring Scheme set up by the former Department of the Environment in 1974. Between the late 1970s and the early 1990s most sites showed reductions in copper, zinc, ammonia and lindane concentrations and biochemical oxygen demand, whereas there were widespread increases in orthophosphate and chloride concentrations (Figure 3.38) (Institute of Freshwater Ecology, 1994).

Figure 3.38 *The percentage of Harmonised Monitoring Scheme sites which have improved or deteriorated between the late 1970s and the early 1990s for 13 determinands*

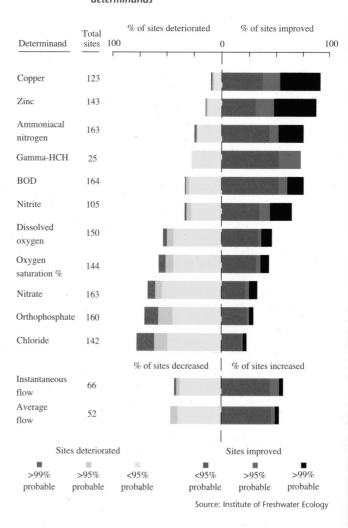

Source: Institute of Freshwater Ecology

Since 1986 the pattern for orthophosphate loads has changed and they now show a decreasing trend overall (Figures 3.39 and 3.41). There have been marked annual variations in the nitrogen load to the sea and current loads are not as high as in

Figure 3.39 *Estimated total riverine inputs to UK coastal waters, 1975 to 1994*

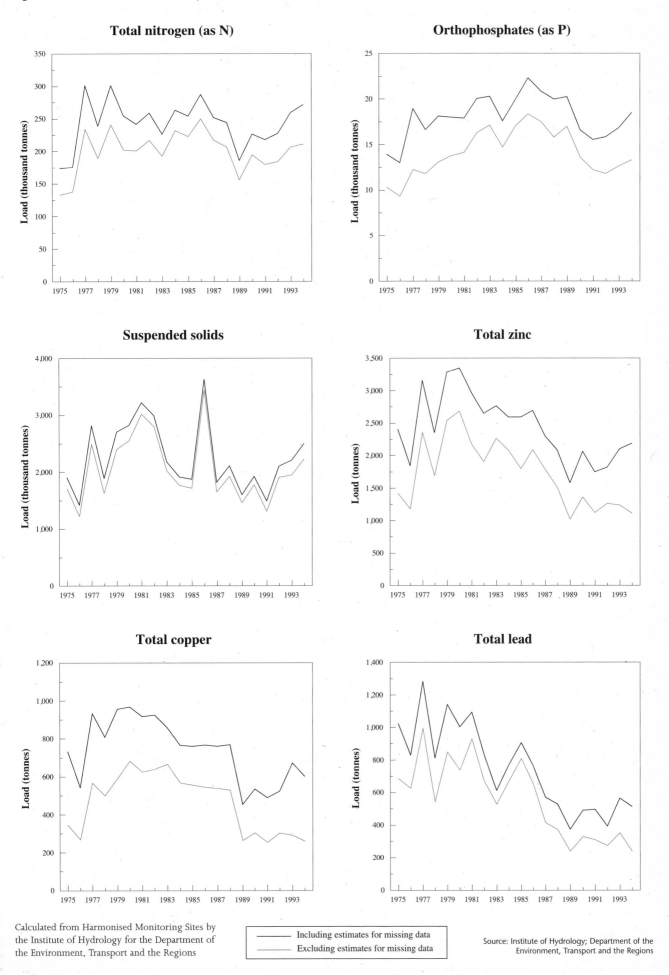

Calculated from Harmonised Monitoring Sites by
the Institute of Hydrology for the Department of
the Environment, Transport and the Regions

Source: Institute of Hydrology; Department of the
Environment, Transport and the Regions

Figure 3.40 *Lindane concentrations and loads*, 1991 to 1997*

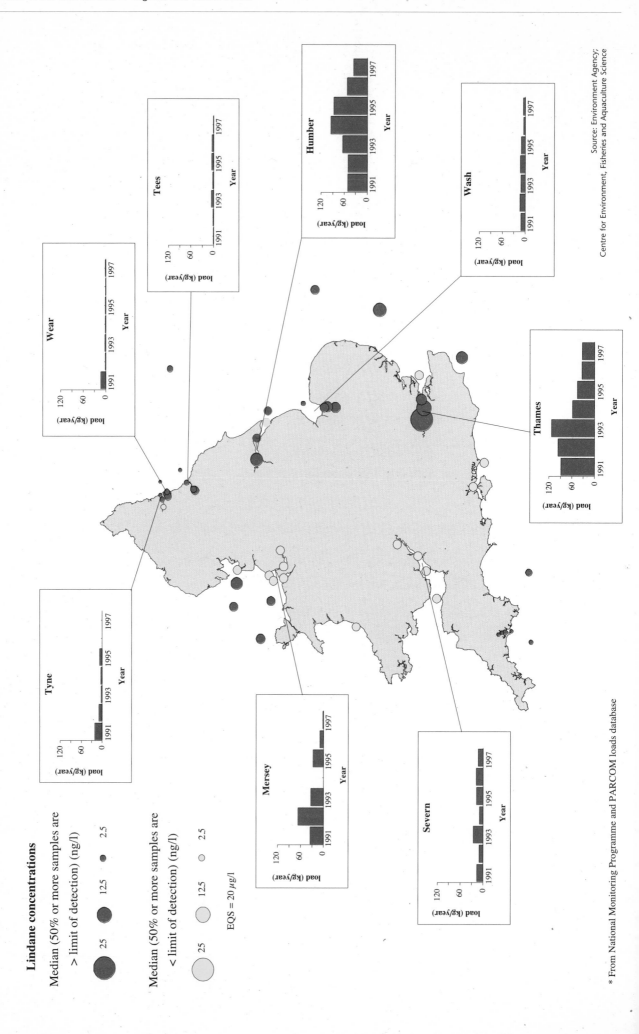

Lindane concentrations

Median (50% or more samples are
> limit of detection) (ng/l)

25   12.5   2.5

Median (50% or more samples are
< limit of detection) (ng/l)

25   12.5   2.5

EQS = 20 μg/l

Source: Environment Agency;
Centre for Environment, Fisheries and Aquaculture Science

* From National Monitoring Programme and PARCOM loads database

the late 1970s. Overall the pattern is fairly stable, but the loads of nitrate, ammonia and orthophosphate from the North West Region to the Irish Sea were all higher in 1996 than in 1993. The loads of copper, zinc and lead have shown steady decreases since the 1970s with a more constant input since the early 1990s (Littlewood *et al.*, 1997; DETR, 1997a; Pentreath, in press).

There can be large uncertainties in the load estimates for individual sites, because:

● few samples are taken (between 12 and 24 per site per year);

● data are sometimes reported below the limit of detection, making load calculations uncertain;

● the chemical sampling point and river flow gauging points are not always in the same place;

● the algorithm used for estimation may be inaccurate or imprecise;

● flow data are usually periodic, and concentration data are frequently taken at irregular time intervals;

● there are inherent errors in multiplying large flows with very small concentrations.

Figure 3.41 *Loads of major contaminants to coastal waters of England and Wales, 1991 to 1997*

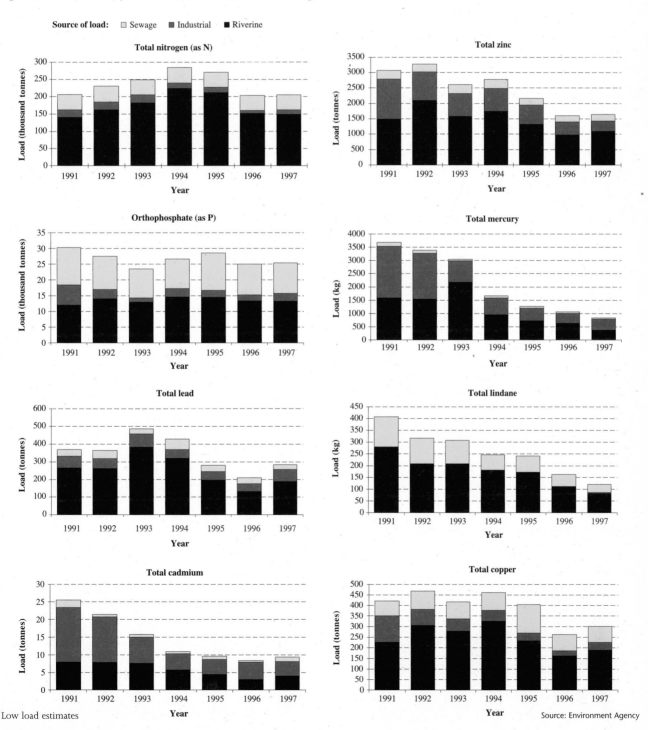

Low load estimates

Source: Environment Agency

67

North Sea ministers made a commitment to reduce aquatic inputs of hazardous substances to the North Sea in the late 1980s (Appendix 1). A target was set to reduce the inputs of 36 substances from rivers and direct discharges by 50 per cent between 1985 and 1995. Total inputs, including atmospheric, of dioxins, mercury, cadmium and lead were to be reduced by 70 per cent. The UK set these targets for inputs to all its coastal waters collectively. A revised strategy for hazardous substances has been developed by the Oslo and Paris Commissions and was approved at the 1998 Ministerial Conference. This sets

Figure 3.42a *Loads of total cadmium to major estuaries, 1991 to 1997*

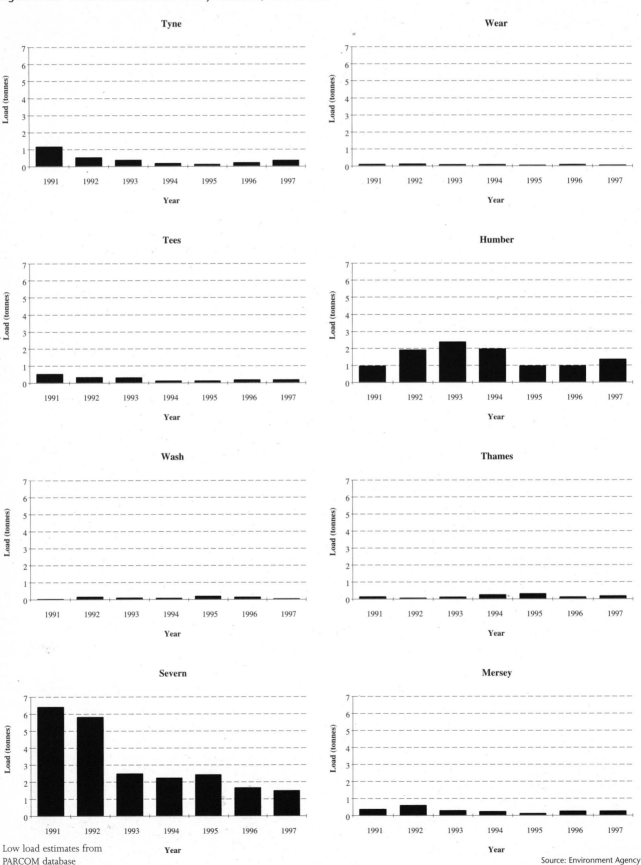

Low load estimates from PARCOM database

Source: Environment Agency

ambitious goals for reducing emissions, discharges and losses of hazardous substances to the marine environment and is likely to influence policy in coming years.

Data for the PARCOM reporting for riverine and direct inputs

from the UK have been assessed. Where substances were not detected in a sample, the load estimates assume that the concentration was equal to the laboratory limit of detection. The data for 1995 indicate the load reductions achieved since 1985; mercury 77 per cent, cadmium 62 per cent, copper 49

Figure 3.42b *Loads of total zinc to major estuaries, 1991 to 1997*

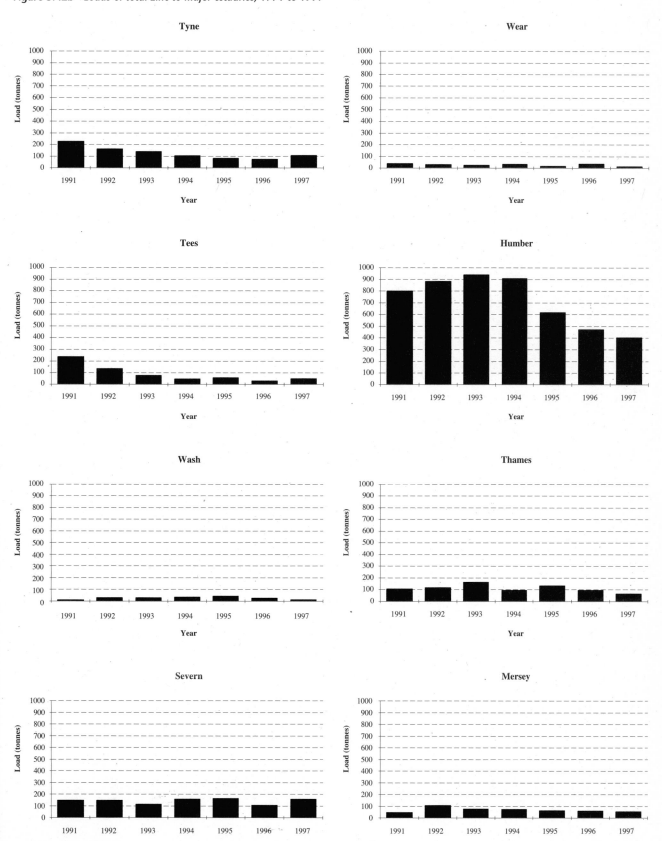

Low load estimates from PARCOM database

Source: Environment Agency

per cent and lindane 61 per cent. These show load reductions in line with the overall targets set in the 1980s. Zinc has been reduced by 23 per cent showing that further progress appears to be needed. Zinc is used in many domestic products as well as in industry. The data for the UK as a whole show that a

significant reduction (of 50 per cent or more) of waterborne inputs of 24 of the 36 substances has been achieved. Reductions exceed 45 per cent for three other substances (DETR, 1997a).

Figure 3.42c *Loads of total copper to major estuaries, 1991 to 1997*

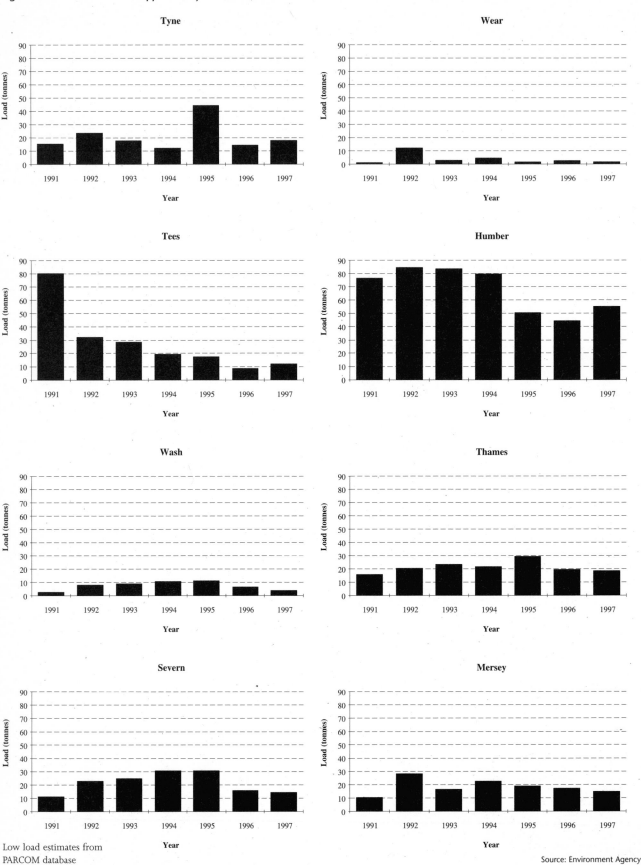

Low load estimates from PARCOM database

Source: Environment Agency

A breakdown of the trends in loads to coastal waters, monitored for PARCOM, reveals that:

● significant direct and riverine inputs of tributyl tin are limited to 14 sites around the country with none in the south and east;

● most of the ammonia load arises from discharges from sewage treatment works into estuaries;

● most of the nitrate load is from riverine sources, rather than from direct discharges to coasts, and while this is stable overall the North West Region shows an increase;

Figure 3.42d *Loads of total nitrogen to major estuaries, 1991 to 1997*

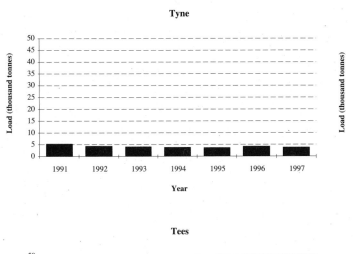

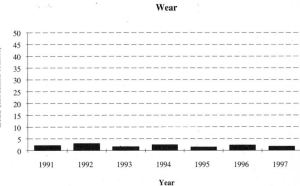

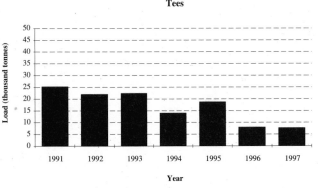

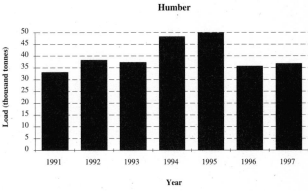

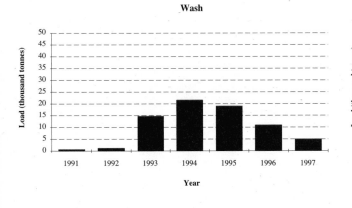

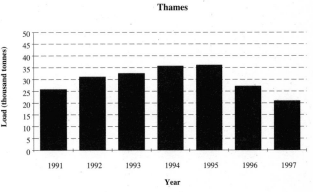

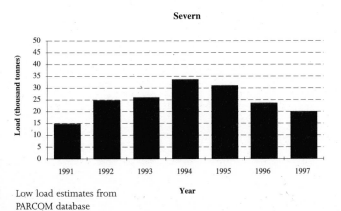

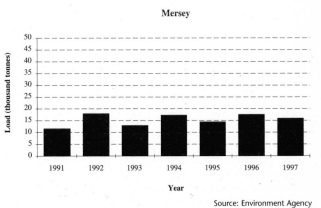

Low load estimates from PARCOM database

Source: Environment Agency

- after reductions in use over the last decade, there are now no significant measured inputs of atrazine or simazine from direct or riverine sources in Wales or the south west of England;

- the overall contribution to reductions in lindane has been

- greatest in the Thames Region (Figure 3.40);

- there are very few measured inputs of dichlorvos or malathion, and those that exist are concentrated in the north and south west respectively.

Figure 3.42e *Loads of orthophosphate to major estuaries, 1991 to 1997*

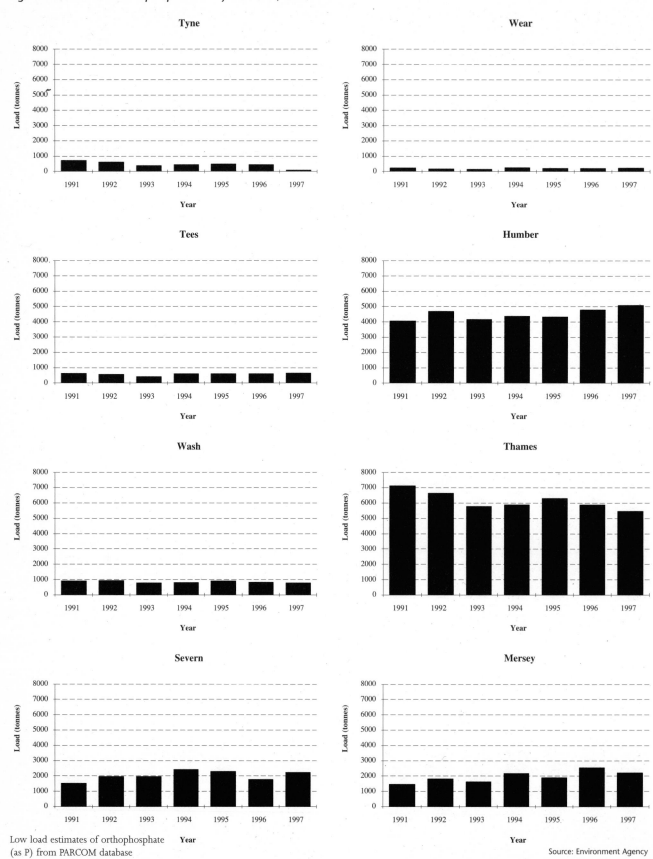

Low load estimates of orthophosphate (as P) from PARCOM database

Source: Environment Agency

Figure 3.43 *Amounts of oil entering the North Sea annually from anthropogenic and natural sources*

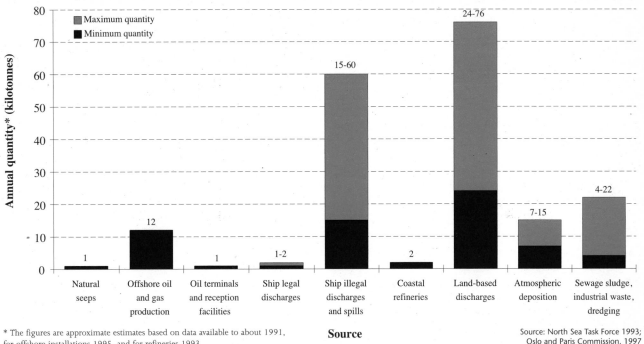

* The figures are approximate estimates based on data available to about 1991, for offshore installations 1995, and for refineries 1993

Source

Source: North Sea Task Force 1993; Oslo and Paris Commission, 1997

These variations reflect differing industrial activity, sewage discharges and diffuse inputs from land use in various parts of the country (Appendix 2 and Figures 3.41 and 3.42).

Land-based discharges to the North Sea provide some 13 to 40 per cent of the total oil discharged, much larger than that arising from refineries or offshore exploration, and perhaps only exceeded by illegal discharges from ships although the figures may not be very accurate (Figure 3.43) (North Sea Task Force, 1993). There is no information to quantify the sources of this oil but contributions from road runoff, illegal discharges of used lubricating oil down surface water drains and pollution incidents from poor storage facilities are likely to be major sources. This requires further investigation (Environment Agency, 1998b).

3.5 Waste arisings and disposals

Disposal at sea

There are hundreds of marine disposal sites in use around the coast of England and Wales at any one time (Figure 3.44). About 130 waste disposal licences were issued by MAFF each year under the Food and Environment Protection Act between 1993 and 1995. Disposal of waste at sea has decreased following the agreement made at the Oslo and Paris Convention in 1992 which prohibited all disposal at sea subject to certain exemptions. In 1989 about 3.8 million tonnes (dry weight) of solid industrial waste were dumped at sea. By 1995 this had fallen to 169 thousand tonnes (dry weight) as a result of the ban on dumping this type of waste (Figure 3.45).

Sewage sludge from treatment works has also been dumped at sea in the past. In 1995/96, 993 thousand tonnes of sewage sludge were produced in England and Wales. Of this, 173 thousand tonnes (dry weight), or 17 per cent, was disposed of

at sea, a reduction of five per cent since 1991/92 (DETR, 1997a). The main disposal grounds in England and Wales were Liverpool Bay, the Thames Estuary and off the north east coast of England. Sewage sludge disposal at sea was banned from the end of 1998.

In 1995 nearly 17 million dry tonnes and 33 million wet tonnes of dredging spoils were dumped at sea. The quantities dumped between 1988 and 1995 varied, with little discernible trend (Figure 3.46). The impact of dumping dredged spoils at sea can be a cause for concern due to the potential for mobilising and releasing pollutants bound to dredged sediments. The mass of metals deposited in the sea with dredged material in the UK annually between 1988 and 1995 is shown in Figure 3.47. Much of the trace metal content was of natural origin and many operations simply relocated the materials rather than constituting a fresh input to the environment (Oslo Commission, 1992).

Unless properly controlled, there is potential for quite severe localised ecological impacts from dumping dredged materials. Increased sea bed elevations caused by dumping material offshore may alter wave properties, leading to changes in sediment erosion and deposition at the coast. Whereas no extractions of material are normally permitted in less than 18m depth of water, dumping is permitted which can have an equally disrupting effect. The deposition of dredged material may also lead to smothering of the bed and increased turbidity from suspended particles in the water which may clog fish gills and disrupt the filter feeding of benthic organisms. There may also be secondary biological effects, resulting in modification of benthic community structures, with consequent effects on the food supply for higher organisms, including commercial fish and shellfish species (English Nature, 1991).

Following the events surrounding the plan to dispose of the Brent Spar in the deep Atlantic in 1995, a scientific group led by the Natural Environment Research Council reported to the DTI on the disposal of large offshore structures (Natural Environment Research Council, 1996). Recommendations were also made to the Government by The House of Lords Select Committee on Science and Technology's report on Decommissioning of Oil and Gas Installations in 1996. The Government has based its approach on sound science and full consultation. The international rules on decommissioning of offshore installations were agreed in Sintra, Portugal in July 1998. The OSPAR Decision 98/3 on the Disposal of Disused Offshore Installations states that the dumping and the leaving, wholly or partly in place, of disused offshore installations within the maritime area is prohibited. The topsides of all installations will now be brought ashore, along with the jackets of heavy steel structures. The decision allows for exceptions to this ban in cases where the regulating government assesses that an alternative disposal method is preferable, following

consultation with the other OSPAR contracting parties. For steel platforms, exceptions can be made on a case by case basis for the footings of installations if the jacket weighs more than 10,000 tonnes in air. Heavy concrete structures may be left in place if, after assessment and consultation, it is agreed that land disposal is neither safe nor practicable. It was also agreed that installations put in place after 9 February 1999 must be completely removed when decommissioned.

Onshore disposal will involve partial or full dismantling of the installation and allow materials such as steel, copper and aluminium to be recycled, while the remainder might be reused or go to landfill. One of the outstanding issues is how to dispose of the drill cuttings that have accumulated around the base of installations. There is currently no tried and tested technology to bring the cuttings safely to the surface without dispersing any contamination into the environment. The UK Government is proposing a strategy for dealing with cuttings piles and the issue is scheduled for discussion by OSPAR. The

Figure 3.44 *Coastal and estuarine waste disposal sites in use from 1990 to 1995*

Source: Ministry of Agriculture, Fisheries and Food; Crown copyright

Figure 3.45 *UK dumping of solid industrial waste and sewage sludge, 1988 to 1995*

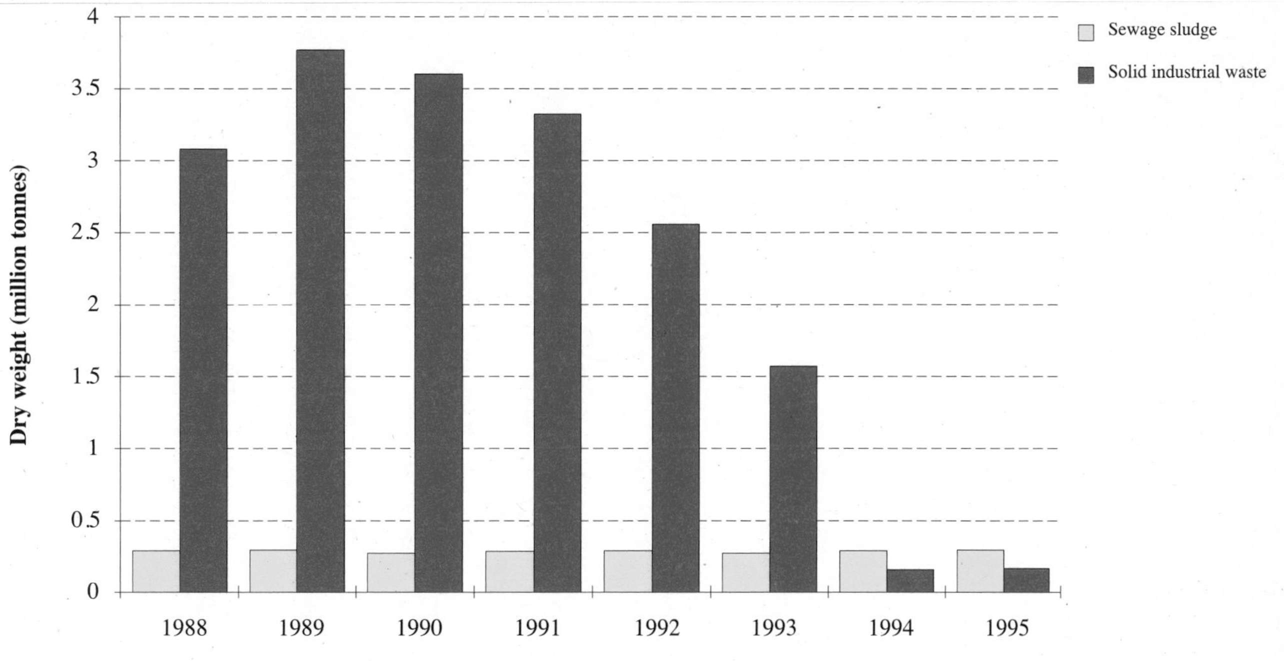

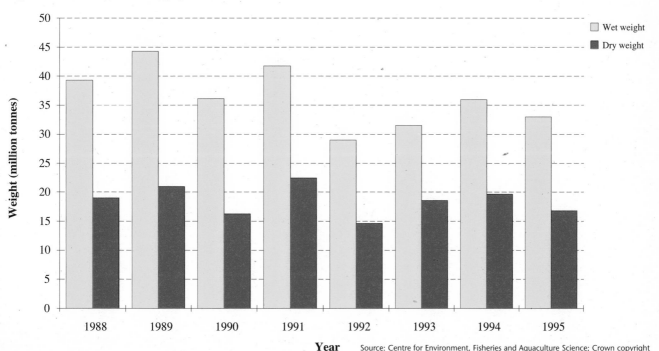

Source: Ministry of Agriculture, Fisheries and Food; Crown copyright

legal status of waste arising in international waters is unclear at present, and the European Union is attempting to resolve this question. The Agency is developing its own guidance on this issue to ensure that it is dealt with consistently and environmental impacts are minimised. This includes the technical issues surrounding the licensing of onshore dismantling sites.

Disposal on beaches

There are a few places in the country where other materials have been dumped on beaches. The dumping of coal mining spoil along the County Durham coastline is an example. This began in the mid-19th century and continued until 1993, when the coal industry collapsed and the last colliery closed. Initially, natural wave action appeared to be sufficient to remove the spoil and up until the Second World War the beaches remained attractive and popular. After the war, however, coal production increased dramatically and the volume of spoil being tipped was too large to be eroded naturally (around two million tonnes per annum).

As a consequence the spoil accumulated, burying the bedrock, raising the beach height several metres and pushing the

Figure 3.46 *UK disposal of dredgings at sea, 1988 to 1995*

Source: Centre for Environment, Fisheries and Aquaculture Science; Crown copyright

Figure 3.47 *Metals in dredged materials dumped at sea in the UK*

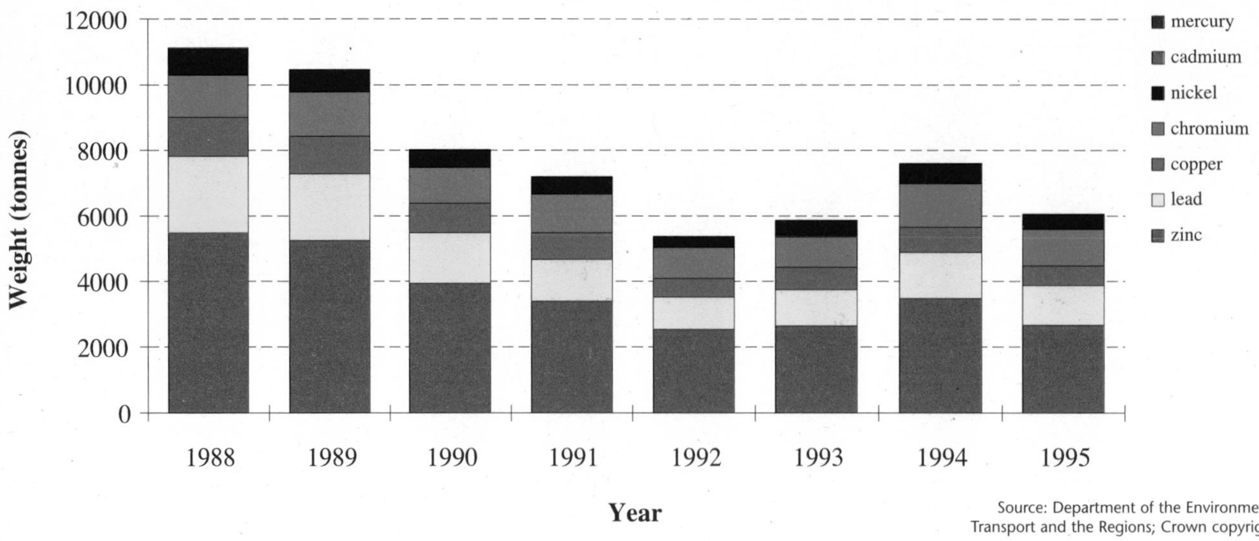

Source: Department of the Environment, Transport and the Regions; Crown copyright

shoreline seaward several hundred metres in some areas. Sediment transport mechanisms associated with the southerly drift spread the spoil southwards from the dumping sites, covering most of the coastline. It is estimated that there could be up to 10 million tonnes of spoil left on the beaches, much of which is in two pit heaps at Easington and Horden. These are separate from the general beach deposits, resting on the upper beaches and obscuring the natural limestone cliffs. If allowed to remain these heaps will eventually be eroded, thus becoming very unstable and re-polluting the beaches. The impact of the coal waste on north eastern beaches was to increase the inputs to the sediment budget. This has now ceased and the sediment budget will decrease, possibly resulting in massive erosion and consequently changing inputs to adjacent parts of the coast.

Disposal of mine waste on beaches has had four major impacts: seabed smothering, increased water turbidity, bioaccumulation of metals and shoreline habitat loss. The Agency is investigating the long-term improvement in ecology following cessation of coal spoil disposal and the clean-up of spoil heaps along the Durham coastline (Proudfoot et al., 1998).

Landfills sites on the coast

There are 541 landfill sites within 10km of the coast (Barne et al., 1995, 1996 and 1998), but a large proportion of these are no longer taking waste. Many estuarine landfills were started in the 1960s or earlier and will have been constructed as part of a land reclamation or sea defence project.

The leakage of leachates from landfill sites may impact on coastal and estuarine water quality if no remedial action is taken. For example, at Walpole Drove site near Bridgwater the mixing of leachates and groundwater had been occurring for some time before a leachate treatment plant with strict discharge consent levels was installed, which synchronises discharges with tidal flow. This site also introduced a system of netting to keep seagulls from the waste being deposited.

It is difficult to quantify the overall impact of landfill leachates

on coastal and estuarine water quality because of the diffuse nature of the pollutant source, but it is believed that landfills exert a much smaller pressure than other sources of pollution. At some sites, landfill gases may cause local air quality problems if uncontrolled. Landfill sites impact on the coastal environment in other ways; land claim, and subsequent loss of habitat and landscape, are also important pressures. Sea level rise and threats to coasts by flooding could also impinge on landfill sites.

Use for artificial reefs

Many waste products can be re-used for other purposes. For example, Southampton University's Oceanography Department has built an artificial reef on the UK coast in Poole Bay. It is an experimental reef, installed in 1989, made of waste fuel ash and concrete. Since installation the reef has been monitored for leaching and the impact on the local lobster population has been assessed. There is preliminary evidence to suggest there are larger animals on the artificial reef compared with the surrounding natural coastal environment, although this is yet to be substantiated (Jensen and Collins, 1995). There is a view that artificial reefs could be created along our coasts as habitats for crabs and lobsters, and to a lesser extent for whelks and spider crabs, and they would also attract fish. In other countries, for example the USA, Australia and Israel, used tyres have made artificial reefs, but it is uncertain as to whether leachates from these contaminate surrounding waters or biota. Artificial reefs are not however a means of waste disposal, and the re-use of material in this way would be considered against there being a clear purpose and net benefit for such a reef. There is also need for an assessment of its impact on the marine environment (Collins et al., 1995).

3.6 Illegal practices

Pollution incidents

Pollution incidents are short-term events or accidents which create a high temporary pollutant load to coastal waters. In contrast to the other continuous pollutant pressures, the elevated pollutant concentrations are usually diluted and dispersed quickly, although they may persist longer in low dispersion areas, in sediments, or at the state of low water in estuaries. Many minor incidents have a local effect which may be difficult to detect, although repeated pollution can cause cumulative long-term damage to marine life. Major incidents can require closure of fisheries, threaten human health and cause extensive biological damage, killing plants and animals over many kilometres of coastline.

Damage to the coastline can also result from physical effects on habitats, for example heavy oil and tar balls from tankers can smother rocky shores and beaches. Chemical effects occur through the spillage of substances which are directly toxic such as paints, pesticides and many industrial chemicals. Other organic substances such as milk, beer, sugar and, more obviously, sewage have equally serious effects when large quantities are released into coastal waters. This is caused by their biodegradation which uses up oxygen dissolved in the water, suffocating fish and other organisms.

The causes of pollution incidents usually relate to equipment failures and management practices which fall short of the required standards and best practice. There is then a greater risk of accidents and natural events (especially heavy rain) triggering a pollution incident.

The Agency uses a standard pollution incident classification system which discriminates major pollution incidents (category 1) from others (categories 2 and 3) and those which were reported to the Agency but are not substantiated by Agency staff (category 4), although this system is currently being reviewed. The pollution incident data collected by the Agency are not usually reported for coasts, estuaries and inland waters separately, but a one-off analysis has been performed for this report using the 1996 data.

During 1996 more than 32,000 pollution incidents were reported in total, of which over 20,000 (63 per cent) were substantiated. In the same year 1,090 substantiated pollution

Figure 3.48 *Substantiated pollution incidents by economic sector for estuaries and coasts, 1996*

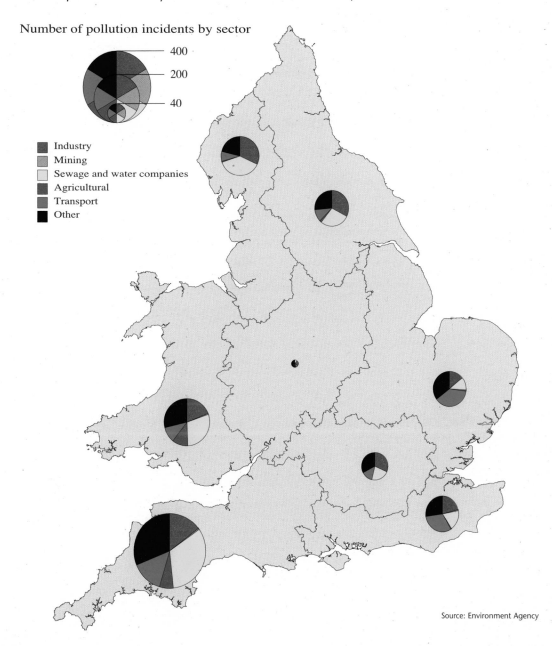

Number of pollution incidents by sector

400
200
40

Industry
Mining
Sewage and water companies
Agricultural
Transport
Other

Source: Environment Agency

incidents impacted directly on the coastal zone, fewer than four per cent of the total. The number of coastal category 1 incidents fell from 10 in 1995 to six in 1996 and the number of category 2 incidents fell from 99 in 1995 to 53 in 1996. The majority of pollution incidents in the coastal zone occur in estuaries (about 70 per cent of substantiated incidents in 1996) where the largest concentrations of people and industries are to be found. This will largely determine both the number of incidents and the number seen and reported.

Regional differences in the number of substantiated pollution incidents partly reflect the length of coastline in each region. The South West Region had about 30 incidents per 100km of coast, Thames had about 60 per 100km and the other regions each had about 10 per 100km (Figure 3.48). Population density does not appear to be a factor, with relatively few incidents in the Thames Region, where 3.6 million live within 10km of the Thames Estuary, and the highest number in the South West Region, where only 3.9 million live in the region as a whole.

Central London has a combined surface water drainage system, so that fewer land based pollution incidents impact on the Thames Estuary, although it is subject to overflows from this system, particularly during summer thunderstorms. The number of incidents which get reported reflect the types of activity taking place in a region. In the relatively industrialised estuary of the Thames, with fewer water-based leisure activities, pollution incidents may be under-reported whereas in the estuaries and coasts of the south west of England, which are popular tourist destinations, there are more incidents reported. The south west also has many small harbours and ports which are prone to pollution incidents involving leisure craft (for example oily bilge waters being spilled).

In 1996 there were large differences between regions in the sources of coastal pollution incidents. Agriculture was responsible for 11 per cent of substantiated incidents in Wales and six per cent in the South West Region, but was rarely a source elsewhere. This is because the other regions have more heavily industrialised or urbanised estuaries. Transport was responsible for 38 per cent of substantiated incidents in the Anglian Region and 32 per cent in the Southern Region, but only eight per cent in the North West Region. Nationally, transport accounts for 17 per cent of all substantiated coastal pollution incidents.

The sewage and water industry accounted for 38 per cent of substantiated incidents in the North West Region, 33 per cent in the South West Region and 30 per cent in the Agency in Wales in 1996. These high figures may be partly explained by the type of sewerage systems in those regions, higher rainfall in the west of the country and the large number of unsatisfactory storm overflows still in use. Nationally, the sewage and water industry was the largest single source of substantiated coastal pollution incidents, accounting for 28 per cent of all such events.

In 1996 other industries accounted for over 30 per cent of substantiated incidents in the North East, North West and Thames Regions, where industries are concentrated, and 20 per

cent of substantiated incidents in England and Wales as a whole. More than 30 per cent of substantiated coastal pollution incidents were from 'other' sources, which include contaminated land, hotels, pubs, hospitals, drainage, residential properties etc.

In terms of pollutant type, coastal pollution incidents involving oil and fuel accounted for 34 per cent of the total nationally in 1996 (Figure 3.49), but were 56 per cent of all substantiated incidents in the Southern Region and 49 per cent in the Thames Region, areas of highest population density. Because oil is more visible as a pollutant than other chemicals, incidents involving it are more likely to get reported.

Sewage was involved in 25 per cent of substantiated coastal pollution incidents in 1996, with the North West Region (38 per cent), South West Region (25 per cent) and the Agency in Wales (25 per cent) having the most sewage-related incidents.

Pollution incidents involving accidental releases to air can also contribute significantly to aerial emissions of some substances. The evaporation from the *Sea Empress* spill of about 29,000 tonnes is equivalent to about one per cent of annual volatile organic compound emissions. Purging of ships' tanks at shore is not a major source of volatile organic compounds but it may be significant for local air quality. The best estimate for 1,3-butadiene emissions from purging is 90 tonnes, about one per cent of the UK total. In July 1995 purging of a ship's storage tanks on the Tees led to high levels of 1,3-butadiene in Middlesbrough, peaking at 83ppb compared with background levels of 0.3ppb (Broughton *et al.*, 1997).

Shipping

Illegal discharges of oil from ships, both tankers and general cargo ships, are detected by regular national and international aerial surveillance. These show that although some slicks occur close to oil and gas installations, the majority of sightings are in the major shipping corridor between the straits of Dover and the German Bight. The estimated amount of oil discharged was up to 2,000 tonnes in some cases. Legal operational discharges of oil from shipping are estimated at one to two thousand tonnes per year, less than one per cent of the total input to the North Sea. Yet overall estimates of the amount of oil discharged each year into the North Sea from ships vary from 15 to 60 thousand tonnes (North Sea Task Force, 1993) to 50 to 100 thousand tonnes (BNSC, 1991).

In 1996 there were 678 confirmed cases of marine oil pollution in UK waters, representing a 16 per cent increase on 1995. Excluding the *Sea Empress* incident, a tanker accident off the Welsh coast, the reported quantity of oil spilled by ships was 106 tonnes. Incidents were clustered in the Humber Estuary, Dover Strait, Thames Estuary and Liverpool Bay. Observations of oil in the open sea accounted for 60 per cent of all reported incidents and direct human error caused 66 per cent of incidents (Advisory Committee on Protection of the Sea, 1997).

The most conspicuous causes of marine oil pollution are tanker accidents. The English Channel and the North Sea are among the busiest sea routes in the world. Very large tankers carry

Figure 3.49 *Substantiated pollution incidents by pollutant type, 1996, for estuaries and coasts*

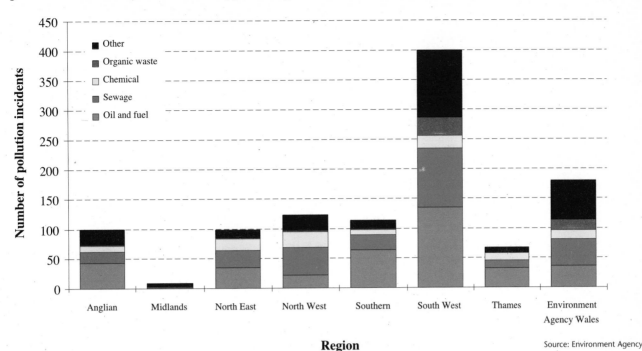

Source: Environment Agency

over 250 thousand tonnes of crude oil, while large container vessels may carry 10 thousand tonnes or more of oil for fuel. The trend over the last 25 years appears to be a reduction in the frequency of spills and the quantity of oil involved due to improved standards of tanker construction (Figure 3.50).

Major tanker disasters are relatively rare, but the impacts can be substantial, depending on the location, the type of oil involved, time of year, wind and tidal conditions. The first wreck of a supertanker was the *Torrey Canyon* which sank west of Land's End in 1967. Two major accidents in the 1990s in UK waters have emphasised the threat from tankers and have also provided some of the best information on what happens when large quantities of oil are released into the marine environment.

On 5 January 1993, under severe wind and wave conditions, the *Braer* was wrecked on south west Shetland, losing its cargo of 84,000 tonnes of light crude oil. Less than one per cent of the oil was stranded on the shore, 35 per cent was deposited in subtidal sediments, 14 per cent evaporated into the atmosphere

and 50 per cent was dispersed in the sea (Davies *et al.*, 1997). The *Sea Empress* ran aground off Milford Haven in Wales on 15 February 1996, spilling 72,000 tonnes of crude oil and 480 tonnes of heavy fuel oil. Only one to two per cent of the oil was collected from the sea surface, 40 per cent was lost by evaporation, five to seven per cent went ashore and 51 to 54 per cent of the oil dispersed in the sea (Sea Empress Environmental Evaluation Committee, 1998).

The initial response to an accident greatly influences the amount and fate of the oil released. Recovery of oil from the stricken vessel is clearly the ideal. Where oil has been spilled, booms and skimmers can protect sheltered inlets in calm conditions and some of the spilled oil can be recovered. Dispersants can be effective on oil, particularly if it is not too heavy or weathered. They remove oil from the surface into the water column and, by breaking the oil into small droplets, accelerate the degradation of the oil by marine micro-organisms. In the *Sea Empress* incident 446 tonnes of chemical dispersants were used, increasing the amount of oil dispersed

Figure 3.50 *Number of oil tanker spills and the quantity of oil spilled worldwide, 1970 to 1997*

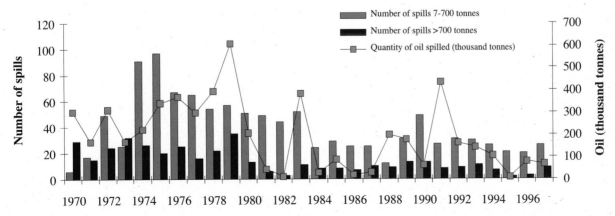

Source: International Tanker Owners Pollution Federation Limited

by at least 18,000 tonnes, or around 50 per cent. Such dispersal is of great benefit as it maximises biological degradation of the oil and significantly reduces the risks of the slick to shoreline habitats and birds. Although dispersants can be very effective in preventing damage to wildlife and recreational amenities in sensitive coastal areas, they increase the volume of oil that is dispersed into the water column. This can adversely affect fish and shellfish and the marine environment in general, particularly in shallow waters where there is limited scope for dilution of dispersed oil. Their manufacture and use is therefore subject to control by MAFF to ensure that only appropriate products are used and that their use is appropriate and of environmental benefit.

Crude oil loses most of its acute toxicity within a few days of being spilled at sea. The mortality of marine organisms declines rapidly thereafter. There are sub-lethal effects in the water column but the observed recovery of the marine ecosystem usually appears to be rapid, particularly when there are nearby sources of organisms to replace the losses.

Clean-up techniques and physical and biological degradation may affect recovery after a spill in the following ways:

- removing shore material, flushing or sandblasting can damage habitats and force oil further into the underlying layers of shoreline material;

- rocky shores cleaned with toxic dispersants can typically take between one and four years to recover biologically;

- the rate of biodegradation will depend in part on how often the microbial population has been exposed to hydrocarbons;

- ecological recovery may be promoted by leaving oiled but biologically active sediments in place and just removing bulk deposits of oil;

- by contrast, bathing beaches may require thorough cleaning, but this process will kill the remaining organisms and damage the habitat so that biological recovery may be prolonged.

The Agency has produced a detailed report on oil and gas in the environment which covers oil-related issues in more depth (Environment Agency, 1998b).

3.7 Summary of the pressures on coastal waters

Table 3.6 summarises the information presented in this chapter. The table draws out the pressures which are increasing and need attention, and shows where pressures have been successfully reduced.

Table 3.6 *Pressures on the coastal environment*

Pressure	Stresses and strains	Trend in pressure (+ increasing, - decreasing, = stable, ? unknown)
Natural forces	**Climate change:** affects temperature, runoff, and storminess. Likely to affect habitats, species, frequency of high water levels, water demand and distribution, demand for recreation. The decade since 1988 has had increased frequency of severe gales	+ UK air temperatures predicted to rise by between 0.1°C and 0.3°C per decade + Severe gales
	Sea level change: affects erosion and deposition, shape of coastlines, frequency of high water levels, extent and cost of coastal defences, coastal squeeze	+ UK average sea levels generally rising, by up to 0.5cm/yr. Highest rates in south and east England.
	Flooding: risk of property loss and lives. Some five per cent of population and 1.5 per cent of land below 5m contour	? Trends will be linked to climate change, sea level change and investment in coastal defences.
	Erosion and deposition: 0.6 to 1m per year eroded on south coast. Defences can affect sediment transport	Variable. Decrease in sedimentation rates in Humber since 1920. Increase in wave heights since 1960 affecting erosion.
Societal influences	**Population and development:** coastal population is about 17 million (one-third of total). Household numbers expected to increase in future. Some 11 per cent coastal area developed	+ 4.6 million new homes needed in England and Wales between 1991 and 2016
	Barrages: loss of intertidal areas and habitats, change in amenity value, but can provide economic regeneration	? Will depend on proposals for development
	Recreation: extensive development in some areas, destruction of some fragile habitats, disruption to wildlife, litter, conflicts between users. Demand for leisure activities growing	+ Over the 1980s increases of: 138 per cent in walking club members, 69 per cent in surfers, 35 per cent in yacht club members. In 1991, there were 500,000 windsurfers and 3,000 jet skis. Tourism growing by seven per cent per year.
	Transport: port developments and potential loss of habitats, pollution from ships' emissions, antifouling paints and road runoff	+ 1 per cent per year increase in goods traffic through ports, 29 per cent of ships' fuel used in ports, 2.7 per cent annual average increase in vehicle flows on roads

Pressure	Stresses and strains	Trend in pressure (+ increasing, - decreasing, = stable, ? unknown)
Abstractions and removals	**Water resources:** about 24,000 Ml/d abstracted from tidal waters, mainly used as cooling water for industry which may cause thermal plumes. Risk of pollution from biocides. Risk of fish entrainment. Freshwater abstraction impacts on dune-slacks, and over-abstraction can lead to saline intrusion	= 93 per cent of cooling water used by the electricity supply industry
	Dredging and mineral extraction: some 27 million tonnes of aggregates dredged from the sea in 1996. Mineral extraction potentially affects sediment transport and shoreline stability, and may disturb subtidal habitats and species	+ 63 per cent increase in aggregate extraction predicted by 2015
	Commercial fishing and aquaculture: overfishing puts strain on fish stocks, which then impacts other species. Fish farms cause localised impacts, and non-native species exert pressures on native species	- Bottom-dwelling species landed since 1940s + Shellfish and open-water species landed + Range of species caught
Usage, releases and discharges	**Point discharges from sewerage system:** over 5,000 discharges to coast in 1997, they are a source of nutrients to coasts. Storm water overflows cause intermittent pollution	- Pollutant loads decreased since 1970s. Over 96 per cent of STWs compliant with consents - Improvements made to many storm overflows and more planned
	Regulated releases and discharges from industry: can affect water quality, air quality and contain dangerous substances. Some 40 per cent of heavy industry located on coast	- Over 25 years to 1995 aerial emissions fell by: 63 per cent for SO_2, 48 per cent for NO_x and 47 per cent for CO_2. Oil discharged from refineries progressively reduced
	Diffuse discharges: includes coastal oil exploration, road runoff, agricultural runoff, minewater and seepage. Land-based discharges of oil are significant source (13 to 40 per cent) of oil in sea	+ Minewaters as mines are abandoned
	Contaminant loads from land to sea: loads from rivers and direct discharges are the major source for most contaminants	- Between 1985 and 1995, reductions of: 77 per cent in mercury, 62 per cent in cadmium, 49 per cent in copper, 61 per cent in lindane = Nutrient loads variable but stable in some areas
Waste arisings and disposals	**Disposal at sea:** sewage sludge until 1998, dredged spoils impact on benthic communities and contribute to contaminant loads	- In 1995/96, 173,000 tonnes of sewage sludge dumped at sea but sea dumping of sewage sludge banned from 1998 = In 1995, 17 million (wet) tonnes and 33 million (dry) tonnes of dredgings were dumped at sea
	Disposal on beaches: historical dumping of colliery spoil (up to 10 million tonnes on Durham beaches) and mine waste smothers sea bed, increases turbidity, adds to metal loads and habitat loss	- Dumping of colliery waste and minestone at sea is now banned.
	Landfill sites on the coast: coastal leachates from landfill could impact on water quality and cause habitat loss	-/? Over 540 landfill sites by the coast, stress largely unknown
Illegal practices	**Pollution incidents:** potential physical, chemical, biological and aesthetic impacts. Over one-third of incidents due to oil and fuel	? In 1996, 1090 incidents recorded on coast (4 per cent of total)
	Shipping: oil spills are significant source of coastal pollution. Tanker disasters are rare but local impacts can be substantial	+ In 1996, 678 cases of marine oil pollution, up 16 per cent from 1995 (but may be due to improved reporting). Up to 100,000 tonnes of oil discharged to North Sea each year.

Section 4 Viewpoints on the state of the coastal environment

Measuring the state of the environment is a fundamental aspect of the Agency's environmental management role. A sound scientific understanding of what the state of the coastal environment is at any one time, and how it is responding to the many and varied pressures placed upon it, is critical to achieving this role. It provides the basis for assessing priorities for action, charting progress with respect to environmental management plans and targets, and producing information on the environment for all those who have an interest in it. It also provides an important part of assessing the rate of progress towards achieving the objective of sustainable development. Although vast amounts of data exist on the coastal environment, there are many gaps and inconsistencies when the information base is considered as a whole. This is partly because there is no coherent national framework for measuring the state of the whole coastal environment. There is a need to adopt an integrated view because some parts of the coastal environment depend on other parts and an improvement in one aspect could be at the expense of another.

This section attempts to answer the question: "What is the general state of the coastal environment and how is it responding to the pressures placed upon it?". This fundamental question gives rise to several further basic questions about how best to describe its state and changes to it. It can be broken down in the following way.

- Assuming that the various types of land and coastal resources can be characterised, how are these resources changing over time?

- How are the various (key) populations and communities of flora and fauna changing over time?

- How is the quality of the environment changing over time, as judged by comparison with physical, chemical and biological standards?

- How is the 'health' of the environment changing over time?

- How is the environment changing in the long term as a result of both natural and human pressures?

- How are aesthetically valued features (landscape, amenities etc.) changing over time?

This framework is discussed in more detail in the Agency's consultation document, *Viewpoints on the Environment - Developing a National Environmental Monitoring and Assessment Framework* (Environment Agency, 1997b).

Each of the above sets of environmental indicators may be affected by one or more pressures placed upon it, quite often with a natural pressure being exacerbated by a more-readily controllable human one. Irrespective of such cause-and-effect relationships (most of which are not fully understood), and bearing in mind that it is impossible to measure everything, this section presents a selection of the information available on the state of the coastal environment in order to answer the questions posed and identify areas where more monitoring and surveillance is required.

4.1 Land use and environmental resources

Land use

This section describes and quantifies the extent of coastal resources in England and Wales, and how they have changed over time. The coastline extends to over 5,000km, which is one of the largest in Europe, and there are over 100 estuaries greater than 2km long. Estuaries vary greatly in size. The Wash (66,600ha) and the Severn (55,700ha) are the largest in areal terms and there are six others greater than 10,000ha. British estuaries form over a quarter of the whole estuarine resource

Figure 4.1 *Sand dunes, shingle structures and saline lagoons in England and Wales*

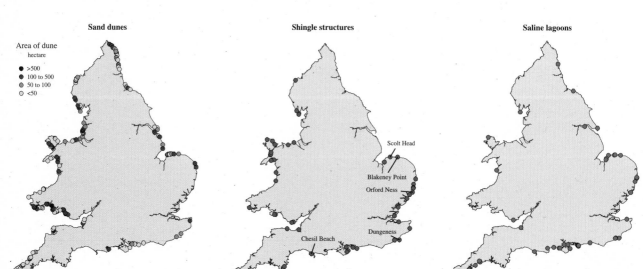

Source: Joint Nature Conservation Committee; Sneddon and Randall, 1993; Barnes, 1989; Elsevier Science

Figure 4.2 *The loss of saltmarshes in Essex and Kent between 1973 and 1988*

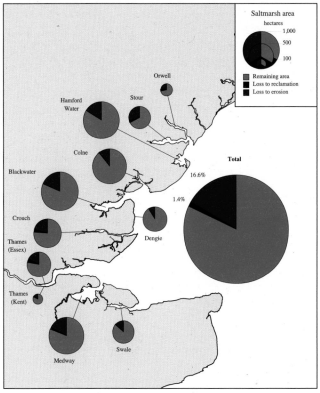

Source: Burd, 1989; Pye and French, 1993b

Some 24 per cent of the English coastline and 11 per cent of the Welsh coastline is covered by saltmarshes, about 14,000ha in total, substantially less than the 200,000ha a few centuries ago (Carpenter and Pye, 1996). The largest areas are in the Thames Estuary, Liverpool Bay, the Wash and Morecambe Bay, although most estuaries have some saltmarshes - they cover about one-sixth of the intertidal zone (Burd, 1989; Davidson *et al.*, 1991). In Essex and Kent 18 per cent of saltmarshes were lost between 1973 and 1988 due to coastal erosion and land reclamation (Figure 4.2), but in other areas, for example north Wales and south Devon, saltmarshes are actively extending (Figure 4.3). Erosion could lead to a further eight per cent loss by 2012 (Pye and French, 1993a). New surveillance techniques are helping to quantify the extent of saltmarshes more accurately (Figure 4.4).

Historically, saltmarshes were enclosed to form grazing marshes with major areas in the Wash, Ouse, Nene, Severn and Thames estuaries, but since the 1930s some two-thirds in the south east have been claimed for other forms of agriculture or development, leaving 200,000ha of freshwater and brackish grazing marsh in England in total (UK Biodiversity Steering Group, 1995a).

In the UK there are over 581,000ha of estuarine and intertidal mud and sand, about 28 per cent of the intertidal area of north west Europe, of which 233,000ha are in England. In some parts there has been much reclamation - none is left on the Tyne now, and 80 per cent has been reclaimed since 1720 on the Tees. The largest intertidal areas are Morecambe Bay (33,750ha) and the Wash (29,770ha). This resource is particularly important for over-wintering birds.

in Europe (Davidson *et al.*, 1991). But cliffs, beaches and mudflats, which we usually associate with the coastline, account for only three per cent of the coastal zone and less than one per cent of the land area of England and Wales.

The physical characteristics of the coastal area vary from place to place as shown by the following facts.

- Cliffs occur along 38 per cent (1,690km) of the coastline, with chalk cliffs along 2.5 per cent (113km). Many have been modified by coastal engineering (Tittley, 1998).

- Sand dunes occur along 400km (nine per cent) of the coast of Great Britain, most frequently in the north and west (Figure 4.1) covering a total area of over 56,000ha. Some 14 per cent of dunes have been afforested in the past 50 years, and the dunes between Liverpool and Southport have been reduced to a tenth of their previous extent by development and industry.

- Shingle occurs on a third of the coastline, mainly on exposed beaches; five are nationally important in terms of biodiversity (Figure 4.1) (Sneddon and Randall, 1993). Dungeness, with over 2,000ha of shingle, is one of the largest shingle areas in Europe.

- There are 37 natural saline lagoons, mainly in the south and east, with a further five behind artificial barriers, covering some 3,300ha although Poole Harbour covers 75 per cent of this; most are less than 20ha (Figure 4.1). The number of lagoons in southern England doubled between 1800 and 1974, largely due to gravel extraction (Gubbay, 1988).

Figure 4.3 *Saltmarsh stability in England and Wales*

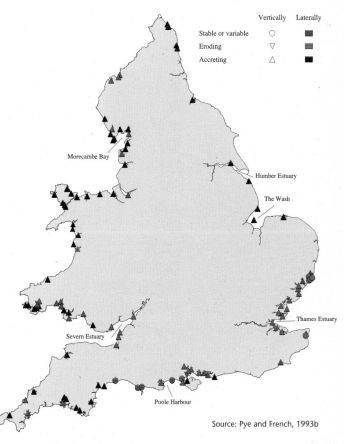

Source: Pye and French, 1993b

Figure 4.4 *Saltmarsh on the Deben Estuary in Suffolk, August 1996*

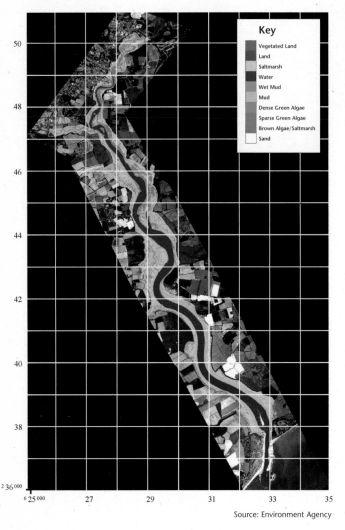

Source: Environment Agency

These statistics relate to natural features in the coastal area. Human uses take up about four-fifths of the 10km wide strip of land by the coast. Development accounts for 11 per cent of land use, agriculture 61 per cent (much of which is grade 1), natural and semi-natural uses 16 per cent, and forestry nine per cent (Figure 4.5). This is based on an Agency analysis of the Institute of Terrestrial Ecology's land cover data.

In the period 1990 to 1993 about 2,500ha of land changed from rural to urban uses in England within 10km of the coast (based on an Agency analysis of DETR's land use change statistics and data from the Institute of Terrestrial Ecology's Land Cover Map of Great Britain). This land use change represents an estimated net loss of 0.12 per cent of rural land in the coastal strip in the period 1990 to 1993 (Figure 4.6). Because of the way that DETR's land use change is recorded this change is probably an underestimate. An alternative approach (based on an Agency analysis of the Institute of Terrestrial Ecology's Countryside Survey data) shows that in the six year period, 1984 to 1990, about 0.8 per cent of rural land changed to urban uses in the 10km coastal strip, compared with 0.58 per cent for England and Wales as a whole. There are large uncertainties in these figures, and so better estimates are required over longer time periods in order to fully assess how land use in the coastal zone is changing.

In recognition of their resource value, many coastal areas have been designated in various ways, such as Heritage Coasts, Areas of Outstanding Natural Beauty, or areas which hold special conservation value. These are described and discussed later in Section 5.5, and shown in Figures 5.2 and 5.3.

State of coastal defences

These land uses have historically led to the construction of defences to protect them from flooding, erosion and storms and

Figure 4.5 *Land cover within 10km of the England and Wales coast, 1990*

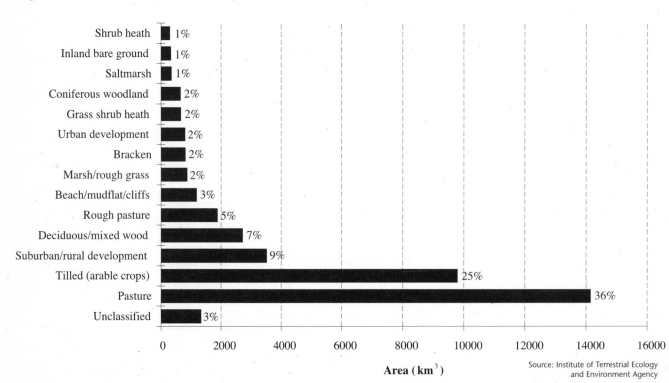

Source: Institute of Terrestrial Ecology and Environment Agency

Figure 4.6 *Net loss of rural land in the coastal strip of England, 1990 to 1993*

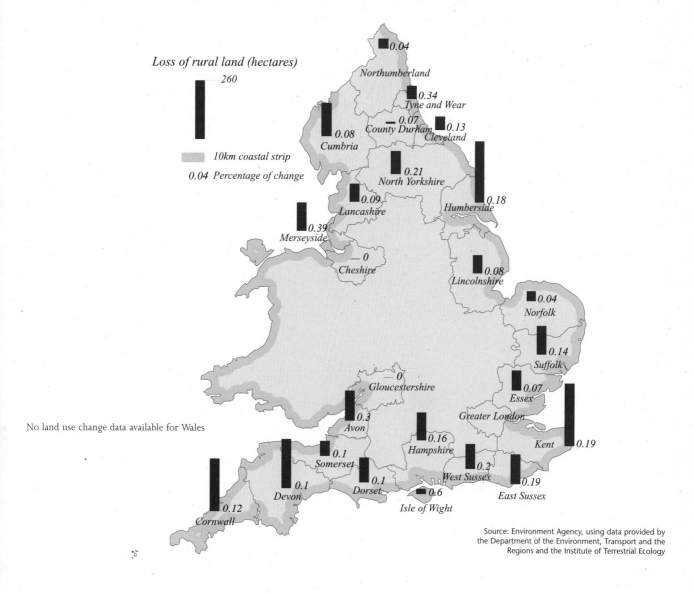

Loss of rural land (hectares)

260

10km coastal strip

0.04 Percentage of change

0.04 Northumberland

0.34 Tyne and Wear

0.07 County Durham

0.13 Cleveland

0.08 Cumbria

0.21 North Yorkshire

0.18 Humberside

0.09 Lancashire

0.39 Merseyside

0 Cheshire

0.08 Lincolnshire

0.04 Norfolk

0.14 Suffolk

0 Gloucestershire

0.07 Essex

Greater London

0.3 Avon

0.16 Hampshire

Kent 0.19

No land use change data available for Wales

0.1 Somerset

0.1 Dorset

0.2 West Sussex

0.19 East Sussex

0.1 Devon

0.6 Isle of Wight

0.12 Cornwall

Source: Environment Agency, using data provided by
the Department of the Environment, Transport and the
Regions and the Institute of Terrestrial Ecology

about one-third of the total length of coastline is protected by artificial or semi-natural defences or both. Sea defences and tidal defences protect low-lying areas against sea flooding and are usually the responsibility of the Agency. Coast protection works prevent the erosion of land and encroachment by the sea and are predominantly the responsibility of local authorities. Coastal defence is the term given to both sea defences and coastal protection works for convenience. Many coastal defences are now essential to the social and economic wellbeing of the landward areas, and to seaward facilities for boating and recreation, and so are essentially part of the coastal resources. Most coastal defences are made up of several 'elements', for example, a foreshore with an earth embankment, or groynes in front of a sea wall, and so a length of coastline 100km long may be defended by more than 100km of defence elements. Analyses of coastal defences sometimes focus on defence elements and sometimes on length of coast defended. The lengths of coast defended are shown in Figure 4.7, which clearly shows their greater density in the east and south of England. The land protected by individual sea defences varies in length, area and use. The total length of coast defended by sea defences is 1260km (NRA, 1992) of which about 350km of

defences (by length of coast) protect areas of less than 100ha, over 510km protect areas between 100ha and 1,000ha, and 390km protect areas above 1,000ha. The lengths defending land use types are:

- dense urban and major transport infrastructure, 94km of defences;

- predominantly urban, 205km;

- high grade agricultural land with residential and industrial property, 481km;

- average grade cropland and pasture, little built property, 361km;

- low grade land use, 119km.

Surveys are done periodically to assess their state of repair, based on the individual elements (Table 4.1). The table shows that over 12 per cent of defences need moderate or significant work and another 40 per cent show signs of wear.

A survey was carried out in 1993 to examine the extent, adequacy and state of repair of coastal protection works in England. This showed:

Figure 4.7 *The length of sea defences and coastal protection around England and Wales*

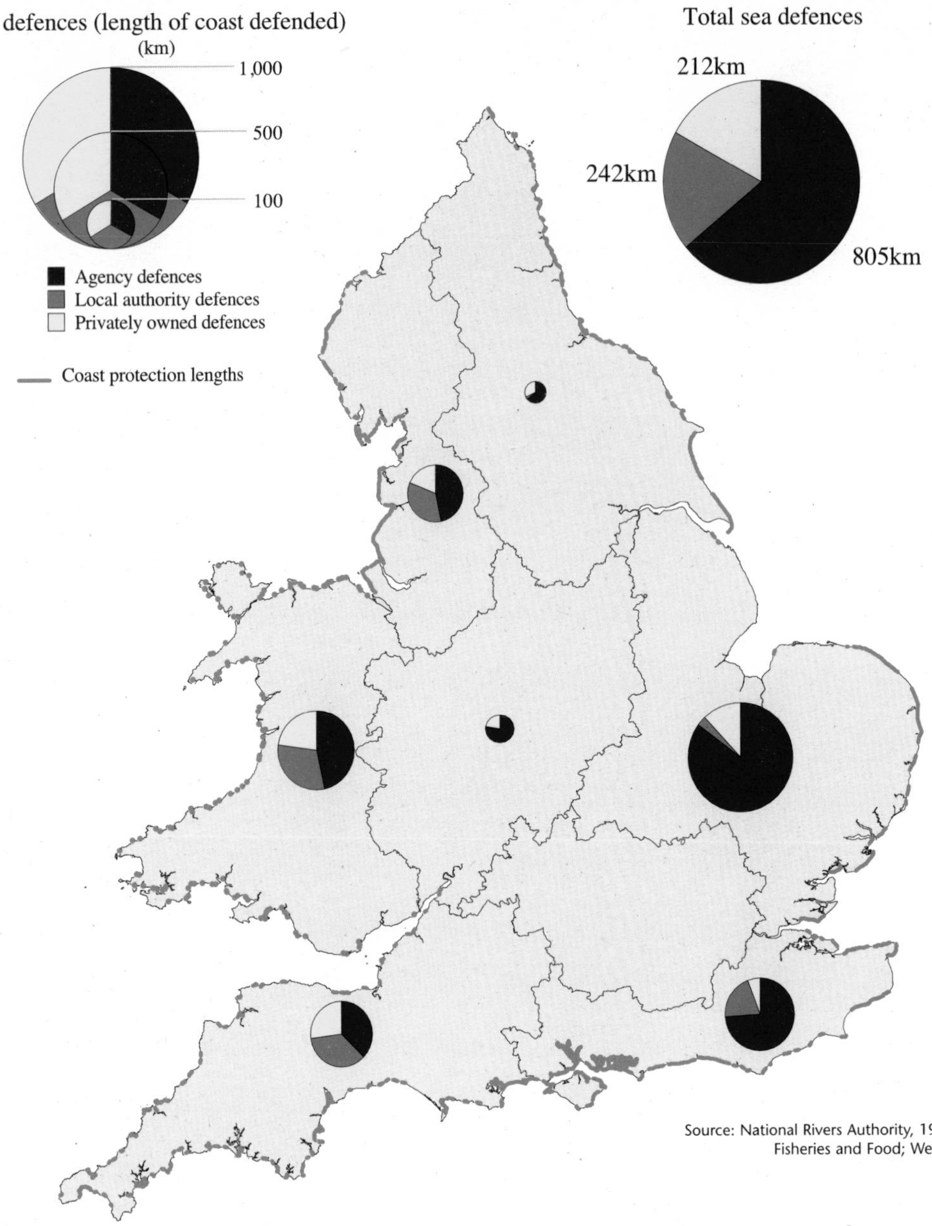

Source: National Rivers Authority, 1992; Ministry of Agriculture, Fisheries and Food; Welsh Office; Crown copyright

Table 4.1 *The condition of sea defences (by defence elements), 1997*

Condition of sea defences	Environment Agency-owned length (km)	Local authorities-owned length (km)	Private ownership length (km)	Total length (km)	Total per cent
Condition as built	664	316	111	1091	48
Some signs of wear	624	111	149	884	40
Moderate works needed	116	14	95	225	10
Significant works needed	23	4	15	42	2
Total	1428	445	370	2242	100

Source: Environment Agency, 1998c

- a total coast protection length of 1,018km, comprising 860km of constructed defences (1,688km of defence elements) and 158km of natural defences (for example cliffs);

- the south east, north west and south west have the greatest lengths of protected coast in England (Figure 4.7);

- some 41 per cent of defence elements (692km) needed significant or moderate maintenance work;

- only 12 per cent (203km) of defence elements were in the 'condition as built';

- nine per cent (152km) of defence elements had a residual life of less than five years and 24 per cent (405km) a residual life of five to 10 years;

- 135km of unprotected coastline were described as significantly eroding and could indicate the potential requirement for new works (MAFF, 1994).

Comparing surveys suggests that on the whole coastal protection works are in a poorer state than sea defences, although it is not known how the condition of coastal protection works have changed since 1993. Also there are cases where the elements are redundant and they are not maintained because it is no longer appropriate to do so. It could be, though, that some 24 per cent (959km) of defence elements (sea and coastal) in total need moderate or significant improvements. There have not been any recent surveys of the state of tidal defences, but there are 2,150km of these too (Hydraulics Research Wallingford, 1997).

Energy resources available from the coastal environment

Oil and gas reserves

At the end of 1995 the oil and gas reserves in the UK continental shelf (onshore and offshore) were 1,890 million tonnes of oil and 1,915 billion cubic metres of gas (DTI, 1997b). Proven UK reserves amount to fewer than one per cent of the world total (Institute of Petroleum, 1997). As a result of continuing discoveries, the remaining reserves of both oil and gas have been roughly constant over the past decade. Present rates of depletion of UK reserves are around 6.5 per cent per year for oil and 4.0 per cent for gas. This suggests that UK reserves have a lifetime of a number of decades, but this is somewhat uncertain.

There are only three areas in England and Wales where oil and gas are produced within 30km of the shore:

- in the south east Irish Sea, some 10km to 20km from the shore;

- in the North Sea off the mouth of the Humber Estuary and Norfolk coast, about 20km to 30km from the shore;

- onshore at Wytch Farm in Dorset.

Many of the areas close to the coast have not been explored yet. Exploration requires licensing from the DTI who offers 'blocks' of the sea bed from time to time. The eastern Irish Sea is due to be explored further in the near future, so the overall extent of our oil and gas reserves close to the coast is unknown.

Wytch Farm in Dorset, owned by BP, produces 90 per cent of the onshore oil in the UK and is the largest onshore production site in Europe. The Wytch Farm oil field stretches out from the land under Poole Harbour and Poole Bay and is estimated to contain 53 million tonnes of oil, of which 27 million tonnes have been used to date (DTI, 1997b).

Alternative energy resources

The coast of England and Wales is in many ways an ideal place for harnessing energy. It has some of the largest tidal ranges in the world, particularly in the estuaries of the west coast. Its shores are exposed to strong winds and the west coasts receive large waves of oceanic origin: the eastern Atlantic has some of the highest wave energy levels in the world. Yet currently there is very little use of these energy sources. The reasons may be partly economic (for example fossil fuels are still cheaper than alternative forms), partly institutional (there are not sufficient incentives) or even cultural, but there are also large uncertainties surrounding the environmental impacts of alternative energy schemes. It is not yet obvious whether the potential damage that may be caused by developing the coast for alternative energy production is offset by the benefits of low emission energy production.

The main methods of generating electrical energy from the coastal environment are turbines, which harness tidal currents; rockers or pistons which harness wave action, and offshore turbines which are driven by the wind. The potential for power generation from these is shown in Table 4.2.

Table 4.2   *The apparent potential for electrical power generation from coastal alternative energy sources in the UK*

Power generation method	Maximum potential (terawatt hours per year)	Maximum potential as a proportion of 1995 consumption (per cent)	Current uses in UK	Countries elsewhere using this method
Tidal barrages	50	16	none	France, Canada, China
Tidal currents	50	16	none	experimental
Wave devices	35 to 48	11 to 16	experimental	Norway, experimental
Wind turbines (offshore)	140	46	Blyth Harbour, and other proposals including Welsh coast	Denmark, Netherlands

Source: Department of Trade and Industry, 1997a; Energy Technology Support Unit, 1994; DeMontfort University, 1997; Crown copyright

Table 4.2 suggests that most of the electrical energy consumed in the UK could be produced at the coast from natural sources, but this would require every location suitable for power generation to be developed with barrages or turbines. The environmental pressures associated with alternative energy production are varied and complex and depend on the production method employed and the scale of development. For example, onshore wind turbines are known to have, for some people, a large aesthetic impact which diminishes the landscape. It is unknown whether this would be the same for offshore wind turbines. Tidal power generation requires a large, permanent structure to be built across an estuary which will modify currents and tides and consequently change sediment movement, ecological systems and flood risk.

The reductions in the emission of gaseous pollutants that could be achieved by producing energy from alternative means are potentially great. For example, if a barrage on the Severn Estuary was used to supply electricity instead of some existing power stations, it is estimated that the UK total carbon dioxide and sulphur dioxide emissions could be reduced by seven to eight per cent on 1998 energy consumption levels.

There are many challenges to be overcome in order to produce alternative energy on a large scale in a sensitive and environmentally protective way. But the potential exists for natural coastal sources of energy to provide a greater contribution to energy production in the UK in future.

4.2 Key biological populations, communities and biodiversity

The status of animals and plants depends on the condition of their habitat and on their interactions with other species. Some of these habitats have been identified in the UK Biodiversity Action Plan for their significance (Table 4.3). Some, like commercial fish, are affected by direct human exploitation. After describing the diversity of coast lands, this section looks at key biological groups - invertebrates, fish, birds and mammals. It concludes by looking at threatened species and the occurrence of non-native species.

Table 4.3 *Priority marine and coastal habitats in the UK Biodiversity Action Plan*

Coastal and floodplain grazing marsh	Littoral and sub-littoral chalk reefs
Maritime cliff and slopes	Sub-littoral sands and gravels
Coastal sand dunes	Tidal rapids
Machair	Maerl beds
Coastal vegetated shingle	Deep mud (seapen and burrowing megafauna communities)
Saline lagoons	*Serpula vermicularis* beds (worm)
Saltmarsh	*Sabellaria alveolata* reefs (polychaete worm)
Mudflats	*Sabellaria spinulosa* reefs (polychaete worm)
Sheltered muddy gravels (intertidal)	*Modiolus modiolus* beds (horse mussel)
Seagrass beds	*Lophelia pertusa* reefs (cold-water coral)

Source: UK Biodiversity Group pers. comm., 1998

Coast lands

The principal habitats of the coastal strip are coastal grassland, sea cliffs, rocky shores, dunes and saltmarsh. Plants and animals typical of these are shown in Table 4.4. In all, coastal habitats hold 121 out of the 624 scarce or rare British species of vascular plants (Doody et. al., 1993). Large seabird colonies exist on Flamborough Head, the offshore islands of south west Wales, the Farne Islands and the Scillies. The major seabird sites are well protected and most cliff-nesting species are on the increase (Table 4.6). Sea cliffs also hold a number of rare insects and cliff caves are important roosting sites for bats.

Table 4.4 *Plants and animals of coastal lands*

Habitat	Examples of plants and animals	Comment
Coastal grasslands	Meadow fox-tail, rye grass, tasselweeds, brackish water-crowfoot	18 scarce or rare plant species; ditches provide an important habitat
Sea cliffs	Wild cabbage, sea lavender, seabirds, peregrine, raven, greater horseshoe bat, mouse-eared bat	16 rare plant species on North Sea cliffs; important for nesting seabirds and caves important for bats
Rocky shores	Lichens, crabs, limpets, starfish, barnacles, blennies	Common throughout England and Wales; resilient to impacts, recover rapidly from disturbance
Dunes	Sea sandwort, sea buckthorn, creeping willow, sea spurge, natterjack toad, sand lizard, smooth snake	16 rare or scarce plant species on North Sea dunes; heavy grazing by livestock and trampling by visitors can damage
Saltmarsh	Sea grass, cord grass, common reed, sea-club rush, Brent goose, shelduck, redshank, mud snails, ragworms, flatfish, bass, mullet	12 rare or scarce plant species; can be eroded if sea defences breached

Figure 4.8 *The distribution of natterjack toads, sand lizards and smooth snakes, pre-1900 to post-1970*

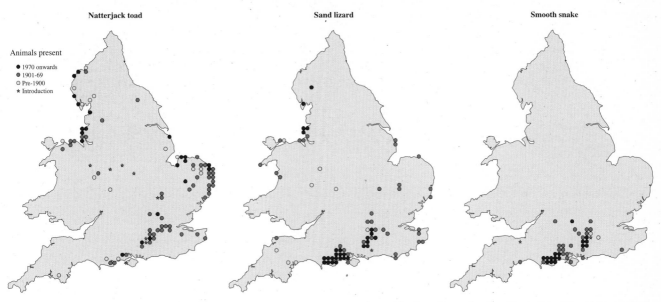

Source: Joint Nature Conservation Committee; Institute of Terrestrial Ecology, 1995

Rocky shore communities can be affected by industrial discharges, particularly in sheltered locations, but population changes tend to be limited to the immediate vicinity of the discharge. In Milford Haven in south west Wales, where four refineries have operated, there were reductions in species such as limpets and barnacles, and increases in the abundance of algae within a few hundred metres of refinery outfalls (Hobbs and Morgan, 1992).

Dunes, which are important sites for mosses and invertebrates, are one of the main habitats for natterjack toads and the sand lizard. Loss of habitat due to development has caused a decline of natterjack toads, and they have become extinct in Wales. They are limited to 35 natural sites in England, although by 1995 they had been introduced to eight sites including one in Wales. The sand lizard, also found on lowland heath and sea cliffs, has been lost from many sites as a result of habitat

Figure 4.9 *The distribution of Spartina-dominated saltmarsh*

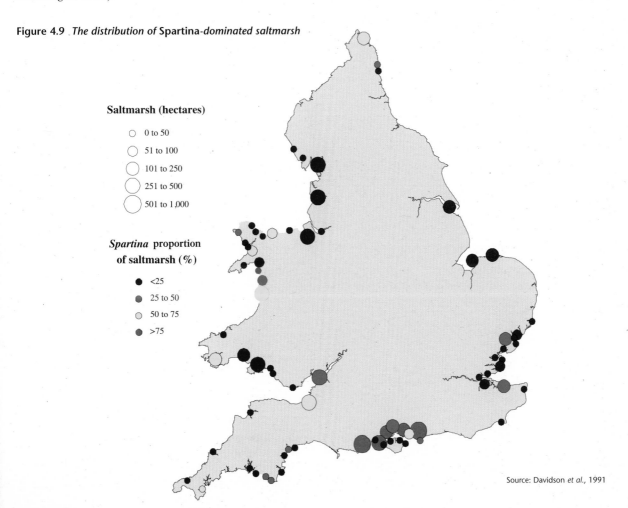

Source: Davidson *et al.*, 1991

damage including encroachment of pines, gorse and other scrub onto open sandy areas. The population in Britain in 1980 was only about 5,000. The smooth snake is another reptile species associated with the coastal zone although it occurs mainly on lowland heath. Its population is now around 2,000. Studland National Nature Reserve on the Dorset coast is the most important site for both of these reptile species (Figure 4.8).

Saltmarsh vegetation is zoned from the sea towards the land and, together with mudflats, it supports important populations of invertebrates, fish and birds. Land reclamation and flood defences have changed the nature of the plant communities. This is shown by a comparison of community types in the north west with those in East Anglia where the proportion of coastal defence is about double. Protection has increased the amount of upper marsh communities at the expense of the more species-rich lower to mid-marsh community types. Extensive change has been caused by the spread of the common cord grass (*Spartina anglica*). This is a newly evolved species which was first recorded in Southampton Water in the late 19th century. It has spread, often with deliberate assistance to reclaim land for grazing, to most of the estuaries in England and Wales (Figure 4.9). It now forms three-quarters or more of some saltmarshes in southern England though it is dying back on some of these sites as it generates anaerobic soils with high sulphide levels which kill the plants. Common cord grass may be associated with the decline in the native *Spartina maritima* and produces a monoculture which has a lower conservation

value than other saltmarsh. Its seaward spread may also have reduced the area of intertidal mud available to fish, birds and other species. In some areas common cord grass is being controlled by spraying with the herbicide glyphosate (Davidson *et al.*, 1991).

Further from shore some 36 per cent of estuaries have beds of sea grass (*Zostera*) on sheltered muddy sands and green algae (*Enteromorpha*) also occur, both of which provide grazing for invertebrates, fish and birds. Calcareous species of red seaweeds form unattached beds of 'maerl' in sheltered waters which support a rich fauna and flora; the Fal Estuary holds the largest maerl bed in England.

Invertebrates

The ecological quality of estuaries is naturally variable reflecting changes in salinity, flow and substrate. Changes in the benthic invertebrates due to human activities are difficult to detect against this dynamic background.

A review of 102 estuaries in the 1980s showed that there is a tendency towards a greater number of estuarine plant and animal communities in the south west, south, and west Wales, with lower numbers in the east and north (Figure 4.10). This pattern is probably related to the warming influence of the North Atlantic Drift in the west, favourable physical substrates and habitats such as rias. Offshore, invertebrate communities vary with depth. The nature of the seabed is particularly

Figure 4.10 *Aspects of biodiversity on coasts and in estuaries*

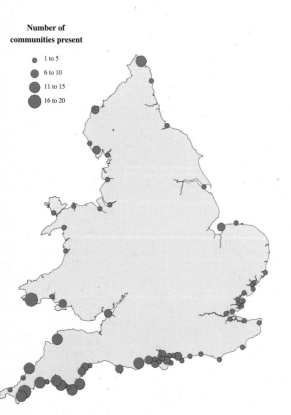

The diversity of plants and animals in estuaries

Number of communities present

- 1 to 5
- 6 to 10
- 11 to 15
- 16 to 20

Source: Davidson *et al.*, 1991

The number of bottom-dwelling animal groups* at National Monitoring Programme sites in 1993 and 1994

Estuarine sites
- 150
- 75
- 15

Intermediate and offshore sites
- 150
- 75
- 15

*For example, worms, crabs, shrimps, shellfish, sea urchins

Source: Environment Agency; Centre for Environment, Fisheries and Aquaculture Science

Figure 4.11 *The number of macroinvertebrate species along the Thames and Humber Estuaries, 1994 and the Mersey Estuary, 1988*

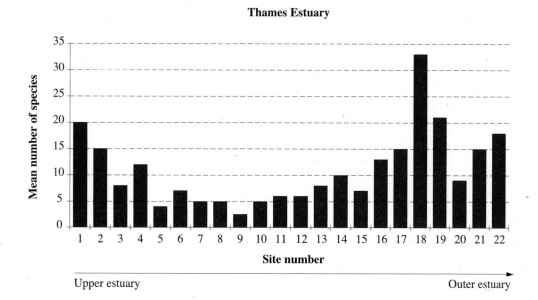

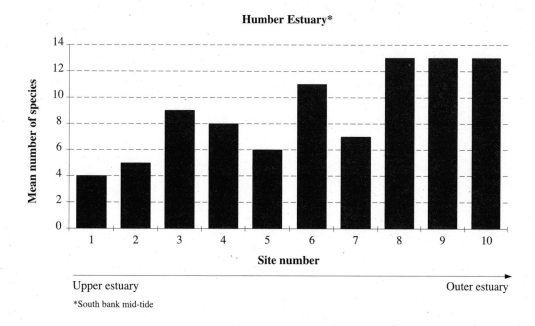

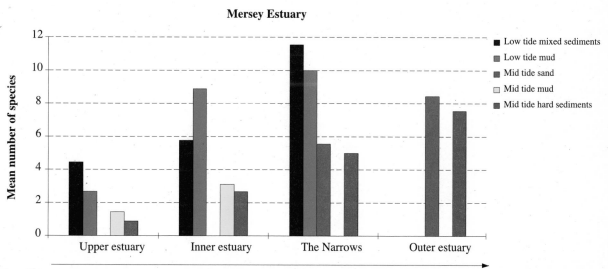

Source: Environment Agency

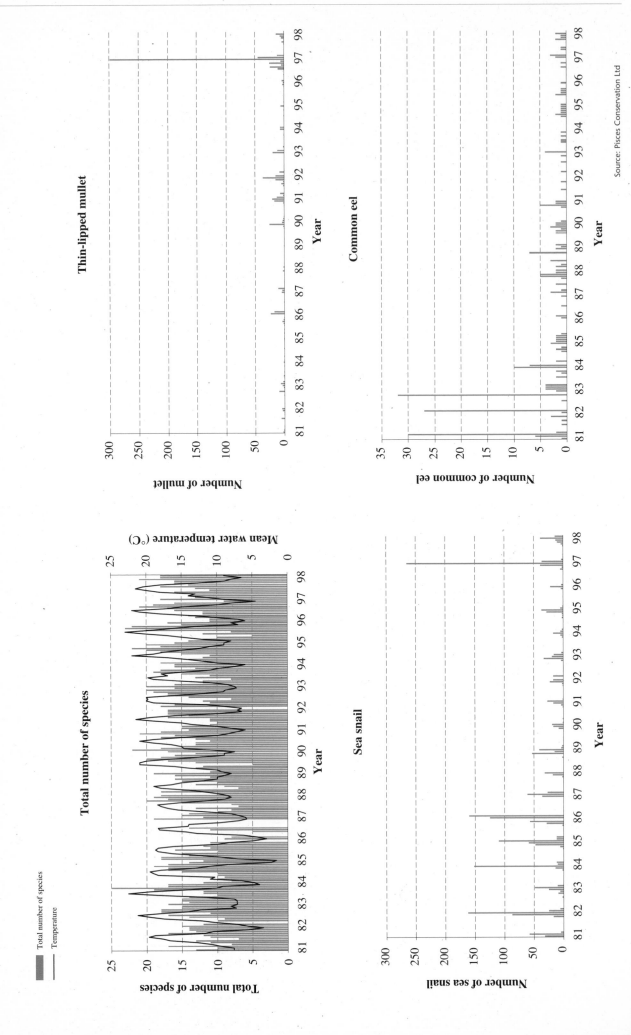

Figure 4.12 *The number of fish species, and the number of mullet, sea snail and common eel at Hinkley Point Power Station, 1981 to 1998*

Source: Pisces Conservation Ltd

important, so that areas around England and Wales with similar bed types, depth and flow hold similar invertebrate communities. Sandy sites in strong tidal currents in the Bristol Channel and southern North Sea have few macroinvertebrate groups. But overall the review concluded that there is a continuing widespread destruction of estuarine ecosystems, implying that the existing conservation safeguards are not effective at maintaining the wildlife resources (Davidson *et al.*, 1991).

More invertebrate groups are found in areas of fine sediment in weaker tidal currents off Plymouth and in the Irish sea, including heart urchins, scallops, Dublin Bay prawn, bivalves and polychaete worms. Reefs of polychaete worms develop mainly on bedrock in strong tidal currents on the open coast, although some have declined greatly, probably due to shrimp trawling. Hard sea beds, which are common near-shore and in areas swept by strong currents such as the north east, English Channel and west coast, support diverse communities including kelp (a seaweed), encrusting sponges, bryozoans, hydroids and tubeworms (Doody *et al.*, 1993). Overall there is a tendency for the number of bottom-dwelling animal groups to be higher towards the south west and lowest in the southern North Sea (Figure 4.10) (Marine Pollution Monitoring Management Group, 1998a).

A few estuaries have been studied intensively and can be used to show the influence of natural factors and pollution. In the Thames Estuary 22 intertidal and subtidal sites from the tidal limit at Teddington Weir to Southend were surveyed in 1989. The numbers of macroinvertebrate groups were greatest at the upper and outer limits, reflecting the physical and chemical features of the estuary (Figure 4.11). In some reaches, scouring flows and extreme salinity variations place natural restrictions on the fauna. In the middle reaches large numbers

of oligochaetes (worms) indicate organic enrichment from sewage treatment works. The Humber Estuary also shows the effects of organic enrichment in the upper reaches where an abundance of the polychaete worm *Capitella* is an indicator of poor quality due to organic pollution. Surveys from 1989 to 1994 of mid-shore and lower shore invertebrates show a richness in the number of families increasing from the upper to the outer estuary (Figure 4.11) (Environment Agency, 1996a).

Intertidal macroinvertebrates in the upper estuary of the Mersey show very low numbers of families. This is probably due to industrial and sewage pollution, some of which is historic, although salinity variations may also limit species' diversity (Figure 4.11). The fauna in the Severn Estuary are related mainly to current velocities and sediment particle size and have shown no obvious changes over time (Mettam, 1979).

Fish

Out of the 330 species of British marine fish, 41 are highly dependent on estuaries and about 140 are marine 'vagrants'. These are species that are mainly freshwater or marine which visit estuaries, those which pass through on migration and those which spend most of their life cycle within an estuary (Potts and Swaby, 1993). Fish that feed in the sea and breed in fresh water include salmon, sea trout, twaite shad and lampreys. Eel and flounder follow the reverse strategy by breeding in the sea and feeding in fresh waters. Estuaries are also important juvenile nursery areas for commercially important marine species including sole, plaice, dab, bass, sprat and herring. Trends in populations of these species are now considered.

There has been an increase in the number of fish species caught on the intake screens at Hinkley Point Power Station near Bridgewater between 1981 and 1998. This may be related to

Figure 4.13 *Bass landings and catch per unit effort in England and Wales, 1985 to 1996*

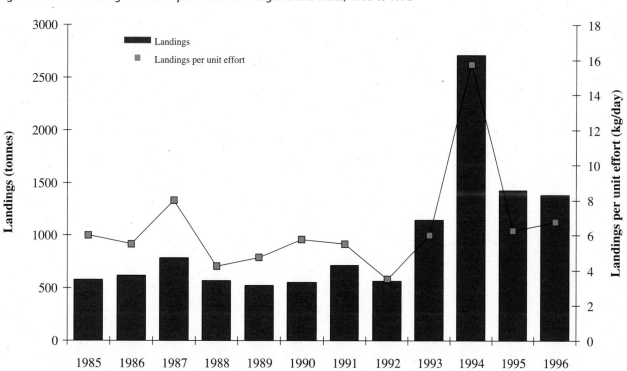

Source: Centre for Environment, Fisheries and Aquaculture Science, 1998; Crown copyright

increasing water temperatures. Mullet, for example, a relatively warm water species, has increased in frequency while another species, the sea snail, shows a decline (Figure 4.12) (Seaby and Henderson, 1998). Water quality can also limit the distribution of fish in estuaries; improved water quality usually results in greater numbers of fish. Some 19 species of freshwater fish and 92 marine fish have migrated to the Thames Estuary over the past 30 years (Environment Agency, 1997a). In the Mersey the number of species recorded increased from 15 to 36 between 1977 and 1988 (Head and Jones, 1991).

Common eels have declined in several European rivers since the early 1980s and this trend includes British rivers such as the River Severn. The cause is unknown but potential factors include natural variation, overfishing, loss of freshwater habitat, bioaccumulation of organic chemicals and infection by a bladder parasite. A similar decline in the American eel suggests that oceanographic changes may be important. Intervention has so far focused on barriers which may impede elver migration. Fish passes have been installed on the Nene, Severn and Thames (Mann and Welton, 1995).

Bass occur mainly in the southern North Sea, Irish Sea and western English Channel. Young fish live in estuarine nursery areas and enter the fishery at about five years old. Bass landings more than doubled between 1985 and 1996 (Figure 4.13). The peak numbers were in 1994 when the fish hatched in 1989 (a strong year class) became catchable. This shows that populations and catches are strongly influenced by natural variations in year class strength which are probably related to climate (CEFAS, 1998a). Management controls imposed by MAFF in 1990 were an increase in the minimum landing size, an increase in permissible net mesh size and prohibition of bass fishing in 34 nursery areas. These measures have reduced exploitation of small bass but the effects on populations have been difficult to demonstrate so far because of the many factors that influence them (Pickett et al., 1995).

Coastal and freshwater salmon and sea trout fisheries are managed by the Agency. Most salmon and sea trout rivers are in the north east, west and south west. Although nets still take the largest proportion of the salmon and sea trout catch, compared with the numbers caught by rod anglers, this is

Figure 4.14 *Salmon and sea trout rod and net catches in England and Wales, 1952 to 1997*

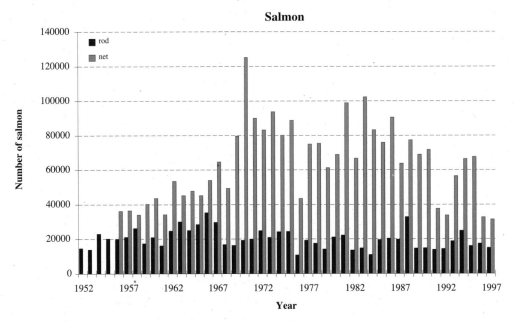

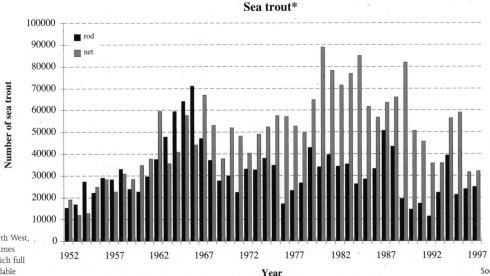

* Excluding North West, Anglian and Thames Regions, for which full data are not available

Source: Environment Agency

Figure 4.15 *Reported salmon catches in the River Wye, 1913 to 1998*

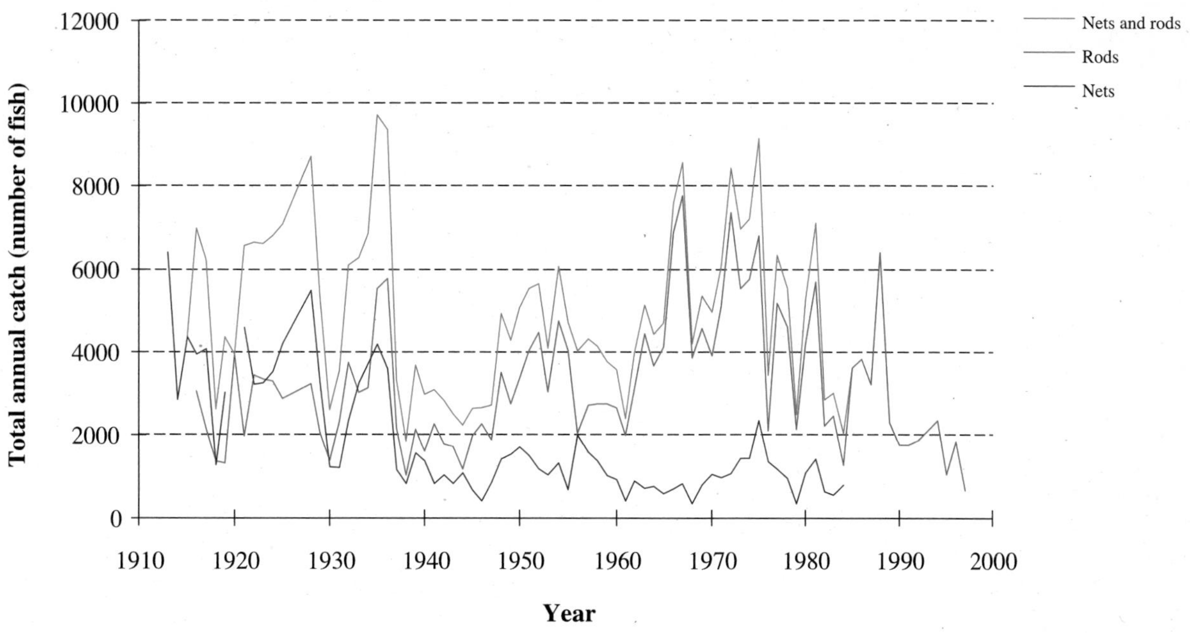

There are no data for nets after 1985 because the net fishery ceased operating

Source: Environment Agency

entirely due to the influence of the north east coast fishery and this proportion has steadily reduced (Figure 4.14). Direct stock assessments of returning adult fish are based on combinations of measures including traps, counters and rod and net catches. Catch data are the most extensive and long-term measure, but need to be interpreted carefully because they are subject to errors from variable reporting rates and fishing effort. Data for the Wye confirm the wide fluctuations in catches and the difficulty of identifying trends in overall catch. Since the 1930s rods have taken an increasing share of the catch on the Wye while net catches have remained at a lower level than in the early part of this century (Figure 4.15).

Since the 1960s there has been a general decline in abundance of salmon in many rivers, a pattern seen in many other areas of the North Atlantic. The reduction is particularly apparent in the numbers and proportion of multi-sea winter fish (those spending two to four winters at sea) which enter rivers before June. The cause of this decline is uncertain but reduction in marine survival is thought to be a likely contributory factor, probably coupled with changing conditions in the freshwater environment of juveniles (ICES, 1996). Early running multi-sea winter fish are also subject to higher selective exploitation by rod fisheries. Long-term cycles in salmon abundance, probably driven by environmental factors, are known to occur but at this stage the effects of human influences cannot be reliably disentangled from such long-term changes. Despite the general decline, some estuaries have shown significant increases in numbers of salmon since the 1970s. For example, catches in the Thames Estuary have increased from zero in the 1970s to a few hundred per year since 1982 as pollution has been reduced and salmon restocked.

More rivers contain salmon now than in the past 200 years, because of improving water quality, access and active management of freshwater habitats. Rivers such as the Tyne have re-established large and increasing runs of salmon and sea trout.

About 70 fish species spend part of their lives in coastal waters, including gobies, dragonet, pogge and juvenile sole and plaice (Rogers and Millner, 1996). The number of families increases from the north east coast to the south and fluctuates annually, partly in response to sea temperatures. Good population data are available only for the main commercial fish stocks for the fishing areas defined by the International Council for the Exploration of the Sea (ICES, 1997). The bulk of the fished stocks are outside the coastal zone but there are important coastal fisheries including those for cod, bass, sole and plaice. The changes in the main commercial fish stocks in relation to fishing are summarised in Table 4.5 and Figure 4.16.

Most of these species are near to sustainable levels or below them. Some are showing limited recruitment of young fish due to the low spawning stock biomass. Other stocks which are above safe levels are dependent on the continued occurrence of good years for recruitment which is vulnerable to natural variations. Less familiar species are also now threatened. Common skate are now virtually extinct in the Irish Sea due to overfishing and it is not known whether they will recover (North Sea Task Force, 1993). Sharks are especially vulnerable to over-exploitation by commercial and recreational fishing because of their slow reproductive rates. Blue sharks, for example, mature at over 2m in length and produce only four to 135 young per year. Recreational catches of blue shark at Looe in Cornwall have fallen from 6,000 in 1960 to only a few hundred per year since 1978. These figures suggest a decline in stocks but the changes in catch per unit effort, which is a better indicator of abundance, are unknown (Vas, 1995). The basking shark has been identified as a threatened species and is on the priority species list of the UK Biodiversity Group. This Group has also recently proposed an action plan to cover groups of marine commercial fish species (UK Biodiversity Group, 1998).

Figure 4.16 Trends in the spawning stock biomass and landings of fish and Dublin Bay prawn in the North Sea

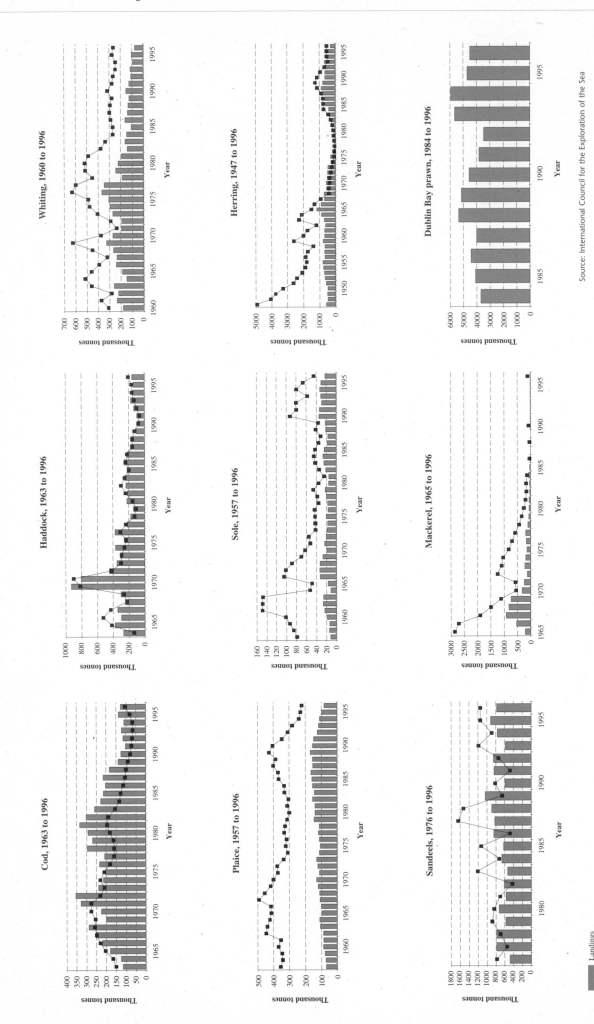

Source: International Council for the Exploration of the Sea

Table 4.5 *Change in fish stocks*

Species	Status of stock	Trend in fishing
Cod	Half sustainable level	Steady increase since 1960s
Haddock	Record lows in the early 1990s, above safe level in 1996	High fishing pressure in North Sea, substantial losses due to discarded catch
Whiting	Constant in 1980s and 1990s though lower than the 1960s and 1970s	Part of mixed fisheries and taken as by-catch. Present rates may be sustainable
Plaice	North Sea stock at record lows in 1990s and below safe level in 1996. Close to sustainable levels in other areas.	Steady increase since 1960s due to increase in beam trawling
Sole	North Sea stock varied around safe level in 1970s and 1980s. Fell below safe level in 1996	Steady increase since 1960s due to increase in beam trawling
Herring	Collapsed in 1960s, recovery during 1980s, below safe levels in North Sea and Channel in 1990s	Rapid increase in 1960s, fishery closed 1977 and re-opened 1981
Sandeel	Natural fluctuations over past 20 years, now above safe levels	Fishing at sustainable rates
Mackerel	Collapse in spawning stocks in 1990s to about one per cent of that in the mid-1960s	Increased in 1990s
Dublin Bay prawn	Stock over-exploited off east coast and in Celtic Sea. Irish Sea stock fully exploited	Increased over past decade

Source: International Council for the Exploration of the Sea, 1997

Birds

British estuaries are internationally important for their populations of wading birds and wildfowl. Around one-fifth of the migratory population stop-over in Britain each spring and autumn, and over one-third of waders wintering on the Atlantic coast of Europe are found here. The birds feed on the high densities of invertebrates in the intertidal muds and saltmarshes and on coastal grassland. Other birds found on estuaries in winter include flocks of finches and buntings which feed on seeds in saltmarshes and the strandline, and predatory birds like hen harriers, short-eared owls, merlin and peregrine. British coastal wetlands are also important in the summer months for 12 species of breeding waders, shelduck, gulls and terns (Davidson *et al.*, 1991).

The over-wintering birds include 26 species of wildfowl and 18 species of wader. In January Britain holds more than one-tenth of the world population of 20 of these species. Bird counts in England and Wales from 1970 to 1995 show that populations of waders, for example, are increasing or fairly constant (Figure 4.17). This hides some regional and local variations. There is a slight decline in wader populations in south west England and Wales offset by a general increase in south east England. It is not known whether these changes are related to natural causes such as climate or to human activities.

The number of waders wintering on different estuaries is related to the intertidal area (Davidson *et al.*, 1991 and Rehfisch *et al.*, 1997). Despite the loss of intertidal areas over the past 30 years there has been a general increase in estuarine bird populations. This may be because wintering populations on most estuaries have not yet reached their 'carrying capacity' because numbers are limited by mortality during migration or on the breeding grounds (Goss-Custard, 1995).

Pollution has occasionally led to substantial mortalities of birds in estuaries, although this has not been of long-term significance to populations. Oil is one of the greatest hazards because spills initially float, exposing birds to oiling of their plumage. The Mersey pipeline oil leak in 1989 killed over 4,000 birds, most of which were common species of gull.

Birds are disturbed to varying degrees by walkers, bait diggers, dogs, windsurfers and low-flying aircraft, and one person can disturb birds in an area of 10 to 50ha. But birds can compensate to some degree by feeding at different times and places. There is no evidence of effects on populations although there may be local and temporary reductions in bird numbers (Davidson and Rothwell, 1993). While there is no evidence of a general problem at the moment, any substantial rises in recreational pressures in the future might be of concern unless managed. Similarly, wildfowlers kill over a million birds annually but there is no evidence of population reduction from this activity, partly because the participants often maintain habitats which support bird populations.

In terms of seabirds, England and Wales hold more than 10 per cent of the world population of manx shearwater, gannet and lesser black-backed gull and significant numbers of several other seabird species. Of the species for which the population trends are known, 13 are increasing, four are declining and one is constant (Table 4.6). Seabirds have benefited this century from controls on hunting and egg collecting which were prevalent in the 19th century for sport, food and feathers. In the past three decades increases in the quantities of offal and fish discarded by fishing vessels are likely to have significantly enhanced food supplies. It is also possible that long-term changes in the climate and oceans have affected populations of both fish and birds (Lloyd *et al.*, 1991).

Figure 4.17 *Populations of waders in England and Wales, 1970 to 1996*

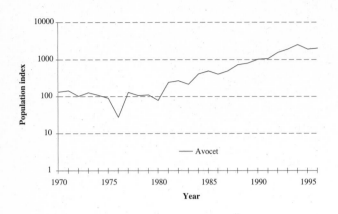

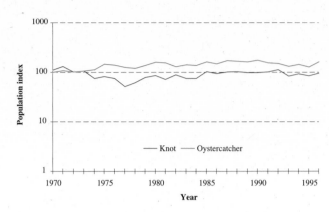

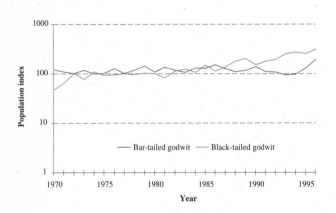

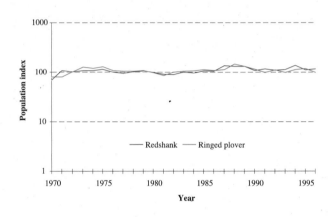

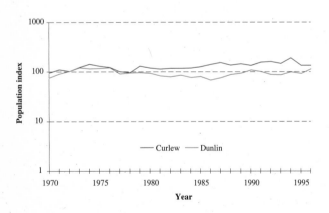

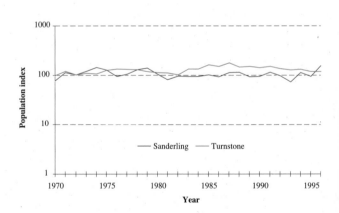

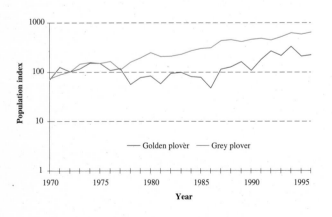

The data in each year show the winter population, e.g. 1996 data are from the winter of 1996/97. The population index shows the size of the population relative to that in the winter of 1972/73 and then rescaled so that 1972 = 100

Source: British Trust for Ornithology

Table 4.6   *Population trends in seabirds in England and Wales between 1969/70 and 1985/87[1]*

Species	Population trends from 1969/70 to 1985/87 (pairs of birds[2])		Comment
Fulmar	3,900 to 9,200	++	Many new colonies in 1970s. Possible causes of population explosion include availability of discarded fish, climate warming, species evolution
Manx shearwater	220,000 to 250,000, 94 per cent of world population nest in British Isles. Colonies on the south west Wales islands and Scillies	?	Rats on Cardigan Island led to extinction. Their removal has allowed recolonisation and re-introduction
Storm petrel	20,000 to 150,000, 28 per cent of the world population breed in the British Isles, including a small proportion on the Isles of Scilly, Skokholm and Skomer	?	
Gannet	31,000 including an important colony at Grassholm off south west Wales. 36 per cent increase in Britain and Ireland from 1969/70 to 1994/96	+	Bird protection laws in the last century reduced shooting and egg collecting, allowing population growth
Cormorant	2,700 to 3,300 (coastal and inland colonies)	+	Some are shot by fish farmers and fishermen
Shag	3,200 to 5,700	++	Susceptible to changes in local food supply, for example herring, sandeel stocks. On Farne Island, 80 per cent killed in 1968 and 60 per cent in 1975 by dinoflagellate toxins ('red tides')
Black headed gull	Majority breed inland. On the coast in 1938 there were 16,000, in 1969 54,000 and in 1987 69,000	+	Protection from egg collecting and persecution this century. Have exploited safe roosting on gravel pits and reservoirs
Common gull	Mainly inland. Only 35 (up from 10) in England and Wales out of British Isles total 15,700	+	
Lesser black-backed gull	36,000 to 45,000, 20 per cent of world population	+	Feed on offal and discarded fish which have increased, and often now overwinter on gravel pits and reservoirs instead of migrating. Culled on many nature reserves
Herring gull	115,000 to 42,000, having previously increased from 1940s to mid 1970s	--	Increase this century was due to abundant food from rubbish tips, sewage, offal etc. There have been mortality incidents from botulism at tips since 1975 and some of the food sources may have reduced. Herring gulls are not fully legally protected; they are culled on nature reserves to protect other bird species such as terns
Great black-backed gull	2,800 to 2,200, after increasing earlier this century	-	Previous increase due to abundant food from rubbish tips, sewage, offal etc. Local decreases due to botulism and culling on some nature reserves in the 1970s and early 1980s
Kittiwake	57,000 to 136,000 (37,000 in 1959). 84,000 are at Flamborough Head	++	Increase related to cessation of hunting and egg collecting, and increased fishing offal availability
Sandwich tern	7,400 to 11,800. Notably in Northumberland and Norfolk	++	Possibly due to protection on reserves and winter survival in West Africa

Species	Numbers	Trend	Notes
Roseate tern	557 to 110. Rare and in decline over past 20 years, was close to extinction in Britain in late 1800s, numbers peaked in 1950s/60s. Colonies on north east coast, Anglesey, Scilly Isles. 80 per cent decrease from 1969/70 to 1996. 40 in 1996	--	Recovered early this century after shooting and egg collecting ceased. Now causes of decline unknown, though vulnerable to natural predators and trapping in West Africa
Common tern	6,500 to 5,800. Population small but widespread	-	Pressures on populations not understood
Arctic tern	5,300 in 1987. Farne Islands most important colony outside Scotland	0	Natural predators can cause significant mortality
Little tern	1,300 to 2,000, the majority on the south east coast	++	Human disturbance and natural predation appear major threats, and tidal flooding can cause catastrophic losses.
Guillemot	36,000 to 96,000, despite a decline between 1975 and the 1980s	++	Trends unexplained. Vulnerable to oiling and fishing net capture
Razorbill	9,000 to 21,000 birds. Between 1900 and 1969 numbers constant or may have declined	++	Trends unexplained. Vulnerable to oiling and fishing net capture
Puffin	11,000 to 32,000 birds	++	Affected by predation, oil pollution, food availability

Source: Lloyd et al., 1991; Thompson et al., 1997

[1] Gannets and roseate tern have been updated to 1996
[2] Numbers are pairs except for guillemot, razorbill and puffin which are individuals

0   less than 10 per cent change
+, -   between 10 and 50 per cent increase or decrease
++, -- greater than 50 per cent increase or decrease
?   unknown trends

Herring gulls, greater black-backed gulls, roseate terns, and common terns show the most serious declines. Seabirds may be affected by the availability of undisturbed nesting habitat, human competition for fish, changes in the amounts of fisheries offal and discarded fish, oiling mortality and net entanglement. The Sea Empress spill is known to have killed at least 7,000 birds. This included some 3,500 over-wintering common scoters, and the population in the following winter was 10,000 fewer than the 1995/96 peak and one-third lower than the long-term mean (Sea Empress Environmental Evaluation Committee, 1998).

Mammals

Twelve species of whales and dolphins are regularly seen in British coastal waters, including the harbour porpoise, bottle-nosed dolphin and Risso's dolphin. Minke whales occur in coastal waters off north east England and there is a resident population of bottle-nosed dolphins in Cardigan Bay, but harbour porpoises are by far the most common species around England and Wales. Harbour porpoises are widely distributed in coastal and offshore waters with relatively high frequencies in the Irish Sea and off the north east coast. The population in the North Sea, Channel and Celtic Sea is about 350,000, but in some coastal areas around the UK populations have fallen since the 1960s. Over 2,000 harbour porpoises are taken annually in hake gill net fisheries off south west Britain, equivalent to six per cent of the population in the Celtic sea. The International

Whaling Commission threshold of concern for fishing mortality is one per cent and two per cent is considered the maximum sustainable mortality rate. There is significant uncertainty over these assessments so better population and catch data are needed (Northridge et al., 1995).

British coasts support about 25,000 common seals and 94,000 grey seals, about five per cent and 42 per cent respectively of the world population. In England and Wales there are fewer than 2,000 common seals which occur only on the east coast of Lincolnshire and Norfolk. The 10,000 or so grey seals around England and Wales are more widely distributed (Doody et al., 1993). Seal populations have increased this century as a result of controls on hunting. In 1988 phocine distemper virus killed half of the common seals in the Wash and the population is recovering slowly towards the pre-epidemic level. Few grey seals were affected by the disease.

There is limited evidence of the effect of any human activities on seal populations (Hammond, 1992). Of about 6,000 seals tagged in the Farne Islands since the 1960s, at least two per cent have died in fishing gear. The cost to fishermen of seal damage to nets and fish may be significant as studies of the north east drift net fishery and an inshore set net fishery indicated that grey seals removed or damaged around five per cent of the fish caught (Northridge, 1988).

Threatened species

The Biodiversity Action Plan identifies species which are rare, threatened or vulnerable (UK Biodiversity Steering Group, 1995b; UK Biodiversity Group, 1998). Of the 116 action plans which have already been prepared there are 20 for coastal species, including the harbour porpoise, sand lizard, natterjack toad, twaite shad, bright wave moth, starlet sea anemone and Lundy cabbage (Table 4.7). In 1998 the UK Biodiversity Group announced its intention to produce a second round of 276 species action plans, covering individual species or groups of species, which will eventually bring the total number of plans to about 400 (UK Biodiversity Group, 1998).

The action plans that are being developed specify targets to maintain and improve status where possible. Sites are managed to protect existing populations and include measures such as water resource management and pollution reduction. Landowners' awareness and co-operation is vital for habitat management. In many cases knowledge of the present distribution is incomplete so surveys are required to show where they occur, for example allis shad, and to identify suitable sites for re-introduction, for example natterjack toad and several plant species. Research is needed to understand the requirements of some species, such as the harbour porpoise. Other management plans include re-creation of habitats, for example seagrass beds, and monitoring programmes are essential to show progress against targets.

Non-native species

There are 51 non-native species which have been reported as colonising British coastal waters. Over half arrived in ballast

Table 4.7 *Priority coastal species in the UK Biodiversity Action Plan*

Species	Status	Likely pressures
Harbour porpoise (*Phocoena phocoena*)	Population in North Sea, Channel, Celtic Sea c.350,000; possible decline since 1940s	Entanglement, pollution, disturbance, reduced fish stocks
Sand lizard (*Lacerta agilis*)	Lost from Wales, New Forest, many coastal dunes and heaths	Loss/deterioration of heathland and dune habitat, scrub encroachment
Natterjack toad (*Bufo calamita*)	Substantial decline from heathland, dune, upper saltmarsh, extinct in Wales; 35 natural sites in England, introduced to 13 sites including one in Wales	Habitat loss by development, agriculture, sea defence
Allis shad (*Alosa alosa*)	Small numbers around coast, no evidence of spawning stocks	Pollution, habitat destruction
Twaite shad (*Alosa fallax*)	Lost from several rivers, spawns in Wye, Usk, Severn, Tywi	Pollution, habitat destruction
Cathormiocerus britannicus (a broad-nosed weevil)	Found at a few cliff sites in south west England	Lack of grazing of cliff tops
Black-backed meadow ant (*Formica pratensis*)	Disappeared from cliff tops and heaths near Bournemouth; found on Channel Islands	Urban spread, scrub encroachment
Bright wave moth (*Idaea ochrata*)	Sandy shingle beaches, found in three areas in south east England	Tidal erosion, recreation
Panagaeus crux-major (a ground beetle)	Three UK sites including two in dune systems. Formerly widespread	Lack of grazing sites
Sandbowl snail (*Catinella arenaria*)	Three sites in England including one dune system	Drainage of habitats
Ivell's sea anemone (*Edwardsia ivelli*)	One world site, Widewater Lagoon in West Sussex, last seen 1983	Reduced seawater penetration, diffuse pollution
Starlet sea anemone (*Nematostella vectensis*)	A few coastal lagoons in south and south east	Drainage, pollution
Lundy cabbage (*Coincya wrightii*)	Endemic to Lundy Island, 3,000 to 5,000 flowering plants	Overgrazing, spread of bracken and rhododendron
Eyebrights (*Euphrasia spp*)	Maritime heaths and grassland, dune grass, saltmarsh. Taxonomic status unclear	Loss of heaths, lack of grazing
Fen orchid (*Liparis loeselii*)	Declined from 40 to four sites, including two dune systems in south Wales.	Sand dune stabilisation

Shore dock (*Rumex rupestris*)	Anglesey, Devon, Cornwall, Isles of Scilly. Over last century declined 80 per cent to ten 10km squares	Loss of habitat by sea defences and recreation, spread of other species
Pseudocyphellaria aurata (a lichen)	Oceanic species found on Sark and in Ireland, formerly in southern England and Channel Islands	Heathland damage
Weissia multicapsularis (a moss)	11 sites south west England and Wales, including cliff tops in Cornwall	Unknown
Atlantic lejeunea, liverwort (*Lejeunea mandonii*)	Six 10km squares in UK including three in Cornwall, in sheltered coastal sites	Water quality, rhododendron spread, recreation
Petalwort (*Petalophyllum ralfsii*)	19 sites in Britain, mainly dune slacks	Development, drainage, recreation

water or on ships' hulls and a further one-third may have been introduced by mariculture (Eno *et al.*, 1997). The effects of these invasions range from negligible to substantial ecological and commercial impacts (Table 4.8). The Japanese weed, *Sargassum muticum* for example, was probably brought to north west Europe with oysters from Canada or Japan about 30 years ago. It grows rapidly in warm waters, displacing native species, and has spread along the entire English Channel coast. The species is a pest because it fouls boat propellers and intakes, fishing nets and oyster beds. It is usually not possible to

eradicate such pest species so they create a long-term problem for mariculture, fishing and recreational users as well as damage to ecosystems. It is difficult to prevent the transport of exotic species to Britain, but steps could be taken to reduce certain stresses on ecosystems which make them less able to resist invasions or make conditions more favourable to the colonising species. The American hard-shelled clam, *Mercenaria mercenaria*, was introduced in 1925 to Southampton Water and it may have benefited from power station discharges of cooling water, which create warmer water conditions.

Table 4.8 *Some non-native marine species and their effects in British waters*

Species	Effects
Japanese weed plants, (*Sargassum muticum*)	Occurs on entire Channel coast and south east coast. Can displace eel grass and other plants, fouls small boats, oyster beds and fishing nets
Hydroides ezoensis (an annelid worm)	Causes severe fouling in the Solent
Pacific oyster (*Crassostrea gigas*)	Widely cultivated commercially, no specific environmental effects reported
Slipper limpet (*Crepidula fornicata*)	Introduced in late 19th century with American oysters. Widespread except in north west. Competition damaging to commercial oyster beds
American oyster drill (*Urosalpix cinerea*)	Essex and Kent coasts. Predates native oysters, severely damaging commercial beds. Its current status is unknown, since its abundance was affected significantly through imposex, caused by tributyl tin
American jack knife clam (*Ensis americanus*)	First found 1989 in Norfolk. Now found from Humber to Rye Harbour and is very common in some locations. Effects unknown
American hard-shelled clam (*Mercenaria mercenaria*)	Introduced 1925 to Southampton Water, where it benefited from the warm cooling water discharge of the (now defunct) Marchwood power station. Occurs sporadically on south coast. Can displace soft-shelled clam. Now depleted by harvesting
Soft-shelled clam (*Mya arenaria*)	Widespread. Effects unknown
Anguillicola crassus (a nematode)	Common in England. Parasite of common eel, infecting swimbladder, can reduce growth and lead to mortality
Elminius modestus (a barnacle)	Arrived about 1940, now widespread. May displace native barnacle species
Chinese mitten crab (*Eriocheir sinensis*)	Humber, Thames, Tyne and Medway estuaries. Burrows cause bank erosion, could undermine flood defences
Leathery sea squirt (*Styela clava*)	Arrived in 1952, now occurs on southern and western coasts. Competes with native species, fouls ships and oyster beds

Source: Eno *et al.*, 1997

4.3 Compliance with environmental standards and targets and classification schemes

There are many different environmental quality standards in existence that relate both to the protection of human health, such as those for bathing waters and shellfish waters, and to the protection of the environment itself, such as the quality required to protect marine life. The standards are often expressed in terms of the concentration of a particular substance which must not be exceeded, according to set statistical compliance criteria. These standards may arise from EC Directives, national legislation or international agreements (Appendix 1). The Agency has extensive monitoring programmes to provide information to assess compliance with the terms of EC Directives and other legislation.

There are a wide range of standards and targets deriving from different sources and for different purposes. In some cases compliance with these standards is an indirect measure of environmental quality or health. For example, in the EC

Directive on bathing water quality (76/160/EEC) standards are set in terms of concentrations of organisms which are indicators of the degree of pollution by human sewage.

To comply with the law, and to meet the basic requirements of environmental protection, chemical compounds must occur in the environment at concentrations below the relevant environmental quality standard. But even if individual chemicals do occur at concentrations below their environmental quality standards, it does not necessarily mean that the environment is healthy. Biological effects may occur if several contaminants act together. Hydrocarbon residues alone contribute thousands of individual compounds, most of which have additive toxicity. Biological effects are discussed in Section 4.4.

There is also a classification scheme which is used to assess whether the principle of maintaining or improving estuarine water quality is being achieved. This section looks at compliance with statutory and non-statutory standards as well as trends in the classification scheme.

Figure 4.18 *Bathing water quality, 1998*

Bathing waters meeting guideline coliform and faecal streptococci standards

Bathing waters meeting mandatory coliform standards

Non-compliant bathing waters

Whitby
Scarborough
Morecambe
Blackpool
Southport
Skegness
Rhyl
Pwllheli
Great Yarmouth
Aberystwyth
Southend-on-Sea
Margate
Tenby
Barry
Oxwich Bay
Weston-super-Mare
Brighton
Bude
Lyme Regis
Hastings
Newquay
Bognor Regis
Torquay
Bournemouth
Penzance

Source: Environment Agency

103

Figure 4.19 *Compliance with the standards of the EC Bathing Waters Directive, 1988 to 1998*

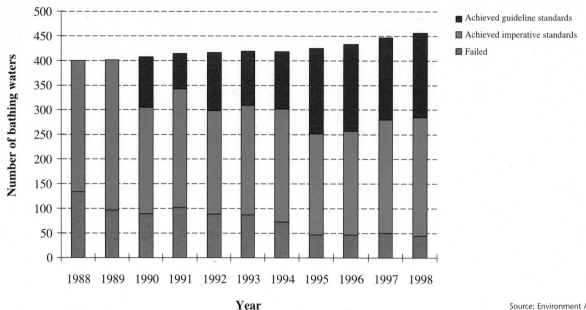

Source: Environment Agency

Bathing water quality

In accordance with the EC Bathing Waters Directive (76/160/EEC) the Agency monitors water quality every summer at designated bathing waters around the coast of England and Wales. In 1998 there were 458 beaches around the coast which were designated as bathing waters (ten more than designated in 1997). Most of the analyses performed on the samples are for bacteria that may indicate contamination with sewage. Details are given in Appendix 1.

In 1997, 88.8 per cent of bathing waters passed the Directive's imperative standards and 37.1 per cent passed the more stringent guideline standards. In 1998, the proportions were 90.4 and 36.1 per cent respectively. Figure 4.18 shows how each bathing water fared and the summary results for the 1998

season are shown in Appendix 1. In 1997 the area with greatest problems was the north west with some failures in the north east, south and south west. In 1998 the north west and north east had the greatest problems with some pockets of problems in the south west.

From the late 1980s to the present the water services companies have been building and improving sewage treatment works at many sites around the coast. They have had to ensure that their discharges do not cause bathing waters to fail to comply with EC Directive standards. Some of the improvements are not yet complete and the improved bathing water quality expected from some of the new works has yet to be observed. However, there has been a general improvement in overall bathing water compliance with time across England and Wales, despite some interannual variability. Figure 4.19 shows the proportion of

Figure 4.20 *Consistency in compliance with the standards of the EC Bathing Waters Directive, 1988 to 1998*

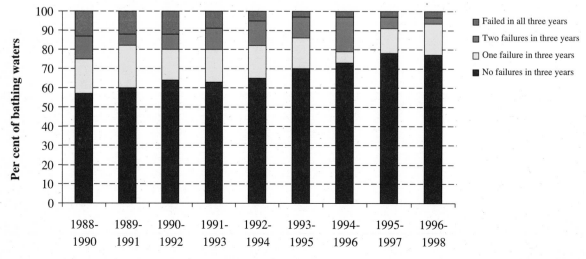

Three-year rolling periods

Source: Environment Agency

bathing waters achieving compliance with the imperative and guideline standards each year from 1988 to 1998. Prior to 1990 there were not many data collected on *faecal streptococci* so calculations on compliance with the more stringent guideline standards are only given from 1990. The figure shows that improvements have been significant. Some 34 per cent of bathing waters failed in 1988 compared with 9.6 per cent ten years later.

It has always been the case that a number of bathing waters pass the Directive's imperative standards in one year and fail the next (or vice versa). This may happen in bathing waters which are of marginal quality, but it can also happen because of the inherent variability of the data collected over the bathing season, and the way in which compliance is assessed statistically. During the 1997 bathing season, for example, 16 previously compliant bathing waters became non-compliant for the first time in several seasons. The laws of chance can play a significant part in determining the overall compliance level, as can weather conditions which affect bacterial survival and contamination from non-human faeces.

Figure 4.20 shows the proportion of bathing waters achieving consistent compliance, which is when a bathing water has complied for each of three years in a rolling three-year period. There is a clear and continuing trend with time showing that, when interannual variability and chance variations are taken into account, the compliance of bathing waters improved significantly across England and Wales from 1988 to 1998.

Bathing water quality and compliance with Directive standards depend on many factors. The most important is whether nearby coastal waters receive sewage discharges and the level of treatment applied to those discharges. Other factors include the strength and duration of daylight (which kills off many microscopic organisms), temperature, salinity, turbidity, storms (which may resuspend contaminated sediments or cause storm overflows on sewer networks to operate) and contamination from non-human faeces (for example, dogs exercised on beaches, farm stock grazing nearby and indicator organisms transported to the coast from river catchments). The Agency is concerned about the non-compliance of bathing waters. Details of how we are addressing the issue are given later, in Section 5.1.

Figure 4.21 *Dangerous Substances Directive statutory monitoring sites*

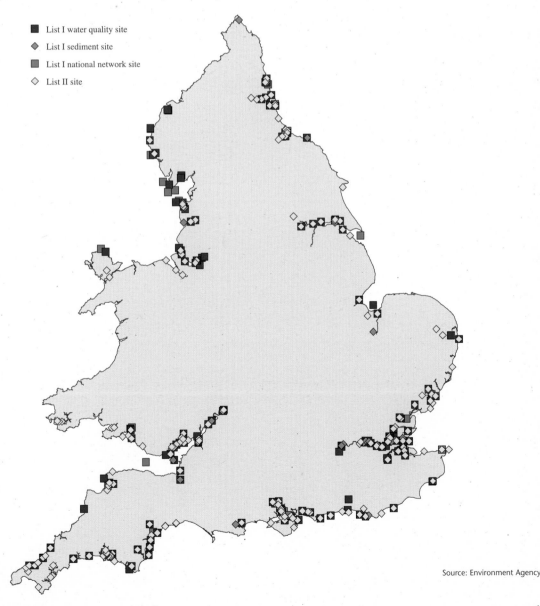

- List I water quality site
- List I sediment site
- List I national network site
- List II site

Source: Environment Agency

Figure 4.22 *Non-compliance with the Dangerous Substances Directive, 1992 to 1997*

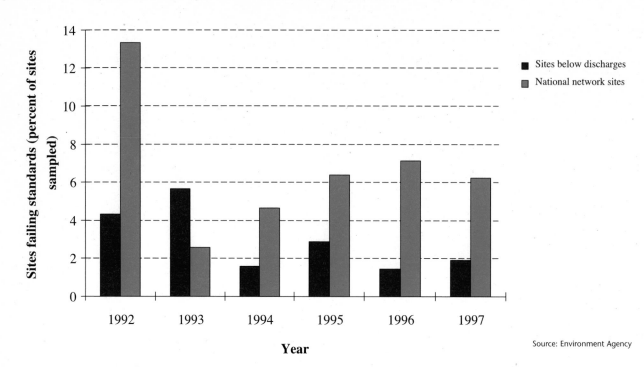

Source: Environment Agency

Figure 4.23 *Failing standards at Dangerous Substances Directive monitoring sites in coastal and estuarine waters in 1997*

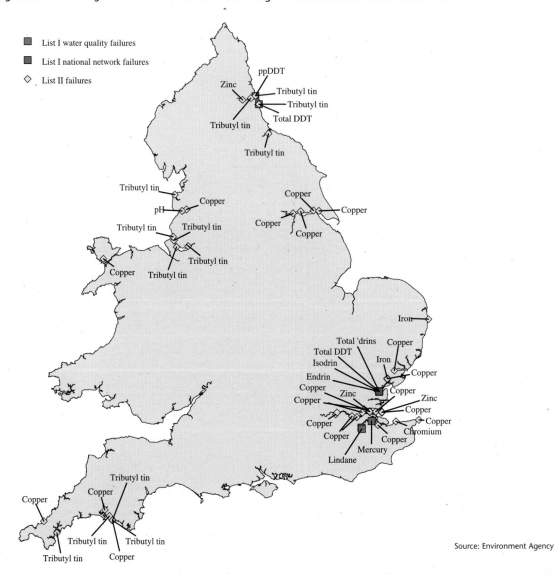

Source: Environment Agency

Dangerous substances

In accordance with the EC 'Dangerous Substances' Directive (76/464/EEC), the Agency monitors coastal and estuarine waters and sediments receiving List I substances from point source discharges containing these substances. Such sources include all industrial plants liable to handle and discharge these substances and all significant discharges of·these substances from sewage treatment works. As well as monitoring for List I substances in the vicinity of discharges, monitoring takes place for 'background' concentrations at sites remote from discharges, known as 'national network' sites (Figure 4.21). Sampling is performed monthly or quarterly and results are reported annually against environmental quality standards (EQSs) (Appendix 1).

Overall compliance with EQSs for List I is high; three per cent of sites failed the standards in 1997. Compliance has improved over the last six years; in 1992, six per cent of sites failed (Figure 4.22). In 1997, there were three failures in the vicinity of discharges in the Medway Estuary, two for HCH (lindane) and one for mercury (Figure 4.23). There were also three national network sites that failed the standards. These were for pesticides; DDT in the Tyne, Wear and Blackwater Estuaries and for isodrin, endrin and total 'drins in the Blackwater. The reasons for these failures are being investigated. The results from the List I sediment sampling sites have been supplied to the Government for the purposes of determining the load standstill requirement, but these assessments have not yet been finalised.

The Agency also monitors coastal and estuarine waters receiving List II substances against EQSs and advisory quality standards (Appendix 1). In 1994, some 34 per cent of sites failed the standards set. About 20 sites failed List II standards in 1995 and 1996, some 11 per cent of sites (Figure 4.24). However, in 1997 the number of failing sites rose to 39, some 18 per cent of sites sampled, although the number of sites sampled has

trebled since 1994. In 1997, the List II failures were dominated by copper, tributyl tin and zinc. The South West, Thames, North West and North East Regions show most failures (Figure 4.23). The majority of copper failures correspond roughly with the major inputs of copper measured in the PARCOM loads monitoring programme (see Section 3.4), although this is not the case in the Thames Estuary and along the Essex coastline. The sources of copper in these places include industries, sewage treatment works not monitored under PARCOM and copper derived from antifouling paints. In the Tyne and Tees estuaries copper inputs from industry have reduced since 1990 as a result of stricter discharge consent conditions. Tributyl tin failures also show a very sketchy correspondence with PARCOM inputs and these are most likely to be caused by antifouling paints leaching from ships' hulls or boat yards, or recontamination of over-lying waters from tributyl tin contaminated sediments. In the Mersey, tributyl tin is still used at a number of large shipyards and mitigation measures are being introduced.

Titanium dioxide

Since the 1930s titanium dioxide has been increasingly used as a white pigment by industry. Being virtually non-toxic and inert, and of high opacity and brilliant whiteness, it has replaced the earlier toxic white pigments such as white lead and zinc oxide. Its unique properties have resulted in the safe use of titanium dioxide in a wide range of industrial and domestic applications, for example from the manufacture of paint, plastics, paper and printing inks, to use in the production of cosmetics, toiletries, food and packaging.

The production of titanium dioxide from ores can result in highly acidic, metal-rich effluents. For this reason titanium dioxide plants have traditionally been located on large estuaries to obtain the maximum dilution of the waste liquid discharges. In the 1970s and 1980s European Community legislation was

Figure 4.24 *Non-compliance with standards for List II substances, 1994 to 1997*

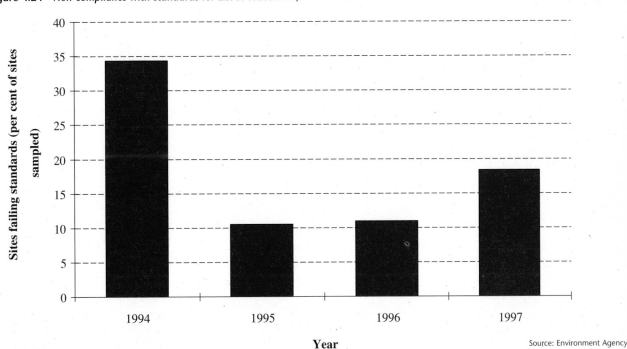

Source: Environment Agency

introduced to minimise the environmental impact from titanium dioxide plants.

There are only three industrial plants in England and Wales that are covered by the EC Directive on titanium dioxide (78/176/EEC, 82/883/EEC, 83/29/EEC, 89/428/EEC, 92/112/EEC). Two of these discharge into the Humber Estuary and the other discharges into the Tees Estuary. In the 1980s there was evidence of localised pollution near the two discharges in the Humber, due principally to ferrous iron and acid. These discharges damaged the life inhabiting the bed of the estuary and water in the estuary was acidic at large distances from the discharge points. Both the plants in the Humber discharged at the low-water mark, where dilution was limited. They caused an impoverishment of biological life on extensive intertidal mudflats adjacent to the outfalls and produced heavy iron staining of the sea wall with no growth of brown seaweed, which would normally be expected. After changing the location of the discharge to a deeper offshore area, and

complying with the terms of the Directive, there has been a significant reduction in the staining of the foreshore and the acidity of the estuary is only elevated very close to the discharge points (NRA, 1993).

The Teesside plant has not caused a significant environmental impact as a result of the cleaner process technology employed at the site. This is evidenced by diverse fish and invertebrate communities found in the vicinity of the plant and a small, recovering seal population which has been re-established nearby on Seal Sands.

For the purposes of the Directive monitoring of water quality, sediments and benthic fauna and an assessment of fish population health are carried out in the immediate vicinity of these three discharges and at reference sites in waters deemed to be away from the influence of the discharges. In the period 1988 to 1997 there were no failures against environmental quality standards, but sediment monitoring results show higher

Figure 4.25 *Shellfish Waters Directive statutory monitoring sites and failures for 1997*

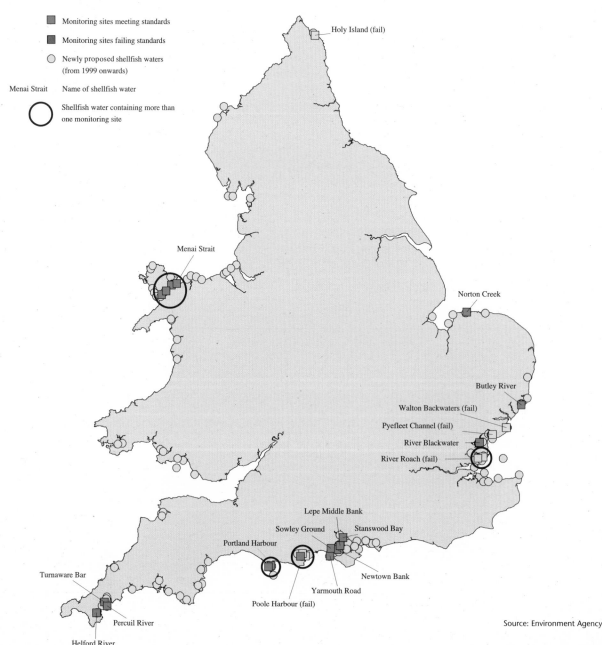

Source: Environment Agency

Figure 4.26 *Compliance with the EC Directive on shellfish water quality in 1991, and from 1993 to 1997*

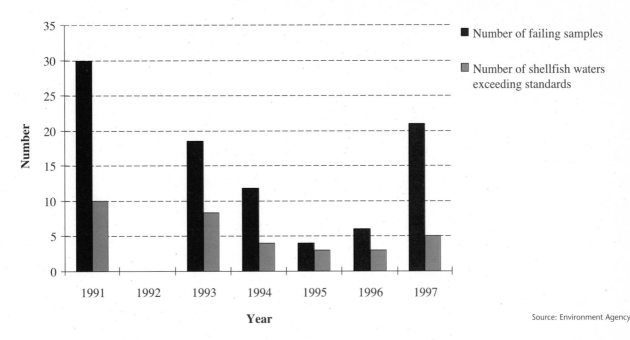

Source: Environment Agency

metals concentrations at outfall sites, compared with the reference sites, and biological monitoring results show localised effects at all three discharges.

Shellfish water quality

Early in 1998, there were 18 shellfish waters designated under the EC Directive in England and Wales on shellfish water quality (76/923/EEC) but subsequent to the recent DETR consultation exercise the Agency has proposed that this should be substantially increased. The Agency is the competent authority for the purposes of providing the basic monitoring information to the DETR and Welsh Office on the Directive. There are standards for 12 parameters ranging from metals to dissolved

oxygen (Appendix 1). There may be several monitoring sites within each shellfish water and compliance with the standards must be achieved at each site for the whole shellfish water to comply with the Directive (Figure 4.25). The number of shellfish waters failing to meet the imperative standards fell from 10 in 1991 to three in 1996 but increased to five in 1997 (Figure 4.26). The failures in 1997 were at Walton Backwaters, River Roach, Pyefleet Channel, Poole Harbour and Holy Island (Figure 4.25). The number of failing samples decreased from 35 in 1991 (1.4 per cent of all samples) to six in 1996 (0.3 per cent of all samples), but they rose again to 21 in 1997 (1.1 per cent of all samples).

Under the rules for compliance with the Directive and with our

Figure 4.27 *Individual sample failures in the EC Directive on shellfish water quality in 1991, and from 1993 to 1997*

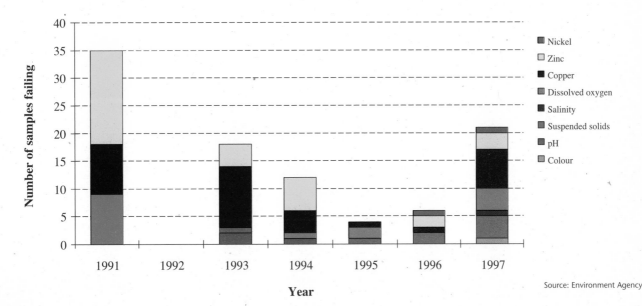

Source: Environment Agency

current sampling regime, a single sample failure for any determinand will cause the whole shellfish water to fail. The range of determinands causing failure increased between 1991 and 1997 (Figure 4.27). In 1991, the three determinands that caused all the sample failures against imperative standards were zinc (17 sites), copper (nine) and dissolved oxygen (nine). In 1997, the failures were caused by colour (one), salinity (one), nickel (one), zinc (three), suspended solids (four), dissolved oxygen (four) and copper (seven). Shellfish waters are typically shallow and muddy, or sandy, and may experience high temperatures, low oxygen levels or high turbidity through natural processes alone. There is no obvious relationship between the copper and zinc failures and direct inputs of these metals from sewage treatment works, industries, marinas or docks. Diffuse inputs, which are mostly uncontrolled, probably account for the high concentrations observed. For example, copper-based antifouling paints are widely used on yachts and commercial vessels and zinc occurs in many household and industrial products.

Figure 4.28   *EC Shellfish Hygiene Directive classification of designated harvesting sites in 1997*

Class A	Shellfish can be collected for human consumption without any treatment or cleaning process
Class B	Shellfish can only be placed on the market after relaying in clean sea water or treatment in an approved purification centre
Class C	Shellfish can only be placed on the market after prolonged relaying in clean sea water or after intensive purification

Source: Centre for Environment, Fisheries and Aquaculture Science

The water quality of shellfish waters improved significantly from 1991 to 1996, but there has been a deterioration at some sites in 1997. Under this Directive shellfish water quality is determined by monitoring a relatively small number of chemical determinands. The implementation of the Directive in England and Wales was reviewed in 1998 to include new standards and monitoring requirements (Appendix 1).

Shellfish hygiene

The EC Directive on shellfish hygiene (91/492/EEC) is concerned with the quality of the shellfish themselves, rather than the environment in which they live. The Directive requires the designation of shellfish production areas and a classification system based on the level of treatment that the shellfish require before sale for human consumption. The classes range from A, which means that shellfish can be collected for direct human consumption, to C, which means that shellfish require extensive purification (Appendix 1). The monitoring of shellfish is conducted by local authorities and the results are collated nationally by MAFF. The 1997 classifications are shown in Figure 4.28.

Radioactivity

Most of the major nuclear licensed sites are located on the coast and radioactivity from their discharges can be measured in the local environment. Their concentrations and radiological impact have been measured by MAFF since the 1960s. Previous reports by Her Majesty's Inspectorate of Pollution, one of the Agency's predecessor bodies, addressed:

- surveys of radioactivity in the Ribble Estuary, Lancashire, as a consequence of discharges from nuclear sites at Springfield and Sellafield;

- radioactivity in the Esk Estuary, Cumbria.

Historic discharges of radioactivity from Sellafield in Cumbria can be detected around most of the coastal area of the UK. Since the 1970s discharges from Sellafield have reduced over 100-fold, and are much less radiologically significant. However, recent increases in the discharges of one radionuclide, technetium-99, are increasing although it is of minimal radiological significance. This radionuclide concentrates in lobsters (Figure 4.29) and increased levels of technetium are being found around the shoreline of the Irish Sea and further afield. The Agency has recently re-examined the Sellafield authorisation and has proposed a significant overall reduction in the permitted levels of discharges of technetium-99 and the imposition of strict conditions requiring the development and application of new abatement techniques to drive down discharges further.

In most cases radiation exposures from natural radioactivity far exceed those from human sources. The average annual effective dose to the UK population has been estimated by the National Radiological Protection Board to be 2.6 milliSieverts. Radiation of natural origin accounts for 86 per cent of human exposure. Of the remainder, 14 per cent is accounted for by medical procedures and discharges of waste from nuclear establishments contribute less than 0.1 per cent (NRPB, 1993).

Radiation exposures from environmental materials not involving food pathways, which may have been incurred by members of the public in 1997 remain similar to those in previous years. In all cases exposures have been substantially less than the principal dose limit of 1 milliSievert per year.

Seafood and other foodstuffs produced in and around the UK in 1997 were radiologically safe to eat and the exposure of consumers to artificially produced radioactivity via the food chain remained well below UK and EC limits. Natural radionuclides are the most important source of exposure in the average diet of consumers. Artificial radionuclides contributed less than five per cent of the dose. Radioactivity in UK coastal

Figure 4.29   *The trend in radionuclide levels in lobsters from Sellafield, 1989 to 1997*

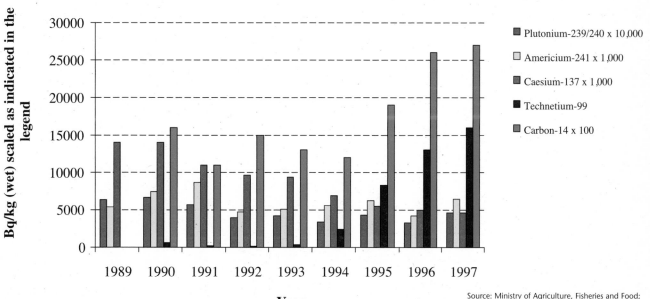

Source: Ministry of Agriculture, Fisheries and Food;
Scottish Environmental Protection Agency

Figure 4.30 *The quality of estuaries in England and Wales by length, 1995*

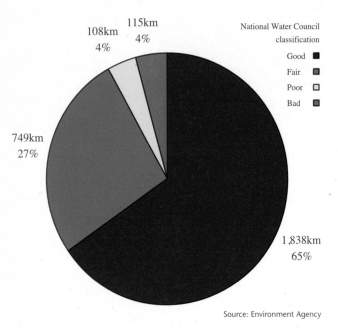

108km
4%

115km
4%

749km
27%

1,838km
65%

National Water Council classification

Good ■
Fair ■
Poor □
Bad ■

Source: Environment Agency

waters and its impact have been extensively studied (Kershaw *et al.*, 1992; Pentreath, 1988)

Estimated doses to consumers of fish and shellfish in the vicinity of Sellafield from artificial radionuclides in the diet decreased from 14 per cent of the dose limit of 1 milliSievert in 1996 to 10 per cent in 1997. The decrease was largely due to changes in the consumption of shellfish by these people. The highest dose to members of the public in the UK from both artificial and natural radioactivity was estimated to be 0.49 milliSieverts to consumers of fish and shellfish in the Whitehaven area (MAFF and SEPA, 1998).

Estuary classification scheme

Every five years, from 1980 to 1995, the Agency (or its predecessors) conducted surveys of estuary quality according to the classification scheme developed by the National Water Council (NWC) in the 1970s. This is a non-statutory scheme which aims to provide measures of estuarine water quality based on dissolved oxygen concentrations, aesthetic quality and biological quality. It is a highly subjective scheme and is not

Figure 4.31 *The quality of estuaries in England and Wales, 1995*

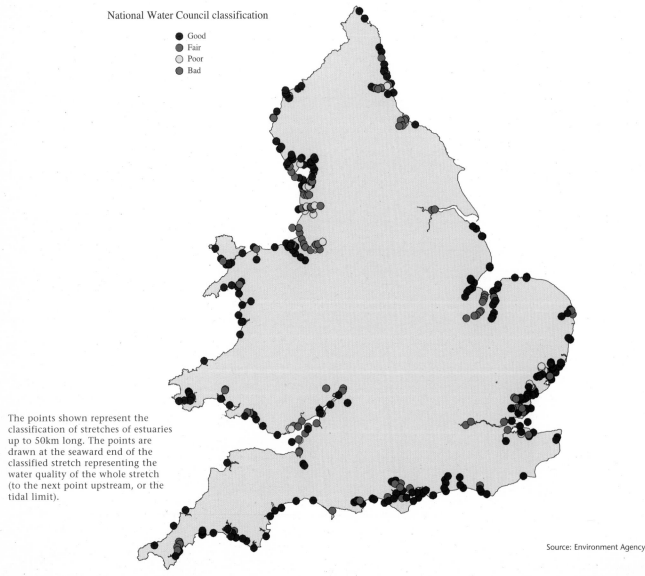

National Water Council classification

● Good
● Fair
○ Poor
● Bad

The points shown represent the classification of stretches of estuaries up to 50km long. The points are drawn at the seaward end of the classified stretch representing the water quality of the whole stretch (to the next point upstream, or the tidal limit).

Source: Environment Agency

Figure 4.32 *The quality of the Tyne Estuary, 1975 to 1995*

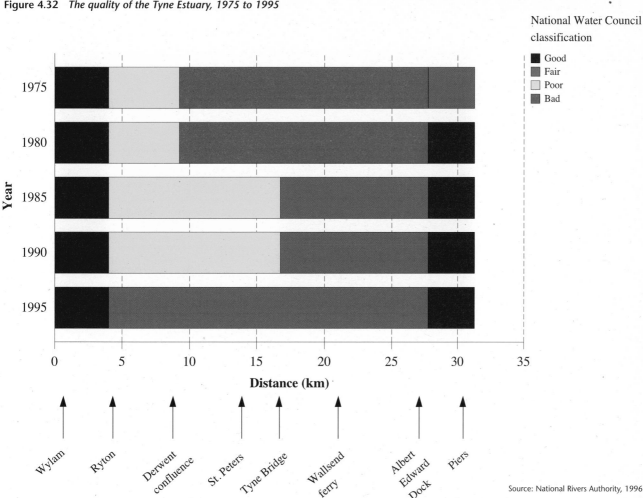

National Water Council classification

- ■ Good
- ■ Fair
- ■ Poor
- ■ Bad

Source: National Rivers Authority, 1996

sensitive enough to show all but the most dramatic changes in water quality.

In the 1960s and 1970s the quality of many estuaries appeared to improve, particularly the most grossly polluted estuaries, as a result of investments in sewerage and sewage treatment works, the construction of new sea outfalls and the diversion of unsatisfactory industrial discharges to sewers or treatment works. Between 1980 and 1985 estuarine quality remained much the same, but there was a small deterioration in quality between 1985 and 1990. This is partly explained by the effect of dry weather in 1989 and 1990 which reduced freshwater flows into estuaries, which is important for flushing and dilution, and by changes in survey methodology. The most recent survey in 1995 (Figures 4.30 and 4.31) shows a similar quality to 1990, and 92 per cent of estuaries are classified as good or fair. In terms of lengths, the 1995 position is worse than 1980 with fewer 'good' and more 'bad' lengths of estuaries (NRA, 1995; Environment Agency, 1996a; Environment Agency, 1997a).

The NWC classification scheme was not very comprehensive or precise. It was useful for discriminating between grossly polluted waters and those of better quality, but its usefulness in classifying a wide range of estuaries with very different properties or problems was limited. The water quality improvement brought about in the Tyne Estuary is a good

example of where the scheme worked (Figure 4.32). In the early 1970s the Tyne was grossly polluted, and large parts of it were biologically inert and very much in need of regeneration. Twenty years later, after much work, its entire length of 32km was classified as 'good' or 'fair'.

Although the Tyne is a good example of improvements being reflected in the NWC class, it is also a good illustration of the limitations - all the estuary may now be 'good' or 'fair' but there is imposex in dog-whelks caused by exposure to tributyl tin, feminisation of flounders and incidence of disease and seasonal salmon deaths. On the other hand, the presence of these organisms indicates the general clean-up of the Tyne reflected in the NWC class.

Research and development is being carried out by the Agency to develop ways of assessing coastal water quality. This will include sanitary determinands, nutrients, biology and aesthetics.

Non-statutory monitoring

This section draws together information from many sources on the chemical quality of coasts and estuaries. The lack of consistent information was recognised by the Marine Pollution Monitoring Management Group in the late 1980s which set up a programme to address the shortfalls (Marine Pollution Monitoring Management Group, 1998a; CEFAS, 1998b;

Figure 4.33 *Selected metals in water* at National Monitoring Programme sites, 1990 to 1995*

Cadmium
EQS = 2500ng/l

Median (50% or more samples are
  > limit of detection) (ng/l)

400 200 40

Median (50% or more samples are
  < limit of detection) (ng/l)

400 200 40

Lead
EQS = 25 μg/l

Median (50% or more samples are
  > limit of detection) (μg/l)

5 2.5 0.5

Median (50% or more samples are
  < limit of detection) (μg/l)

5 2.5 0.5

Copper
EQS = 5 μg/l

Median (50% or more samples are
  > limit of detection) (μg/l)

5 2.5 0.5

Zinc
EQS = 40 μg/l

Median (50% or more samples are
  > limit of detection) (μg/l)

50 25 5

Source: Environment Agency;
Centre for Environment, Fisheries and Aquaculture Science

* All analyses carried out on filtered water

Figure 4.34 *Metal contamination in estuarine sediments*

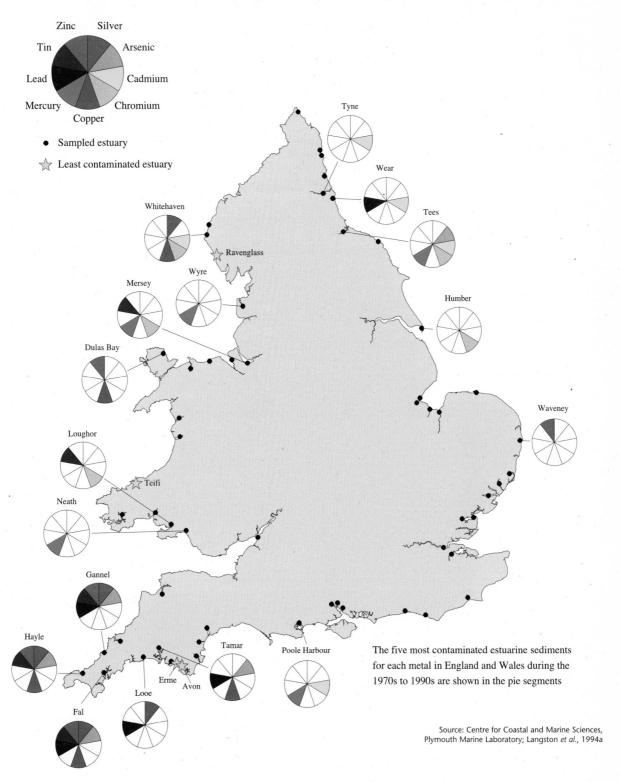

The five most contaminated estuarine sediments for each metal in England and Wales during the 1970s to 1990s are shown in the pie segments

Source: Centre for Coastal and Marine Sciences, Plymouth Marine Laboratory; Langston *et al.*, 1994a

Appendix 3). Various other research organisations have looked at specific issues in the environment and these have been considered where relevant.

Metals in water

Results for selected metals from the 1990 to 1995 National Monitoring Programme are shown in Figure 4.33 and show that concentrations are generally very low. Of all the median metal concentrations in water, only zinc exceeded the environmental quality standard at any sites; this was in the Dee

Estuary and the Tyne Estuary. However, these median results were based on very few samples and there were no failures of the EC Dangerous Substances Directive for zinc in these estuaries in 1996.

Metal concentrations in water in estuaries were higher than at intermediate and offshore sites. This is interpreted as being a direct consequence of the proximity of estuarine sites to inputs, from rivers and point discharges, as well as less dilution by sea water with lower natural levels of metals. Within estuaries there was also a general tendency for metal concentrations to decrease with increasing salinity, again reflecting dilution with sea water. Where information is available, concentrations tended to be higher in those estuaries which receive large inputs from industrial or sewage sources. Examples are cadmium (Severn Estuary), lead (Tyne, Tees and Thames estuaries) and zinc (Tyne, Wear and Mersey estuaries).

Metals in sediments

Metal contamination of estuarine sediments has been monitored by the Agency and the Centre for Coastal and Marine Sciences' Plymouth Marine Laboratory throughout the 1970s, 1980s and 1990s. The estuaries found to be most contaminated over this period were those which received large inputs of metals from industrial effluents (for example in the north east and north west) and those which are downstream of metalliferous catchments, some of which have been mined extensively (for

example in the south west). While there are many estuarine sites whose sediments are contaminated with metals, it is almost impossible to find sediments in England and Wales which are uncontaminated by human activities (Figure 4.34) (Langston et al., 1994a).

Organic contaminants

Many of the organic compounds such as atrazine, simazine and pentachlorophenol, monitored in the water column as part of the National Monitoring Programme, were found at concentrations below the limit of detection and most positive results were below the relevant environmental quality standard. The insecticide lindane has the most complete dataset in terms of spatial coverage and quality. Median concentrations of lindane were below the environmental quality standard at all sites except one in the Thames Estuary (Figure 3.40).

Figure 4.35 *Total polycyclic aromatic hydrocarbon levels in sediments at National Monitoring Programme sites, 1993 to 1995*

Total polycyclic aromatic hydrocarbon level

g/kg

30

15

3

Source: Environment Agency;
Centre for Environment, Fisheries and Aquaculture Science

Individual lindane concentrations above the environmental quality standard were found in the Ouse, Thames, Tamar and Mersey estuaries, which all have major conurbations or large agricultural catchments. Generally, concentrations of lindane decline with distance offshore. Occasional high concentrations of other compounds were found but these were not repeated on other monitoring occasions.

The National Monitoring Programme also did some analysis of organic compounds in sediments which suggested very little contamination. But there were some difficulties in the types of sediments sampled and analytical procedures, so further work is needed (Marine Pollution Monitoring Management Group, 1998a).

Polycyclic aromatic hydrocarbons (PAHs) are ubiquitous environmental contaminants. Although they can be formed naturally (for example in forest fires), their predominant source is anthropogenic emissions and the highest concentrations of PAHs are generally found around urban centres. Their widespread occurence results largely from formation and release during the incomplete combustion of coal, oil, petrol and wood, but they are also components of petroleum and its products. PAHs reach the marine environment via sewage discharges, surface runoff, industrial discharges, oil spillages and deposition from the atmosphere. PAHs can be acutely toxic to aquatic organisms and some are carcinogenic. Elevated PAH concentrations in seawater and sediments may present a risk to aquatic organisms and also to human consumers of fish and shellfish.

At offshore locations in the National Monitoring Programme, PAH concentrations in seawater were mostly below the limit of detection. In coastal and estuarine water samples total PAH concentrations above 1μg/l were found at sites in the Tees, Humber, Great Ouse and Thames estuaries. Other studies have highlighted the Mersey, Tees, Thames and Tyne (Law and Klungsøyr, 1998). There are considerable uncertainties in conducting a risk assessment of PAHs in seawater, but evaluation of the data suggests that about 15 per cent of the samples

analysed came from waters that may have the potential to affect the long-term well-being of a range of aquatic organisms. About 30 per cent of samples were obtained from waters in which some human food items such as bivalve molluscs may be locally contaminated to an unacceptable level due to bioaccumulation. Almost all these samples originated from industrialised estuaries rather than the open sea, often close to effluent outfalls (Law et al., 1997).

PAH monitoring in sediments was also carried out in the National Monitoring Programme survey. The number of samples was limited and many data were reported below the limit of detection. Nevertheless, an idea of the spatial extent of PAH contamination of sediments has emerged with the highest concentrations found in the formerly highly industrialised estuaries of north east England, particularly in the muddy sediments of the Tyne and Wear estuaries (Figure 4.35).

There were negligible PAH concentrations in the marine environment prior to the industrial revolution, and the burning of fossil fuels since then has been the primary source. A sediment core from the Tamar Estuary in south west England shows a steady increase in PAH concentrations in the 1930s and 1940s followed by an exponential growth from the 1950s to 1980 (Figure 4.36). Copper, zinc and lead concentrations were also found to increase at the same time. The most important contributory factor to PAH emissions around the Tamar during this time period is probably the increase in petrol and diesel-driven vehicles. A particularly marked increase in PAH concentrations in Tamar sediments was noted following the opening of the Tamar Road Bridge in 1961, which enabled unrestricted entry into Cornwall from Plymouth. This is the major route of vehicles into the south west and has increased traffic in the area (Readman et al., 1987).

4.4 The health of the coastal environment

Environmental quality standards are usually based on physical or chemical criteria, but it is also useful to look at the biological effects of physical or chemical factors as an indication of

Figure 4.36 *Concentrations of polycyclic aromatic hydrocarbons in sediments in the Tamar Estuary, 1925 to 1980*

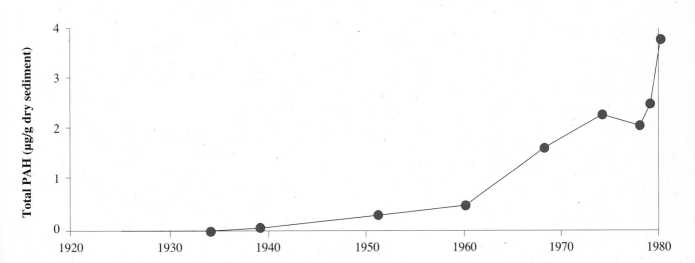

Source: Readman et al., 1987; Elsevier Science

environmental quality. In other words, how 'healthy' is our environment? There are not yet many ways of measuring 'health' so this section concentrates on specific issues of concern such as eutrophication and bioaccumulation.

Eutrophication

Eutrophication is a sign of poor 'health' in estuarine and coastal waters. The definition of eutrophication adopted by the Agency is:

> *"The enrichment of waters, by inorganic plant nutrients, which results in the stimulation of an array of symptomatic changes. These include the increased production of algae and/or other aquatic plants, affecting the quality of the water and disturbing the balance of organisms present within it. Such changes may be undesirable and interfere with water uses"* (OECD, 1982 modified).

The growth of algae, associated with eutrophic water, is often limited by lack of sunlight, low temperatures, lack of nutrients or insufficient residence time. Summer conditions tend to favour algal growth provided nutrients are sufficient. When nutrients limit growth in marine waters, nitrogen is usually lacking. Algal growth in estuarine ecosystems tends to be restricted by phosphorus at the freshwater end, grading through to nitrogen-limitation at the seaward end, but suspended sediments often mean that a lack of light actually limits algal growth in estuaries. This is the case for many estuaries around England and Wales, particularly the Thames, Humber, Mersey and Severn.

Nutrient levels in estuaries were monitored in the National Monitoring Programme (Appendix 3) and spatial variations tend to reflect differences in catchment areas and input loads (Figures 4.37 and 4.38). A proper understanding of the relevance of estuarine nutrient levels requires nutrient budgets and information on processes which are unique to each estuary.

Coastal waters are considered to be nutrient enriched if the winter concentration of dissolved available inorganic nitrogen is more than 169µg/l in the presence of more than 6.2µg/l of dissolved available inorganic phosphorus (CSTT, 1997). Based on this definition, nutrient enrichment is widespread in coastal waters, as shown by results from surveys conducted by the Agency from 1993 to 1997, in which nutrients, chlorophyll-a and other water quality parameters were measured. These surveys took the form of simultaneous measurements from boats and remote sensing from aircraft four times per year. The surveys show how nutrient concentrations are higher in winter than summer because they are not consumed by biota in the winter. They also show that the highest nutrient concentrations occur near the Severn Estuary, Thames Estuary, the Wash, along the north east coast and in the south eastern Irish Sea (NRA, 1996; Environment Agency, 1997d).

Nutrient enrichment does not necessarily lead to excessive algal growth so it is also essential to monitor algae. Chlorophyll-a is used as an indicator of the amount of phytoplankton present. The UK interpretation of the EC Urban Waste Water Treatment Directive (91/271/EEC) suggests the 10µg/l value as being

Figure 4.37 *Total oxidised nitrogen concentrations in estuaries and coastal waters*

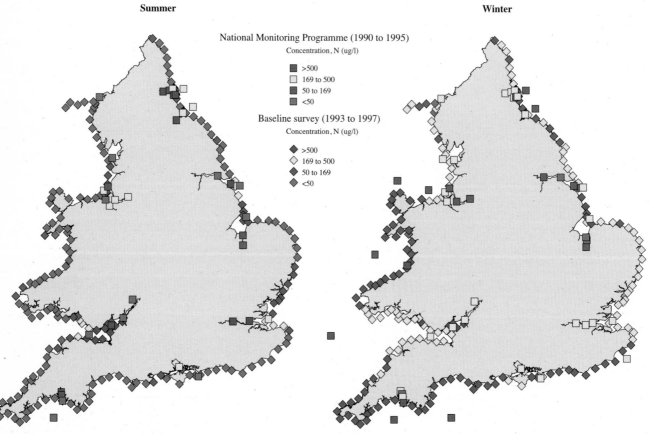

Source: Environment Agency

Figure 4.38 *Orthophosphate concentrations in estuaries and coastal waters*

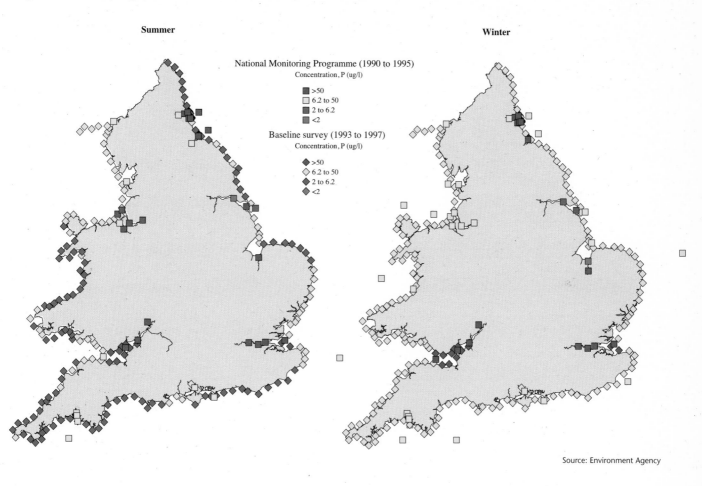

Source: Environment Agency

Figure 4.39 *Chlorophyll-a concentrations in estuaries and coastal waters*

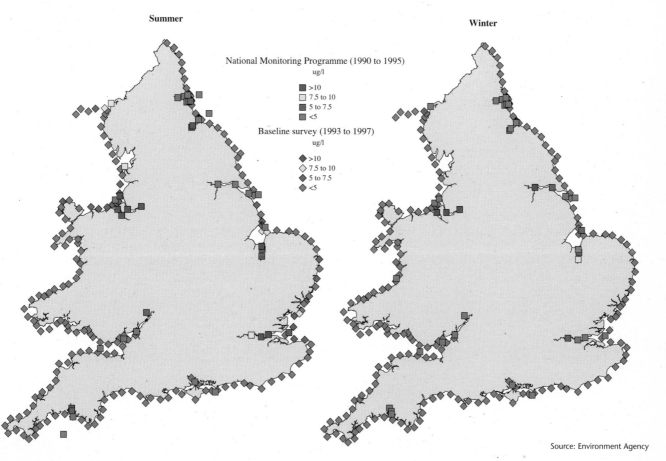

Source: Environment Agency

Figure 4.40 *Remote-sensing image of Langstone Harbour, showing saltmarsh (yellow) and algae (green), taken in August 1996*

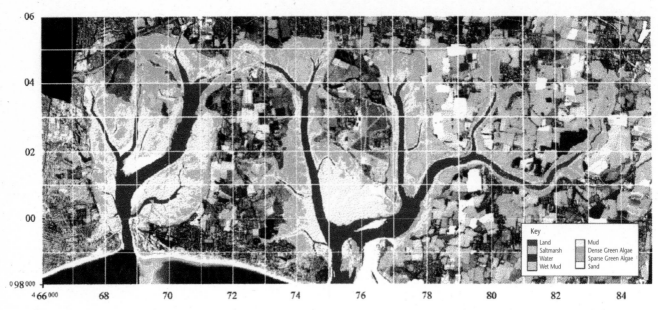

CASI (Compact Airborne Spectrographic Imager)

Source: Environment Agency

indicative of the presence of algal blooms, although not necessarily indicative of eutrophication. Data from the National Monitoring Programme show concentrations in excess of 10μg/l in the Dee and Mersey estuaries, the Ouse, Wash, Tees and Thames (Figure 4.39). The Agency's coastal survey shows that the north Wales coast and parts of the north west and east coast exceed this value, particularly in the spring. The information from these surveys is very limited because the results will very much depend on the conditions when the four samples were taken.

The highest chlorophyll-a concentrations occurred on the largest scale in the south eastern Irish Sea. Due to the restricted circulation in the Irish Sea the flushing time of Liverpool Bay is estimated to be between seven and 16 months; there is therefore potential for contaminants to build up in these waters.

The Compact Airborne Spectrographic Imager (CASI) images from the baseline surveys show algae occurrence in detail (Figure 4.40). The Agency is currently exploring the operational use of new technologies for monitoring the marine environment, but to get a better picture more frequent monitoring is needed. While remote sensing has provided a much greater spatial coverage, the time dimension still needs to be addressed (Environment Agency, 1997e).

The most obvious sign of eutrophication in our coastal waters, particularly in certain sheltered or enclosed estuaries, such as some of those on the south coast, is the excessive growth of green macro-algae. These can form benthic mats that displace less competitive species and lead to the deoxygenation of sediments. While the direct impacts on sediment-dwelling fauna are well documented, the effects higher up the food chain on fish and wading bird populations, are to a greater extent inferred. Marine blooms of planktonic algae can also cause nuisance through depositing foams (commonly from *Phaeocystis pouchetti*) on beaches, or discolouring the water (red tides).

While they occur more often on the eastern side of the North Sea, algal foams of limited scale and duration occur in other locations around England and Wales.

Reports of exceptional algal events in coastal waters of England and Wales date back at least to the early part of this century, when regular plankton observations began. It is probable that of all the events that have occurred relatively few have been documented. Records of exceptional algal blooms from various sources have been drawn together to find those species whose occurrence is more regular or widespread (Figure 4.41) (Lewis, 1997).

The Agency takes samples of microalgae at EC-designated bathing waters each year in the period May to September, either routinely or whenever significant algal blooms appear. The total number of blooms observed on these beaches increased from 143 in 1993 to 162 in 1994 and 227 in 1995. The Southern Region and the Agency in Wales recorded more than half the total number (Figure 4.42). The number of potentially toxic blooms observed also increased from one in 1993, to eight in 1994 and 15 in 1995 (Figure 4.43). The south and west of England and Wales recorded the most potentially toxic microalgal bloom occurrences over this period. However, there were large differences in the number of bathing waters visited by each region (South West Region having the most bathing waters), in the number of samples taken each year, and in the monitoring effort applied (Wales making the most frequent observations). This uneven monitoring effort should be taken into account when comparing regions.

In 1997 fifty-one estuarine and coastal waters were assessed to establish their eutrophication status for the purposes of the EC Nitrates Directive (91/676/EEC) and the EC Urban Waste Water Treatment Directive (91/271/EEC). Five estuaries were designated as eutrophic sensitive areas under the Urban Waste Water Treatment Directive - Langstone Harbour, Chichester

Figure 4.41 *Location of major blooms (and potential impacts) of selected species of algae*

———— Location of occurrences

Phaeocystis
Attheya armatus and related species
Foam formation

Gyrodinium, Gymnodinium
Fish and invertebrate deaths

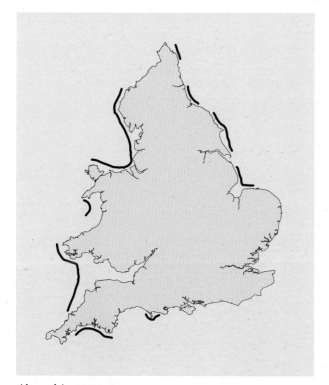

Alexandrium tamarense
Paralytic shellfish toxins

Noctiluca scintillans
'Tomato soup'-coloured water in red tides

Source: Lewis, 1997

Figure 4.42 *Marine microalgal blooms by Agency Region, 1993 to 1995*

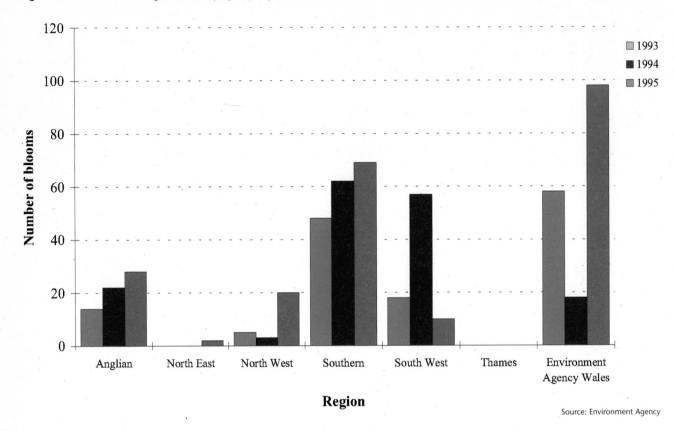

Source: Environment Agency

Harbour, the Fal Estuary, the Taw Estuary and the Tawe Estuary - but no nitrate vulnerable zones were identified under the Nitrates Directive (Figure 3.35). The indicative standards for identifying eutrophic sensitive areas are expressed in terms of nitrate, phosphate, dissolved oxygen, plant biomass, clarity, retention time and biological effects, with different criteria applying to estuaries and coastal waters. There is now a requirement for nutrient removal from qualifying discharges into these areas (DETR and Welsh Office, 1997).

In 1998 OSPAR agreed a *Strategy to Combat Eutrophication* (OSPAR, 1998a) which requires contracting parties to develop and apply common assessment criteria for identifying coastal waters as non-problem areas, potential problem areas or problem areas with regard to eutrophication. Actions to prevent or eliminate the causes of eutrophication must then be applied as appropriate.

On-going research on nutrient fluxes in estuaries is being conducted jointly by government departments and universities.

Figure 4.43 *Potentially toxic marine microalgal blooms by Agency Region, 1993 to 1995*

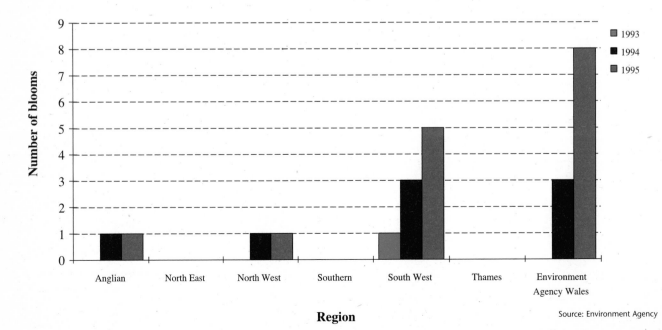

Source: Environment Agency

The Joint Nutrient Study (JONUS) and Southampton Water Nutrients Study (SONUS) are research projects which aim to estimate nutrient fluxes in estuaries and coastal waters and to improve understanding of the fate and behaviour of nutrients as they are carried through estuaries to coastal waters. This research is helping to demonstrate the complexity of mechanisms determining nutrient fluxes in estuaries and to counter over-simplified assumptions about risks of eutrophication.

The Agency has recently produced a consultation document proposing a strategy for managing eutrophication in inland and coastal waters (Environment Agency, 1998d).

Shellfish poisoning

Shellfish may become unfit for human consumption by accumulating hazardous or toxic substances in their flesh. For example, toxins produced by algae are sometimes taken up by shellfish in enough quantities to render them unsafe. The human consumption of shellfish containing accumulated algal toxins may result in ill health, with symptoms ranging from diarrhoea to vomiting, paralysis and death. In 1968 seventy-eight people were hospitalised as a result of ingesting contaminated mussels from the north east coast of Britain. Since that time regular monitoring has been conducted by CEFAS (previously MAFF's Directorate of Fisheries Research) in high-risk areas for toxins which may produce paralytic shellfish poisoning, and more recently for toxins which produce diarrhetic shellfish poisoning and amnesic shellfish poisoning. In the event of these being found, the shellfisheries are closed until the risk has passed. The programme, based on the collection and testing of shellfish, has worked well and there have been no recorded incidences of paralytic or diarrhetic shellfish poisoning of humans in England and Wales since monitoring for each type of toxin began (Lewis, 1997).

Since 1992 shellfishery closures have been implemented at the following times and locations:

- in March 1994 a temporary prohibition order was put in force at Maryport on the Solway Firth because widespread diarrhetic shellfish poisons were detected;

- from June to July 1997 there was a voluntary closure of the Fal Estuary shellfishery because paralytic shellfish poisons were detected;

- in September 1997 there was a voluntary closure of the Pacific oyster farm near Holy Island after diarrhetic shellfish poisons were detected.

Paralytic shellfish poisons are frequently detected along the north east coast of England from April to September and very occasionally in the south west of England. Few commercial molluscan shellfisheries are present in this area so closures are not necessary but when appropriate the local authorities have to place warning notices to inform casual shellfish gatherers of the possible danger.

Bioaccumulation

Many substances, such as polychlorinated biphenyls (PCBs) and certain pesticides, are persistent in the environment and accumulate in biological tissues where they may exert toxic effects. For these reasons DDT was banned from use in the UK in a phased approach over the period 1964 to 1984, and dieldrin was banned in 1989. With respect to PCBs, UK manufacture ceased in 1976 but production continued in many other countries until the late 1980s and they could be sold for use in electrical transformers until 1986. Some of these are still in use although there is a move for a phased reduction in use. Other chemicals implicated in health problems, for example lindane, are still used and other pesticides may bioaccumulate or cause effects not yet identified. For invertebrates, like mussels, hydrocarbons are important organic contaminants. Some metals may also accumulate in biological tissues and produce health problems, and although they may not be as persistent as PCBs, for example, their concentrations in marine organisms are still of concern.

Data on metal accumulation in selected estuarine organisms in the 1970s, 1980s and 1990s have shown the extent of pollution due to industrial and mining activity. The seaweed bladderwrack has been shown to accumulate metals dissolved in water, whereas ragworms and clams accumulate metals predominantly from sediments, their food and also from water. The concentration of metals measured in the tissues of organisms from different areas of an estuary gives a general indication of the extent to which they have been incorporated into estuarine ecosystems (Figure 4.44). Metal concentrations in biota follow the same general trends as water quality and sediment quality - highest concentrations occur mostly near industrial and mining areas - but there are some differences. This is because bioavailability is not always a direct function of environmental contamination, but can be modified by a variety of physical, chemical and biological factors (Langston et al., 1994a).

It is not clear what effect metal contamination of sediments is having on estuarine ecosystems because other contaminants often accompany metals, for example hydrocarbons. There are examples where gross contamination has led to the exclusion of several species. In the Fal Estuary larval settlement of bivalves was inhibited by high levels of copper and zinc in the sediment. Embryonic and larval stages of organisms are usually far more sensitive to metals than the adults, often by orders of magnitude, and the conditions for successful settlement and establishment of larval organisms are often quite critical (Bryan and Langston, 1992). Some animals have adapted to metal contamination by inducing detoxification processes and some populations have become metal tolerant (for example ragworms in the Fal Estuary).

High metal concentrations in tissues are often a feature of metal-tolerant species and may pose problems for predators through biomagnification up food chains. In particular, birds may be responsible for the consumption of a large proportion of the annual production of estuarine mudflats. For example, bird mortalities in the Mersey Estuary between 1979 and 1982 were almost certainly caused by lead compounds accumulating

Figure 4.44 *Metal contamination of seaweed and clams*

Mercury
ug/g dry tissue

2

■ Seaweed (*Fucus vesiculosus*)
■ Clam (*Scrobicularia plana*)

Lead
ug/g dry tissue

100

■ Seaweed (*Fucus vesiculosus*)
■ Clam (*Scrobicularia plana*)

999

Source: Centre for Coastal and Marine Sciences,
Plymouth Marine Laboratory; Langston et al, 1994a

in food species in the vicinity of a factory which manufactured additives for petrol (Bryan and Langston, 1992).

Generally, the data on metal contamination in estuarine waders are too limited to deduce any patterns except in a few locations. For seabirds, the most contaminated specimens have been collected in and around industrial centres, including the north east Irish Sea, Severn Estuary, Thames Estuary and north east England. Much lower contaminant burdens were detected in birds from offshore islands and the Welsh coast. There is evidence of elevated mercury and cadmium concentrations in certain pelagic species, especially skuas and petrels, but overall the data are rather limited (Bryan and Langston, 1992).

It is not only the direct consequences of metal toxicity which pose a threat to predators but also the indirect effects which result from the disappearance of food species. This may be the case in estuaries which are heavily contaminated with tributyl tin, where several species of bivalves have declined. For example, while some birds (for example, the dunlin) can eat a variety of prey species, others are less adaptable. The knot, for example, feeds almost exclusively on bivalves (Bryan and Langston, 1992).

There is large variation in levels of pollutants in seabirds and their eggs, both between species and between different parts of an individual species range. Studies in the 1980s found that petrels, gannets, divers, grebes and saw-billed ducks contained high levels of many contaminants, and there were high levels of mercury and organochlorine in eiders. Levels of some organochlorines, for example dieldrin, aldrin and DDT, have fallen since the early 1970s when their use was statutorily restricted (Tasker and Becker, 1992). The decline in PCBs has been less pronounced although the toxic effects of PCBs on birds remain unclear, and are possibly minor. The accumulation of metals in seabirds is not widespread and toxic effects are rare, although some local populations may be at risk in areas where prey species are highly contaminated.

Overall, the increases in many seabird populations since the 1970s (see Section 4.2) indicate that toxic residues are not having adverse effects. Effects which occur in heavily contaminated areas are not great enough to reduce the overall population (Tasker and Becker, 1992).

Measurements of various contaminants (for example metals, tributyl tin, PAHs, PCBs, pesticides) in mussel tissues were made along the North Sea coast and offshore sites in 1990 and 1991 and in the Irish Sea in 1996 and 1997. These elevated tissue concentrations indicate reduced water quality near obvious sources of pollution such as large coastal towns, harbours and industrialised areas. Shallow semi-enclosed coastal areas (for example the Irish Sea and southern North Sea) all had signs of chemical contamination (Widdows et al., 1995).

A limited amount of data on selected contaminants in common mussels were collected over the period 1993 to 1996 for the National Monitoring Programme (Appendix 3). From these data mussels had relatively high concentrations of:

- cadmium in the outer Severn Estuary;

- mercury in the Thames Estuary;

- zinc in the Mersey Estuary;

- PCBs in the Humber.

As part of the National Monitoring Programme selected contaminants were also measured in fish tissues, using dab and flounder as the target species. Although some substances, for example mercury, arsenic, lead, PCBs, dieldrin and the DDT group of pesticides, were present in fish at many sites the highest concentrations were for:

- mercury in fish muscle in Liverpool, Morecambe and Cardigan Bays;

- cadmium in fish livers off the Humber Estuary;

- PCBs in fish livers in Liverpool Bay;

- DDT in fish livers off the north west and north east coasts of England.

PCBs and PAHs have also been found in porpoises and dolphins which are resident in UK coastal waters. Current understanding of the diet and behaviour of these animals is not good enough to determine exactly how they receive these contaminants, but they may have accumulated them through the food chain. These mammals are generally found in less industrialised and less developed areas, for example Cardigan Bay in Wales, which receive few direct discharges of effluents. It seems unlikely that PCBs and PAHs affect porpoises or other marine mammals except on an individual basis, in contrast to other influences such as being caught in fishing nets or over-exploitation of fish stocks. Further information on the occurrence and effects of these contaminants is necessary before a full assessment of their significance can be made (Law and Whinnett, 1992; CEFAS, 1997).

Disease outbreaks with high mortality rates among seals and dolphins around the world in the 1980s and 1990s attracted considerable attention. Although in most cases viral infections were the primary cause of the disease outbreaks, it was speculated that pollution-induced suppression of the immune system in some species had played a role. In particular, organochlorine compounds (for example DDT, dieldrin and PCBs) have been implicated in several notable events, such as the 1988 phocine distemper epidemic which killed 18,000 common seals in the North Sea.

The limited amount of data that exist suggests that populations of seals inhabiting estuaries near large conurbations (for example the Tees and the Dee) may be exposed to higher levels of contaminants (like PCBs and metals) than animals in remote locations such as Shetland and Orkney (Hall et al., 1992; De Swart et al., 1994).

Endocrine disruption

Chemical substances that interfere with the hormone systems of animals are known as endocrine disruptors. Interference with normal hormonal systems can cause physiological damage resulting in effects on the form or structure of animals (morphology) and their reproductive capacity (for example a decrease in the number of young produced).

These types of effects have been demonstrated using ecotoxicological methods (laboratory and field exposures) and by field community surveys. Laboratory tests have indicated that many substances have endocrine-disrupting properties. These substances include naturally occurring substances such as phyto-oestrogens produced by plants, steroid substances (both natural and man-made) and synthetic substances. Synthetic substances which are thought to be endocrine disruptors include pesticides such as DDT and lindane, biocides such as tributyl tin, detergents such as alkylphenol ethoxylates, plasticisers such as alkyphenols, polychlorinated biphenols (PCBs; used in old electrical components), bisphenol A (used in the lining of tin cans and in dental fillings) and ethynyl oestradiol (synthetic steroid used in the oral contraceptive pill). The most widely reported effect from endocrine disruption is a feminising or oestrogenic effect (so called because the effects are the same as those caused by the female hormone

Figure 4.45 *The extent and severity of imposex in dog whelks caused by tributyl tin contamination*

Source: adapted from Spence *et al.*, 1990; Blackwell Science Ltd; original data from Davies *et al.*, 1987; Bailey and Davies, 1988; Elsevier Science

Figure 4.46 *Tributyl tin in seawater in the Test, Itchen and Hamble estuaries*

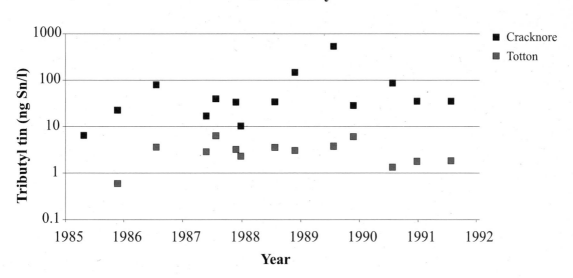

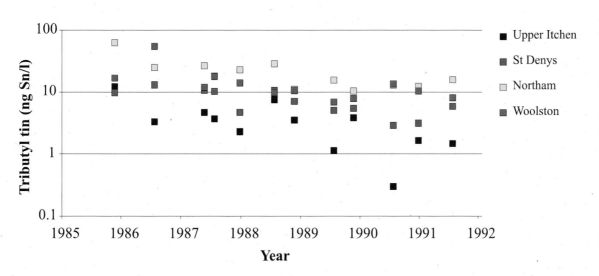

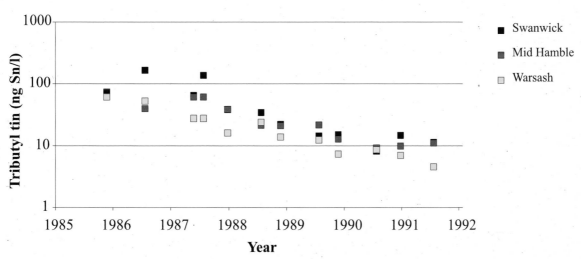

Source: Centre for Coastal and Marine Sciences, Plymouth
Marine Laboratory; Environment Agency; Langston *et al.*, 1994b

Figure 4.47 *Tributyl tin in sediments in the Test, Itchen and Hamble estuaries*

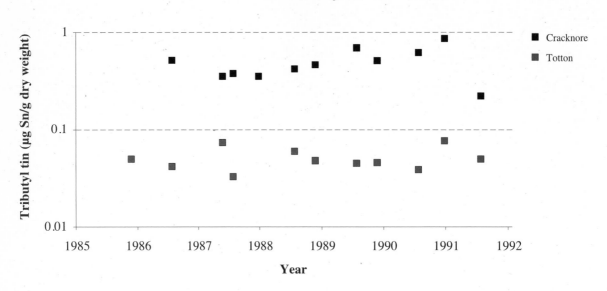

Test Estuary

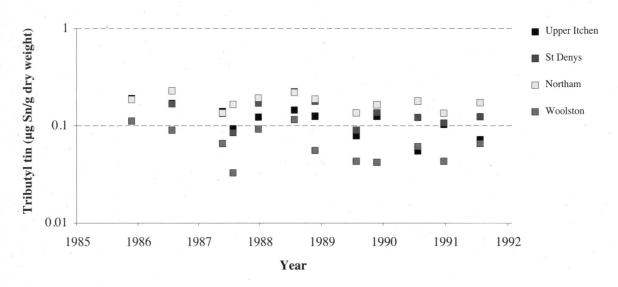

Itchen Estuary

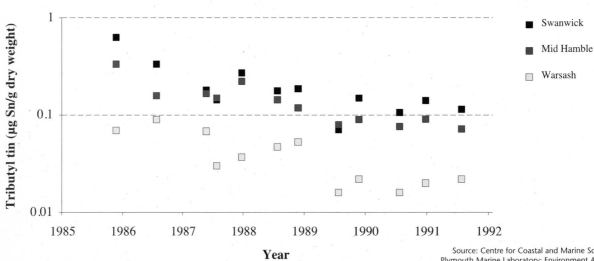

Hamble Estuary

Source: Centre for Coastal and Marine Sciences,
Plymouth Marine Laboratory; Environment Agency;
Langston *et al.*, 1994b

oestrogen). Other endocrine disrupting effects that result from exposure to the chemicals described above have been identified and reported, for example masculinising or androgenic effects (so called because the effects are the same as those caused by the male hormones androgens).

One early and most striking example of the effect of pollution by endocrine-disrupting substances on wildlife in the UK was the identification of changes in the structure of the reproductive organs in a marine snail, the dog whelk. Exposure resulted in female whelks acquiring male characteristics that physically prevented them from laying eggs, known as imposex. Imposex has lead to large decreases in the numbers (and in some areas the complete disappearance) of dog whelks on the UK coast (Figure 4.45).

By the late 1980s it was clear that imposex was causing the observed widespread decline in dog whelk populations around the coast of the UK and that this condition was caused by tributyl tin, the antifouling agent used in paints applied to the hulls of boats and ships. Tributyl tin was subsequently banned for boats less than 25 metres in length in 1987. Since this ban, populations of the dog whelk have shown signs of recovery in some areas but not in others (for example, the Solent). In Southampton Water between 1986 and 1992 there was a decline in tributyl tin concentration in seawater in areas where small boats predominated (that is, ones on which tributyl tin could no longer be used after 1987) in the Hamble and Itchen estuaries. However, in areas frequented by ships (larger than 25 metres), for example on the Test Estuary, there was no decline in tributyl tin concentrations in seawater (Figures 4.46). In the areas used mostly by small boats there was a slight decline in tributyl tin concentrations in sediments and clam body tissues, whereas in the Test Estuary sediment and clam tributyl tin concentrations increased slightly (Figure 4.47) (Langston et al., 1994b).

Full recovery of affected dog whelk populations is likely to take some time because of continuing inputs from commercial shipping and residues of tributyl tin which remain in the environment, particularly in the sediments. Although these residues will disappear gradually natural recolonisation of animals to restore populations may be a slow process, particularly in areas where dog whelks disappeared completely.

Other species of shellfish have been affected by tributyl tin. For instance Pacific oysters which are bivalve (two-shelled) molluscs, have been observed to grow abnormally thick shells when exposed to tributyl tin. A study in Poole Harbour, which is used mostly by small boats, has demonstrated that the tributyl tin levels in seawater have remained above the environmental quality standard and bivalve populations have hardly recovered at all (Langston et al., 1994b).

Endocrine disruption has also been observed in fish. For instance male flounder from the estuaries of the Thames, Tyne, Tees, Mersey and Solway Firth have shown signs of feminisation and other physiological abnormalities thought to have resulted from exposure to endocrine-disrupting substances (Allen et al., 1997; Lye et al., 1997). Of 11 estuaries studied between 1996

and 1998, the degree of oestrogenic contamination in male flounder was found to be greatest in the Tees, Mersey and Tyne with two estuaries - the Tamar and Dee - where the fish appeared entirely normal. The substances causing these effects are not known, but there is a clear relationship with the volume of industrial effluent (Matthiessen et al., 1998). The full spatial extent and significance of these effects in the environment is not yet clear and the implications for marine fish populations are unknown. It is not known whether a low number of animals in an ambiguous sexual state significantly affects the ability of a population to breed and remain stable.

The Agency, among others, is investigating these gaps in current knowledge. For example, one four-year collaborative programme called Endocrine Disruption in the Marine Environment (EDMAR, carried out with DETR, MAFF, SNIFFER and industry) which started in 1998 is researching the effects of endocrine-disrupting chemicals on marine fish and invertebrate species. The programme includes surveys for abnormal fish, the development of new methods that allow rapid screening of changes in the hormone systems of fish and invertebrates and the development of models to predict the effect of endocrine-disrupting substances on fish populations.

In addition to targeted research programmes the Agency is progressing other strategic approaches. It is working with industry to encourage and identify options for reducing emissions of these substances at source to minimise the exposure of animals in the environment. Priority substances are being identified and environmental quality standards are being developed for the most significant endocrine-disrupting substances. These two approaches were applied to the detergent nonylphenol where precautionary action was taken in advance of setting an environmental quality standard. Another group of detergents, the alkylphenol ethoxylates, have also been banned from use in the offshore oil industry. It is not possible to remove steroids at source because these chemicals are excreted by humans, therefore better sewage treatment processes are needed to remove them before they are discharged into the environment.

As many substances appear to have endocrine-disrupting effects at low concentrations, it may be appropriate in the future to control and monitor the release of these substances in complex discharges, using biological effect-based methods (ecotoxicological methods). Whole effluent-based ecotoxicological assessments and limits (Direct Toxicity Assessment) allow effluent discharges to be controlled on the basis of the 'biological harm' that the whole effluent is likely to cause in the environment as opposed to the complementary approach of controlling individual priority chemicals (Environment Agency, 1998e).

Ecotoxicological studies

Bioassays can be used for measuring the environmental quality of environmental samples by observing the response of indicator organisms following exposure. The tests integrate the combined effects of known and unknown chemicals and other physicochemical conditions. Bioassays also provide an early

Figure 4.48 *Scope for growth in mussels in UK coastal waters**

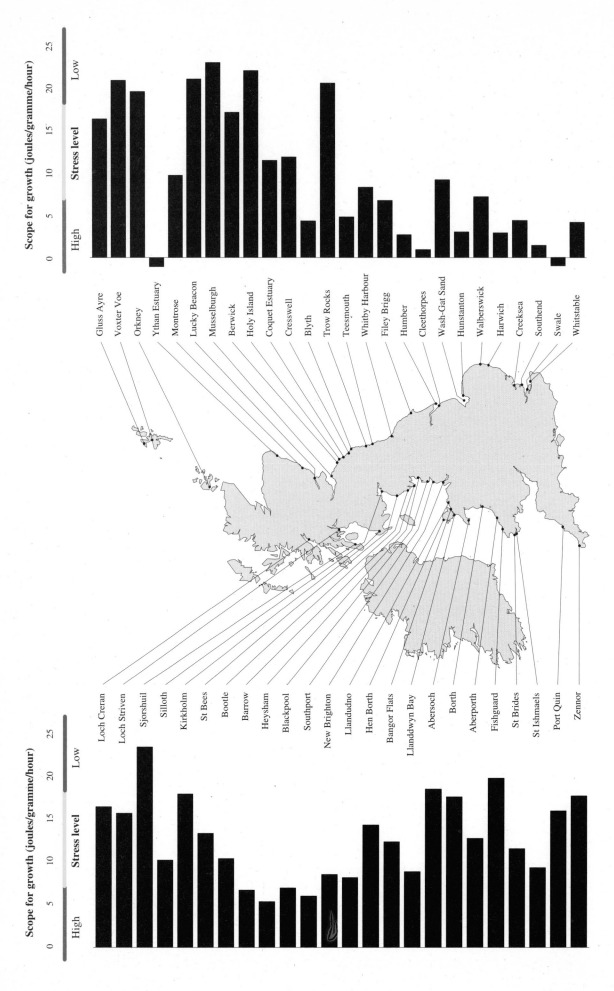

Source: Centre for Coastal and Marine Sciences, Plymouth Marine Laboratory; funded under contract to DETR

* North Sea coast surveyed in 1990 to 1991 and the Irish Sea coast in 1996 to 1997

warning or prediction of potential environmental damage, whereas biological community survey techniques tend to demonstrate damage after it has occurred. If chronic sublethal tests are used, the long-term impact of water quality can be measured and its effects on biological communities predicted. As with chemical spot samples single water samples taken for ecotoxicological assessment provide information on the quality of the sample at the point in time when it was taken and only for a limited spatial area. Sediment and in-situ ecotoxicological tests better reflect the quality of the environment over a longer time.

Organisms vary in their sensitivity to different chemicals so it is important to use combinations of complementary tests to obtain a measure of general quality. Responses which are specific to individual species can be of benefit as they allow cause-effect relationships to be determined (for example imposex caused by tributyl tin in molluscs). Generally, however, current single bioassays are not able to identify the substances causing any effects. Batteries of tests and laboratory toxicity identification procedures and biomarkers can provide powerful diagnostic tools to link effects with causative agents. Bioassays also show great promise for assessing the quality of

Figure 4.49   *Oyster embryo bioassay at National Monitoring Programme sites*

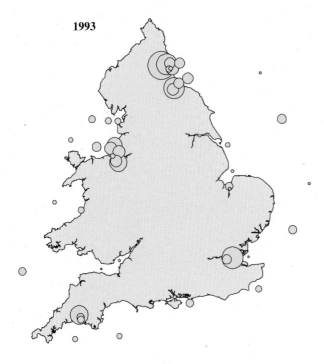

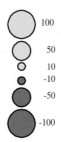

Percentage Net Response

100
50
10
-10
-50
-100

A Percentage Net Response (PNR) is a measure of how many larvae develop to the normal D-shape and hence will survive after exposure to environmental samples compared with a control sample.

A PNR of 100 means that all the larvae failed to develop normally after exposure to the environmental sample.

A PNR of zero means that the same number developed as compared to the control sample.

A PNR below zero means that more larvae developed normally in the environmental sample compared to the control sample.

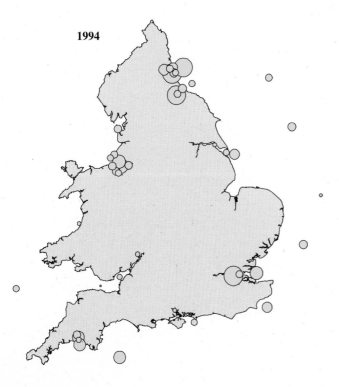

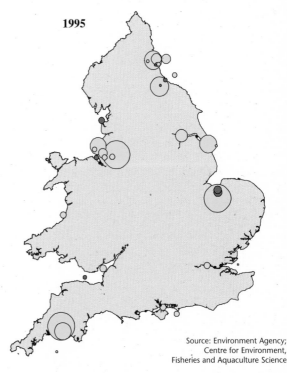

Source: Environment Agency;
Centre for Environment,
Fisheries and Aquaculture Science

environments where biology cannot be used or biological classification schemes are poorly developed (for example soil, contaminated land, sewage sludge, dredged material, heavily impacted sites, 'poor' substrates, marine and estuarine sites).

A bioassay which has been used in coastal waters is the common mussel *Mytilus edulis* 'scope for growth' assay. Scope for growth is a measurement which determines the energy available for growth rather than a direct measurement of growth itself. It can be interpreted as an indicator of stress due to pollution. The scope for growth assay has been applied along the North Sea coast and offshore sites in 1990 and 1991 and in the Irish Sea in 1996 and 1997. These studies indicated that scope for growth was lowest near obvious sources of pollution such as heavily urbanised and industrialised areas and in shallow semi-enclosed coastal seas rather than in the open sea (Figure 4.48). At the majority of sites elevated PAH concentrations in mussel tissues could help to explain a substantial part of the reduced scope for growth, but the combined effects of often unidentified substances probably also reduced scope for growth at many sites (Widdows *et al.*, 1995).

Another bioassay that has been used successfully to demonstrate pollution gradients in estuaries is the viability of copepod eggs. The hatching success of copepod eggs removed from sediments in the Exe (92 per cent), Humber (48 per cent) and Mersey estuaries (14 per cent) in 1995 was found to be closely linked to measured concentrations of toxic substances in the sediments (Lindley *et al.*, 1998).

The oyster embryo larval bioassay has also been used widely to measure biological effects in estuarine and coastal waters. Fertilised eggs for the test are produced following mixing of sperm and eggs from adult male and female oysters. When grown in good quality water the eggs undergo cellular division and develop into characteristic D-shaped larvae. In poor quality water the embryos will not develop into the D-shape. The test involves assessing the percentage of normal D-shaped larvae that develop in a sample (for example seawater, sediment, effluent) relative to a 'clean' control.

Oyster embryo larval bioassays were performed as part of the National Monitoring Programme (Appendix 3) between 1991 and 1995. The oyster embryos were exposed to estuarine and coastal waters and sediment samples. Biological effects using oyster embryos were rarely detected in coastal or offshore water samples, the exception being samples from a few sites in the North Sea where slight effects were detected (Figure 4.49). Significant effects were detected when exposed to water samples from the Tyne, Great Ouse, Tamar, Mersey, Wear, Humber, Thames and Dee estuaries, in at least one of the three years from 1993 to 1995. This is likely to be a result of industrialisation in these areas. Effects detected from samples from the Great Ouse did not appear to be related to large-scale industrial activity, and may be associated with agricultural runoff, although this has not been investigated further. Oyster embryos exposed to sediment samples detected significant effects with samples from the Tees, Tyne and Wear estuaries.

Results using oyster embryo larval bioassays alone suggest that coastal and offshore water and sediment quality is generally

good but there may be concern with the quality of water and sediments in many industrialised estuaries. Samples from some sites produced acutely toxic effects in oysters which could result in lethal or serious sublethal effects. The combined use of biological effects, chemical and biological community data generated from the National Monitoring Programme can be used to give 'weight of evidence' to these observations. Available data suggest that no single contaminant is responsible for the detected effects which are likely to be due to several contaminants acting together. The sources of these materials are unknown, but probably consist of both contemporary sewage and industrial discharges and historically contaminated sediments (Marine Pollution Monitoring Management Group, 1998a).

Detailed analysis of strategic monitoring datasets and integrated control and monitoring programmes should, in the future, be able to better link source, cause and effect allowing more effective control of the release of harmful substances. Ecotoxicological methods are likely to play a significant role in these activities.

4.5 Long-term reference sites

Environmental processes often act over very long time periods and the effect of human activities may not be noticed for several years or decades. Furthermore, natural changes may evolve over hundreds of years. There is a need to take a long-term perspective if sustainable development is to be achieved and if long-term changes are to be detected. This section looks at existing monitoring.

The National Monitoring Programme has been running since the early 1990s and was designed specifically to address the need for long-term monitoring of water quality in marine waters. To date only a spatial survey has been done, but the programme offers to provide the backbone of long-term coastal and marine pollution monitoring in the UK (Marine Pollution Monitoring Management Group, 1998a). At present, the only long-term information comes from site-specific studies across the country. We have drawn on these to look further back in time.

Long-term sediment quality

Saltmarshes accumulate sediments under normal conditions. Over time, a build-up of sediments can occur along with any contaminants bound to them, and cores from these can provide a very useful long-term record of water quality and contamination in estuaries and coasts.

Over the past 120 years metals accumulated in the saltmarsh sediments of the Mersey Estuary have shown elevated concentrations in response to increased mining or industrial activity (Figure 4.50). Mercury levels in recent Mersey sediments, from 1974 to 1997, show a decline as a direct response to changes in industrial activity and improved regulation of industry and clean-up of effluents (Figure 4.51).

Metal levels in sediment cores from elsewhere show a similar picture. In Swansea Bay levels of zinc, copper and lead in

Figure 4.50   *Concentrations of metals at Widnes Warth, in the Mersey Estuary*

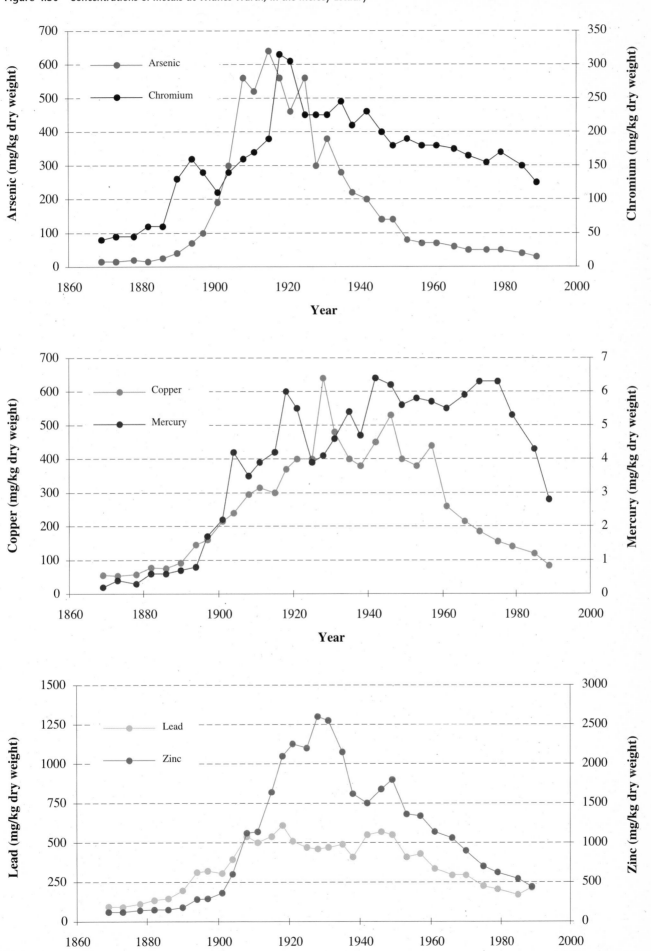

Source: Environment Agency

Figure 4.51 *Mercury contamination of Mersey Estuary sediments, 1974 to 1997*

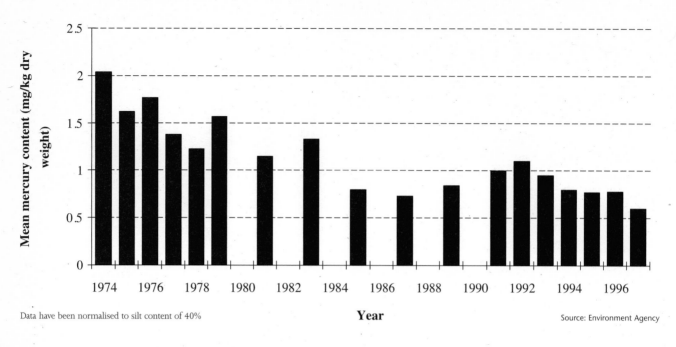

Data have been normalised to silt content of 40%

Source: Environment Agency

Figure 4.52 *Metal contamination of Swansea Bay sediments in the 19th and 20th centuries*

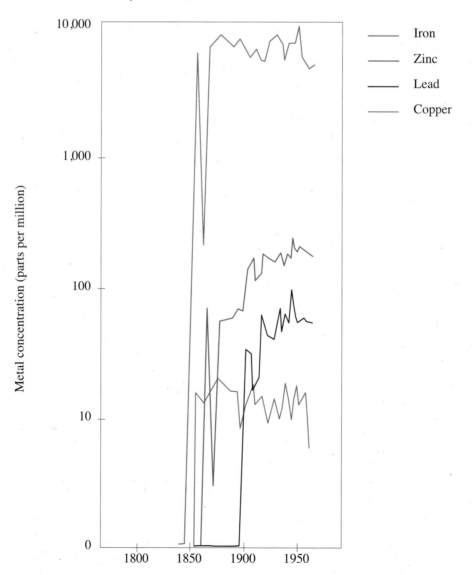

Source: Clifton and Hamilton, 1979; Academic Press

Figure 4.53 *Southampton Water sediment contamination from 1950 to 1989*

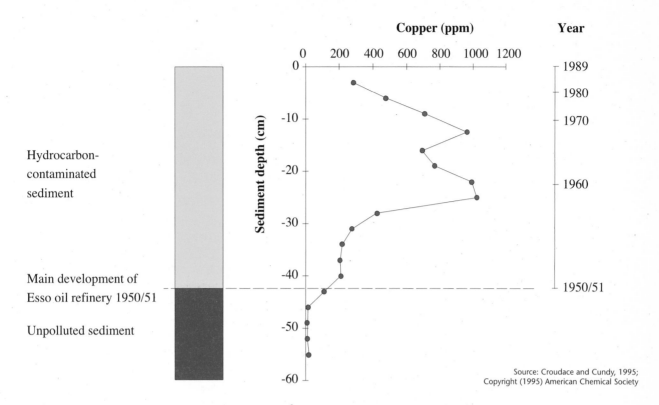

sediments can be traced back several hundred years but show a rapid increase from the mid-19th century onwards (Figure 4.52) (Clifton and Hamilton, 1979; Allen and Rae, 1986). In Southampton Water the sediment record shows pollution following the expansion of Fawley oil refinery in 1949 to 1951 and the first appearance of hydrocarbon contamination (Figure 4.53) (Croudace and Cundy, 1995), although the clean-up since 1970 is also very evident.

Long-term water quality

There are very few long-term data sets of water quality in estuaries and coastal waters. Those that exist are from isolated sites or they have been collected over relatively short periods, leaving us without a coherent unbroken long-term record of coastal water quality. Some estuaries have been monitored more or less continuously for the past five decades and these data show large improvements in water quality as measured by sanitary determinands (ammonia, dissolved oxygen and BOD), which reflect the huge efforts that have been put into cleaning up industrial and sewage discharges since the Second World War. The Thames (Figure 3.29) and the Mersey (Figure 3.30) estuaries are good examples.

The University of Liverpool has maintained a monitoring station at the Port Erin Marine Laboratory in the central Irish Sea since 1954. The data from this station show that nutrient concentrations have risen steadily from the 1950s to the 1990s and that chlorophyll-a concentrations at the time of the main bloom have increased since the mid-1960s (Figure 4.54). These data show clearly that the influence of increases in nutrient inputs can be observed well away from the major sources (Allen *et al.*, 1998).

Long-term plankton data

The Sir Alister Hardy Foundation for Ocean Science collects and holds data on plankton community composition and relative species abundance in the North Sea and North Atlantic since the 1930s. These data are collected using the Continuous Plankton Recorder, which is a high-speed plankton sampler designed to be towed from commercially operated 'ships of opportunity' over long distances. The plankton survey methodology has changed a little over time but comparable data exist for zooplankton from 1948 to the present day and for phytoplankton from 1958 to the present day. By 1994 Continuous Plankton Recorders had been towed for over six million kilometres, resulting in the acquisition of over 160,000 samples (Warner and Hays, 1994).

Although the plankton data are collected at a distance from the coast they show long-term trends in important biological parameters which characterise the marine environment that surrounds the British Isles and which impinge on coastal waters. For example, 'phytoplankton colour', a coarse index of the level of chlorophyll-a in water samples, has been increasing in the North Sea. The sea has been getting 'greener' since 1960, with a much longer season of elevated phytoplankton colour since 1988.

There has been a declining trend in most of the zooplankton from 1948 and the majority of phytoplankton taxa since 1958, in the north east Atlantic and North Sea. In these seas zooplankton numbers have declined substantially over the last 35 years. There have also been studies which have successfully correlated changes in plankton variables, measured by the Continuous Plankton Recorder, to changes in the Gulf Stream and the North Atlantic Oscillation. The driving forces and

135

Figure 4.54 *Long-term nutrient concentrations in the Irish Sea*

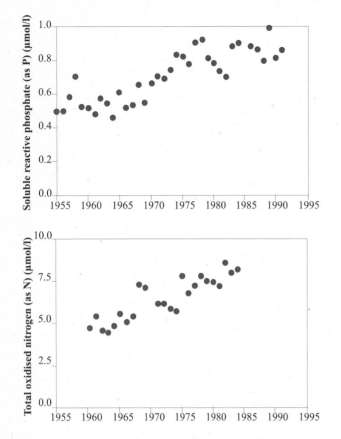

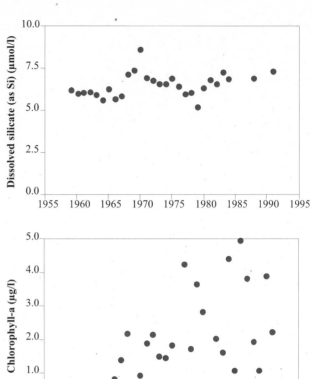

Median nutrient concentrations for January and February and median chlorophyll-a concentrations for May and June

Source: Port Erin Marine Laboratory, University of Liverpool

mechanisms behind these and other phenomena are still being researched (Sir Alister Hardy Foundation for Ocean Science, 1995).

There is still clearly a need to develop sensible long-term reference sites for the principal concern affecting our coastline - that of climate change.

4.6 Aesthetic quality

The aesthetic quality of the coastal environment is what is most readily seen, heard or smelt and as such ranks highly in the public's perception of overall quality. Issues such as the amount of litter, the presence of an intrusive odour and the general look and feel of a place are often the first things that users of the coastal environment notice. Therefore aesthetic quality is an important indicator of the state of the coastal environment. The tourist industry in the UK is very important and so the aesthetic quality of the coastal environment is not only of interest in itself but can also have a large local economic impact. For example, if coastal areas are polluted or badly littered tourists will either move away to other areas or go abroad. The Agency is working with other organisations on schemes for assessing the aesthetic quality of the coastal environment and is working towards solutions to control marine litter, for example, through both enforcement of legislation and education. A major on-going initiative is the development of a standard protocol to be used by any organisation for assessing and classifying beach litter pollution.

Figure 4.55 *Sources of litter in the 1997 Beachwatch Campaign*

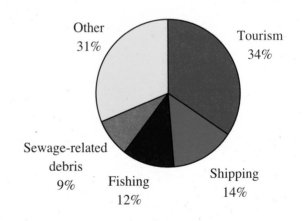

Number of items = 262,349
Length surveyed = 169km
Mean items/km = 1,554

Source: Marine Conservation Society

In 1997, assessments of the type and quantity of beach litter were made by several organisations who are testing a national protocol for monitoring litter on a consistent basis. The assessment considers the amount of sewage-related debris, harmful litter, oil deposits and non-human faeces present among other types of litter and then classifies the beaches as A (very good), B (good), C (fair) or D (bad). It is too early to publish any results and the protocol still needs finalising. Full details are given in Appendix 4.

A litter survey in 1997, which covered 169km of beach, collected about 19 tonnes of litter and found an average of 1,554 items per km of beach (Marine Conservation Society, 1997). Most of the items collected were plastic (57 per cent) and the main sources were found to be tourists, shipping and fishing (Figure 4.55).

The Tidy Britain Group Seaside Award scheme is based on the assessment of beaches for their cleanliness, water quality, provision of proper safety and first aid facilities, access for the disabled, control of dogs and free public information. Beaches given the award must meet all of the above requirements. In 1997, 224 beaches were given the award, an increase of 21 on 1996. The scheme provides an assessment of the trend in the aesthetic quality of the coastal environment in that an increasing number of awards is a good indicator of an improved environment for the public. Europe also has the Blue Flag scheme based on good water quality and the provision of standard facilities to the public. The number of Blue Flags awarded to UK beaches has increased over the past few years from 18 in 1995 to 38 in 1997 (Hampson, 1997). Again, the increasing number of Blue Flags is an indicator of the improved aesthetic state of the coastal environment.

Environmental impact of marine litter

The thousands of tonnes of waste discarded into the marine environment every year has a detrimental aesthetic impact, and also has direct impacts on marine life. Animals can become entangled in discarded fishing nets or die after ingestion of waste material. It has been estimated that worldwide over one million birds and up to 100,000 marine mammals die every year from entanglement or ingestion of plastic materials. The litter also affects the benthic flora and fauna by smothering the seabed with waste material, preventing light and oxygen reaching benthic organisms and interfering with the feeding of species which graze the seabed. There is also the potential risk of poisoning by leachates from the debris, either by direct ingestion or slow bioaccumulation in the food chain. Microscopic plastic fragments in marine sediments may have an impact on the environment, either by altering habitat or through toxic effects in the food chain. Up to 10,000 plastic particles of around 0.1mm in diameter per litre of sand have been found in some areas (Thompson and Hoare, 1997).

4.7 Summary of the state of coastal waters

(Please refer to table overleaf)

Table 4.9 *Summary of the state of the coastal environment*

Viewpoint	State	Comments and trends
Land use and environmental resources	**Land cover:** within 10km coastal strip includes agriculture (61 per cent) and development (11 per cent). Natural and semi-natural uses represent 16 per cent. Urban areas are increasing	Decreases in saltmarsh and intertidal areas. Better estimates of land use and land use change are required for managing development pressures
	Coastal defences: 40 per cent of sea defence elements show some signs of wear and 12 per cent need moderate or significant work. Forty per cent of coastal protection elements need moderate or significant work	One-third of the coastline is protected by artificial or semi-natural defences
	Energy resources: oil and gas reserves have been roughly constant over time, new areas close to shore are being explored	Oil and gas exploration and production near to shore carry greater risks for the coastal environment. Concerns about the siting of wind farms. Use of alternative energy sources set to increase
Key biological populations, communities and biodiversity	**Coast lands:** rich and diverse habitats with one-fifth of scarce or rare plants. Natterjack toads extinct in Wales and very limited in England	Coastal habitats are vulnerable to development and recreational pressures
	Invertebrates: distribution reflects oceanography and habitat availability (33 estuarine community types)	Estuaries are important locations. Threats include pollution, nutrient enrichment, habitat removal and bait digging. Trends unknown
	Fish: most commercial fish populations are at low levels through overfishing. Decline in eels and salmon is unexplained. Threatened species include sturgeon, twaite shad, allis shad and many commercial species	Major factors are over-exploitation and loss of habitat. Improvements in water quality have meant re-introduction of salmon to many rivers
	Birds: populations thriving (waders, wildfowl, some seabirds), many are internationally important. Also some seabirds are declining (herring gull, great black-backed gull, roseate tern, common tern)	Human intervention has been important: cessation of hunting and egg collecting, increase in food supply, habitat management
	Mammals: population status is uncertain for many cetaceans and seals. Human impacts are thought to be limited: 2,000 common seals and 10,000 grey seals in England and Wales	Better information is needed on population estimates. Common seals suffered setback in 1988 virus epidemic. Populations of seals perhaps increasing, but poor information
	Threatened species: 20 coastal species have Biodiversity Action Plans so far, 21 significant coastal habitats identified	Action plans being developed by various organisations. Sand lizards have declined to a population of only 5,000
Compliance with environmental standards and targets	**Bathing waters:** In 1998, 90.4 per cent of waters passed imperative standards, 36.1 per cent passed guideline standards	Substantial improvement since 1988. More investment yet to impact on bathing waters. Problems at individual sites under investigation
	Dangerous substances: six sites failed (three per cent) for List I substances in 1997; 39 failures (18 per cent of sites) for List II. Copper accounts for most of these but zinc and tributyl tin significant too	Improved compliance with List I substances, but numbers of List II failures rising
	Titanium dioxide: no failures since 1988	
	Shellfish water quality: 21 failing samples in 1997 at five (28 per cent of all) shellfish waters	Copper, zinc and nickel are among the main causes of failure

	Shellfish hygiene: in 1997, one-quarter of sites required extensive purification of shellfish before consumption	
	Radioactivity: overall exposure from environmental materials is insubstantial and seafood is radiologically safe to consume	Proposed reductions in discharge limits at Sellafield. Technetium-99 increasing in biota around Sellafield
	Estuary classification: in 1995, 92 per cent of estuaries, by length, were good or fair	The existing classification scheme is subjective. A new scheme is needed
	Non-statutory monitoring: most waters and sediments have low concentrations of contaminants. Higher levels occur near historic or known sources of pollution	For some compounds present monitoring is inadequate to allow risks to be quantified. The National Monitoring Programme is addressing this
The health of the environment	**Eutrophication:** five estuaries are designated eutrophic sensitive areas. Algal blooms occur in many coastal areas (for example the Irish Sea)	Need a better understanding of how nutrient enrichment can lead to eutrophication in estuaries. Algal monitoring needs improving
	Shellfish poisoning: shellfisheries are closed periodically but no recorded incidents of human poisoning in recent years	Shellfish toxins are frequently detected in the summer along the north east and south west coasts
	Bioaccumulation: metal contamination is not widespread, although there are higher concentrations in historically polluted estuaries and TBT impacts are still evident. PCBs, PAHs and some pesticides are found in many species around the coast, but mostly at low concentrations	Monitoring for some organic substances is very sparse and the effects on biota are still poorly understood. More research needed
	Endocrine disruption: partial TBT ban leading to slow recovery in small boat areas, not in shipping areas. Feminisation of male flounder in estuaries a recent discovery. Population scale effects unknown	There is a need for a TBT ban for all ships. A four-year research project on endocrine disruption in the marine environment has just started
	Ecotoxicology: many bioassays confirm presence of known pollutants in historically polluted estuaries. Poor mussel scope for growth in some areas is unexplained	Bioassays monitoring the coastal environment are relatively new. New techniques and monitoring methods are being developed and should extend knowledge
Long-term reference sites	**Sediment quality:** sediment cores show increases in pollution with industrialisation and growth of road traffic, but reverse in some trends since 1970s	Metals, pesticides and PAHs in sediments arose from industrialisation and intensification of agriculture. Regulation has helped to reduce these inputs
	Water quality: improvements have been achieved in many areas through investment and regulation	Some evidence to show nutrients increasing in Irish Sea
	Plankton: structure of offshore plankton communities has changed in this century. More chlorophyll-a, less zooplankton and fewer groups of phytoplankton	Reasons are unknown but there are links to long-term climatic and oceanographic factors
Aesthetic quality	**Aesthetic quality:** In 1997, 224 beaches gained Tidy Britain Group Seaside Award, 38 gained Blue Flags. Most litter items were plastic and mainly came from tourists, shipping and fishing	Increased number of beaches with awards. Litter can kill animals, is unsightly and can cause a health risk

Section 5   Responding to the state of the coasts

This section looks at what has been done by various economic sectors, regulators and authorities to manage the pressure of human activities on coasts. Most efforts to reduce pressures involve investment, so the section looks at how much has been spent on taking action and gives a description of the actions already taken. Details of planned investment and actions are also given, where known. Some actions, of course, are not readily quantifiable in terms of monetary cost but can help to reduce pressures, for example voluntary action by conservation groups and waste minimisation. Education and information create an awareness of the issues that threaten sustainable development and should also elicit a response from society. Such a response is hard to measure, as are the benefits of better access to information.

Much of the emphasis in this section is on pollution control and coastal defence because expenditure on these items dominates the others. Information on investment by the water industry has been collated by the regulator of the water industry, OFWAT, since privatisation and so is readily available. OFWAT is also responsible for approving the investment plans of the water companies. All water industry costs from OFWAT have been adjusted to a 1997/98 price base. Later in the section, the expenditure and actions by the fishing and other industries (including the tourist industry) and others on the coastal environment is considered, but investment information has been less easy to collate from these sectors and may be incomplete.

The section then looks at the effectiveness of the overall management of the coastal zone. Because of the diverse range of relevant human activities, there is a need for integrated management and planning if development and use is to be sustainable. This need is widely recognised and various organisations have been working together to produce management plans for the coastal zone. We look at the range of plans that have been and are still being produced and opportunities for further collaboration between organisations working in the coastal zone in order to achieve sustainable development.

The final part of the section looks at how society values the coastal environment. This is difficult to assess but we have compiled several sources of information that relate to this. The results of studies that have investigated how much society is willing to pay for improvements to the coastal environment are also summarised.

5.1   Pollution abatement by the water industry

Investment by the water industry has risen dramatically since 1989 and is now roughly double the average of the 1980s (OFWAT, 1998a). This is leading to substantial improvements in quality as shown in Section 4. Over the past decade or so there have been three main drivers for investment by the water industry at coastal works:

● the need to ensure compliance with the EC Bathing Waters Directive (76/160/EEC);

● the need to phase out the dumping of sewage sludge at sea by 1998 as agreed at the Oslo and Paris Convention in 1992 and specified in the Urban Waste Water Treatment Directive (91/971/EEC);

● the need to improve estuarine quality to meet water quality objectives.

Since 1991 there has also been:

● the need to comply with the requirements of the EC Urban Waste Water Treatment Directive (91/271/EEC) in a phased way with full compliance by the year 2005;

● the need to plan investment to comply with new proposals or modifications to existing Directives and UK regulations.

The capital expenditure to meet these needs are shown in Table 5.1. The reporting categories have changed over the years, so that some used in the early 1990s no longer exist and other categories have been added. The categories for the earlier time

Table 5.1   *Water industry capital expenditure since 1990/91 on sewerage services*

Reason for expenditure		1990/91 to 1994/95 £million	1995/96 to 1997/98 £million
Bathing waters compliance		820	670
Sewage sludge disposal		310	443
Long-term estuarine quality objectives		210	N/A
Other sea outfalls		106	N/A
Urban Waste Water Treatment	- continuous discharges	N/A	597
	- intermittent discharges	N/A	66
Total		**1,446**	**1,776**

Source: OFWAT, 1995 and 1998b; adjusted to 1997/98 price base

period do not include expenditure to reduce the impact of storm overflows (intermittent discharges), unless this was needed to meet any other objectives, such as bathing water compliance or estuarine objectives.

Some £312 million was spent on storm overflows over the earlier period but it is not known what proportion of these discharged to the coastal environment as opposed to fresh waters, although it is likely to be small. There are significant regional differences in the spend - North West and South West Regions have seen the greatest spend on bathing waters, and Thames the greatest spend on sewage sludge. Full details are given in Appendix 5. All the major drivers for investment are now considered in more depth.

Bathing waters

A question that can be posed is "has this money been well spent and what remains to be done?" Almost half has been spent on bathing waters. We have shown in Section 4.3 that the number of bathing waters consistently complying over a three-year period with mandatory coliform bacteria standards has risen from 57 per cent in 1988/90 to 77 per cent in 1996/98. Only three per cent now fail consistently compared with 13 per cent in 1988/90. But compliance is still not good enough and some of the schemes which were designed to remedy problems have not been entirely successful. Sea outfalls were abandoned at the rate of about 20 per year over the period 1991 to 1994, with only eight new sea outfalls per year being commissioned on average (Water Services Association, 1996). In 1995 there were still about 471,000 'population equivalents' served by unsatisfactory sea outfalls, the largest problem being in the north west (OFWAT, 1996). But this is a reduction of 10,000 on the previous year. Improvements are expected to continue as all coastal outfalls serving equivalent populations above 10,000 are required to comply with the Directive, which invariably means the construction of new or upgraded treatment works. Some companies have decided to install tertiary sewage treatment, such as ultra-violet disinfection or microfiltration, at some sites in order to meet the requirements. Thirty-five discharges now receive ultra-violet treatment. Such plants are expensive to run. Figures suggest that about £18 million per year is spent by water companies in maintaining and operating all plant to ensure bathing water compliance (OFWAT, 1998b)

The Agency is very concerned about the continuing poor levels of compliance at certain sites. Exceedances of EC Directive coliform bacteria standards appear to be continuing due to a combination of point source sewage inputs, operation of storm overflows during wet weather, diffuse inputs from farm pollution and riverine sources impacting on the coast, including plumes from the estuaries. The Agency has carried out two major projects to investigate bacterial loads impacting the coast in the north west. These have shown that the Ribble estuary in the North West Region receives about 89 per cent of its total coliform input from rivers during high flow (11 per cent during low flows). In total, sewage treatment works contribute about 42 per cent of the total faecal coliform loading to the estuary, and 14 per cent derives from combined sewer overflows. The balance is derived from riverine sources, which include diffuse and point sources of coliforms in the catchment,

so expenditure on coastal sewage works cannot necessarily ensure bathing water compliance (Fewtrell et al., 1998). In the North West Region as a whole, of the 17 non-compliant bathing waters in 1997 16 have completed remedial schemes and there are no further schemes outstanding, giving some idea of the extent of the problem (13 bathing waters were non-compliant in the North West Region in 1998). Where point source discharges are known to be causing problems the Agency is pursuing improvements, and where reasons for exceedances are not known investigations are continuing and considerable additional money is being spent to identify the causes and clean up the bathing waters in the North West. In addition discussions are taking place with North West Water over inconsistent operation of ultra violet disinfection at two sewage treatment works.

At the end of 2000, following completion of outstanding Bathing Water and major Urban Waste Water Treatment Directive schemes which have been funded through the second asset management programme of the water companies, the Agency estimates that:

● the annual level of compliance with imperative coliform bacteria standards will be about 94 per cent;

● some 85 per cent of bathing waters are expected to comply consistently with imperative coliform bacteria standards every year;

● about three per cent of bathing waters will remain at high risk of non-compliance with imperative coliform bacteria standards.

Another 49 waters (11 per cent) are at an estimated risk of failure of one in five years or less. Details of specific sites are given in Appendix 6. The Government considers that these performance levels are not acceptable and that water charge payers would support action to bring further improvement. It has asked the Agency to devise an action programme to raise consistent compliance with imperative standards to at least 97 per cent by 2005 and to achieve a significant improvement in compliance with guideline standards, particularly at major holiday resorts (DETR and Welsh Office, 1998).

In order to understand why there are still a number of bathing waters at risk, despite the investment programmes undertaken by the water companies, it is necessary to examine the sources of microbiological contamination that can contribute to failures to meet the standards, both imperative and guideline, of the Directive. This will help to establish what can practicably be done in future to manage and minimise the risk of further non-compliance.

Strategy to meet the standards

The Agency's bathing waters strategy addresses the most persistent imperative coliform bacteria standard compliance failures, secures 'no deterioration' of bathing water quality and makes a move towards guideline coliform bacteria standard compliance. The Agency uses its powers under the statutory provisions to ensure compliance with imperative values. While circumstances might arise in which it will be impossible in practice to secure compliance, any failure to achieve a mandatory standard must be rectified as quickly as possible and considerations of cost do not provide a justification for delay in achieving compliance.

But there is also a need to consider the coliform bacteria standards described as 'guideline' values in the Directive which are not mandatory standards, and this is recognised in the statutory provisions. The Agency will endeavour to respect these values as guidelines and, where guideline values are already achieved, will ensure their maintenance under its 'no deterioration' policy. In 1997 some 37 per cent met these guideline standards; this is expected to rise to 47 per cent by the end of 2000 and 50 per cent by 2005. Factors which might inhibit the Agency in securing compliance with guideline values are environmental criteria, physical impossibility and other practical problems, where the cost of surmounting such problems are disproportionate to the degree of improvement in the relevant environmental standard which is likely to be achieved. This is because of the many and diffuse sources of microbial contamination that affect bathing waters. Costs may be taken into account in this respect because guideline values are not mandatory standards, in contrast to the position for imperative values.

In order to ensure compliance with the mandatory and guideline standards the Agency is:

- investigating the occurrence and distribution of enteroviruses and salmonellae in sewage and in the environment;

- investigating monitoring and analytical methodology;

- undertaking research into the reliability and efficacy of sewage treatment techniques;

- developing clear and transparent consenting techniques.

During the period 2000 to 2005 the Agency is seeking to achieve the following actions in relation to bathing waters identified in England and Wales for the purposes of the Directive:

- implementation of the mandatory requirements of the Bathing Waters Directive;

- ensuring that improvement schemes are compliant with the Agency's Bathing Water Policy and are therefore protective of enterovirus and salmonellae standards;

- where the guideline standards have already been achieved, ensuring that we are confident in the effectiveness of the action. This requires full consideration of all potential sources of impact such as:

    i   continuous sewage discharges and combined sewer overflows;

    ii private discharges and diffuse sources, such as agricultural inputs, which are outside the influence of the water companies' investment programmes.

These actions may be achieved not only by improvement works identified under the Bathing Waters Directive in the water companies' investment programmes but also by improvements undertaken to combined sewer overflows and sewage-works as part of the Urban Waste Water Treatment Directive (UWWTD) and the Shellfish Waters Directive. With these actions, compliance with the imperative standards are expected to reach 96 per cent.

We have already shown how about £1.5 billion was spent on improving bathing waters over the period 1990/91 to 1997/98, which amounts to about £9 per household per year. An estimate of a further £93 million may be spent by 1999/2000. In the current round of planning water company investment a further £10 million may be needed over the period 2000/01 to 2004/05, all for improvements at sewage works (OFWAT, 1998a). In total, over the period 1990/91 to 2004/05 about £1.6 billion may have been spent on compliance with the Bathing Waters Directive.

A proportion of the spend on unsatisfactory storm overflows, where improvement will reduce background microbiological levels in rivers and streams, may indirectly affect compliance with imperative standards but will definitely impact on guideline compliance. These unsatisfactory storm overflows are also included for improvement in the investment programmes; estimated costs are given later in the section.

Water companies have also estimated the cost of any new designations of bathing waters and of targeted investment related to the endeavour to observe the guidance values in the Directive, at £210 million capital expenditure with £7 million operating cost over the period 2000/2005 (OFWAT, 1998a).

Use of bathing waters outside the bathing season

Another issue that is often raised is the use of bathing waters outside the 'normal' season. There is evidence of a steady increase in the number of water contact users outside the bathing season. Debate as to whether the current narrow definition of bathers should be extended to include other water contact sports continues. In 1994 the European Commission published proposals for a revised Bathing Waters Directive. In 1996 the European Parliament recommended that the proposed revision should be amended to include all recreational waters, but it is now up for further review. The Agency is increasingly being requested to monitor the quality of EC bathing waters outside the bathing season of 15 May to 30 September, and while a limited number of sites are monitored outside the bathing season, these data are not used for compliance assessment.

When the water quality at bathing waters is improved, either from improvements to nearby sewage discharges or by other pollution prevention measures, there are likely to be improvements to water quality outside the bathing season. This is because conventional sewage treatment is operated year-round. In addition, where disinfection is provided, the Agency's policy states that, for long-term use, disinfection will be required over the whole year except where there are no clear benefits in maintaining the dosing and application system continuously. Seasonal disinfection may be acceptable where the discharger has demonstrated to the Agency that there are no clear benefits to ecological or human interests in maintaining the dosing and application system continuously. In most cases disinfection operates all year.

Meeting new Directives and changes to existing ones

Urban Waste Water Treatment Directive

The implementation of this Directive is expected to improve sewage treatment for 30 million people, many of whom live in coastal areas, by the end of the century. Improvements are required both to continuous discharges (that is the level of treatment provided by sewage treatment works) and storm overflows. So far £663 million has been spent on improving continuous and intermittent discharges from the sewerage system to estuaries and coastal waters to meet the requirements of the legislation (OFWAT, 1998b). The estimated spend over the years 1998/99 and 1999/2000 is £1,058 million, giving a total of £1,721 million by the year 2000. Most of the investment on continuous discharges should be complete by the year 2000. Original estimates to meet the Urban Waste Water Treatment Directive at sewage works discharging to the coast assumed that many areas would be deemed high natural dispersion areas. The Government has subsequently announced its intention to remove the high natural dispersion area designations. OFWAT estimates that this will increase the cost of meeting the Directive by £360 million in capital expenditure, and £18 million in annual operating costs (OFWAT, 1998a).

There are also five estuaries designated as eutrophic sensitive areas under the Directive. These require more stringent treatment of large discharges into the areas, at an estimated cost of £3.6 million. Most of this is for nutrient removal from discharges to the Fal and Taw estuaries; other areas will be improved by investment costed for other reasons.

Unsatisfactory storm overflows

Dealing with unsatisfactory storm overflows to improve aesthetic quality will help meet bathing water standards in many areas but is also a requirement of the Urban Waste Water Treatment Directive. The percentage of unsatisfactory combined sewer overflows is falling as the planned investment programme of the water companies is realised. Improvements are expected to accelerate until the year 2000 (OFWAT, 1996) and as shown already some £66 million has been spent on these in coastal and estuarine areas so far. The Periodic Review in 1994 allowed £1 billion to rectify 60 per cent of the problems over the 10-year period 1995 to 2005. In the current Periodic Review, estimates suggest that £900 million is needed to complete this work across England and Wales over the period 2000 to 2015. This amounts to about £3 to £4 per household (OFWAT, 1998a). There is no breakdown of estimated expenditure on overflows affecting coastal regions, but data suggest that about five per cent of unsatisfactory overflows discharge to estuaries or coasts. We have assumed that five per cent of the expenditure, that is £45 million, will be allocated to these, in the absence of any other knowledge about specific schemes.

Sewage sludge disposal

In 1995/96 some 17 per cent of sewage sludge generated was dumped at sea but water companies have needed to invest in other options with the need to phase out sewage sludge dumping by the end of 1998 (Water Services Association, 1996). Incinerators have been built on the Thames Estuary, at a cost of £165 million, to deal with sewage sludge from the London sewage works. They generate 13.5 MW of electricity. Another incinerator is being built at Widnes in Cheshire, at a cost of £100 million, to treat sewage sludge from Merseyside and Manchester. Discharges from these plants may raise temperatures and metal concentrations locally in estuaries, the ash will also contain these residues, and nitrogen oxides will be emitted to the air. But the load is a lot less than was previously dumped at sea, so the overall impact of the investment has been to reduce inputs of hazardous substances into coastal waters. Other works are disposing of their sewage sludge on land and this may be up to 50 per cent of the sewage sludge generated. The level of metal accumulation in soil is limited by standards. The Agency regulates this process by enforcing the Sludge (Use in Agriculture) Regulations 1989 and is working to ensure that the standards and methods applied protect the environment. It is also involved in a research project looking at the safety of the current limits.

Sewage sludge spreading on agricultural land has raised concerns about the risk of pathogen transfer to the food chain, and retailers are pressing for improved sewage sludge treatment standards. Wessex Water now dry the sewage sludge that was previously sent to sea from Avonmouth. It intends to dry 90 per cent of all its sewage sludge arisings by the year 2002. The granules are largely used for soil improvement. Other water companies are also investing in sewage sludge driers. There has also been investment in other novel solutions such as sewage sludge gasification schemes which can produce electricity. Other solutions are to use the dried materials as light-weight aggregates. The issue of sewage sludge will be looked at more comprehensively in our next report on the state of the land.

Overall, some 23 per cent (£753 million) of the capital investment by water companies in the eight-year period 1990/91 to 1997/98 was on sewage sludge disposal. The planned spend for 1998/99 and 1999/2000 is £297 million and a further £160 million capital and £13 million operating costs over the time period 2000 to 2005 may be required (OFWAT, 1998a). This gives a total of £1.2 billion capital investment on sewage sludge disposal over the 15 years from 1990.

Other Directives

Changes to the implementation of the Shellfish Waters Directive in the UK were the subject of consultation in 1998 (Appendix 1). The costs associated to ensure compliance with the new designations cannot be assessed with any certainty, but it has been estimated that they could be as high as £50 million over the period 2000/01 to 2004/05 (OFWAT, 1998a).

In the on-going Periodic Review there have also been some estimates made of the costs of improvements to effluent discharges to meet the Habitats Directive and resolve problems caused at SSSIs. These are estimated at some £50 million over the period 2000/01 to 2004/05 (OFWAT, 1998a). They cover freshwater and coastal discharges, and so we have assumed some 10 per cent (£5 million) are relevant here but these figures are very uncertain.

Costing has also been estimated by OFWAT for meeting the Water Resources Framework Directive after the year 2005. It suggests a cost of between £1.6 billion and £4.8 billion (OFWAT, 1998a). Some of this should bring about improvements to the coastal environment.

It is clear from this information that compliance with European Directives has been and continues to be a driving force to improve the quality of the coastal environment. But there have been local initiatives too, which are now described.

Long-term estuarine quality

Non-statutory estuarine water quality objectives have been set since the 1970s and many water companies have had long-term programmes over the years to meet them, even though there has not been any statutory need to improve estuary quality. Some 15 per cent of the water company investment in the five years 1990 to 1994 was allocated to long-term estuarine improvements, £210 million in total. The national classification scheme for estuaries has not detected any significant improvement from this investment (Section 4.3) but that is more likely to reflect the inadequacies of the classification scheme rather than lack of actual estuarine improvement. Other assessments - using continuous water quality monitors as shown in Figure 3.29 and biological information, such as salmon returning to the Tyne - show that many estuaries have improved significantly. Furthermore, many sewage works discharging to estuaries are large, so any improvements to them will cost much more than is required for smaller works discharging to fresh waters. For example, Beckton sewage treatment works which serves part of London treats more sewage than all the works in Wales and the south west combined. Some of the large London works have installed better screening to improve aesthetic quality; again this is not reflected in any of the current monitoring data.

In the second investment programme of the water companies which was agreed in 1994, £586 million was allocated to specific environmental schemes for investment over the period 1995 to 1999. These were schemes for specific enhancement, above those required to meet statutory needs. Some £108 million of this sum was for schemes which will bring about improvements in the coastal environment (OFWAT, 1994).

5.2 Pollution abatement by others

Industry

Many of the most technically complex and potentially most polluting industrial processes are located on coasts and estuaries. Standards specified in their authorisations are set by the Agency and reviewed from time to time, with

improvements driven by either international agreements, such as the need to reduce carbon dioxide emissions, or by local needs.

In 1994 about £1.1 billion was spent by industry (excluding the water industry) on the treatment of effluents to water, of which £360 million was capital and £743 million operating costs (figures adjusted to a 1997/98 price base). The largest proportion of this expenditure was by the chemical industry (ECOTEC, 1996). Some 12 per cent of capital spending in the chemical industry was related to environmental protection, although it is not known what proportion of this relates to coastal waters and what proportion to other media (Chemical Industries Association, 1996). Dumping at sea of industrial waste has been prohibited since 1992, following substantial investment by industry to develop alternative methods for recycling waste and disposal on land.

There has been a requirement under the Oslo and Paris Commission for oil refineries to reduce the amount of oil in any discharges to water from their sites to 5mg/l (annual average). This has improved the aesthetic quality around their sites and led to improvements in plant diversity in some locations. Refineries have also reduced their sulphur emissions to air by 18 per cent between 1970 and 1995. The cost to refineries of minimising environmental impacts is about £250 million per year (UK Petroleum Industries Association, pers. comm.), which includes both capital and operating costs. The significant achievement of reducing metal loads to the North Sea, as outlined in Section 3.4, was partly achieved by the tightening of conditions in discharge consents and authorisations of industry. This is a notable success, but there is no information to say how much it has cost. Some substances have been reduced because of industrial process changes or by substitution of materials, but it is not known how much this has cost to achieve. There are cases where 'better housekeeping', and waste minimisation has cleaned up effluents with knock-on benefits for the overall costs of industry.

In the north east there had been a long-standing practice of dumping waste from collieries at sea but this was stopped in 1993, and disposal onto beaches was stopped in 1995, since when a limited amount of minestone material has been licensed for use as an interim coast defence measure. The collieries south of the River Tyne have closed completely. One remains to the north of the River Tyne and this still discharges watery waste to the sea but it has to comply with a new standard for solids in its consent, which has required a £150,000 treatment plant to be installed. There is also a Millennium-funded project to reinstate the coastline which had been affected by past practices, including the clean-up of derelict structures on cliff tops. This is costing £3.3 million which covers removing debris and structures, developing the recreation potential and monitoring (East Durham Task Force, 1995).

In 1998, there was an agreement made at the Ministerial meeting of the Oslo and Paris Commission to continuously reduce discharges, emissions and losses of hazardous substances and radioactive substances, and to prohibit the dumping of all steel installations in the sea with certain derogations (Appendix

1). The cost of meeting these agreements by the target dates set are unknown.

Ports and shipping

The Government has launched a major initiative to cut pollution from all commercial and leisure craft using UK ports. The International Maritime Organization (IMO) is considering recommending that all coastal states take similar steps. All UK ports - including harbours, marinas and terminals - are now required under the Merchant Shipping (Port Waste Reception Facilities) Regulations 1997 to draw up plans to demonstrate they have complied with their duty to ensure that appropriate facilities are available to take waste produced by sea-going vessels. Ports had to submit a waste management plan to Government by 30 September 1998. The International Convention for the Prevention of Pollution from ships (MARPOL 73/78) regulates the types and amounts of wastes that may be discharged at sea. It prohibits the discharge of plastics. In the North Sea, which is a special area, it prohibits the discharge of all garbage waste except food waste. From 1999 a new special area covering all of the UK coast will impose a virtual ban on discharges of oil. The MARPOL discharge regulations apply to all vessels operating in the marine environment, irrespective of size. However, not all ships are operated in compliance with the regulations. This is demonstrated by the fact that some wastes washed up on UK beaches can be traced back to shipping. By improving the provision and use of waste reception facilities in port, the 1997 Regulations should improve the situation.

Since 1986 tributyl tin, an antifouling paint, has been banned from use on small boats, with a consequent improvement in the status of dog whelks and other bivalve molluscs in some areas, which were suffering from sub-lethal effects. Many boat-yards and manufacturers have had to change their operating procedures and substances used. The use of tributyl tin is still allowed on large vessels (over 25m in length) although the International Maritime Organization's marine environmental protection committee has recommended a ban on the application of tributyl tin paints from 2003, and its removal from all ships by 2008. One problem with the proposal to use alternative anti-foulants is the effectiveness of alternatives, the likely high costs and potential pollution problems. Among the alternatives to tributyl tin, copper-based biocides are used in the highest quantities. The Agency is investigating the use of alternative antifouling agents and their potential to cause pollution (WRc, 1998).

In Section 3 we have shown how dredging is essential in many places to maintain navigation routes into ports and harbours. There are some examples of costs. Dredging requirements at both Harwich and on the Tees cost over £1 million per year, at Rye £45,000, at Holyhead £17,500 and at Salcombe £2,000 per year (DoE, 1995a). The national total is unknown, although one estimate suggests £75 million per year (Hydraulics Research Wallingford, 1997) but it is unclear how this was derived.

Local authorities: beach cleaning

We have already shown how about £1.5 billion has been spent on reducing pollution loads to clean-up bathing waters. Money is also spent on removal of litter from beaches. There are no national figures for this but we do have some idea of costs:

- the two beaches at Weston-super-Mare cost about £100,000 per year to clean (Acland, 1995);

- the 40km Suffolk coastline (most of which is shingle) costs £60,000 per year to clean;

- Kent's district councils spend about £800,000 per year cleaning 20 designated beaches;

- Weymouth and Portland spend £39,000 per kilometre of beach cleaned, about £2 per person in the council's area (Hall, 1997);

- the National Trust spends £30,000 per year dealing with litter on Studland Beach in Dorset (National Trust, pers. comm.).

These figures suggest an average cost of £40,000 per year per beach which, if applied to the number of beaches in England and Wales, gives total operating costs of £14 million per year. This figure is probably an overestimation because the Kent beaches, being near to the busiest Channel shipping lanes, and the long beaches at Weston-super-Mare probably have much more litter than remote beaches in Wales. Others estimate a much greater amount, up to £32 million, based on the same data but using different assumptions to estimate a national figure (Marine Pollution Monitoring Management Group, 1998b).

These clean-up costs are small in relation to the benefit to the economy of tourism on the coast, although the process needs to be done in such a way as not to threaten the environment. For example, dunes can be made unstable and 'blow outs' may be formed if there is too much trampling within them. Removing seaweed, perceived by the public as unpleasant, is also destroying the habitat of animals that live on or about the strandline, and has a detrimental effect on sand accretion on beaches. Some shingle and sand is also removed by mechanical cleaning, making the beaches more prone to erosion.

It would obviously be better to prevent litter entering the environment in the first place. The national 'Bag It and Bin It' campaign, run by the water industry, government agencies, sanitary products' manufacturers and various charities, has been working to prevent sewage-derived debris entering the environment. The campaign encourages the public not to flush certain sanitary items such as tampons, towels, cotton bud sticks and condoms into the sewerage system, but to safely dispose of them with general household waste. The new port waste regulations should address the amount of litter derived from ships by providing better facilities for disposal on shore. The role of education will be central. For example, Figure 4.55 shows that a large proportion of litter on beaches is left by the public itself. Education and the provision of proper disposal facilities should reduce the amount of litter in the environment and therefore make a major contribution to the improvement of the aesthetic quality of our coasts, and a reduction in the amount spent on beach cleaning.

The National Aquatic Litter Group (NALG) has been created, under the sponsorship of the Government to bring together organisations with an interest in the subject of marine litter, to look at ways of co-operation, to develop common monitoring procedures and to work together to identify sources of marine litter and remedial actions. It includes members from the Agency, academic institutions, government departments, the Tidy Britain Group, local authorities, the Marine Conservation Society, other non-governmental organisations and the water industry. The NALG is working to develop a harmonised approach to assessing and categorising beach litter, improving identification of the sources of litter, drawing up a communication strategy and recommending actions for the prevention and remediation of the problem (Appendix 4).

Managing pollution incidents: agencies

In the event of a major oil or chemical spill which threatens the UK coastline a number of government agencies, local authorities, non-governmental organisations, port authorities and private companies are required to work together to provide an integrated response.

The Maritime and Coastguard Agency fulfils the Government's emergency planning and response duties for spills, and the National Contingency Plan sets out the organisational framework, principles and procedures for dealing with marine pollution. This plan currently requires a Shoreline Response Centre to be set up to integrate the onshore response of central and local government and national and local plans.

The Sea Empress Environmental Evaluation Committee report into the response to the *Sea Empress* incident in Milford Haven in 1996 provides an insight into the adequacy of current arrangements for dealing with pollution incidents, the clean-up of oil and subsequent environmental impact assessments (Sea Empress Environmental Evaluation Committee, 1998). The report concludes that the National Contingency Plan was basically sound and practical - the Shoreline Response Centre had been set up within 12 hours of the initial grounding of the *Sea Empress*, and adequate resources and equipment were available - and it praises the key participants for their preparation, planning and co-operation on environmental and technical matters. However, a number of points were identified where there could be improvements, and in summary these are:

● more basic research is required into the biology and population dynamics of some species in the coastal zone to enable impacts and risks to be identified;

● more information is needed on the efficacy of bird cleaning and rehabilitation for some species of birds to prevent unnecessary suffering, and to improve planning and management of resources;

● the reasons why a fishery closure order have been imposed or removed should be made clearer, as there

was confusion amongst the fishing community and the public about the basis of these precautionary measures, with some mis-interpretation that fish stocks had been damaged;

● even though the clean-up was successful, there is a need to improve future operations in certain areas (definition of tasks, command and control procedures, documentation, criteria for terminating operations on shorelines, local authority plans and responsibilities, health and safety, use of technology to provide information on oil distribution, relationship with the media, emergency procedures and waste disposal);

● it is imperative that there are plans for assessing environmental impacts and an inter-organisational Impact Assessment Group should be established immediately after an incident to co-ordinate assessments (the report suggests that the Agency and SEPA take the lead roles).

5.3   Managing fisheries

Fishing is an activity that has been associated with the coast for centuries, although it is only in the last century that there has been awareness of the extent to which commercial fishing activity can modify the environment. Coastal sea fisheries must be managed in line with the Common Fisheries Policy of the European Union which has the primary aim of ensuring rational and sustainable exploitation of fish stocks through conservation and management policies designed to protect resources and reflect the needs of the fishing industry (MAFF, 1996). This was originally agreed between member states in 1983 with revisions in 1992 (EC 3760/92), which highlighted the need for fisheries to pay due regard to the environment. The main thrust of the policy is:

● to limit the total allowable catches of fish stocks by a national quota;

● to state the minimum permitted landing size for fish of each species;

● to specify the minimum mesh size allowed in any part of a fishing net.

The enforcement of the policy and management of coastal sea fisheries lies with MAFF and 12 local sea fisheries committees, established in the 19th century - Northumbria, North Eastern, Eastern, Essex-Kent, Sussex, Southern, Devon, Cornwall, Isles of Scilly, South Wales, North Western and North Wales, and Cumbria. In addition, the Agency has sea fisheries powers in certain areas, for example, in Cornish estuaries, and in the Taw, Torridge, Dee, Severn and Thames estuaries.

The committees have to safeguard the interests of the local (inshore) fishing industry through the conservation of coastal fish stocks and the management of the vessels which exploit those stocks. They can make bylaws to manage the fishery but cannot limit non-fishing activity even if it affects the fisheries interests. Owing to the extension of the Common Fisheries Policy to pay due regard to the environment and with the designation of special sites under the Habitats Directive (92/43/EEC) and Wild Birds Directive (79/409/EEC), the committees now have an additional member with expertise in marine nature conservation (Gray, 1995).

Despite the Common Fisheries Policy and the responsibilities given to the Agency, MAFF and the sea fisheries committees, there is evidence that the state of many coastal sea fisheries is not good and declining (Section 4.2). This has been recognised and partly accounts for the extension of the powers of the sea fisheries committees to pay due regard to the environment. As quotas on the traditional target species have become more restrictive fishing attention has switched to non-quota species such as red mullet, black bream, lemon sole, cuttlefish and squid. There is a risk that these species will become over-fished in turn. Many seabirds feed on sandeels, sprats, herring and other fish and changes in fish stocks do not seem to be affecting them, with most populations increasing. An exception was the poor breeding success of seabirds in Shetland in the 1980s which was related to a shortage of sandeels, possibly linked to changing practices in the sandeel fishery.

Whales, dolphins and porpoises rely on fish prey and seem likely to have been affected by the severe depletion of some stocks, but changes in their populations have not yet been proven to be caused by fish availability, or by anything else. Their populations are, in any case, very difficult to estimate and are not known with certainty. In view of these uncertainties a precautionary approach should be used to manage fishing rates so that spawning stocks are maintained at sustainable levels in order to ensure their protection and availability for both human consumption and the support of fish-eating wildlife.

But there has been little progress. The Government Panel on Sustainable Development has drawn attention to the decline in fish stocks and lack of coherent policies on various occasions, but says that "*the scandal continues*". It recommends that the Government establish a new advisory forum to promote consensus on controls to achieve sustainable fisheries and the creation of an Intergovernmental Panel on the Oceans (DETR, 1998b).

Migratory salmonids are not covered by the Common Fisheries Policy and the Agency regulates these. The Agency is concerned that conditions at sea may be affecting the return rates of migratory species. The numbers of salmon in particular are declining, especially those which have spent more than one winter at sea.

The issue has been raised internationally, and the International Council for the Exploration of the Sea (ICES) considers that salmon stocks are "*outside or close to safe biological limits, and extreme caution should be exercised in the management of these stocks, particularly in mixed-river stock fisheries. A significant reduction in exploitation rate should be achieved in 1999, and reduced exploitation should continue until the pre-fishery abundance has recovered*" (North Atlantic Salmon Conservation Organisation, 1998).

Through the implementation of its National Salmon Management Strategy, the Agency has already been producing salmon action plans for individual rivers, and there is now a ministerial directive from MAFF for all rivers to have salmon action plans by the year 2002. Even prior to the adoption of the strategy, relevant actions had been taken, namely:

- the phasing out of mixed stock fisheries (off the north east coast, the Anglian Region and in Wales);

- the introduction of rod and net bylaws to increase protection, especially of spring salmon (Wye, Usk, Dee, Hampshire Avon, Taw, Torridge);

- habitat protection and enhancement schemes;

- stock protection through reduction in illegal fishing.

But significant further reduction in exploitation by both rod and net fisheries is needed. Multi-sea-winter salmon, especially early-run fish, should receive the greatest additional protection. Reductions might be achieved through national bylaws if given a high priority by both the Agency and Government and introduced for 1999. The Agency has consulted on the following options:

- closure of the net and rod fisheries for salmon until early summer;

- mandatory catch-and-release for the rod fishery during the same period with method restrictions;

- measures for additional protection of larger salmon in the later part of the season;

- extension of stock protection measures.

The Common Fisheries Policy is next due for review in 2002 and the Agency considers that some dramatic changes are needed. The European Commission is consulting on possible approaches which include a system of regional fisheries management. One of the key issues in the review is the continuation of the derogation that restricts fishing within the six and 12-mile (10 and 20km) limits to UK boats. The Agency wishes to see this derogation retained. This is because any illegally netted salmon will then be landed mainly at UK ports. If foreign vessels are allowed access this will cease to be the case which will make law enforcement much less effective.

An example of efforts to try to develop a better understanding between the fishing industry and marine conservation is provided by trials in a new approach to managing the Thames herring fisheries. It is an initiative which promotes responsible fishery management through a marketing scheme by the award of an eco-label. The scheme is being developed by the Marine Stewardship Council, which was established by World Wildlife Fund International and Unilever.

The Thames herring fishery is a small one with a small number of boats but is of significant value to local communities. Regional fisheries management may enable a greater feeling of ownership over inshore fish resources to be created, by restricting access more than at present and so removing some of the competition to catch fish. The scheme should provide an opportunity to improve the marketing of the Thames herring and so improve the meagre income from the fishery. Conservation and people could benefit - a good example of sustainable development (Midlen, 1998).

5.4 Coastal defence

Aims and standards

The aim of the nation's coastal defence policy is to reduce the risks to people and the developed and natural environment from flooding and erosion:

● *"by encouraging the provision of adequate and cost-effective flood warning systems;*

● *by encouraging the provision of adequate, technically, environmentally and economically sound and sustainable flood and coastal defence measures;*

● *by discouraging inappropriate development in areas at risk from flooding or coastal erosion"* (MAFF and the Welsh Office, 1993).

Sea defences alleviate - but do not eliminate - all risk of flooding or erosion, and a Storm Tide Forecasting Service exists to warn of high surge tides. This service was set up as a result of the 1953 flood. Predetermined danger levels have been set for various reference points along the coast. By combining tidal information and surge predictions, the Storm Tide Forecasting Service can assess whether danger levels are likely to be exceeded at any point and a warning can be issued to the Agency in order that the secondary, local warning service can be activated.

The Agency designs its defences to protect against a storm with the risk of recurrence which is cost-effective and commensurate with current land use. Generally, there is greater protection for urban areas than rural areas (Table 5.2). Many cities, including London and Cardiff, have significant defences against tidal flooding and coastal towns such as Blackpool are defended from the sea. Out of a total of 491 coastal defence schemes approved for grant over the two financial years 1990/91 and 1991/92, only 65 schemes (13 per cent) gave protection to agricultural land alone, and the majority provided urban benefits alone. In the other cases, residential and commercial property as well as urban areas benefitted from coastal protection.

In autumn 1997 MAFF introduced a new pilot scheme

(Priorities for Grant Aid Scheme, PGAS) to structure the allocation of funding for coastal defence works in England. This is based on a points system allocated according to three criteria - priority, urgency and economics - and then ranked on total points. Schemes exceeding a given number of points (set according to funds available) would get grant-aid. The criteria take into account land use, including environmental assets of international importance, the state of repair of existing defences and hence urgency, and the economic benefits of the scheme.

This scheme is aimed at using limited funds to protect human lives and areas of greatest economic value as opposed to rural areas, although it fails to take into account long-term pressures on overall coastal resilience (Turner et al., in press).

In July 1998, MAFF announced adjustments in Government funding arrangements to provide protection for internationally designated habitats from flooding and erosion.

Costs of providing and maintaining defences

The cost of storm damage can be high. Storms in 1989 and 1990 caused damage to defences and beaches which cost £60 million; the cost of the breach in the sea wall at Towyn alone being £35 million (DoE, 1995a). The cost of the 1953 storms, if repeated today, have been estimated at £5 billion.

Major urban defences include the Thames Barrier, owned and operated by the Agency, which was completed in 1982 at a cost of £600 million out of a total of £1 billion for the Thames tidal defences. It costs £4 million per year to operate and protects over a million housing equivalents. It was designed to contain a one in 1,000 year flood event and allows for a continued rise in sea levels of 8mm per year to 2030. The barrier has been closed 30 times in the 15 years from 1982 to 1997. If operating conditions remain the same (closing the barrier whenever sea levels are forecast to rise to within 450mm of defences in central London), and with current projections of sea level rise, forecasts show that there will be 10 barrier closures per year by the early part of the next century and 325 barrier closures per year by 2100.

Expenditure on sea and tidal defences was planned to increase in the 1990s following the 1989 and 1990 storms when some of them failed. Over the six-year period 1990/91 to 1995/96

Table 5.2 *Indicative standards of protection against tidal flooding for grant-aided schemes*

Current land use	Return period (years)
High-density urban containing significant amount of both residential and non-residential property	200
Medium-density urban. Lower density than above, may also include some agricultural land	150
Low-density or rural communities with limited number of properties at risk. Highly productive agricultural land	50
Generally arable farming with isolated properties. Medium productivity agricultural land	20
Predominantly extensive grass with very few properties at risk. Low productivity agricultural land	5

Source: MAFF, 1993b; Crown copyright

the Agency and its predecessors spent £56 million on sea defences and £80 million on tidal defences (figures adjusted to a 1997/98 price base), which is about £23 million per year and some 25 per cent of its total flood defence budget. Of this, about 70 per cent (£95 million) was capital costs and 30 per cent (£41 million) operating and maintenance costs. Over the same period £253 million (adjusted to a 1997/98 price base) has been spent on capital projects for coast protection in England and Wales, an average of £42 million per year. There will also be operating costs associated with coastal protection which are largely spent by the local authorities and do not appear to be collated nationally but based on the cost of maintaining sea defences, could be as much as £100 million over this six-year period. Adding these figures for sea defences, tidal defences and coast protection gives a total capital spend of £348 million on coastal defence for the six-year period, 1990/91 to 1995/96, about £58 million per year, with estimated operating costs of £24 million per year.

The Agency's investment programme for the period 1998/99 to 2007/08 identifies the needs for capital spends of £22 million per year on sea defences and £29 million per year on tidal defence amounting to a total of £51 million per year which is more than treble its expenditure in the early 1990s. This includes several large-scale schemes where there is a need for the injection of capital sums over a relatively short time-scale. The emphasis in the early 1990s was on river schemes; there is now a need for relatively more expenditure on sea and tidal defences to protect against increased storminess.

Long-term strategy

In some parts of the country, the cost of maintaining coastal defences is increasing substantially. This has been due in some cases to the loss of saltmarshes which provided a natural sea defence. A sea wall with no saltmarsh may need to be 12m high and cost around £5,000 per metre to construct, whereas a wall fronted by 80m of saltmarsh may need to be 3m high and cost only £400 per metre (Environment Agency, 1996b). In Essex 84 per cent of the 440km of sea wall relies on saltmarsh to help maintain protection (Toft et al., 1995). With sea level rise the width of saltings is reducing, causing an ever-increasing cost of maintaining sea walls, especially on the East Anglia coast. In other cases, hard sea defences have affected erosion and deposition patterns. One could reasonably ask whether this continued spend on coastal defences is worth it, and whether we are fighting a losing battle against natural forces.

Coastal defences must therefore be seen in the context of an extremely changeable environment, where modification of one part can have serious consequences locally and on other parts some distance away (MAFF, 1993a).

The Government is committed to effective coastal defence but the ways in which that commitment is put into effect are constantly evolving and improving. A developing understanding of physical processes, recent and on-going changes in land use and changes in attitude towards the environment have all reinforced the need to take a more strategic view of the planning of coastal defences. It is important to avoid placing an additional burden of responsibility on future generations by increasing unnecessarily the number of areas to be artificially protected. Sound planning decisions are needed to control development in risk areas. With the increasing pressures of climate change, sea level rise, and development all impinging on the coastal zone, the Agriculture Select Committee (1998) commented:

"We are of the opinion that flood and coastal defence policy cannot be sustained in the long term if it continues to be founded on the practice of substantial human intervention in the natural processes of flooding and erosion".

It continues to say that the legacy arising from existing practices may combine to present organisations with *"insuperable difficulties"* in future.

The automatic replacement or improvement of existing defences will not necessarily address the long-term needs of the community, and Section 4 has already shown how over 12 per cent of sea defence elements and 40 per cent of coastal protection elements need at least moderate works carried out if they are to remain effective. There are some cases where these elements are redundant but there will be cases where they have to be replaced or improved to reduce the risk of loss of life and damage to homes, businesses, land and the environment (MAFF and the Welsh Office, 1993). Sea walls in Essex provide an example of where costs have risen substantially, perhaps beyond the benefit received.

Some £200 million has been spent on rural sea walls between 1953 and 1993, amounting to some £14,700 per hectare of land protected. The market value of this land is between £3,000 and £4,000 per hectare. The annual maintenance cost for sea walls in Essex averages about £150 per hectare of rural land protected, in some sections rising to over £40,000 per ha, so the flood defence 'subsidy' for this land is substantial (Dixon and Weight, 1997).

Some studies have been done to assess the economic implications of sea level rise to determine whether or not sea defences should be abandoned, maintained or increased further. One model, for Great Britain at an aggregated level, predicts that the optimal degree of protection varies between 92 per cent and 98 per cent (for a predicted sea level rise of between 0.2m and 1m over the next 100 years) for open coasts and beaches, and between 98 per cent and 99 per cent for developed areas. For the whole of Great Britain, the combined protection and damage cost estimate lies between £1.9 billion and £10.3 billion using a three per cent discount rate (Fankhauser, 1994).

This work was done at a national level and there was some concern it could mask significant regional and local differences. So a study in East Anglia looked in more detail at predicted sea level rises to the year 2050 and considered the costs and benefits of three coastal defence strategies:

- retreating - abandoning existing uses and resettling elsewhere;

- accommodating - maintaining existing defences but allowing some overtopping;

●   protecting - full robust and reliable defences.

Using a discount rate of six per cent, it found that the protection strategy was economically justifiable on a region-wide basis, but a combination of management options including retreating was the optimal economic approach at a more localised scale (Turner *et al.*, 1995).

The option of managed retreat or managed realignment has recently been emphasised. This is where the defences are breached and the intertidal zone is allowed to move landward to some pre-determined set-back line (Figure 5.1) (MAFF, 1993a). Such an approach might be suitable where the long-term provision of hard defences is economically or environmentally unsustainable and may be feasible for limited areas of agricultural land. The cost savings on defence, and the cost of realignment, need to be set against the loss of agricultural land, which in most cases is likely to be used for grazing. Payment may be available under agri-environment schemes, for example if saltmarsh is created by managed realignment. The payment by MAFF, of up to £525 per hectare per year for creating saltmarsh, is generally considered by landowners to be an inadequate incentive.

So far managed realignment has not been widely practised. By 1997 there were only four managed realignment schemes creating saltmarsh. At Orplands, on the Blackwater Estuary in Essex, which suffered erosion to the saltmarsh and damage to the sea wall, it would have cost up to £600,000, or £16,000 per hectare of land, to maintain protection for the next 20 years, compared with a market value for the land of £3,700 per hectare. The managed realignment scheme involved re-routing public access and changing the drainage system at a cost of only £100,000. The scheme has successfully created a new marsh for wildlife and a saline flood control zone which will absorb storm wave energy (Dixon and Weight, 1997).

In some places managed realignment is not viable because the existing defences protect sites which have become designated as sites of conservation value, some as Special Protection Areas, designated under the EC Wild Birds Directive (79/409/EEC), or as Special Areas of Conservation designated under the EC Habitats Directive (92/43/EEC). Legislation requires that they are protected whatever the cost or replaced elsewhere, so there is not always a realistic option to allow a breach of the defences, but this will depend on the approach taken to resolve the conflict. There is an example provided by Cley-Kelling in north Norfolk, where a simple barrier ridge provides flood protection for the two villages as well as grazing marshes and reedbeds designated as a Special Protection Area. The simple barrier has been breached several times in recent years and an understanding of natural processes suggests that this will continue, requiring a decision on what to do for the future. Widespread consultation took place involving all the stakeholders with an agreement reached to create a secondary line of defence further back and to recreate the habitat lost elsewhere (O'Riordan and Ward, 1997). Funding had been allocated but this was postponed when the new Priorities for Grant Aid Scheme was introduced in 1997.

Figure 5.1   *Managed retreat for flood defence*

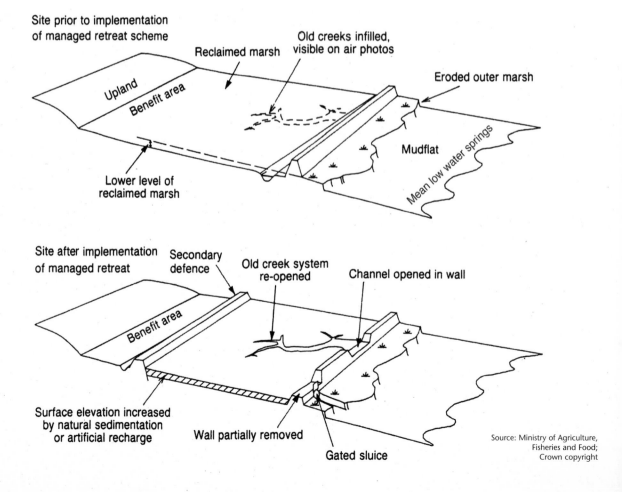

Source: Ministry of Agriculture, Fisheries and Food; Crown copyright

An overview of the potential nature and extent of impacts of natural processes and coastal defence policies on habitats over the next 50 years, within designated sites, has recently been completed. If the 'most likely' coastal defence policies are implemented and if the predicted natural coastal changes occur, then the following important habitat changes are possible:

- a net gain of intertidal habitats of about 770ha (total gains of 12,500ha due to managed retreat but balanced by losses due to coastal squeeze and erosion);

- a loss of 120ha of sand dunes, mainly in Northumberland, the south west, Cardigan Bay and Sefton;

- a loss of 130ha of shingle bank habitats (four per cent of the existing resource);

- a net loss of freshwater and brackish habitat of about 4,000ha, including 500ha of coastal lagoons.

The likely cost of freshwater and brackish habitat replacement was estimated at £50 to £60 million (1998 prices). Some habitats are likely to be irreplaceable, for example sand dunes and shingle banks, whereas others need a simple change of management practice (for example from arable use to grazing marsh).

The study also identified a number of important coastal defence related issues which could constrain the successful implementation of the Habitats Directives. These include: the conflict between maintaining the favourable conservation status of the saltmarsh resources through managed retreat, and the resulting losses of freshwater habitats; saltmarsh recreation may not necessarily lead to the production of habitats that would be integral to a site of international importance; and the future management of sand dune and shingle bank systems needs to find an appropriate balance between habitat diversity and flood defence (Lee, 1998).

In England and Wales there are around 160 organisations which can undertake coastal defence works, causing concern that this has led to a piecemeal approach which has inhibited a more strategic view (National Audit Office, 1992). Other groups, such as planning authorities, also have an interest in the development and use of coastal areas. Co-ordination between organisations is important because of the impact of defences on the natural processes which shape the coast.

Two national fora and several coastal groups have been created to help overcome these difficulties. These groups are based on the natural coastal cells for coarse sediment transport within which any decisions on defence measures are likely to have a wider impact. Since 1995 the groups have developed 'shoreline management plans' for the cells in question and considered natural processes, planning pressures, current and future land use, defence needs and environmental considerations. These plans now need to be integrated into the statutory plans of local authorities through coastal zone management plans to avoid inappropriate development, and then implemented. English Nature and many Wildlife Trusts have questioned whether these

plans will make significant changes towards achieving a sustainable shoreline, and they may be too local to reflect the long-term strategic needs of the coastline (House of Commons Agriculture Committee, 1998). Others have questioned whether involvement of groups in the development of the plans has been sufficiently widespread, because the success of shoreline management plans will depend upon informed consent and widespread support among interested parties. Consultation has been common practice for years but it is often seen as imperfect and takes time and money. It is therefore important that it is an effective process. The way forward could be a move towards more participatory consultation which is more active, face-to-face, close and responsive and involves people in local partnerships where trust is built between parties. Such an approach has been tried in the development of the north Norfolk coast Shoreline Management Plan with some success (O'Riordan and Ward, 1997).

In 1998 the Agriculture Select Committee reported on the effectiveness of MAFF's current expenditure and policy on flood and coastal defence in England, focusing on the efficiency of implementation of policies by the many organisations involved (House of Commons Agriculture Committee, 1998). It has also looked at the social, economic and environmental implications of coastal defence policy and recommended a package of planning, administrative and financial measures. It has based its recommendations on three general principles:

- a desire to change the widespread public culture of intolerance to naturally occurring and unavoidable risk associated with flooding;

- that strategic policy should be set at national level but implementation at regional (not local) level;

- a need to reform the national planning system to attach greater importance to flood and coastal defence priorities.

If these recommendations are adopted, they are likely to have a significant effect on the design of coastal defence works.

Of the recommendations made, the Agency has welcomed:

- simplification of the funding arrangements to deliver the flood and coastal defence service by cutting out unnecessary bureaucracy and administration;

- the need to encourage a more sustainable approach by putting in place suitable compensation arrangements to enable managed realignment of the coast;

- the need to develop methodologies addressing social and environmental criteria by broadening MAFF's Project Appraisal Guidance Notes which set out the procedures by which operating authorities obtain grants for projects. They also recommend the identification of the best practicable options and greater transparency in the process;

- a clear distinction between policy guidance by MAFF and separate clear implementation by the Agency;

- the emphasis placed on development control, the production of flood hazard maps and the continued improvement to flood warning.

In its response to the report the Government was not persuaded that there should be a radical change in the present institutional arrangements. It did accept that there should be a review of the present funding arrangements. MAFF is to pursue with the Agency and other operating authorities the adoption of high level targets to measure their achievement of the Government's aim on flood and coastal defence. The Government's response also stated that there will be action to define the Agency's general flood defence supervisory duty in relation to the monitoring of plans of other operating authorities, and in achieving widespread adoption of best practice between and within authorities (MAFF, 1998).

5.5 Managing development pressures

We have shown there are many development activities causing pressures on land in coastal areas which include:

- increasing number of households;

- the siting of a range of industries, many of them heavy;

- increasing demand for tourist activities and attractions;

- increasing trade at ports;

- new demands for wind farms, barrages and other economic developments, such as oil exploration in coastal waters.

All of these activities have to be considered against a background of rising sea levels in some parts of the country, making land below 5m unsuitable for development, increased risk of storm severity, plus the fact that much of the agricultural land in coastal areas is grade 1 (high quality) and an important resource for future generations.

So what should the balance be between different forms of coastal and estuarine development? The foreshore is often seen as a vast undeveloped resource or open space in crowded cities

Figure 5.2 *Designations in coastal areas*

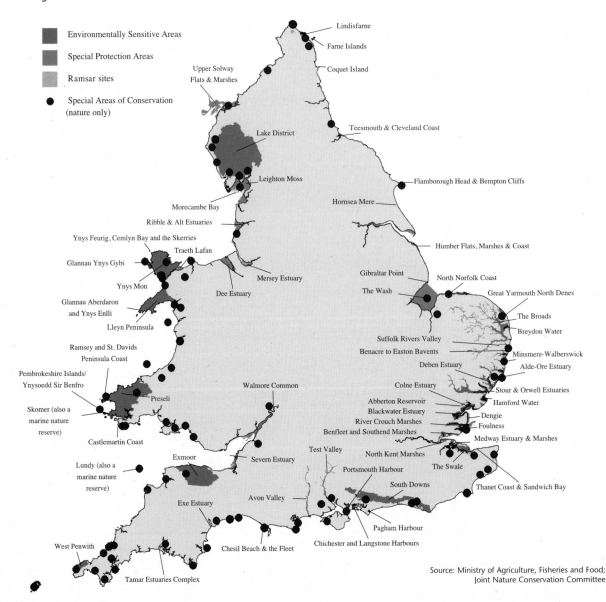

Source: Ministry of Agriculture, Fisheries and Food;
Joint Nature Conservation Committee

like London and there needs to be a balance struck between development, recreational use, and the conservation of coasts and estuaries.

The Government's guidance on coastal development recognises the many and conflicting pressures on the coastal zone. There are some clear statements about the policy for development: *"In the coastal zone, development plan policies should normally not provide for development which does not require a coastal location"*, and it is essential to demonstrate that a coastal location is required before any major developments are permitted. It mentions that it is reasonable to expect provision of land for housing and employment to be made in parts of the local authority not in the coastal zone. The guidance also says, *"new development should not generally be permitted in areas which would need expensive engineering works, either to protect developments on land subject to erosion by the sea or to defend land which might be inundated by the sea."* The guidance covers other aspects such as tourism and recreation saying, *"public access to the coast should be a basic principle, unless it can be demonstrated that this is damaging to nature conservation or impractical."* The guidance sets the framework for

managing the coastal environment (DoE and Welsh Office, 1992)

It is important to protect the coastal environment, so that the economic and social benefits it gives can continue, whilst maintaining the intrinsic value of the coast. The tourist industry, for example, depends on an aesthetically pleasing and healthy environment - one of the attractions for tourists of coastal areas - but development pressures can conflict with this dependence. One way of protecting the environment has been in designating areas which have special value of one form or another, and there are now a plethora of these arising from various regulations. They are shown in Table 5.3. Planning restrictions apply in some of these types of designations but not all. The agri-environment schemes in the table are entirely voluntary and do not impose planning restrictions. They have been included in the table to show the extent of such sites which have been recognised to be of some specific value. In total, between a third and a half of the coastline is designated in one form or other. The extent of coastal Special Protection

Figure 5.3 *Protected coastal areas*

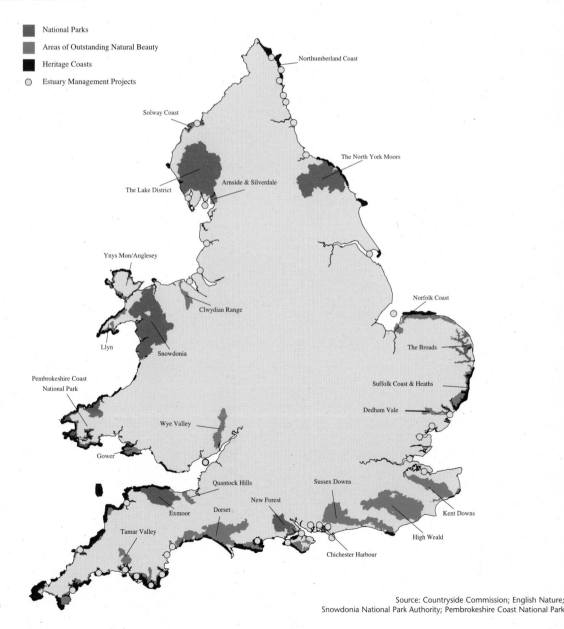

Source: Countryside Commission; English Nature;
Snowdonia National Park Authority; Pembrokeshire Coast National Park

Table 5.3 *Conservation designations in coastal areas*

Type	Designation	Legal status	Extent on coasts
Wildlife	Special Protection Areas (EC Wild Birds Directive)	statutory	53 (coastal or intertidal)
	Special Areas of Conservation (EC Habitats Directive)	statutory	47 proposed (including 50 per cent of the Welsh coast)
	Sites of Special Scientific Interest	statutory	67 per cent estuarine intertidal zones
	Wetlands of International Importance (Ramsar sites)	international	37
	Marine Nature Reserve	statutory	2 (Lundy and Skomer)
	Biosphere reserves	international	2 (Braunton Burrows, north Norfolk coast)
	Sensitive Marine Areas	non-statutory	27
Landscape	National Parks	statutory	3
	Areas of Outstanding Natural Beauty	statutory	35
	Heritage Coasts	non-statutory	45; 1,500km
Agri-environment	Environmentally Sensitive Areas	statutory	10
	Habitat Scheme: saltmarsh creation	non-statutory	four agreements so far, covering 54 hectares

Areas, Special Areas of Conservation and Environmentally Sensitive Areas is shown in Figure 5.2. Some of these areas lie within others. For example, all Special Protection Areas, Special Areas of Conservation and Ramsar sites will have first been designated as SSSIs. Taken together, Special Areas of Conservation and Special Protection Areas will form the proposed Europe-wide network of sites known as the *Natura 2000* series, and where the designated area includes sea or seashore it is described as a 'European marine site'. (The term *Natura 2000* comes from the 1992 EC Habitats Directive - it symbolises the conservation of precious natural resources for the year 2000 and beyond). Under present proposals an estimated 76 per cent of UK estuaries will form part of *Natura 2000* and 75 ports will be located within or adjacent to a designated site (Townend, 1997).

Heritage Coasts have no formal statutory basis but are defined by local authorities for the purpose of conserving undeveloped coasts for public enjoyment. Significant stretches occur both within National Parks and Areas of Outstanding Natural Beauty (Figure 5.3) and most Heritage Coasts contain one or more Sites of Special Scientific Interest. As with Areas of Outstanding Natural Beauty, protection is afforded through policies in local development plans.

The UK Biodiversity Action Plan has identified the need to protect 21 priority habitats found in coastal areas. Costed action plans have been produced for six habitats, showing that about £102 million needs to be spent protecting five of these six habitats (those which occur in England and Wales) over the

next 10 years, most of this on grazing marsh land (Table 5.4). Draft costed plans for the remaining 15 have also been prepared but have yet to be confirmed (Baker et al., 1988).

Both small and large estuaries depend for their survival on the co-operation of conservationists, decision-makers and estuary users over the protection and management of this important part of Britain's natural heritage. The National Trust has recently announced its intention to increase its ownership (by purchase) of the English coastline to one-third.

The overall management of development pressures on the coast is not down to one regulator. Many organisations are involved and local authorities have a key role in exercising planning control and produce statutory plans, but many other organisations also produce plans or strategies to assist in their roles. Six of the most significant types of plans which consider the coast are:

- development plans of the local authorities;

- management schemes for marine Special Areas of Conservation prepared by relevant authorities with guidance from English Nature and the Countryside Council for Wales, and management plans for Special Protection Areas prepared by English Nature and the Countryside Council for Wales;

- management plans for the 45 Heritage Coasts, prepared by the local authorities together with the Countryside Commission and other interested bodies;

Table 5.4 *Spending on five key habitats within the UK Biodiversity Action Plan*

Habitat	Total 10 year cost, £million 1997 to 2006[1]
Grazing marsh (coastal and floodplain)	78.0
Saline lagoons	14.1
Sea grass beds	3.6
Saltmarsh	4.9
Vegetated coastal shingle	0.9
Total	101.5

[1]Prices at 1997/98 cost base

- Local Environment Agency Plans prepared on a river-basin catchment basis including the coastal zone where appropriate;

- shoreline management plans to identify sustainable coastal defence policies for the entire shoreline, prepared by the Agency and maritime local authorities (and a prerequisite for grant-aid for coastal defence schemes);

- estuary management plans prepared by English Nature which provide integrated plans for the sustainable use of estuaries, and developed in collaboration with local authorities and others with interests in estuaries. Figure 5.3 shows the extent of these.

The ways in which the plans interact are given in Appendix 7. Most of these plans follow specific guidelines, aspects of which are relevant here. The guidance for shoreline management plans states: "*The key to a strategic approach to the management of the shoreline is knowledge of the coastal processes in the area concerned*". It continues to say: "*An understanding of the inter-relationship between coastal processes and coastal defence is fundamental to the effective management of the shoreline*" (MAFF and the Welsh Office, 1993). The planning guidance issued to local authorities states that new development should be avoided in areas at risk from coastal processes or adequate precautions must be taken. Such precautions must be sustainable.

Because there are so many plans and people involved, local managers and decision-makers are apparently becoming fatigued by the process of producing plans. Furthermore, development in one area could impinge on other areas so overall coastal zone management is essential. This is "*the process which brings together all those involved in the development, management and use of coasts within a framework which facilitates the integration of their interests and responsibilities to achieve common objectives*" (DoE, 1996b). Coastal zone management has evolved within the context of the growing awareness of environmental issues and the desire to achieve a proper balance between securing future economic prosperity and maintaining environmental quality. It depends on effective integration, communication and planning under five key headings:

- ensuring that full account is taken of guidance, plans or strategies from the international and European scale, through national and regional levels down to the local context;

- bringing together within an area policies and practice from all sectors and seeking integration of their different characteristics and timescales:

- bridging management across the sea/land interface;

- establishing clear aims and objectives, and assigning responsibilities within a common and agreed framework;

- accepting that the management of the coast is a continuous task which goes beyond the production of any plan or strategy and focuses on implementation and action.

Emphasis is placed on voluntary agreements because thay can help promote consensus through participation and choice; compliance is encouraged where those affected are involved in drawing up schemes of regulation and can help to enforce them; and changing circumstances can secure a more rapid response. The need for such agreements is also emerging through codes of practice prepared by a wide range of coastal industry, commerce and recreation groups, as well as through non-statutory management plans for the coastal zone (DoE, 1996b).

The Government's guide *Coastal Zone Management - Towards Best Practice* suggests that anybody can take the lead in integrating plans. Often the local authority does, but it could be another organisation such as English Nature and the Countryside Council for Wales which may lead on estuary plans. Clear objectives need to be set in forming an integrated plan including the identification of issues that need to be resolved, what agencies can do within their existing powers and making sure that false expectations are not raised. In order to help promote discussion on coastal issues and networking between a wide range of organisations, a 'Coastal Forum' was set up in England in December, 1994. This is run by DETR on behalf of the Inter-departmental Group on Coastal Policy. It brings together more than 60 representatives from bodies with interests in the coast including Government, leisure, conservation, commerce and industry. In particular it seeks to:

- promote understanding of coastal zone management and initiatives;

- assist evaluation of coastal zone initiatives and disseminate good practice;

- complement, but not overlap, the work of other bodies with interests in coastal issues;

- maintain close links with the coastal fora for Northern Ireland, Scotland and Wales and build on other liaison arrangements at international, national, regional and local level (DETR, 1997d).

National coastal fora were established in Scotland and Wales in 1997 and close liaison has been established between DETR, the Scottish Office and the Welsh Office, as reflected in the joint newsletter *"Wavelength"*. But is coastal zone management working? We now present two case studies to address this question.

Case study: Humber Estuary management

The Humber Estuary Management Strategy Group was set up to integrate needs for the Humber. It is a partnership of key interests around the estuary which includes industry, local authorities, agriculture, conservation and the ports. The partnership has identified 13 key issues which affect the long-term sustainability of the estuary. The Agency has responded by producing an action plan which states how it will work towards the resolution of each issue. Importantly the objectives for achieving success in each of these are not the Agency's alone but also those of the partnership. The clear consequence of this is that many of the issues are most effectively resolved by partners working together. For example, the aims and objectives for flood defence have been identified between the Agency, MAFF and English Nature. By meeting these objectives the Agency is therefore also going to secure wider acceptance for its actions, a fact that is very important in developing long-term strategic approaches.

There are over 230km of flood defences around the Humber Estuary and their management determines the behaviour of the whole estuary as well as the security of the people who live and work there. A major part of the work has been identifying a long-term approach to flood defence. This has involved developing an approach (agreed by the group) for preparing a strategy, and work is underway on the many studies and projects which comprise it. These studies include the development of an Estuary Shoreline Management Plan (ESMP) and an investigation into the geomorphology of the estuary. The results of these will be used to determine how the estuary will be managed for many years by working with the processes that shape it rather than continually fighting them. This is of considerable importance in establishing cost effectiveness. At the same time, a set of procedures for developing urgent flood defence works was developed, to ensure that the Agency continues to meet its flood defence obligations and these are now in use for all engineering works around the estuary, ensuring consistency of approach.

Environmental quality is a major issue in this area of dense population, industry and agriculture and in the rivers which drain into the estuary, the Trent and Ouse. Considerable improvements have been made to the quality of effluents discharging to the estuary, and industry has spent about £300 million in the last five years to achieve them. A significant amount of work remains to be done, much of which is already underway. It involves many facets of the Agency, working with industries on waste regulation and management, process regulation and water quality. The integration of these towards estuary-wide objectives is proving very valuable in raising awareness of the environment and demonstrating cost-effectiveness.

Contaminated land is also an issue in this estuary with its industrial past and many initiatives are taking place with external partners to do some remediation work where contaminants have been found in flood bank material during flood defence work. At one site, where improvements were made to 5km of defences, the cost of removing this material to landfill was £1.5 million. Information about contaminants therefore becomes a very important part of the project appraisal process. Biological data collected primarily for water quality monitoring is increasingly being used to ascertain the health of intertidal habitats. This is important if the Agency is to develop long-term strategies for flood defence which works with natural forces.

There are a number of areas where further work is required to complete the shift towards management of the estuary as a whole. These include:

- the need to develop monitoring programmes to demonstrate success;

- the need to do more to inform and involve everyone who has an interest in the estuary;

- the need to continue to develop best practices and to be innovative.

Similar groups work elsewhere, such as the Severn Estuary Strategy Group. Again, they suggest that partnership is the underlying theme of their strategy.

Case study: Wales

A further example is provided from Wales. In 1997 the Countryside Council for Wales commissioned a review of coastal management in Wales. While non-statutory national and regional coastal fora have been developed, the study revealed some inadequacies in the management of the coastal zone. Its recommendations included the short, medium and long-term priorities shown in Table 5.5, but it concluded, *"whatever integrated coastal management system develops, it should be flexible"* (University of Wales, Cardiff, 1997).

Overall, coastal zone management provides a framework for competing demands and tries to strike an appropriate balance for uses. It cannot predict all demands or development proposals, and does not replace statutory planning controls. But it can operate at a level divorced from local needs which is thwarting its usefulness. One critic suggests:

"The fragmented institutional structure and the dominance of a top-down policy approach have led to a lack of commitment to integrated coastal management, and inadequate incorporation of potential environmental change impacts into decisions...[there is] a need for integration at the government level, while including stakeholder consultation in the decision process" (Turner et al., in press).

Table 5.5 *Coastal management in Wales*

	Priorities
Short-term	Wider dissemination of information on the benefits and characteristics of integrated coastal management.
	Increased co-ordination and liaison among and within organisations with coastal responsibilities and coastal programmes.
	More effective public participation in the development of coastal planning and management.
	Increased training opportunities for coastal practitioners.
	Development of coastal fora to cover the complete Welsh coast and address all coastal issues.
	Improvements in the quality and availability of information for coastal management.
	Improvements in the scientific basis for coastal management.
	Development of multi-sectoral, non-statutory coastal strategies for the developed coasts.
	Mechanisms to improve strategic planning, especially in relation to developing planning.
	Public awareness and education programmes.
	Research into funding opportunities for coastal management.
Medium-term	Development of multi-sectoral coastal strategies for the entire Welsh coast.
	More secure funding arrangements for coastal management programmes.
	The development and use of sustainability indicators for coastal management.
	The implementation of strategic environmental assessment for coastal, including marine, areas.
	Improved techniques for economic assessment and resource accounting.
	Increased private sector involvement in coastal management.
Long-term	Fully integrated coastal management programmes.
	Harmonisation of plan boundaries.
	Reduction of the gaps between disciplines.
	Utilisation of sustainability indicators and other methods for plan monitoring.
	Welsh coastal management lying centre-stage and being involved in the international development of integrated coastal management.

Source: University of Wales, 1997

European initiatives

While the UK Government is encouraging coastal zone management, the European Union is concerned that planning for sustainable development is being implemented too slowly in an area where problems are complex. It initiated a demonstration programme in 1995 (European Commission, 1995a). The objectives of the programme are to show what practical conditions must be met if sustainable development is to be achieved in coastal zones. The programme depends on:

- co-operation between all parties concerned which needs to be organised and maintained;

- the availability of information on the state of the environment, the origin of changes affecting it, the implication of policies and measures at the various levels, and the options (European Commission, 1997)

Four sections of the English coast have been selected within this demonstration programme - Kent, the Isle of Wight, Dorset, and Devon and Cornwall. They were selected because of the range of pressures in these areas and the need for integrated management. The Kent area, for example, has wide stretches of saltmarsh and grazing marsh of international significance alongside tiny fishing harbours, ferry and cargo ports, major industries including paper-making, oil refining and chemical products, as well as famous traditional seaside resorts. With such a range of interests there is considerable potential for conflict, so there is a need for an integrated strategy and to bring together the many existing plans.

The results anticipated from these programmes include detailed integrated management strategies, improvement of information provision within the areas and among organisations, and the establishment of a co-operation-management process. All of these should help towards maintaining and improving the coastal environment for future generations.

5.6 Summary of investment in the coastal environment

The previous parts of Section 5 have included various facts and figures about investment on the coastal environment which we have drawn together here. There are some broad assumptions made about the investment by industry because the only information is from a study of expenditure in 1994. This figure has been multiplied by five to give the estimated spend over the same five-year period for comparison with other sectors. This figure has then been factored by 0.4 to represent the proportion of industry found in the coastal zone. The figure for industry is, therefore, very uncertain.

Table 5.6 *Summary of actual and projected capital investment to protect the coastal environment[1]*

Sector		1990/91 to 1994/95 (£million)	1995/96 to 1997/98 (£million)	Planned (£million) (estimates)
Water industry	bathing waters	820	670	103 (1998/99 to 2004/5)
	sewage sludge	310	443	457 (1998/99 to 2004/5)
	Urban Waste Water Treatment Directive	nil	663	1,467 (1998/99 to 2004/05) [2]
	Shellfish Directive	nil	nil	50
	Habitats Directive	nil	nil	5
	other	316	nil	108 (environmental schemes, 1995 to 1999)
Water industry total		**1,446**	**1,776**	**2,190**
Industry		720	Unknown	
Coastal defence		290	170	510 (1998/99 to 2007/08) (sea and tidal defences)
Farming		Unknown	Unknown	
Biodiversity Action Plans		nil	Included in planned	102 (on five habitats, over 10 years from 1997)
Total		**2,456**	**1,946**	**N/A**

Source: University of Wales, 1997

[1] All figures adjusted to a 1997/98 price base.

[2] This total is derived from £1,058 million on continuous and intermittent discharges from 1998/99 to 1999/00; £45 million on intermittent discharges from 2000 to 2004; £360 million on high natural dispersion areas; £4 million on eutrophic sensitive areas.

In total, the capital investment over the five years 1990/91 to 1994/95 is estimated to have been £2,456, about £491 million per year, of which over half has been spent by the water industry (Table 5.6). The following three years show a much higher rate of investment, some £649 million per year and this does not include any figures for industry. These figures exclude operating costs which can be substantial, for example some £24 million per year is spent on operating and maintaining the coastal and estuarine sewerage systems by the water companies, £23 million on coastal defences and £75 million on navigation dredging. Operating costs by industry are also likely to be substantial. While this amount of investment is large, it is interesting to compare it with the amount invested on the freshwater environment - some £1,300 million per year (Environment Agency, 1998a).

The Agency needs to be better informed on investment on the environment, especially that by industry, and is developing a database of economic figures, but often the information is not available to feed into this.

5.7 The value of the coastal environment

The investment on protecting the coastal environment can be justified by reference to the value people attach to it, although these values will vary depending on peoples views. For at least 2,000 years the coast has been inextricably linked with the development of England and Wales. The sea and the shore has been and continues to be an important source of food, and the fishing and shellfish industries still make a valuable contribution to the coastal economy. The coastline provided suitable conditions to develop the ports that were established to ensure the UK's position at the centre of world trade until the early 1900s. The growth of industry on the estuaries took advantage of a plentiful supply of water for power and cooling and the ease of transportation.

Over the last 200 years the coast has become increasingly popular for the 'taking of the sea air', bathing, scenery and wildlife, walking, sailing and many other water-based recreational activities. It is evident that people like to be by the sea; they retire to coastal resorts and many people like to take day trips to the sea if not their annual holiday. The tourist trade is a very important part of the economy and for some parts of the country, such as Cornwall, it is its main industry.

So the coast is indisputably a valuable asset. Its value can be assessed both in direct terms (the amount that it contributes to economic activities) and indirectly (by what value it is judged to have by those who make use of it). In terms of foreign trade, of the £290 billion worth of imports and exports in 1992, about £177 billion (61 per cent) was moved through ports. Given that 69 per cent of this was shipped through estuarine ports, their significance in facilitating trade and sustaining economic activity is great. UK marine-related activities had a total turnover of £51 billion in 1994/95, accounting for about five per cent of Gross Domestic Product, and the total value added was about £28 billion. About 50 per cent of this can probably be attributed to activities carried out in estuaries alone. The value of leisure and tourism at the coast was estimated at about £8.8 billion in 1994/95 and contributed an estimated 3.8 per cent to Gross Domestic Product (Hydraulics Research Wallingford, 1997; Pugh and Skinner, 1996; European Commission, 1995b; Turner *et al.*, 1998).

The UK fishing industry contributed £590 million (including £128 million of shellfish landings) to Gross Domestic Product in 1995 (less than 0.1 per cent) but is of particular socio-economic importance in parts of Wales, and in south west and northern England (MAFF, 1996).

Many goods and services are produced in or provided by the coastal zone, and are of significant value to present and future generations. The capacity to assimilate wastes, biodiversity and the storm-buffering function of coastal wetlands are not priced but they nevertheless represent very valuable resources. Globally, such services have been approximately valued at £760 billion per year, or 71 per cent of the Global Gross National Product (Costanza *et al.*, 1997). This type of estimate is of course extremely uncertain, but serves to highlight the importance of the coast and its resources.

Expenditure on environmental improvements can be justified by the value placed on the coastal environment and the economic benefit derived by its use within the boundaries of sustainable development. Some areas of expenditure are more easily justified than others. The cleaning up of bathing water quality can probably be justified from the value placed on the coastal environment as a place to live, bathe or visit for recreation or sightseeing. The value is reduced by pollution by litter and oil as well as pollution which may risk public health. But expenditure on an eroding cliff-top footpath may not be justified when the value of the path is confined largely to local use and the prediction is for continuing coastal erosion, which will mean regular costly maintenance of the defences.

The National Trust has campaigned to bring attention to the intrinsic value of the coast line and the need to protect it. A survey of the coast of England, Wales and Northern Ireland which was completed in 1963 concluded that about a third had been spoilt beyond redemption, another third was of no particular interest and that at best, the final third, about 1,450km or so, was worthy of urgent protection (Evans, 1992). In 1965 the Enterprise Neptune campaign was launched to acquire unspoilt coastline. It caught the public's attention and the response was good, with over £0.5 million raised in a year. By 1973 the Trust's original target of £2 million was realised, but it then estimated that 3,000km of coastline was beyond redemption. By 1998 £30 million had been raised and brought protection to more than 920km of coast and some 50,000ha of coastal hinterland and foreshore. The Trust has also acquired spoilt coastline and restored it, for example parts of the Durham coast ruined by decades of colliery spoil dumping. On average, the Trust spends £10 million per year protecting its 920km of coastline, some £11,000 per kilometre. The success of this campaign demonstrates that people value the coastline and there is a willingness to pay voluntarily to protect it (National Trust, pers. comm., 1998).

There is now considerable debate on how to value environmental assets and put them in perspective compared with alternative services that the public value, such as health and education. One possible framework is cost-benefit analysis, where attempts are made to determine how much the public is willing to pay as a measure of relative value. There are many different ways of valuing a commodity but the most widely used technique for obtaining a monetary value of environmental problems is the 'contingent valuation method' which uses surveys to assess the 'willingness to pay'.

None of the techniques is without problems, either theoretical or practical. Nevertheless they can add some insight to the process of environmental protection. The Agency has been developing techniques to assess the value of water quality improvements to put cost into perspective (Foundation for Water Research, 1996). Others have looked at techniques for valuing the coast with respect to flood defence and coastal protection. And survey work undertaken in the late 1980s found that sea bass anglers were willing to pay over £25 per year to prevent the closure or loss of a fishery. Multiplying this by the estimated 490,000 bass anglers in England and Wales indicates a value associated with the protection of this recreational fishery of over £12 million (Hydraulics Research Wallingford, 1997).

Valuing coastal defence

The benefits of flood alleviation projects are the expected value of the losses that would otherwise be anticipated to result from flooding. The assessments of the benefits of coastal defences are complicated by the effect of erosion of the coast. All that coastal defence can do is slow down or prevent erosion during the life of the project and reduce the risks of loss of life.

Several surveys have looked at the value attached to a visit to a beach in order to achieve a baseline valuation against which to assess changes to the beach (Table 5.7) (Penning-Rowsell *et al.*, 1992). The table shows a wide range of valuations with a tendency for the beaches in the north of England to be valued at a lower rate than those in the south. Incomes can bias the value given to a commodity.

The results from such surveys are used in the decision-making process of which coastal defence options to pursue. For example, a case study into the benefits that might arise from an erosion problem and a proposed protection project was undertaken at Peacehaven in East Sussex. The site, although part of a long-distance footpath, was predominantly used by local residents. A residents' survey was carried out on their enjoyment of the cliffs and their willingness to pay increased rates and taxes to prevent erosion of the land. The result showed that the locals valued their cliff-top recreation and were willing to pay a certain amount to protect it. Although it was likely that loss of access to the cliff top as a result of erosion would result after 50 years, there was considerable uncertainty about the

Table 5.7 *Contingent valuation surveys of coastal recreation, 1987 to 1990*

Coastal amenity and year	Sites	Size and type of sample	Per cent of people able to put a value on a site	Value (£) (mean)
Beaches and promenades, 1988	Scarborough	101 users	83	4.93
	Clacton	170 users	90	9.96
	Dunwich	101 users	61	6.87
	Filey	88 users	88	3.64
	Frinton	178 users	70	9.56
	Hastings	247 users	66	7.72
	Spurn Head	97 users	80	8.50
Beaches and promenades, 1989	Bridlington	151 users	86	5.91
	Clacton	146 users	67	10.52
	Hunstanton	152 users	90	8.74
	Morecombe	150 users	92	5.76
Beaches and promenades, 1990	Herne Bay	127 users	88	12.34
	Herne Bay	189 residents	83	3.59
Cliff tops, 1988	Peacehaven	214 residents	54	3.50

Source: Penning-Rowsell *et al.,* 1992

future rate of erosion and hence the time at which access would be lost and the benefits would come on stream. It was not therefore possible to arrive at a total benefit figure for protecting the coast. Given that the number of people benefiting was not large, and the benefits were likely to be realised only after a considerable number of years, total discounted benefits were unlikely to be substantial. This result led to the decision not to proceed with protection on this stretch of coast (Penning-Rowsell *et al.*, 1992).

Another survey, in 1991, assessed the potential amenity benefits of a beach recharge scheme between Mablethorpe and Skegness, using a contingent valuation method to value the benefits of both maintaining and raising the existing beach levels. The average value was estimated at between £1.11 per visit for holidaymakers and £1.36 per visit for day-trippers. The study also looked at alternative beaches to determine whether or not it would be more economical for beach users to travel to an alternative site and avoid the beach recharge. It concluded that it was more efficient to maintain the beach levels as an amenity resource than to encourage people to travel to alternative sites (Posford Duvivier Environment, 1991).

The willingness to pay for conserving the Broadlands in East Anglia against salt-water flooding was assessed. This study was one of the first UK studies to attempt the estimation of non-use values, and a key finding was that people from all over the country did hold values for the preservation of the Broadlands even though they were unlikely to visit the area. Estimates of

between £67 and £140 per household per year were found, giving a total use (recreation and amenity) value of the area of between £5 million and £15.5 million per year (Batemen *et al.*, 1993).

Valuing water quality

We have shown how large the cost of cleaning up bathing waters has been. Here we draw upon a study which set out to assess whether it was worth it in terms of whether people were willing to pay for it. Visitors and locals were interviewed at Lowestoft, which met the bathing water standards, and at Great Yarmouth which, at the time, did not meet the bathing water standards. They were asked whether they would be willing to pay higher water rates to preserve or meet the standards at all Britain's beaches. At Great Yarmouth 57 per cent answered 'yes' to the question and at Lowestoft 58 per cent, a clear majority in each case.

The amount that people were willing to pay averaged £18.19 per household per annum at Great Yarmouth and £16.21 at Lowestoft (both allowing for those who refused to pay) (Georgiou *et al.*, 1996a). These amounts are substantially more than has been spent on bathing water improvements per household (£9) although it is not known whether this study of only two resorts in East Anglia reflects the general views held.

The results from this study were analysed further to assess why some people were unwilling to pay for improvements, and what the overall perception of risk from bathing water quality was. Some 12.75 per cent of the people in the survey stated that they, or a family member, have suffered an illness as a result of bathing in the sea. This does not mean that the water quality was responsible for the illness but that it was perceived to be so.

Actual epidemiological evidence suggests a much lower incidence of illness and it is unclear why the perceived incidence is greater, although one suggestion is that individuals over-assess the risk of low probability events, such as bathing water risks, and under-assess the risk of high probability events. This was borne out by the replies to the question, 'How risky do you think the following activities, products and technologies are to people in the UK?', whereby bathing water quality was perceived to be more risky than driving (Table 5.8).

Table 5.8 *Perceived risk of various types*

Risk type	Mean rating[1]
Food additives	2.59
Air pollution	3.70
Smoking	4.40
AIDS	3.66
Nuclear power	3.16
Bathing water quality	3.16
Driving	3.13
Sunbathing	3.34

[1]Rating: 5 very high, 1 very low   Source: Georgiou *et al.,* 1996b

Further work needs to be done, but the findings on willingness to pay must reflect these perceptions of risk (Georgiou *et al.,* 1996b).

Results of some other surveys have assessed the value of water quality improvements per trip. Having assessed the overall value of a day's recreation on the coast at £8.93 per person per trip as a baseline, values were derived for the willingness to pay for increased benefits (Table 5.9). The values found in the surveys differ but give an order of magnitude of the value attached to these improvements.

Attitude surveys

In 1997 the Agency commissioned a survey to establish the importance to water company customers of protecting and improving the environment. This was precipitated by the review of water company prices, due in 1999. Telephone interviews were held with 2,500 water bill payers across England and Wales. The main findings were:

● environmental improvements and an adequate supply of water are key issues to customers with some 69 per cent who said they would be willing to pay more, an average of £36 per year, to achieve these objectives;

● the quality of water in rivers and seas was regarded as very important by 86 per cent of customers;

● ninety-five per cent of customers would prefer to have the same water bill in the year 2000 as now and have environmental improvements, rather than receive a lower bill and have no environmental improvements;

● customers believe that water companies are working towards improving the environment, but 59 per cent think that they should do more (NOP Social and Political, 1997).

The OFWAT National Customers Council (ONCC) suggests, that with environmental improvements being the main cost driver on water and sewerage bills, the system should be changed so that costs do not always fall on the customer. The chairman of the ONCC said: *"Cleaner rivers and beaches are national assets. There is a strong case for a proportion of funding for environmental improvements to come from general taxation. There is also a case for local authorities to contribute to the funding of environmental improvements where they produce benefits for tourism and contribute to the local economy"* (OFWAT, 1998c).

The Agency is also looking at other techniques to help put a value on the environment including consensus building approaches, which attempt to build a community perspective on value. These will inform the way in which the Agency reports on and prioritises its actions in the protection of the coastal environment.

In 1996/97, DETR commissioned MORI to carry out a survey of 2,000 people in England and Wales to investigate attitudes

Table 5.9 *Willingness to pay for recreational activities*

Value	Activity and location	Improvement needed
£1.52/person/trip	Informal recreation on beaches in the north east of England	To comply with EC Bathing Waters Directive
£4.01/person/trip	Informal recreation on estuaries in Scotland	Further investment in sewage treatment to discharges from small conurbations
£0.76/person/trip	Informal recreation on beaches at Yarmouth	To comply with EC Bathing Waters Directive
£1.07/person/trip	Informal recreation on beaches at Lowestoft	To avoid future non-compliance with EC Bathing Waters Directive

Source: Foundation for Water Research, 1996

161

to, and knowledge of, environmental issues. This was the fourth such survey, after those carried out in 1986, 1989 and 1993. There were some results relevant to the coast.

● Some 88 per cent of people are concerned about the environment. Three aspects of coastal pollution - chemicals put into rivers and the sea, and oil and sewage on beaches - rank highly in the list of issues about which people are very worried, with over half the people interviewed being concerned (Figure 5.4).

● Some 30 per cent are very worried about over-fishing. This was the first time that this had been listed as an environmental issue in the surveys.

● Thirty-four per cent of people suggested they did not bathe in rivers or the sea in this country owing to pollution, an increase since 1993 when the number was 26 per cent.

Other findings were that people are generally very optimistic

Figure 5.4 *Percentage of people 'very worried' about environmental issues, 1996/97*

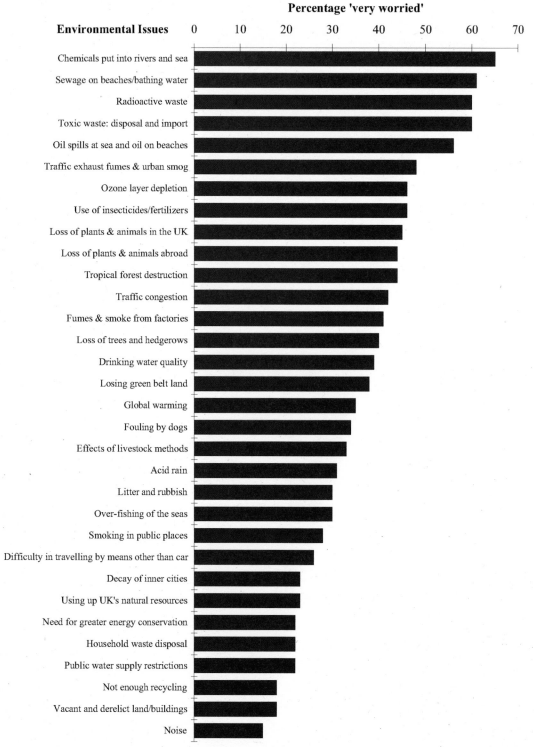

Source: Department of the Environment, Transport and the Regions; Crown copyright

that a lot can be done about environmental issues, although there is considerable confusion and lack of understanding about causes of environmental problems. People supported a wide range of environmental policy options but tended to oppose measures involving a direct cost to individuals (DETR, 1998c).

The last finding listed above is particularly interesting because bathing water quality has actually improved over the same period (Section 4.3). This could suggest that people are unaware of the improvements made, or that awareness of the potential risks has increased, amongst other factors.

All the information presented in this section shows that the coast is a valuable asset, although the actual value varies from person to person and from site to site. It provides an important insight into one element of the appraisal and decision-making process, and should help to inform future work.

Section 6 Conclusions: the Agency's opinion on the state of the coastal environment

A reasonable question to ask now is, 'What does all this information add up to?' Bearing in mind that measuring the state of the environment provides the basis for assessing priorities for action and charting progress with respect to environmental management plans and targets, analyses continually need to be done to decide which pressures and states cause the greatest concern and what are the priority issues to which strategies and actions need to be targeted. But concern will also depend on value judgements, and the value of the coastal environment will depend on its ability to meet the needs of the human population and of other species. Some of the most difficult value judgements will be those where a view is needed, often based on incomplete information or scenario planning, on the need for action to both protect the environment and prevent a rapid growth in the exposure of life and property to the potentially catastrophic risks of coastal inundation.

Stresses and strains

The information on pressures on the coastal environment shows that the polluting load from sewerage systems has reduced over the last decade or so due to better sewage treatment following investment by water companies. Pollution from combined sewer overflows is set to decrease with further investment planned by 2005. The load of some priority dangerous substances to estuaries and coastal waters from industry, sewerage and riverine sources has also reduced. Though nutrient loads to coastal waters have in general declined, there are still areas where loads have not decreased and are even increasing. Dumping of industrial and mine wastes and sewage sludge at sea has ceased altogether. The number of tanker accidents at sea has also reduced, although those that do occur can be catastrophic locally.

On the other hand, many more pressures are growing. The pressures exerted by society and lifestyles are increasing, with the demands for a planned 4.6 million new households in England and Wales above 1991 levels by 2016 of particular significance. Many of these new households are expected to be on the coast in the south and east of England where it is already highly urbanised. The rate of coastal habitat loss because of human uses has historically been very high and continues, albeit at a lower rate. Where development occurred in low-lying areas in the past, sea defences were built to protect lives, property and land. In places, 'hard' sea defences are exerting a pressure on the environment as naturally dynamic coastlines cannot adjust in response to erosional forces and sea level change, leading to problems such as loss of natural habitats and an interruption in the natural movement of sediments having a knock-on effect elsewhere. Some parts of the coastline might benefit from managed retreat, but this may not always be practical and there may not yet be sufficient understanding of the natural processes involved. Unless the pressure to further develop within flood risk areas is strongly resisted, the demand for flood defences, the risk to life and property, and the

associated pressures on the natural environment will increase dramatically.

Lifestyles are also changing rapidly, with many people having more leisure time and more disposable income to spend on recreational activities, including travel. The coast has always been attractive to tourists and many coastal leisure activities are gaining in popularity, further increasing the demand for facilities. The coastal environment offers an opportunity for meeting the needs of these changing lifestyles but local problems can arise if conflicts among users, and between users and the environment, are not managed.

Goods and ships passing though our ports are increasing, as is the motorised traffic on coastal roads (many of which are narrow), bringing added emissions of aerial pollutants, congestion and inconvenince to the local population. Some ports are thriving and may wish to expand into estuaries which have already lost a substantial proportion of their natural habitats. Any increases in demand for land for industrial, port and urban development or leisure facilities will present great challenges for planners, environmental regulators and conservation organisations.

In terms of abstractions and removals from the coastal environment, there is likely to be a growing demand for marine aggregate, mainly for construction but also for beach replenishment and for export.

The tonnage of fish landed by the UK fleet has fallen for most species but has risen for shellfish, and many fish stocks are now near or below levels considered 'safe' for the sustainability of the species.

There are significant numbers of coastal pollution incidents, and illegal dumping of oil from ships is a significant source of oil to the North Sea. Pressures from diffuse pollution are also giving cause for concern. These include leaching of antifouling paints from ships, urban and road runoff, and problems caused by abandoned mines.

On top of this, climate change is a growing concern because it naturally affects the weather and river catchment processes which impact upon the coastal environment. Climate change is predicted to impact upon river flows into estuaries. The maintenance of adequate river flows is required to sustain estuarine ecology and sediment transport. Climate change may also affect other aspects such as biodiversity, eutrophication in coastal bays and lagoons, the frequency and severity of storms and tidal and sea flooding.

Overall, the pressures caused by the changing climate, sea level change, changing lifestyles, diffuse pollution and increasing urbanisation pose the greatest challenges to the future management of the coastal environment. Equally, the associated uncertainties present considerable challenges to those charged with decision making and policy setting.

Viewpoints

Significant improvements have taken place in water and sediment quality and in compliance with European Directives. Since the 1970s changing industrial and agricultural practices, combined with investments in effluent quality by the water industry and other industries, and the establishment of independent regulation, have resulted in large improvements in both the chemical and biological quality of many estuaries and coastal waters. The 1990s have seen a steady improvement in the quality of bathing waters and shellfish waters with reductions in the concentrations of the most dangerous substances in water and sediments, reducing health risks to humans and wildlife. Nevertheless, a few areas have high, local concentrations of some hazardous substances arising from historical contamination and diffuse sources. Metal contamination of plants and animals around our coast does not, in general, appear to be widespread, but there are problems with individual substances.

Despite widespread nutrient enrichment of estuaries and coastal waters, nuisance algal blooms tend to be localised and only five coastal areas have been designated by the Government as eutrophic. Human poisoning from algal toxins in shellfish has not been recorded for many years due to strict regulation.

The coastline of England and Wales is part of our natural heritage and has a rich and varied flora and fauna. This is reflected in the many important designations conferred upon it, both for landscape (National Parks, Areas of Outstanding Natural Beauty and Heritage Coasts) and wildlife (Special Areas of Conservation, Special Protection Areas and Sites of Special Scientific Interest) and conservation purposes. In addition, an ever-increasing number of beaches gain awards for their amenities and aesthetic qualities, including Blue Flags and Seaside Awards from the Tidy Britain Group. However, marine litter continues to cause nuisance and harm to animals, and visitors are among the major contributors.

Some 16 per cent of the land in the coastal zone supports natural and semi-natural cover (which includes rough pasture). Development has encroached onto saltmarshes and intertidal areas, and rural land is continually being put under pressure for development. In parts of England, saltmarshes are eroding significantly and yet these provide a natural defence from the sea. About one-third of the coastline is defended from erosion and flooding. Many defences are in need of moderate or significant improvement, all require maintenance and many modern 'soft' defences require continual recycling and periodic renourishment.

The energy resources available from the coast are principally oil and gas, and wind and waves. The known reserves of oil and gas remain relatively constant despite production and new areas are being explored close to shore, with the potential for adding to the pressures on the coastal environment. Coastal alternative energy schemes are still in their infancy. They have great appeal because of the promise of cleaner energy production, but there are concerns about their environmental and aesthetic impacts if they are not planned and managed effectively.

While the populations of some coastal or marine animals, such as many seabirds and waders, are increasing, other species appear to be declining. The number of eels and salmon, which migrate through estuaries, have declined dramatically in recent years. Sand lizards and natterjack toads have declined over a longer time period. Over 50 non-native species have colonised British coastal waters. One-fifth of the UK's priority species are dependent upon coastal habitats, and many fish species are now considered to be threatened including shad and many commercial species.

There is great uncertainty about the 'health' of marine ecosystems. Contamination by metals, organic substances (including pesticides, polychlorinated biphenyls and polycyclic aromatic hydrocarbons) and other synthetic chemicals appears to be occurring at low levels. A number of these substances are already banned but they still persist in the environment, bound up in sediments. In some heavily industrialised or urbanised estuaries there is evidence of stress in marine life caused by exposure to combinations of contaminants. The long-term effects of these stresses, and their consequences for whole populations, are not well understood. For example, there is increasing concern over the effects of endocrine-disrupting chemicals in the environment. The ban on the use of the antifouling agent tributyl tin on small vessels has brought about gradual improvements in some affected areas, but in other areas recovery has not occurred because it is still used on large vessels. Tributyl tin does not degrade rapidly, and sediments are still contaminated. A complete ban on tributyl tin would at least stop any further contamination of water, sediments and biota. Endocrine disruption has been observed in several marine species, but the causes have yet to be fully substantiated (apart from the case of tributyl tin and its effects on shellfish). Although there have been major studies of individual species and communities, or at specific locations, there is no coherent national picture of the state of our coastal and marine plants and animals. Better and more integrated information on health, populations, community structures and biodiversity is required to determine the state of, and risks to, coastal biota.

While existing monitoring programmes, scientific tools and assessment schemes have provided much valuable information on the state of the coastal environment, there are many aspects which need improvement. The existing estuarine classification scheme only demonstrates general differences in environmental quality. More comprehensive approaches need to be developed to assess the state of estuaries and coastal environments, taking account of different viewpoints. Powerful monitoring technologies, like remote sensing, need to be more widely used over larger areas. Established technologies, continuous water quality monitors, could be deployed at more sites, at relatively low cost. There is also a need to develop rapid techniques for monitoring biological health. Future coastal monitoring will require greater ingenuity, more efficient use of resources and co-operation of effort between organisations to more clearly define the state of the coastal environment.

The Agency's overall opinion

What actions therefore need to be taken to reduce the pressures, and to protect and improve the state of the coastal environment? Because many of the pressures are interlinked there is a need for integrated coastal management to ensure that improvements in one sector or area do not cause problems elsewhere. While this need has been recognised for several years, real stakeholder participation in the planning processes has only just started.

The Agency has developed an environmental strategy to address major issues in an integrated way, recognising the interactions between different media (Environment Agency, 1997f). The principal themes of the strategy in the context of the coastal environment are:

- addressing some of the causes of, and helping to ameliorate the effects of, climate change;

- ensuring that the impacts on the coastal environment from major industries are progressively reduced, both for the benefit of industry itself and for the enjoyment of coastal areas by everyone;

- improving air quality and thus a specific source of pollutant loads to the coast;

- managing wastes so that they do not add to the polluting pressures on coasts;

- ensuring long-term and integrated approaches to the management of water resources which will have an impact on residual flows to estuaries;

- delivering an integrated approach to the management of river basins, which includes impingement on the coastal environment;

- conserving the land which includes working with nature to reduce coastal flooding and reporting regularly on the state of flood defences;

- managing our freshwater fisheries (many fish migrate through estuaries) in a sustainable way;

- improving the biodiversity of coastal habitats.

There are a number of specific issues relating to the coastal environment which have been drawn out in this assessment that need to be addressed if a more sustainable balance between the needs of society and the health of coastal ecosystems is to be achieved.

- ### Sea level changes and increased storminess

    In the 20th century global surface air temperatures have risen by between 0.3°C and 0.6°C, and they are predicted to continue to rise by between 0.1°C and 0.3°C per decade in the UK, affecting weather patterns. Many of the most serious storms have occurred in the last decade and climate change predictions suggest that the UK climate could become stormier and experience increasing flooding, erosion and damage. At the same

time sea levels have been rising in some areas by up to 50mm per decade, especially in the south and east of England.

These factors are putting pressure on coastal defences. As the sea level rises and natural barriers such as saltmarshes are destroyed, both by natural forces and human activities, maintenance costs are increasing. In some areas the costs of maintaining defences can outweigh the benefits and so managed retreat may have to be the way forward. But this could mean local losses of land and possible livelihood for people. In many urban areas, maintaining defences is cost-beneficial but defences can disturb natural processes such as sediment transport with consequences elsewhere on the coast which become starved of sediment. In other cases sea defences now protect habitats designated as Special Protection Areas and it is unclear how to work with nature in these circumstances. All these issues suggest that there is a need to review coastal defence policy. There is a need for a better understanding of coastal processes and for greater involvement of local people in the decision-making process. While shoreline management plans were developed to address the issue, their effectiveness has yet to be fully demonstrated, and further consideration needs to be given to how they integrate with all the other plans in the coastal zone.

There is also a lack of accurate and precise information on the height and shape of coastal areas subject to inundation with rising sea levels. The Agency is addressing this issue by developing airborne techniques for improved mapping of low-lying coastal areas at risk from sea level changes and is considering the setting up of a network of long-term reference sites against which to measure sea level change. The Agency is also addressing the need to improve existing sea defences against predicted increases in storminess with a large capital investment programme. In planning these schemes, the Agency will consult widely and find ways of resolving any conflicts between conservation interests, natural processes, landowners and other coastal users.

- ### The quality of bathing waters and beaches

By far the largest investment on the coast in the 1990s has been on improvements to sewerage and sewage treatment to ensure that waters comply with the European Bathing Water Quality Directive. Despite this several areas in the north west, one of the most popular destinations for seaside trips, and other parts of England still fail to comply with the mandatory standards. Diffuse sources of contaminants may be the cause but more work is needed to establish this with certainty. There are also issues surrounding the achievement of stricter guideline standards, the meeting of standards outside the designated bathing season and the consequences of possible revisions to the Directive. The Government has announced that further improvements must be allowed for in the capital investment programme of the water companies in the next millennium in order to achieve a higher level of compliance. The Agency has developed a strategy for dealing with this issue which includes local investigations of contaminant sources, pollution prevention campaigns, undertaking research and development and advising Government on the proposed changes to the Directive.

Attitude surveys show that most people are concerned about pollution on beaches and in the sea. But surveys have shown that visitors contribute much of the litter on beaches which adds to the waste materials derived from shipping and activities offshore. Beach cleaning can help to a certain extent although this can affect the natural flora and fauna. It would obviously be better to stop the pollution in the first place. There is a need for better information for the public to help them play their part in resolving these issues. The success of the new port waste management regulations in reducing litter from shipping will need to be assessed in due course.

Loss of habitats and implications for biodiversity

England and Wales have a long history of destruction or modification of coastal habitats, linked to the reclamation of flat land for food production. Historically, large intertidal areas and saltmarshes have been reclaimed or altered; many sites are reported to be at risk of further deterioration. The use of hard sea defences, which stop sediment supply to such areas resulting in coastal land loss, is in some places exacerbating the problem. Erosion has been the main cause of saltmarsh loss in the last 15 years. Insensitive development on the coast can contribute to habitat degradation. The Agency is working with others to implement the EC Habitats Directive. Changes to some discharge consents and sea defence regimes may be needed to enhance the protection of some of Europe's most important wildlife sites. The Agency also has an important role to play in ensuring that habitats are protected and it will work with others to restore coastal habitats that have been degraded. As mentioned previously, a review of coastal defence policy must take into account the impacts on habitats and biodiversity.

The decline in habitats is one factor that has put some coastal plants and animals under stress; others include invasion by non-native species and pollution. The Agency will play its full part in helping to implement the UK Biodiversity Action Plan which is now being extended to coastal habitats and species.

Decline in fisheries

Despite the Common Fisheries Policy of the European Union, there is evidence that the state of fisheries is not good and many species are declining. The Agency is particularly concerned that conditions at sea may be affecting the return rates of migratory species. The numbers of salmon are declining especially those which have spent more than one winter at sea. This issue has been raised internationally and the Agency has already taken action through implementing salmon action plans.

But the Agency also considers that some changes are needed to the Common Fisheries Policy, including the continuation of the derogation that restricts fishing within the coastal zone limits to UK boats. There is a need for greater understanding of the different factors that impact upon the dynamics of fish populations, with particular emphasis on the impact of rising sea temperatures, fishing activities, and the impact of low concentrations of hazardous substances.

Pollution by hazardous substances

While many estuaries have recovered from serious historic industrial and sewage pollution, and loads of many hazardous substances such as metals to the sea have reduced significantly, there are still localised exceedances of standards, especially for copper, zinc and tributyl tin and the target reductions for some metals in common use, such as zinc, have not yet been met. Furthermore, the range of chemicals used by society has increased significantly, such that it is not practical or affordable to include them all in routine monitoring and surveillance programmes. However, biological monitoring has shown the sub-lethal effects of pollution on some species such as changes to the 'scope for growth' in mussels, endocrine-disruption in fish and shellfish, and impairments to the growth of oyster larvae. Most pollution control effort to date has been focused on point-source discharges, and there is now a greater awareness of the potential impact of diffuse pollution arising from road and land runoff and atmospheric sources, all of which accumulate in estuaries and the coastal zone.

The Agency is addressing the issue of hazardous substances through the implementation of integrated pollution prevention and control to achieve environmental quality standards, the development of toxicity-based consents and taking precautionary action where necessary in cases where risks may be high but scientific knowledge is incomplete. The Government has recently been consulted on its strategy for the use and production of chemicals and the Agency will play its part in delivering the final strategy, especially those moves which will achieve environmental benefits. One way of reducing diffuse pollution is to raise awareness of the potential risks. The Agency will continue to run targeted pollution prevention campaigns, but there is a need to raise general awareness too. The Agency will continue to monitor for the impact of hazardous substances and continue to support the development of techniques to assess their impact on the health of ecosystems.

Development pressures on the coast

With increasing urbanisation and mobility and more leisure time, the pressures on the coastal zone and conflicts between users are growing. Port traffic and the demand for larger ports are increasing. Habitats have been disappearing rapidly although designations under the Habitats Directive are attempting to recognise areas which are important for biodiversity. The short to medium term pressure to develop low-lying coastal areas for domestic and industrial use is considerable. There is a need to develop, through a risk based approach, robust land use policies that both protect the environment and prevent a rapid growth in the exposure of life and property to the potentially catastrophic risks of coastal inundation.

There are many different kinds of coastal plans and many different types of designated areas relating to the coastal zone and there is a perceived need for better integration. Integrated coastal zone management should be the way forward although it does not appear to have been very successful to date. There have been a number of joint plans produced, and there needs to be more analysis to determine why they have not been perceived as successful. European initiatives may help to highlight the difficulties in the process, but clearly there is a need for organisations to work much more closely together than currently happens. Planning is one thing; further action by the many players involved is now required. There is also a need for more collaborative involvement of local people through partnerships. The Agency is committed to close and responsive relationships with the public, local authorities and other organisations, and is carrying out research and development into better involvement of stakeholders in the decision-making process. Whilst local partnerships have started to be made, there is also a need for integration at policy level. In particular, the planning authorities need to be aware of the state of the environment in order to develop sustainability plans for the future. The Agency recognises it needs to work more closely with the DETR, all planning authorities and regional development agencies to ensure the information is in a form that can be directly used to fully influence the planning process. Within the Agency itself, the 'breaking down' of functional barriers has started as the Agency moves towards full integration, but better communication between players is essential.

● **Understanding of the coastal environment**

Decisions on the future management of coasts should be based on sound scientific information. In this report, an attempt has been made to compile and assess a wide range of relevant information at a national level. This has shown that there are gaps which require further work to improve decision-making processes. In particular there is currently no reliable way of saying, in an integrated way, how good or how poor the quality of estuaries and coasts are.

There is a need for a set of indicators to assess trends in the state of the coastal environment and for reporting to decision-makers and the public alike. Many such indicators have been developed for other environments, such as for fresh waters, but the coastal environment seems to have been forgotten despite its importance to the nation's social and economic well-being. Periodic reporting using key indicators would also help

understanding of the nature of coasts and how human activities are affecting them, and whether policies are working towards achieving sustainable development.

By artificially maintaining our coastline, there are many places where natural processes have been changed with detriment elsewhere so that the existing position is unsustainable. Natural processes need to be understood to avoid conflict between coastal users and the environment, and to find better ways of working in harmony with nature. This is particularly important in protecting against sea level rise and increased storminess, in reducing erosion of areas dependent on natural accretion, in licensing the extraction of more aggregates, and in addressing further development needs such as port and marina developments.

The Agency is sponsoring a wide range of research and development to achieve a better understanding of coasts generally, including the development of novel monitoring techniques. There is a need for continued co-operation with others, including European partners, on scientific and technical developments to ensure that the best available scientific data are used to inform decisions.

Appendix 1   National and international standards and targets

EC Directives

Directives of relevance to this report are given in Table A1.1. The key Directives are discussed in the relevant sections of this report.

Table A1.1 *EC Directives relevant to this report*

EC Directive		Directive number
Dangerous substances	Pollution caused by the discharge of certain dangerous substances into the aquatic environment	76/464/EEC
	Limit values and quality objectives for mercury discharges by the chlor- alkali electrolysis industry	82/176/EEC
	Limit values and quality objectives for mercury discharges by sectors other than the chlor-alkali electrolysis industry	84/156/EEC
	Limit values and quality objectives for cadmium discharges	83/513/EEC
	Limit values and quality objectives for discharges of hexachlorocyclohexane	84/491/EEC
	Limit values and quality objectives for discharges of certain dangerous substances included in List I of the Annex to Directive 76/464/EEC	86/280/EEC
	Amending Annex II to Directive 86/280/EEC on limit values and quality objectives for discharges of certain dangerous substances included in List I of the Annex to Directive 76/464/EEC	88/347/EEC
	Amending Annex II to Directive 86/280/EEC on limit values and quality objectives for discharges of certain dangerous substances included in List I of the Annex to Directive 76/464/EEC	90/415/EEC
Bathing waters		76/160/EEC
Quality required for shellfish waters		79/923/EEC
Shellfish hygiene		91/492/EEC
Titanium dioxide	Waste from the titanium dioxide industry	78/176/EEC
	Amendment	83/29/EEC
	Procedures for the surveillance and monitoring of environments concerned by waste from the titanium dioxide industry	82/883/EEC
	Procedures for harmonising the reduction and elimination of pollution caused by waste from the titanium dioxide industry	92/112/EEC
Urban waste water treatment		91/271/EEC
Protection of waters against pollution caused by nitrates from agricultural sources		91/676/EEC
The conservation of natural habitats and of wild fauna and flora		92/43/EEC
Conservation of wild birds		79/409/EEC
Integrated pollution prevention and control		96/61/EEC

Bathing Waters Directive (76/160/EEC)

As the competent authority for England and Wales, the Agency plays an important role in the implementation of the EC Bathing Waters Directive. Each year during the bathing season which runs from 15 May to 30 September, samples are taken at regular intervals to monitor the quality of designated bathing waters. The Agency policy is that 20 samples are taken at predetermined sites from the beaches of every designated bathing water. Each sample is then analysed and compared against the standards set out by the Directive (see Table A1.2). The Directive also gives reference methods for analysis. The main parameters (1 to 5, Table A1.2) aim to give an indication of the extent to which a bathing water is contaminated by sewage-derived material. Samples must meet standards at least as stringent as I values, with member states of the European Community endeavouring to observe the more stringent G values. A bathing water is deemed to have complied if 95 per cent of samples taken there meet these standards.

Table A1.2 *Quality requirements for bathing waters*

	Parameters	Guideline standard	Imperative standard	Minimum sampling frequency
1	total coliforms/100 ml	500	10,000	fortnightly (1)
2	faecal coliforms/100 ml	100	2,000	fortnightly (1)
3	faecal streptococci/100 ml	100	-	(2)
4	salmonella/litre	-	0	(2)
5	enteroviruses PFU/10 litres	-	0	(2)
6	pH	-	6 to 9 (0)	(2)
7	colour	- -	no abnormal change in colour (0) -	fortnightly (1) (2)
8	mineral oils mg/l	- ≤0.3	no film visible on the surface of the water and no odour -	fortnightly (1) (2)
9	surface active substances reacting with methylene blue mg/l lauryl sulphate	- ≤0.3	No lasting foam -	fortnightly (1) (2)
10	phenols mg/l	- ≤0.005	no specific odour ≤0.05	fortnightly (1) (2)
11	transparency metres	2	1 (0)	fortnightly (1)
12	dissolved oxygen per cent saturation O_2	80 to 120	-	(2)
13	tarry residues and floating materials,for example wood, plastic, bottles, rubber or any other substance. Waste or splinters	absence		fortnightly (1)
14	ammonia mg/l NH_4			(3)
15	nitrogen Kjeldahl mg/litre N			(3)
16	pesticides mg/l			(2)
17	heavy metals, for example As, Cd, Cr, Pb, Hg mg/l			(2)
18	cyanide mg/l			(2)
19	nitrate & phosphate mg/l			(2)

(0)　Provision exists for exceeding the limits in the event of exceptional geographical or meteorological conditions.

(1)　When sampling in previous years gives results appreciably better than those in the Annex and no new factors likely to lower water quality have appeared; the sampling frequency can be reduced by a factor of two.

(2)　Concentration to be checked when an inspection shows the substance may be present or the water quality has deteriorated.

(3)　Must be checked when there is a tendency toward eutrophication in the water.

The summary results from the 1998 bathing season are shown in Table A1.3.

Table A1.3 *Numbers of bathing waters complying with the imperative standards for microbiological quality in 1998*

Region	Number of bathing waters	Number complying	Per cent complying	Number not complying	Per cent not complying
Anglian	36	36	100	0	0
North East	56	47	83.9	9	16.1
North West	34	21	61.8	13	38.2
Southern	77	75	97.4	2	2.6
South West*	183	167	91.3	16	8.7
Thames	3	3	100	0	0
Environment Agency Wales	68	64	94.1	4	5.9
Total*	457	413	90.4	44	9.6

* excludes Redgate, which was closed due to safety reasons

Source: Environment Agency

Dangerous Substances Directive (74/464/EEC)

Standards have been set for 18 substances under this Directive and daughter directives (Table A1.4). The environmental quality standards (EQS) have limits given as annual means.

Table A1.4 *List I environmental quality standards (EQS) - downstream monitoring*

List I substance	Annual mean (µg/l)		
	Inland	Estuary	Marine
mercury and compounds	1	0.3 (D)	0.3 (D)
cadmium and compounds	5	2.5 (D)	2.5 (D)
hexachlorocyclohexane (all isomers)	0.1	0.002	0.02
carbon tetrachloride	12	12	12
para-para DDT	0.01	0.01	0.01
total DDT	0.025	0.025	0.025
pentachlorophenol	2	2	2
total `drins	0.03	0.03	0.03
aldrin	0.01	0.01	0.01
dieldrin	0.01	0.01	0.01
endrin	0.005	0.005	0.005
isodrin	0.005	0.005	0.005
hexachlorobenzene	0.03	0.03	0.03
hexachlorobutadiene	0.1	0.1	0.1
chloroform	12	12	12
1-2-dichloroethane	10	10	10
trichloroethylene	10	10	10
perchlorethylene	10	10	10
trichlorobenzene	0.4	0.4	0.4

Standards are for total concentrations, unless indicated by (D) for dissolved.

For the purposes of estuarine or marine List I monitoring, samples should be taken at least 12 times per year or four times per year when a greater frequency is not practical.

Environmental monitoring of List I substances is also required at a national network of sites chosen to reflect the ubiquity of a substance. These are generally located to correspond with registered discharges or in the vicinity of diffuse inputs known to have a measurable effect on concentrations. Where possible these sites coincide with those covered by the UK National

Table A1.5 *Environmental quality standards for List II substances in saline waters*

Substance	EQS (µg/l)	Substance	EQS (µg/l)
1,1,1-trichloroethane	100 AT	bentazone	500 AT
1,1,2-trichloroethane	300 AT	benzene	30 AT
arsenic	25 AD	chloronitrotoluenes	10 AT
tributyl tin	0.002 MT	demeton	0.5 AT
triphenyltin and its derivatives	0.008 MT	dimethoate	1 AT
4-chloro-3-methyl-phenol	40 AT	linuron	2 AT
2-chlorophenol	50 AT	mecoprop	20 AT
2,4-dichlorophenol	20 AT	naphthalene	5 AT
(2,4-dichlorophenoxy)acetic acid (2,4-D ester)	1 AT	toluene	40 AT
(2,4-dichlorophenoxy)acetic acid (2,4-D non-ester)	40 AT	triazaphos	0.005 AT
		xylene	30 AT
trifluralin	0.1 AT	atrazine and simazine	2 AT (for the two substances in total)
endosulphan	0.003 AT		
fenitrothion	0.01 AT	azinphos-methyl	0.01 AT
malathion	0.02 AT	dichlorvos	0.04 AT 0.6 M (24 hours after dosing at fish farms)
biphenyl	25 AT		

A = Annual average
M = Maximum allowable concentration in any sample
D = Dissolved
T = Total

Table A1.6 *Advisory quality standards for List II substances in saline waters[1]*

Substance	EQS (µg/l)	Substance	EQS (µg/l)
lead	25 AD	boron	7000 AT
chromium	15 AD	iron	1000 AD
zinc	40 AD	pH	6.0 - 8.5 P
copper	5 AD	vanadium	100 AT
nickel	30 AD	cyfluthrin	0.001 PT
permethrin	0.01 AD	sulcofuron	25 PT
polychloro chloromethyl sulphonamido diphenyl ether (PCSDs)	0.05 AD	flucofuron	1.0 PT

[1] Taken from DoE Circular 7/89 and Welsh Office Circular 16/89

A = Annual average
P = 95% of samples must lie within the range shown
D = Dissolved
T = Total

Marine Monitoring Programme (Appendix 3).

The Directive provides a definition for List II substances, for which pollution reduction programmes have to be established with deadlines for implementation. The identification of List II substances and setting of standards is left to member states. Those relevant to saline waters are given in Table A1.5 (statutory standards) and A1.6 (advisory standards).

List I and List II substances have a 'standstill' requirement in the Directive for which samples of sediment or biota must be taken at least once per year to monitor any changes in concentrations of substances in sediments.

Shellfish Waters Directive (79/923/EEC)

Under the Directive, member states were required to designate

Table A1.7 *Quality parameters for shellfish waters*

	Parameter	Guideline standard	Imperative standard	Minimum sampling frequency
1	pH	-	7-9	quarterly
2	temperature °C	a discharge affecting shellfish waters must not cause the waters to increase by 2°C above background temperature	-	quarterly
3	colouration (after filtration) mg Pt/l	-	a discharge affecting shellfish waters must not cause the colour to deviate by >10mg Pt/l from background level	quarterly
4	suspended solids mg/l	-	a discharge affecting shellfish waters must not cause an increase of >30 per cent of the background concentration	quarterly
5	salinity ‰	12 to 38‰	≤ 40‰ a discharge affecting shellfish waters must not cause their salinity to exceed 10 per cent of the background salinity	monthly
6	dissolved oxygen saturation %	>= 80%	> 70% (average) measurements repeated if individual result indicates value < 70% individual measurement may not indicate a value < 60% unless no harmful consequences to shellfish	monthly minimum of one sample representative of low DO on day of sampling. Minimum of two samples in one day if major daily variations suspected
7	petroleum hydrocarbons	-	hydrocarbons must not be present in such quantities as to: - produce visible film on water and/or deposit on shellfish - have harmful effects on shellfish	quarterly
8	organohalogenated substances	concentration of each substance in shellfish flesh must be so limited that it contributes to the high quality of shellfish products	concentration of each substance in water or shellfish flesh must not reach or exceed levels harmful to shellfish and larvae	half-yearly
9	metals mg/l Ag, As, Cd, Cr, Cu, Hg, Ni, Pb, Zn	as in 8	as in 8, the synergic effects of these metals must be taken into consideration	half-yearly
10	faecal coliforms per 100 ml	< 300 in shellfish flesh and intervalvular liquid[1]	-	quarterly
11	substances affecting the taste of shellfish	-	concentration lower than that liable to impair the taste of the shellfish	-
12	saxitoxin (produced by dinoflagellates)	-	-	-

[1]In accordance with EC Directive on Shellfish Hygiene (91/492/EEC)

coastal and brackish waters needing protection or improvement to support shellfish and set values for parameters listed in the Annex to the Directive (Table A1.7). The standards set were not to be less stringent than the imperative (I) values and member states were to endeavour to observe the guideline (G) values. When setting values, standards already set in the Dangerous Substances Directive were to be taken into account.

The parameters specified generally relate to substances that can inhibit growth or survival. Imperative values are judged to have been complied with if standards are not exceeded on an annual basis and minimum sampling frequencies are set:

(i)   100 per cent of samples for organohalogenated substances and metals, sampled half- yearly;

(ii)   95 per cent of samples for salinity and dissolved oxygen, sampled monthly;

(iii)   75 per cent of samples for other parameters, sampled quarterly.

Member states may reduce the sampling frequency if it can be demonstrated that water quality is better than that described by the guideline values. If there are no pollution sources and no risk of deterioration, zero sampling may be permitted.

This Directive was originally implemented administratively in England and Wales. The Directive was transposed into legislation in June 1997 by the coming into force of the Surface Waters (Shellfish) (Classification) Regulations 1997 and the Surface Waters (Shellfish) Directions 1997. The Regulations set mandatory minimum standards equal to the imperative values in the Directives. However, through the Directives, the Agency has the task of deciding how far it is possible to go beyond the imperative values towards achieving non-mandatory guideline values in designated waters in the light of local circumstances. In setting standards the Agency must also take into account the current water quality and the principle that implementation of the Directive must not lead to increased pollution. In deriving these operational standards, the Agency will not promote expenditure which is disproportionate to the expected degree of environmental improvement.

In July 1998 the Government issued a consultation paper concerning the implementation of the Shellfish Waters Directive which proposed a revised policy on the designation of waters in need of protection or improvement. It made proposals on standard setting for some parameters for which the Directive does not set a numerical value. The consultation period ended in September 1998.

Shellfish Hygiene Directive (91/492/EEC)

The Shellfish Hygiene Directive was adopted in order to protect consumers of shellfish. It sets quality criteria for shellfish taken from shellfish harvesting areas including live bivalve molluscs, echinoderms, tunicates and marine gastropods. In the UK the Directive has been implemented into national legislation by the Food Safety (Live Bivalve Molluscs and Other Shellfish) Regulations 1992.

The Directive requires member states to designate bivalve production areas and classify them according to the level of treatment they require prior to their sale for human consumption (see Table A1.8). The Directive also lays down regulations for the handling of live molluscs, introducing a 'paper trail' which allows batches of shellfish to be traced from harvesting to sale. This allows any illness through consumption to be traced back to the harvesting area.

Table A1.8 *Shellfish hygiene classification*

Class A:	Areas producing shellfish which can be collected for direct human consumption without any treatment or cleaning process. Shellfish should conform to the End Product Standard (see below).
Class B:	Areas producing shellfish which can only be placed on the market after relaying in clean sea water or treatment in an approved purification centre. Shellfish must conform to the End Product Standard and not exceed: (i) 6,000 faecal coliforms per 100g flesh or (ii) 4,600 E. coli per 100g of flesh in 90 per cent of samples taken.
Class C:	Areas from which shellfish can only be placed on the market after prolonged relaying in clean sea water or after intensive purification. Shellfish from these areas must not exceed 60,000 faecal coliforms per 100g of flesh.

End Product Standards are given as requirements for live bivalve molluscs intended for immediate human consumption. They must:

(i)   be fresh, alive and free from dirt;

(ii)   contain fewer than 300 faecal coliforms or fewer than 230 E. coli per 100g of mollusc flesh;

(iii)   contain no Salmonella in 25g of mollusc flesh;

(iv)   not contain toxic or objectionable compounds (as listed in the Annex to the Shellfish Waters Directive (79/923/EEC) (Table A1.7) in such quantities that permissible daily intake may be exceeded or taste impaired;

(v)   contain a total paralytic shellfish poison content of less than 80g per 100g of mollusc flesh;

(vi)   not contain detectable levels of diarrhetic shellfish poison;

(vii)   not contain radionuclides in excess of limits for foodstuffs laid down by the EC.

The Directive gives methodologies to be used for monitoring but concedes that in the absence of routine virological procedures and standards viral health checks must be based on faecal bacteria counts.

Titanium dioxide Directives

The first Directive (78/176/EEC) required any discharge of titanium dioxide to be authorised. The effects on receiving waters were to be monitored and a programme for the progressive reduction of pollution implemented. There was also a requirement for new plants to have a full environmental impact assessment prior to construction.

The monitoring Directive (82/883/EEC) required regulatory bodies to complete a monitoring programme of all environmental media based on the requirements of the first Directive. The Amendment Directive (83/29/EEC) changed the first Directive to allow more time for proposals for harmonisation of the pollution reduction programme to be submitted. Harmonisation of monitoring programmes between member states was required to eliminate distortions to competition.

The Harmonisation Directive (92/112/EEC) required extra controls on production processes to further limit polluting loads. The dumping of solid, strong acid (pH <5.5), treatment, weak acid or neutralised waste into coastal or surface waters was prohibited from 1993. Discharge of strong acid and solid wastes was also prohibited, and discharges of weak acid or neutralised waste had to be reduced. The level of restriction depended upon the process used to extract titanium dioxide.

In the UK, waters receiving a relevant discharge are sampled at a minimum frequency of three times per year. Samples are taken in the immediate vicinity of the discharge point and in a neighbouring zone not affected by the discharge. The Directive also requires a biological survey to be carried out and sediment samples taken once every year.

Urban Waste Water Treatment Directive (91/271/EEC)

The Urban Waste Water Treatment Directive (91/271/EEC) sets out to protect the environment from the adverse effects of discharges arising from urban areas and certain industrial sectors. It lays down minimum standards for the provision of sewerage systems and sewage treatment. It also requires an end to the dumping of sewage sludge at sea.

Under the Urban Waste Water Treatment Directive all significant discharges of sewage must be treated before they are discharged to estuaries or coastal waters. For coastal waters a significant discharge is one that serves an agglomeration with a population equivalent of more than 10,000 and for estuaries it is a population equivalent of 2,000 (Table A1.9). The Directive also requires appropriate treatment to be provided for discharges from smaller agglomerations. Sewage will normally be treated to secondary treatment standards (typically a biological process).

Higher (tertiary) treatment is required for discharges to sensitive areas, for example waters subject to eutrophication, or where other Directives require improved treatment such as the Bathing Waters Directive (76/160/EEC).

The Directive allows provision for less sensitive estuarine or coastal areas to receive discharges where primary treatment is sufficient, subject to comprehensive studies demonstrating low risk to the environment. In the UK less sensitive areas are referred to as high natural dispersion areas. Studies into the effects of discharges in these areas are carried out at the expense of the discharger and audited by the Agency. Discharges of greater than 15,000 population equivalents had to be assessed by the end of 1997, and evaluations of smaller discharges are to be completed by the end of 2005.

Table A1.9 *Treatment requirements and deadlines for the Urban Waste Water Treatment Directive*

Size of urban area (population equivalent)	Nature of receiving water	Compliance deadline			Eligible less-sensitive areas
		31 Dec 1998	31 Dec 2000	31 Dec 2005	
< 2,000	coastal			A	
	estuarial			A	
	fresh water			A	
2,000 - 10,000	coastal			A	
	estuarial			S	P
	fresh water			S	
10,000 - 15,000	coastal	T		S	P
	estuarial	T		S	
	fresh water	T		S	
15,000 - 150,000	coastal	T	S		P
	estuarial	T	S		
	fresh water	T	S		
> 150,000	coastal	T	S		P*
	estuarial	T	S		P*
	fresh water	T	S		

A = Appropriate treatment to meet quality objectives and requirements of relevant EC Directives.
P = Primary treatment in less sensitive areas only.
S = Secondary treatment.

T = Tertiary, or more stringent treatment in sensitive areas.

* Exceptional, where member state provides prior proof that more stringent treatment will not produce any environmental benefit.

The date by which discharges must comply with the terms of the Directive range from 1998 to 2005, depending on the size of the agglomeration and location of the discharge. Separate provisions in the Directive refer to a number of industrial sectors, the discharges from which are of a similar nature to domestic sewage (DETR and Welsh Office, 1997).

Protection of waters against pollution caused by nitrate (91/676/EEC)

The Directive requires member states to identify waters affected by pollution and waters which could be affected by pollution from nitrates including estuarine, coastal and marine waters. Once such waters have been identified, all areas of land draining into these waters which are known to be contributing to the problem are designated as 'nitrate vulnerable zones'. In these areas an action programme is established which includes limits for the quantities of fertiliser that can be applied and times at which application is limited, and promotes a code of good agricultural practice.

Member states are obliged to monitor estuarine, coastal and marine waters to identify which ones are eutrophic and affected by nitrate pollution.

In coastal waters, monitoring points are located in areas thought to be eutrophic and are sometimes supplemented by monitoring in bathing waters and shellfish waters. This approach includes taking algal samples in the event of a bloom occurrence. In addition, non-routine samples are taken if blooms are reported. Shorelines are monitored for excessive algal growth in the summer in areas with known problems, such that if areas greater than 10ha have more than 25 per cent algal cover, quantitative information is recorded on the extent of cover. Also, winter nutrient levels in areas of concern are recorded three times per year.

A similar regime is used for estuarine monitoring, with more stringent surveying being carried out on areas identified as being at risk from eutrophication through the incidence of excessive phytoplankton blooms or intertidal macroalgal growth. These data are then collated as evidence of eutrophication.

Habitats and Species Directive (92/43/EEC)

The aim of the Directive is to contribute towards maintaining biodiversity within member states through the conservation of habitat types along with flora and fauna. Natural habitats are defined as 'terrestrial or aquatic areas distinguished by geographic, abiotic and biotic features whether entirely natural or semi-natural'. Two Annexes to the Directive list habitat types and animal or plant species of Community interest. The intention of the Directive is to set up a European ecological network of designated sites by 2004, known as Natura 2000. This network will consist of three site types:

i.   sites hosting habitat types listed in Annex I of the Habitats Directive;

ii. sites comprising the habitats of animal and plant species listed in Annex II of the Habitats Directive;

iii. Special Protection Areas for birds classified under the Birds Directive.

Member states have an obligation to protect all sites on the Commission's list in the following ways:

i.   deterioration of habitats and disturbance of designated species must be avoided;

ii. any plans or projects likely to have significant effects on sites should be assessed in terms of implications for the conservation value of the site;

iii. where an assessment indicates a plan or project will damage the conservation interest of a site but no alternative solutions are available, compensating measures must be taken to protect the overall coherence of Natura 2000.

Conservation of Wild Birds Directive (79/409/EEC)

The Directive places a general duty on member states to maintain the population of all species of naturally occurring birds in the wild state at a level corresponding to particular ecological, scientific and cultural requirements. This should also take into account any economic or recreational requirements.

Member states should preserve, maintain or re-establish a sufficient diversity and areas of habitat for birds. This is achieved primarily through creating protected areas, known as Special Protection Areas (SPAs), managing habitats both inside and outside protected areas, re-establishing destroyed biotypes and creating new ones. In particular, the following are prohibited although licensed exceptions are permitted, for example to protect crops or human health:

i.   deliberate killing or capture by any method;

ii. deliberate destruction of, or damage to nests and eggs or removal of nests;

iii. taking of eggs in the wild and keeping them, even if empty;

iv. deliberate disturbance, particularly during breeding and rearing;

v.   keeping birds whose hunting and capture is prohibited.

The Wildlife and Countryside Act and Conservation (Natural Habitats) Regulations 1994 (the Habitats Regulations) transpose the requirements of this Directive into national law and provide for the protection of wildlife and the designation and protection of Special Areas of Conservation and Special Protection Areas in Great Britain.

Responsibility for reporting and monitoring of the above two Directives is shared between a number of organisations, including English Nature, the Countryside Council for Wales, the Joint Nature Conservation Committee, the Royal Society for the Protection of Birds and the Environment Agency.

International commitments

There are international commitments which require routine monitoring. These relate to the achievement of agreed targets and arise from the following:

- the Paris Commission (PARCOM) which, in 1988, reached an agreement on surveys of the riverine inputs of certain substances into the sea;

- the North Sea Conference Declarations, which have resulted in a similar need to make regular estimates of the loads of certain materials entering coastal waters from various land-based sources. These materials were listed in Annex 1A of the 3rd North Sea Conference. The UK has undertaken to apply the targets to the whole of its coastline. Inputs of 36 dangerous substances from direct discharges were to be reduced by 1995 to 50 per cent of the 1985 inputs. In addition to reducing inputs from point discharges by applying best available technology, diffuse inputs of dioxins, mercury, cadmium and lead from all sources, including atmospheric and land runoff, were to be reduced by 70 per cent;

- the 'Sintra Statement' which was agreed at the 1998 Ministerial meeting of the OSPAR Commission. There was agreement to prevent pollution of the maritime area by continuously reducing discharges, emissions and losses of hazardous substances, with the ultimate aim of achieving concentrations near background values for naturally occurring substances and close to zero for synthetic substances. A target of 2020 was set for this, based on "*every endeavour*". There was also an agreement to prevent pollution from ionising radiation through progressive and substantial reductions of discharges, emissions and losses of radioactive substances, with the ultimate aim of achieving concentrations in the environment near background values for naturally occurring radioactive substances, and close to zero for artificial radioactive substances. A further part of the agreement was to eliminate eutrophication from anthropogenic inputs. Dumping of steel installations in the sea was also prohibited with some grounds for derogations recognised (OSPAR, 1998b).

- the UN Convention on Biodiversity was signed at the UN Conference on Environment and Development at Rio de Janeiro in 1992. The Convention promotes the restoration of degraded ecosystems and the recovery of threatened species. It requires each contracting party to develop or adapt national strategies, plans or programmes for the conservation and sustainable use of biological diversity. The Government's response to the Convention is the UK Biodiversity Action Plan.

National standards and targets

The UK has maintained a long-held stance in Europe over its preference for the use of environmental quality objectives and standards as the basis for pollution control, related to the uses which waters meet. The Surface Waters (River Ecosystem) (Classification) Regulations 1994 introduced a scheme whereby river stretches could be assigned one of five classes relating to the type of ecosystem that should be maintained in that stretch. Further classification schemes may, in time, be developed for other types of controlled waters, for example lakes, estuaries and groundwaters, and for other uses, such as abstractions for industry and agriculture, watersports, and special ecosystems. The Agency continues to use non-statutory estuary quality objectives as a widespread basis for planning water quality improvements and to set discharge consents accordingly.

The UK Biodiversity Action Plan is the Government's response to its commitments under the Convention on Biodiversity, signed at the United Nations Conference on Environment and Development at Rio de Janeiro in 1992 (DoE, 1994b). The goal is to conserve and enhance biological diversity within the UK. The action plan brings together existing and new programmes for the designation and management of sites and species. A UK Biodiversity Group has been established to develop costed targets for key species and habitats, and to improve information co-ordination and public awareness (UK Biodiversity Steering Group, 1995b). The first tranche of plans for 116 priority species and 14 key habitats were published in 1995 and have been endorsed by the Government (UK Biodiversity Steering Group, 1995a). A further set of action plans for 56 species were published in 1998 (UK Biodiversity Group, 1998) and it is intended to have published plans for about 400 or so priority species and around 40 key habitats by 1999.

Appendix 2 Parcom loads to estuaries and coastal waters

TOTAL Nitrogen (thousand tonnes)								
	Tyne	Wear	Tees	Humber	Wash	Thames	Severn	Mersey	Total
1991	5.338	2.152	25.25	33.09	0.766	25.84	14.90	11.68	119.0
1992	4.406	2.992	22.04	38.24	1.270	31.04	24.84	17.95	142.8
1993	4.052	1.649	22.49	37.29	14.66	32.59	26.03	12.96	151.7
1994	3.882	2.462	14.10	48.28	21.56	35.61	33.58	17.27	176.7
1995	3.755	1.500	18.77	49.84	19.10	36.08	31.01	14.49	174.5
1996	4.214	2.321	7.942	35.70	10.88	27.19	23.59	17.54	129.4
1997	3.777	1.761	7.762	36.74	5.019	21.00	19.98	16.03	112.1

Orthophosphate (tonnes)								
	Tyne	Wear	Tees	Humber	Wash	Thames	Severn	Mersey	Total
1991	717.0	231.0	644.6	4061	915.6	7122	1525	1459	16675
1992	627.8	187.2	569.8	4694	936.6	6648	1972	1833	17468
1993	379.0	165.2	433.6	4165	802.4	5781	1959	1628	15314
1994	457.2	266.5	612.2	4383	815.7	5893	2421	2179	17027
1995	493.5	224.8	621.1	4350	927.5	6304	2306	1912	17139
1996	443.6	217.9	618.9	4790	833.6	5888	1773	2561	17126
1997	104.2	234.9	651.9	5089	797.7	5486	2251	2224	16838

Mercury (tonnes)								
	Tyne	Wear	Tees	Humber	Wash	Thames	Severn	Mersey	Total
1991	0.373	0.096	0.226	0.026	0.043	0.048	0.064	1.762	2.639
1992	0.151	0.026	0.103	0.049	0.058	0.032	0.016	1.630	2.065
1993	0.218	0.033	0.131	0.070	0.024	0.010	0.025	0.817	1.329
1994	0.007	0.000	0.018	0.030	0.374	0.061	0.043	0.704	1.236
1995	0.004	0.003	0.039	0.078	0.079	0.061	0.165	0.605	1.034
1996	0.004	0.010	0.017	0.138	0.109	0.042	0.068	0.515	0.903
1997	0.003	0.000	0.044	0.137	0.014	0.012	0.055	0.309	0.574

Cadmium (tonnes)								
	Tyne	Wear	Tees	Humber	Wash	Thames	Severn	Mersey	Total
1991	1.145	0.088	0.518	0.967	0.027	0.144	6.406	0.372	9.666
1992	0.517	0.107	0.331	1.892	0.164	0.054	5.808	0.601	9.474
1993	0.357	0.075	0.303	2.388	0.108	0.117	2.476	0.304	6.127
1994	0.163	0.080	0.114	1.965	0.082	0.252	2.245	0.233	5.134
1995	0.111	0.035	0.121	0.965	0.204	0.318	2.423	0.120	4.296
1996	0.212	0.073	0.178	0.968	0.143	0.124	1.669	0.257	3.624
1997	0.342	0.024	0.174	1.340	0.049	0.179	1.481	0.260	3.850

Copper (tonnes)								
	Tyne	Wear	Tees	Humber	Wash	Thames	Severn	Mersey	Total
1991	15.38	1.163	80.43	76.60	2.692	15.80	11.18	10.46	213.7
1992	23.60	12.18	32.39	84.65	8.026	20.40	22.87	28.10	232.2
1993	17.80	2.979	28.74	83.80	8.942	23.51	24.70	16.47	206.9
1994	12.30	4.557	19.35	79.94	10.75	21.66	30.57	22.57	201.7
1995	44.47	1.735	17.36	50.47	11.31	29.41	30.58	18.91	204.3
1996	14.47	2.607	8.744	44.41	6.489	19.56	15.66	17.36	129.3
1997	18.04	1.665	12.15	55.13	3.933	18.53	14.43	14.73	138.6

Zinc (tonnes)								
	Tyne	Wear	Tees	Humber	Wash	Thames	Severn	Mersey	Total
1991	228.7	38.63	236.0	802.2	10.17	106.5	149.2	47.94	1619
1992	162.5	29.21	136.1	883.3	29.27	117.1	149.3	107.8	1615
1993	140.6	24.15	76.75	941.9	29.20	164.8	116.4	76.67	1570
1994	104.4	34.56	48.73	907.6	35.00	95.82	160.7	76.03	1463
1995	83.84	15.96	57.19	618.6	42.08	132.8	165.8	62.71	1179
1996	74.65	36.25	31.20	471.2	26.04	95.69	106.8	62.08	903.9
1997	106.0	15.14	50.31	402.6	13.26	65.37	160.6	56.93	870.1

Lead (tonnes)								
	Tyne	Wear	Tees	Humber	Wash	Thames	Severn	Mersey	Total
1991	66.93	3.619	39.73	134.4	0.809	11.08	14.58	8.814	279.9
1992	34.49	14.90	22.65	101.2	4.383	15.78	23.47	33.24	250.1
1993	17.85	10,46	64.06	178.0	4.065	19.51	23.02	63.77	380.7
1994	11.31	16.50	17.38	97.32	5.217	18.28	31.10	41.08	238.2
1995	16.91	7.343	19.36	54.07	3.600	23.64	39.32	36.44	200.7
1996	8.198	17.06	7.839	38.26	2.416	13.46	17.30	41.04	145.6
1997	17.62	3.213	15.90	107.3	0.937	11.58	13.67	10.02	180.3

Lindane (kilogrammes)								
	Tyne	Wear	Tees	Humber	Wash	Thames	Severn	Mersey	Total
1991	21.88	13.21	1.095	50.58	10.39	89.24	16.14	35.15	237.7
1992	9.529	0.800	1.649	49.39	13.41	95.87	10.14	66.48	247.3
1993	3.180	2.410	6.390	64.20	10.67	113.3	25.01	33.25	258.4
1994	4.110	2.090	2.390	94.65	12.16	57.66	9.040	0.450	182.6
1995	7.940	2.050	5.460	87.24	9.750	45.88	17.34	27.76	203.4
1996	0.470	0.660	4.900	52.38	4.380	33.23	17.89	9.410	123.3
1997	0.761	0.968	0.546	35.23	5.260	32.38	12.42	2.371	89.94

Low load estimates and totals for the 8 major estuaries

Source: Environment Agency

Appendix 3   National Monitoring Programme

The Marine Pollution Monitoring Management Group (MPMMG) is a management group with representation from all government organisations with statutory marine environmental protection monitoring obligations. The group is chaired by a representative from MAFF. Its aim is to ensure that monitoring of the marine environment is conducted in a co-ordinated way, is as cost-effective as possible and meets national and international requirements.

In 1987 and 1988 the MPMMG reviewed the monitoring carried out in UK estuaries and coastal waters and concluded that there would be considerable merit in the regular sampling of a network of coastal monitoring stations. It was agreed that the network of stations should include both sites that may be significantly contaminated and others that are free from human-derived inputs. It was envisaged that the uncontaminated sites, which were expected to lie in offshore locations, would serve as reference sites and would also provide information on the extent of natural variability in the marine environment (DoE, 1991a).

In its formal response to the MPMMG review the Government accepted the need for a minimum core programme of marine monitoring to national standards for all UK waters (DoE, 1991b). A network of 87 coastal monitoring stations in estuarine, intermediate and offshore locations around the UK was established. The competent monitoring authorities for the programme are: the Environment Agency for England and Wales; the Scottish Environment Protection Agency; the Environment and Heritage Service, Northern Ireland; the Fisheries Research Services Marine Laboratory (Aberdeen); the Scottish Office (Agriculture, Environment and Fisheries Department); the Centre for Environment, Fisheries and Aquaculture Science; the Department of Agriculture for Northern Ireland; and the Department of the Environment, Transport and the Regions.

The National Monitoring Programme was initiated to co-ordinate marine monitoring in the UK with a view to establishing a clear overall picture of the spatial distribution of contaminants and their biological effects. This information provides a basis for decisions as to future monitoring requirements, especially the need to continue spatial distribution studies and the selection of key sites at which trend monitoring should be undertaken.

The objectives of the National Monitoring Programme were:

(1) to establish as precisely as practicable the spatial distribution of contaminants in different areas of UK waters and to define their current biological status, thus identifying any areas of specific concern, for example areas where the concentrations of one or more contaminants might affect biological processes or render fish and shellfish unfit for human consumption;

(2) to detect with appropriate accuracy trends in both contaminant concentrations and biological well-being in those areas identified as being of concern;

(3) to measure long-term natural trends in physical, biological and chemical parameters at selected areas.

In achieving these objectives it was necessary to establish a central computerised database for contaminants in all media and for biological effects in the UK marine environment. This was established in 1996 and is located in the Agency's National Centre for Environmental Data and Surveillance.

Considerable progress has been made in co-ordinating the monitoring activities of responsible organisations in the UK. This ranges from improved dialogue between organisations to collaboration between the individual laboratories responsible for practical implementation of the work. In parallel with the co-ordination effort, quality control procedures have been developed to ensure that data from one laboratory are comparable to those from another.

The results from the first phase of the National Monitoring Programme are presented in a progress report *Survey of the Quality of UK Coastal Waters* (Marine Pollution Monitoring Management Group, 1998a). The second phase of the programme, which will commence in 1999, will concentrate on temporal trend monitoring in line with the initial objectives, and introduce new biological effects studies. Specific areas have been identified for long-term monitoring and new objectives for the second phase have been established. Since many of the objectives of the second phase will be achieved over a long time, scale the programme will be reviewed annually.

The second phase will seek to integrate national and international monitoring programmes across UK agencies and to complement the marine monitoring programmes of those agencies. The first phase of the programme focused on estuaries with known environmental impacts. During the second phase some monitoring effort will be directed at identifying trends and spatial variability in other estuaries.

Appendix 4   Aesthetic quality monitoring

There are several schemes in place to monitor the aesthetic aspects of the coastal environment. Most are primarily concerned with measuring the extent of litter on the beaches, identifying amounts and sources, and reporting on trends over time.

The National Aquatic Litter Group (NALG)

The NALG has developed a document entitled *Guidance on a Standardised Approach for Comparing Beach Litter Pollution* (Earll and Jowett, 1998). The Agency is using this initiative to develop its own methodology for the assessment of the aesthetic quality of coastal and bathing beaches. This scheme will be used as the basis for the general aesthetic quality assessment for coastal and estuarine waters. The document is developing a standard monitoring and classification protocol for beach litter assessments, based on a standard sampling unit comprising the zone from the current strandline to the edge of the usable beach, along a standard transect length of 100 metres. Categories of litter that are assessed are sewage-related debris, harmful litter (for example sharp broken glass, medical waste), gross litter (items greater than 50cm in one dimension), general litter (items less than 50cm), oil deposits, faeces (non-human origin) and accumulations of litter. Items are counted and each category is placed within one of four grades, A to D.

The protocol was tested by NALG member organisations during 1998 with a view to the results being used to finalise the monitoring methodology and the classification bandings. The final scheme will be agreed by the NALG and adopted as the standard protocol for future surveys.

The major benefit of this initiative is that results from beach litter surveys undertaken by any organisation will be directly comparable.

Coastwatch Europe

Coastwatch Europe is a large-scale survey of beaches in 22 countries. Its aims are to collect baseline data on the extent of marine litter on beaches, gain an insight into the potential threats to the coastline, raise public awareness of the problem and promote environmental education. The survey is conducted by volunteers from the end of September to the first week of October, over a 0.5 kilometre section of coastline. Surveyors record the presence or absence of 17 general litter items and record the actual numbers of items. In 1994 6,000 people participated in the UK, surveying 404 half-kilometre sections of coastline (Rees and Pond, 1994).

Appendix 5 Capital expenditure by the water companies on coasts and estuaries, 1995/96 to 1997/98

Discharges	Type	Expenditure	Anglian	Dŵr Cymru	North West	Northumbrian	Severn Trent	South West	Southern	Thames	Wessex	Yorkshire	Total
Estuaries (UWWTD)	I	CAP	6774.55	5519.68	3306.77	0.00	250.36	32.00	1080.39	5620.52	0.00	0.00	22584.28
Estuaries (UWWTD)	C	CAP	10956.62	139091.30	83323.57	86772.23	0.00	94.16	18602.51	6457.83	19589.97	16791.77	381679.95
Estuaries (UWWTD)	I&C	OP	1139.31	2392.59	3227.39	269.40	0.00	5.65	11.00	303.00	243.22	0.00	7591.56
Coastal (UWWTD)	I	CAP	0.00	622.01	298.34	6018.08	0.00	1.00	31973.88	0.00	2645.19	1674.63	43233.13
Coastal (UWWTD)	C	CAP	7311.74	33354.18	18791.11	43848.95	0.00	2683.81	80058.02	0.00	16088.43	13362.62	215498.58
Coastal (UWWTD)	I&C	OP	122.21	2703.41	3252.68	0.00	0.00	241.11	0.00	0.00	14.00	0.00	6333.40
Coastal (bathing waters)	I	CAP	62251.67	613.37	5118.06	7418.61	0.00	11863.04	39382.83	0.00	21079.99	0.00	147727.58
Coastal (bathing waters)	C	CAP	53089.26	93356.14	197603.63	12378.97	0.00	101493.84	62190.20	0.00	2030.76	0.00	522142.79
Coastal (bathing waters)	I&C	OP	10377.04	2002.48	15605.08	1399.19	0.00	13109.55	10411.35	0.00	0.00	1186.02	54090.71
Sludge disposal (UWWTD)		CAP	33597.90	13660.48	94687.72	55804.13	0.00	7336.00	39522.90	159720.26	2083.75	29917.99	436331.13
Sludge disposal (UWWTD)		CAP	1353.38	1183.67	1077.89	0.00	0.00	47.00	0.00	1680.00	540.95	1022.08	6904.97
												Total	1844118.09

£thousand (97/98 prices)

Key
I = Intermittent discharges
C = Continuous discharges
CAP = Capital expenditure
OP = Operational expenditure

Source: Compiled from OFWAT data, 1998b

Appendix 6   EC bathing waters at risk of non-compliance with the imperative standards

Table A6.1 *Bathing waters at risk of non-compliance with imperative standards*

Region	Risk of future non-compliance of <1 in 5 years	Risk of future non-compliance of 1 in 5 years	Risk of future non-compliance of 2 or 3 in 5 years	Risk of future non-compliance of 4 or 5 in 5 years
Anglian		Heacham	Cleethorpes	
North East		Marsden South Shields Staithes		
North West	Southport Meols St Annes North St Annes Blackpool South Ainsdale Bardsea	New Brighton Silloth Skinburness	Roan Head Fleetwood Morecambe South Walney W. Shore New Biggen St Bees Seascale Heysham	Morecambe North Ashkam-in-Furness Haverigg
Southern		Pevensey Bay Seagrove	Totland Bay	
South West	Christchurch (Avon) Christchurch (Friars Cliff) Sidmouth (Town) Seaton (Cornwall) East Looe Coverack Porthluney Porthcothan Polurrian Woolacombe (Putsborough) Clevedon Ilfracombe (Hele)	Wembury Mothecombe Bude (Summerleaze) Charmouth West Lyme Regis (Church) Trevaunance Cove Combe Martin Readymoney Cove Bovisand Beer Porthallow	Kimmeridge Mawgan Porth Ilfracombe (Capstone)	
Thames		Thorpe Bay Westcliff Bay		
Wales	Southerndown Amroth Central Borth Trearddur	Newport Sands North Aberdyfi Prestatyn		

Appendix 7 Interactions between major types of coastal plans

The table illustrates the impact and effect of the plans named in the columns, on the plans listed in the rows.

	Development plan	Marine SAC management	Heritage coast plans	LEAPs	Harbour authorities	SMPs	EMPs
Development plan		Provides information on environmental sensitivity and management measures within relevant area.	Defines protected landscape areas; provides guidance on recreation.	Illustrates areas liable to flood.	Advice on port management and impact of development proposals.	Advice on areas liable to flood, erosion and instability. Areas best suited to development. Advice to mineral plans.	Provides monitoring data; management of land/sea interface; provides general management context.
Marine SAC management	Provides development context and identifies threats from land.		Provides broad context; management of access and recreation especially on land.	Information on water quality, fisheries, pollution etc.	Advice on long-term natural processes; impact of defence measures.	Provides wider conservation and management context.	
Heritage coast plans	Advice on supporting infrastructure - transport etc. Development context and support for strategy.	Provides information on implications of management measures on onshore recreation activities and facilities.		Water quality, water and beach pollution; water-based recreation issues.	Little correspondence.	Relationship of natural processes to landscape strategy; advice on access.	Environmental context; sensitive sites; interaction of onshore and water-based recreation.
LEAPs	Trends in population, development patterns, transport demands. Potential sources of pollution; links with development control.	Provides information on conservation interests and management measures within the relevant area.	Impact of pollution from visitors, recreation etc.		Impact of major port development; demands for water; possible sources of pollution.	Knowledge of sediment movements will affect strategies at river mouths.	Exchange of common information requirements.
Harbour authorities	Provides development policy context; provision of infrastructure, especially transport links.	Advice on conservation constraints on development proposals, dredging etc.	Likely to be little coincidence.	Pollution monitoring and information.		Need for marine aggregate wharves; advice on availability of dredged material.	Environmental context for port development and management.
SMPs	Pressures for development. Environmental constraints. Interaction with strategy in areas of managed set back etc.	Advice on environmental constraints; sources of marine aggregates etc.	Landscape assessment; impact of recreation.	Impact of sediment transport by rivers.	Need to protect port facilities; dredging and dumping requirements.		Exchange of common information; environmental issues.
EMPs	Development policy context; transport and open space strategies.	Detailed advice on conservation management and provision of environmental data.	Recreational background. Advice on management; signing etc. Landscape assessment.	Pollution information; impact on fisheries etc.	Impact of port development; shipping movements. Contingency/emergency information.	Defence strategy; background on environmental resources and impact of management units.	

Source: Department of the Environment, 1996b; Crown copyright

References

Acland, R, 1995. *Resort Management*. In: Earll, R C (Editor). Proceedings of the workshop on coastal and riverine litter: problems and effective solutions. Marine Environmental Management and Training, Kempley, Gloucestershire, pp18-20.

Advisory Committee on Protection of the Sea (ACOPS), 1997. *Oil pollution survey around the coasts of the United Kingdom, 1996.* ACOPS, London, 54pp.

Allen, Y, Thain, J, Matthiessen, P, Scott, S, Haworth, S and Fesit, S, 1997. *A survey of oestrogenic activity in UK estuaries and its effects on gonadal development of the flounder platichthys flesus.* CM 1997/U:01. International Council for the Exploration of the Sea.

Allen, J R L and Rae, J E, 1986. *Time sequence of metal pollution, Severn Estuary, southwestern UK.* Marine Pollution Bulletin, 17, 9, pp427-431.

Allen, J R, Slinn, D J, Shammon, T M, Hartnoll, R G and Hawkins, S J, 1998. *Evidence for eutrophication of the Irish Sea over four decades.* Limnol. Oceanogr. 43(8): 1970 - 1974.

Bailey, S K and Davies, I M, 1988. *Tributyl tin contamination around an oil terminal in Sullom Voe (Shetland).* Environmental Pollution, 55, pp161-172.

Baker, J M, 1997. *Differences in risk perception: how clean is clean?* An issue paper prepared for the 1997 International Oil Spill Conference, American Petroleum Institute Technical Report IOSC-006, Washington, 51pp.

Baker, Shepherd and Gillespie, 1998. *Costing UK biodiversity habitat action plans.* Marine and Coastal Habitats Consultation Draft, prepared for English Nature.

Bamber, R N, 1995. *Pembroke Power Station assessment: impacts of impingement and entrainment.* Fawley Ltd, Southampton.

Barne, J H, Robson, C F, Kaznowska, S S, Doody, J P and Davidson, N C (Editors), 1995a. *Coasts and seas of the United Kingdom. Region 5, North-east England: Berwick-upon-Tweed to Filey Bay.* Coastal Directory Series. JNCC, Peterborough, 194pp. ISBN 1-873701-79-9.

Barne, J H, Robson, C F, Kaznowska, S S, Doody, J P and Davidson, N C (Editors), 1995b. *Coasts and seas of the United Kingdom. Region 6, Eastern England: Flamborough Head to Great Yarmouth.* Coastal Directory Series. JNCC, Peterborough, 220pp. ISBN 1-873701- 80-2.

Barne, J H, Robson, C F, Kaznowska, S S and Doody, J P (Editors), 1995c. *Coasts and seas of the United Kingdom. Region 12, Wales: Margam to Little Orme.* Coastal Directory Series. JNCC, Peterborough, 239pp. ISBN 1-873701-86-1.

Barne, J H, Robson, C F, Kaznowska, S S, Doody, J P, Davidson, N C and Buck, A L (Editors), 1996a. *Coasts and seas of the United Kingdom. Region 10, South-west England: Seaton to the Roseland Peninsula.* Coastal Directory Series. JNCC, Peterborough, 217pp. ISBN 1-873701-84-5.

Barne, J H, Robson, C F, Kaznowska, S S, Doody, J P and Davidson, N C (Editors), 1996b. *Coasts and seas of the United Kingdom. Region 9, Southern England: Hayling Island to Lyme Regis.* Coastal Directory Series. JNCC, Peterborough, 249pp. ISBN 1-873701-83-7.

Barne, J H, Robson, C F, Kaznowska, S S, Doody, J P, Davidson, N C and Buck, A L (Editors), 1996c. *Coasts and seas of the United Kingdom. Region 11, The Western Approaches: Falmouth Bay to Kenfig.* Coastal Directory Series. JNCC, Peterborough, 262pp. ISBN 1-873701-85-3.

Barne, J H, Robson, C F, Kaznowska, S S, Doody, J P and Davidson, N C (Editors), 1996d. *Coasts and seas of the United Kingdom. Region 13, Northern Irish Sea: Colwyn Bay to Stanraer, including the Isle of Man.* Coastal Directory Series. JNCC, Peterborough, 284pp. ISBN 1-873701-87-X.

Barne, J H, Robson, C F, Kaznowska, S S, Doody, J P, Davidson, N C and Buck, A L (Editors), 1998a. *Coasts and seas of the United Kingdom. Region 7, South-east England: Lowestoft to Dungeness.* Coastal Directory Series. JNCC, Peterborough, 258pp. ISBN 1-873701-81-0.

Barne, J H, Robson, C F, Kaznowska, S S, Doody, J P, Davidson, N C and Buck, A L (Editors), 1998b. *Coasts and seas of the United Kingdom. Region 8, Sussex: Rye Bay to Chichester Harbour.* Coastal Directory Series. JNCC, Peterborough, 196pp. ISBN 1-873701-82-9.

Barnes, R S K, 1989. *The coastal lagoons of Britain: an overview and conservation appraisal.* Biological Conservation, 49, pp295-313.

Bateman, I J, Langford, I H, Willis, K G, Turner, R K and Garrod, G G, 1993. *The impacts of changing willingness to pay question formats in CVM.* CSERGE WP GEC 93-05. CSERGE University of East Anglia, Norwich and University College London.

Brady Shipman Martin, 1997. *Coastal zone management: a draft policy for Ireland.* Brady Shipman Martin, Dublin, 166pp.

British Aggregate and Construction Materials Industry (BACMI), 1996. *BACMI's Statistical yearbook 1996.* BACMI, London.

British Marine Aggregate Producers Association (BMAPA), 1995. *Aggregates from the sea: why dredge?* Second edition. BMAPA, London.

British National Space Centre (BNSC), 1991. *Civil marine applications of remote sensing data.* Earth Observing Systems, London, 134pp.

British Tourist Authority (BTA) and English Tourist Board (ETB), 1998. *Tourism intelligence quarterly.* Volume 19 No. 3. BTA and ETB, London. ISSN 0309-8958.

Broughton, G F J, Bower, J S, Willis, P G and Clark, H, 1997. *Air pollution in the UK: 1995.* Report AEA/RAMP/20112002/002 for the Department of the Environment. AEA Technology plc, Culham, 455pp.

Bryan, G W and Langston, W J, 1992. *Bioavailability, accumulation and effects of heavy metals in sediments with special reference to United Kingdom estuaries: a review.* Environmental Pollution, 76, pp89-131.

Burd, F, 1989. *The saltmarsh survey of Great Britain.* Research and Survey in Nature Conservation no.17, Nature Conservancy Council, Peterborough.

Burt, N and Watts, J (Editors), 1996. *Barrages: engineering design and environmental impacts.* Proceedings of an international conference, 10 to 13 September 1996, Cardiff, UK. Wiley, Chichester, 504pp. ISBN 0-471-96857-9.

Carpenter, K and Pye, K, 1996. *Saltmarsh change in England and Wales - its history and causes.* Environment Agency R&D Technical Report W12 by HR Wallingford Ltd., and Foundation for Water Research, Marlow, 181pp.

Carter, R W G, 1988. *Coastal environments - an introduction to the physical, ecological and cultural systems of coastlines.* Academic Press, London, 617pp. ISBN 0-12-161856-0.

Centre for Environment, Fisheries and Aquaculture Science (CEFAS), 1997. *Monitoring and surveillance of non-radioactive contaminants in the aquatic environment and activities regulating the disposal of wastes at sea, 1994.* Aquatic Environmental Monitoring Report No. 47. CEFAS, Lowestoft, 59pp. ISSN 0142-2499.

Centre for Environment, Fisheries and Aquaculture Science, 1998. *UK bass monitoring report 1997.* CEFAS, Lowestoft, 14pp.

Centre for Environment, Fisheries and Aquaculture Science (CEFAS), 1998b. *Monitoring and surveillance of non-radioactive contaminants in the aquatic environment and activities regulating the disposal of wastes at sea, 1995 and 1996.* Aquatic Environmental Monitoring Report No. 51. CEFAS, Lowestoft, 116pp. ISSN 0142-2499.

Central Statistical Office, 1996. *Annual abstract of statistics 1996 edition.* HMSO, London. ISBN 0-11-620771-X.

Chemical Industries Association, 1996. *The UK indicators of performance 1990-1995.* Chemical Industries Association, London, 34pp. ISBN 1-85897-052-0.

Clifton, R J and Hamilton, E I, 1979. *Lead-210 chronology in relation to levels of elements in dated sediment core profiles.* Journal of Estuarine and Coastal Marine Science, 8, pp259- 269.

Climate Change Impacts Review Group (CCIRG), 1996. *Review of the potential effects of climate change in the United Kingdom.* HMSO, London, 247pp. ISBN 0-11-753290-8.

Collins K J, Jensen A C and Albert S, 1995. *A review of waste tyre utilisation in the marine environment.* Chemistry and Ecology, Vol. 10, pp205-216.

Comprehensive Studies Task Team, 1997. *Comprehensive studies for the purposes of Article 6 and 8.5 of Directive 91/271/EEC, the Urban Waste Water Treatment Directive.*

CONCAWE, 1994. *The contribution of sulphur dioxide emissions from ships to coastal deposition and air quality in the Channel and southern North Sea area.* The Oil Companies' European Organisation for Environmental and Health Protection (CONCAWE), Brussels, September 1994, 25pp.

Construction Industry Research and Information Association (CIRIA), 1996. *Beach recharge materials - demand and resources.* Report 154. CIRIA, London. ISBN 086017-439-5.

Costanza, R, d'Arge, R, de Groot, R, Farber, S, Grasso, M, Hannon, B, Linbury, K, Naeem, S, O'Neill, R V, Paruelo, J, Rastin, R G, Sutton, P and van den Belt, M, 1997. *The value of the world's ecosystem services and natural capital.* Nature 387, pp253-60.

Croudace, I W and Cundy, A B, 1995. *Heavy metal and hydrocarbon pollution in recent sediments from Southampton Water, southern England: a geochemical and isotopic study.* Envionmental Science and Technology, 29, pp1288-1296.

Crown Estate, 1990 to 1997. *Marine aggregates, Crown Estate licences - summary of statistics.* Years 1989 to 1996. Crown Estate, London.

Davidson, N C, d'A Laffoley, D, Doody, J P, Way, L S, Gordon, J, Key, R, Pienkowski, M W, Mitchell, R and Duff, K L, 1991. *Nature conservation and estuaries in Great Britain.* Nature Conservancy Council, Peterborough, 422pp. ISBN 0-86139-708-8.

Davidson, N C and Rothwell, P I, 1993. *Disturbance to waterfowl on estuaries: the conservation and coastal management implications of current knowledge.* Wader Study Group Bulletin 68, pp97-105.

Davies, I M and McKie, J C, 1987. *Accumulation of total tin and tributyl tin in muscle tissue of farmed Atlantic salmon.* Marine Pollution Bulletin, 18, pp400-404.

Davies, J M, McIntosh, A D, Stagg, R, Topping, G and Rees, J, 1997. *The fate of the Braer oil in the marine and terrestrial environments.* In *The impact of an oil spill in turbulent waters: the Braer,* edited by Davies, J M and Topping, G, The Stationery Office, London, pp26-41.

DeMontfort University, 1997. World Wide Web site visited on 31 July 1997 at http://www.iesd.dmu.ac.uk/~slb/wcwave.html.

Department of the Environment (DoE), 1991a. *The principles and practice of monitoring in UK coastal waters.* A report from the Marine Pollution Monitoring Management Group. Department of the Environment, London.

Department of the Environment (DoE), 1991b. *The principles and practice of monitoring in UK coastal waters.* The Government response to a report from the Marine Pollution Monitoring Management Group. Department of the Environment, London.

Department of the Environment (DoE), 1994a. *Guidelines for aggregate provision in England.* Minerals Planning Guidance Note No. 6. HMSO, London.

Department of the Environment (DoE), 1994b. *Biodiversity: the UK action plan.* CM 2428. HMSO, London, 188pp. ISBN 0-10-124282-4.

Department of the Environment (DoE), 1995a. *The occurrence and significance of erosion, deposition and flooding in Great Britain.* HMSO, London, 178pp. ISBN 0-11-753118-9.

Department of the Environment (DoE), 1995b. *Projections of households in England to 2016.* HMSO, London, 99pp. ISBN 0-11-753055-7.

Department of the Environment (DoE), 1995c. *Coastal planning and management: a review of earth science information needs.* HMSO, London, 187pp. ISBN 0-11-753111-1.

Department of the Environment (DoE), 1996a. *Household growth: where shall we live?* Cm 3471. HMSO, London, 72pp. ISBN 0-10-134712-X.

Department of the Environment (DoE), 1996b. *Coastal zone management - towards best practice.* A report prepared by Nicholas Pearson Associates for the DoE. Department of the Environment, London, 74pp.

Department of the Environment (DoE) and Welsh Office, 1992. *Planning policy guidance: coastal planning,* HMSO, London. ISBN 0-11-752711-4.

Department of the Environment, Transport and the Regions (DETR), 1997a. *Digest of environmental statistics, No.19, 1997.* HMSO, London, 284pp. ISBN 0-11-753399-8.

Department of the Environment, Transport and the Regions (DETR), 1997b. *Port statistics 1996.* HMSO, London, 107pp. ISBN 0-11-551974-2.

Department of the Environment, Transport and the Regions (DETR), 1997c. *National road traffic forecasts 1997.* The Stationery Office, London.

Department of the Environment, Transport and the Regions (DETR), 1997d. *Wavelength.* The newsletter of the National Coastal Fora in the UK. (1) Autumn 1997. DETR, Bristol.

Department of the Environment, Transport and the Regions (DETR), 1998a. *Cleaner seas.* DETR leaflet on the World Wide Web, 21 September 1998.

Department of the Environment, Transport and the Regions (DETR), 1998b. *British government panel on sustainable development: fourth report.* Department of Environment, Transport and the Regions, London, 24pp.

Department of the Environment, Transport and the Regions (DETR), 1998c. *Digest of environmental statistics, No. 20.* The Stationery Office, London, 338pp. ISBN 0-11-753466- 8.

Department of the Environment, Transport and the Regions (DETR) and the Welsh Office, 1997. *The urban waste water treatment (England and Wales) regulations 1994: working document for dischargers and regulators.* DETR and Welsh Office, 98pp.

Department of the Environment, Transport and the Regions (DETR) and the Welsh Office, 1998. *Raising the quality: guidance to the Director General of Water Services on the environmental and quality objectives to be achieved by the water industry in England and Wales 2000-2005.* DETR, London, 40pp.

Department of Trade and Industry, 1997a. *Digest of United Kingdom energy statistics.* HMSO, London.

Department of Trade and Industry, 1997b. *The energy report: oil and gas resources of the United Kingdom.* Volume Two. The Stationery Office, London, 196pp. ISBN 0-11-515429- 9.

Department of Transport, 1994. *Safer ships, cleaner seas.* Report of Lord Donaldson's inquiry into the prevention of pollution from merchant shipping. HMSO, London, 522pp.

Department of Transport, 1996a. *Road traffic statistics Great Britain.* HMSO, London, 62pp. ISBN 0-11-551837-1.

Department of Transport, 1996b. *Transport statistics Great Britain.* HMSO, London, 209pp. ISBN 0-11-551823-1.

De Swart, R, Ross, P S, Vedder, L J, Timmerman, H H, Heisterkamp, S, Van Loveren, H, Vos, J G, Reijnders, P J H and Osterhaus, A D M E, 1994. *Impairment of immune function in harbor seals (Phoca vitulina) feeding on fish from polluted waters.* Ambio, 23, pp155-159.

Devon County Council, Research and Intelligence Service, 1998. Personal communication.

Dixon, A M and Weight, R C, 1997. *Managing coastal realignment.* Case study at Orplands sea wall, Blackwater Estuary, Essex.

Doody, J P, Johnston, C and Smith, B, 1993. *Directory of the North Sea coastal margin.* JNCC, Peterborough, 262pp.

Earll, R and Jowett, D, 1998. *Guidance on a standardised approach for comparing beach litter pollution.* Consultation Draft 6. National Aquatic Litter Group.

East Durham Task Force, 1995. *Turning the tide, restoring the coast of County Durham.* A project for Millennium Commission funding. East Durham Task Force.

ECOTEC, 1996. *Environmental protection expenditure by industry: a survey of environmental protection expenditure by extraction, manufacturing, energy and water supply industries in the UK.* Prepared for the Department of the Environment. HMSO, London, 76pp. ISBN 0-11-75300-9.

Energy Technology Support Unit, 1989. *Severn barrage project detailed report: ecological studies, landscape and nature conservation.* Volume IV. ETSU TID 4060 P4.

Energy Technology Support Unit, 1994. *An assessment of renewable energy for the UK.* HMSO, London.

English Heritage, 1997. *England's coastal heritage: a survey for English Heritage and the Royal Commission on the Historical Monuments of England.* English Heritage, London, 268pp.

English Nature, 1991. *Marine conservation handbook.* Edited by Eno, N.C. English Nature, Peterborough.

Eno, N C, Clark, R A and Sanderson, W G (Editors), 1997. *Non-native marine species in British waters: a review and directory.* JNCC, Peterborough, 152pp.

Environment Agency, 1996a. *Humber Estuary quality report 1994.* Unpublished.

Environment Agency, 1996b. *East Anglian salt marshes: the meadows of the sea.* Environment Agency, Peterborough, 11pp.

Environment Agency, 1997a. *The water quality of the tidal Thames.* The Stationery Office, London, 70pp. ISBN 0-11-310125-2.

Environment Agency, 1997b. *Viewpoints on the environment - developing a national environmental monitoring and assessment framework.* Environment Agency, Bristol, 48pp.

Environment Agency, 1997c. *Bathing water quality in England and Wales in 1997 - a summary report.* Environment Agency, Bristol, 20pp.

Environment Agency, 1997d. *National coastal baseline survey 1996 results.* Unpublished.

Environment Agency, 1997e. *Aerial surveillance of fourteen estuaries in England and Wales.* Unpublished.

Environment Agency, 1997f. *An environmental strategy for the Millennium and beyond.* Environment Agency, Bristol, 28pp.

Environment Agency, 1998a. *The state of the environment of England and Wales: fresh waters.* The Stationery Office, London, 214pp. ISBN 0-11-310148-1.

Environment Agency, 1998b. *Oil and gas in the environment.* Environmental Issues Series. The Stationery Office, London, 104pp. ISBN 0-11-310152-X.

Environment Agency, 1998c. *National sea defence survey 1997 update.* Summary Report. Environment Agency and Halcrow.

Environment Agency, 1998d. *Aquatic eutrophication in England and Wales: a proposed management strategy.* Environmental Issues Series. Environment Agency, Bristol.

Environment Agency, 1998e. *Endocrine-disrupting substances in the environment: what should be done?* Environmental Issues Series. Environment Agency, Bristol, 16pp.

Environment Agency, in press. *Radioactivity in the environment: a summary and radiological assessment of the Environment Agency's monitoring programmes, report for 1997.*

Environment Agency and Centre for Environment, Fisheries and Aquaculture Science (CEFAS), 1998. *Annual assessment of salmon stocks and fisheries in England and Wales.* CEFAS, Lowestoft, 43pp.

European Commission, 1995a. *Communication of the commission to council and the European Parliament on the integrated management of coastal zones.* COM(95)511 final, 31 October 1995.

European Commission, 1995b. *Tourism in Europe.* Eurostat DG XXII. European Commission, Brussels.

European Commission, 1997. *Better management of coastal resources.* European Commission, Luxembourg, 48pp. ISBN 92-828-0609-X.

Fankhauser, S, 1994. *Protection vs retreat: estimating the costs of sea level rise.* CSERGE WP GEC 94-02. CSERGE University of East Anglia, Norwich and University College London.

Fewtrell, L, Kay, D, Wyer, M, Crowther, J, Carbo, P and Mitchell, G, 1998. *Faecal indicator budgets discharging into the Ribble Estuary.* Centre for Research into Environment and Health, Leeds University. Prepared for the Environment Agency, Bristol.

Field Studies Centre Oil Pollution Research Unit, 1994. *The recent history of the Fawley saltmarsh and the Esso refinery.* Report for Esso Petroleum Company Limited.

Foundation for Water Research (FWR), 1996. *Assessing the benefits of surface water quality improvements.* Manual, FR/CL 0005. FWR, 617pp.

Fowler, S L, 1989. *Nature conservation implications of damage to the seabed by commercial fishing operations.* Contract surveys no.79. Nature Conservancy Council, Peterborough.

Fowler, S L, 1992. *Survey of bait collection in Britain.* Report no.17. JNCC, Peterborough.

Georgiou, S, Langford, I, Bateman, I and Turner, K T, 1996a. *Economic and epidemiological investigation of coastal bathing water health risks.* CSERGE working paper PA 96-01. CSERGE University of East Anglia, Norwich and University College London.

Georgiou, S, Langford, I, Bateman, I and Turner, K T, 1996b. *Determinants of individuals' willingness to pay for reductions in environmental health risks: a case study of bathing water quality.* CSERGE working paper GEC 96-14. CSERGE University of East Anglia, Norwich and University College London.

Goss-Custard, J D, 1995. *Effect of habitat loss and habitat change on estuarine shorebird populations.* Coastal zone topics: process, ecology and management, 1, pp61-67.

Goudie, A S, 1990. *The landforms of England and Wales.* Blackwell, Oxford.

Goudie, A S and Brunsden D, 1994. *The environment of the British Isles: an atlas.* Clarendon Press, Oxford, 184pp.

Graff, J, 1981. *An investigation of the frequency distributions of annual sea level maxima at ports around Great Britain.* Estuarine, Coastal and Shelf Science, 12, pp389-449.

Gray, M J, 1995. *The coastal fisheries of England and Wales. Part III: a review of their status 1992-1994.* Fisheries Technical Report No.100. MAFF Directorate of Fisheries Research, Lowestoft, 99pp.

Gubbay, S, 1988. *A coastal directory for marine nature conservation.* Marine Nature Conservation Society, Ross-on-Wye, 319pp.

Hall, A J, Law, R J, Wells, D E, Harwood, J, Ross, H M, Kennedy, S, Allchin, C R, Campbell, L A and Pomeroy, P P, 1992. *Organochlorine levels in common seals (Phoca vitulina) which were victims and survivors of the 1988 phocine distemper epizootic.* The Science of the Total Environment, 115, pp145-162.

Hall, K, 1997. *Economic costs of beach cleaning to local authorities.* Proceedings of one day conference Coastal and Riverine Litter, Developing Effective Solutions, 2 December 1997. Available from Earll, R. Coastal Management for Sustainability, Candle Cottage, Kempley, Gloucestershire.

Hammond, 1992. *Marine mammals.* In: Duncan, KA, Kazanowska, S and Laffoley, D (Editors), Marine Nature conservation in England - challenges and prospects. Proceedings of a seminar held by English Nature and the Marine Forum, April 1992. JNCC, Peterborough, 55pp. ISBN 1-85716-078-9.

Hampson, P, 1997. *Tourism and images - issues faced by local authorities.* Proceedings of a one-day conference Coastal and Riverine Litter, Developing Effective Solutions, 2 December 1997. Available from Earll, R. Coastal Management for Sustainability, Candle Cottage, Kempley, Gloucestershire.

Head, P C and Jones, P D, 1991. *The Mersey Estuary: turning the tide of pollution.* In Proceedings of an international conference on environmental pollution, Lisbon.

Hobbs, G and Morgan, C I, 1992. *A review of the current state of environmental knowledge of the Milford Haven waterway.* Field Studies Council Research Centre report FSC/RC/5/92 to the Milford Haven Waterway Environmental Monitoring Steering Group. Field Studies Council, Angle, Pembroke.

House of Commons Agriculture Committee, 1998. *Flood and coastal defence.* Sixth report HC707-I (1997-98). The Stationery Office, London, 154pp.

House of Commons Committee of Public Accounts, 1992. *Coastal defences in England.* Thirteenth report. HMSO, London, 34pp. ISBN 0-10-208593-5.

House of Commons Environment Committee, 1992. *Coastal zone protection and planning.* Second report, Vol 1. HMSO, London, 54pp. ISBN 0-10-290492-8.

House of Commons Environment Committee, 1995. *The environmental impact of leisure activities.* Fourth report, Vol 1. HMSO, London.

Howard, A E, 1996. *Shellfish production.* England and Wales. MAFF, Weymouth.

Howarth, W, 1992. *Wisdom's law of watercourses.* Fifth edition. Shaw and Sons Limited, Crayford, 550pp. ISBN 0-7219-0083-6.

Hulme, M and Barrow, E, 1997. *Climates of the British Isles: present, past and future.* Routledge, London, 454pp.

Hulme, M and Jenkins, G J, 1998. *Climate change scenarios for the UK: scientific report.* UKCIP Technical report No. 1, Climatic Research Unit, Norwich. 80pp.

Hydraulics Research Wallingford, 1997. *Estuaries: the case for research into morphology and processes.* Report SR 478. Prepared for MAFF, Environment Agency, EPSRC, NERC and English Nature.

Institute of Petroleum, 1997. *Oil and gas.* Institute of Petroleum, London, 12pp.

International Council for the Exploration of the Sea (ICES), 1992. *Ecosystem effects of fishing activities.* ICES Advisory Committee on Marine Pollution report to Oslo Paris Conventions for the Protection of Marine Pollution, ICES, North Sea Task Force, Bergen, 3 to 6 November 1992. ICES, London, 24pp.

International Council for the Exploration of the Sea (ICES), 1996. *Report of the ICES Advisory Committee on Fishery Management, 1995.* ICES Co-operative Research Report No.214, Part 2, 355pp.

International Council for the Exploration of the Sea (ICES), 1997. *Report of the ICES Advisory Committee on Fishery Management 1997 Parts 1 and 2.* ICES Co-operative Research report.

International Tanker Owners Pollution Federation Limited, 1998. World Wide Web site visited on 19 June 1998 at http://www.itopf.com/stats.html.

Institute of Freshwater Ecology, 1994. *Harmonised monitoring data for England and Wales: a statistical appraisal.* Prepared for the National Rivers Authority. Unpublished.

Institute of Freshwater Ecology, 1995. *Annual Report, 1994 -95.* IFE.

Institute of Terrestrial Ecology (ITE), 1995. *Atlas of amphibians and reptiles in Britain.* ITE research publication No. 10. HMSO, London, 39pp. ISBN 0-11-701824-4.

Jelliman, C, Hawkes, P and Brampton, A, 1991. *Wave climate change and its impact on UK coastal managment.* Report SR 260. HR Wallingford, Wallingford.

Jensen, A C and Collins, K J, 1995. *The Poole Bay artificial reef project 1989 to 1994.* Biologia Marina Mediterranea, 2, pp111-122.

Kaiser, M J, Hill, A S, Ramsay, K, Spencer, B E, Brand, A R, Veale, L O, Prudden, K, Rees, E I S, Munday, B W, Ball, B and Hawkins, S J, 1996. *Benthic disturbance by fishing gear in the Irish Sea: a comparison of beam trawling and scallop dredging.* Aquatic Conservation: Marine and Freshwater Ecosystems, 6, pp269-285.

Kershaw, P J, Pentreath, R J, Woodhead, D S and Hunt, G J, 1992. *A review of radioactivity in the Irish Sea: a report prepared for the Marine Pollution Monitoring Management Group.* Aquat Env Monit Rep, MAFF Direct Fish Res, Lowestoft (32). 65pp.

Langston, W J, Bryan, G W and Burt, G R, 1994a. *Heavy metals in UK estuaries: Plymouth Marine Laboratory data and mapping programme.* National Rivers Authority and NERC, Plymouth Marine Laboratory. National Rivers Authority, Project A06(91)10, R&D Note 280.

Langston, W J, Bryan, G W, Burt, G R and Pope, N D, 1994b. *Effects of sediment metals on estuarine benthic organisms.* National Rivers Authority and NERC, Plymouth Marine Laboratory. National Rivers Authority, Project 105, R&D Note 203.

Law, R J, Dawes, V J, Woodhead, R J and Matthiessen, P, 1997. *Polycyclic aromatic hydrocarbons (PAH) in seawater around England and Wales.* Marine Pollution Bulletin, 34 (5), pp306-322.

Law, R J and Klungsøyr, J, in press. *The analysis of polycyclic aromatic hydrocarbons in marine samples.* International Journal of Environment and Pollution.

Law, R J and Whinnett, J A, 1992. *Polycyclic aromatic hydrocarbons in muscle tissue of harbour porpoises (Phocoena phocoena) from UK waters.* Marine Pollution Bulletin, 24, No. 11, pp550-553.

Lee, E M, 1998. *The implications of future shoreline management on protected habitats in England and Wales.* Environment Agency R&D Technical Report W150, prepared by the Department of Coastal Management, University of Newcastle. 48pp.

Lewis, J, 1997. *Nuisance microalgae in tidal waters.* Report of the Toxic Algae Task Group, Environment Agency, Peterborough, 133pp.

Lindley, J A, George, C L, Evans, S V and Donkin, P, 1998. *Viability of calanoid copepod eggs from intertidal sediments: a comparison of three estuaries.* Marine Ecology Progress Series, Vol. 162, pp183-190.

Littlewood, I G, Watts, C D, Green, S, Marsh, T J and Leeks, G J L, 1997. *Aggregated river mass loads for Harmonised Monitoring Scheme catchments grouped by PARCOM coastal zones around Great Britain.* A Report to the Department of the Environment (EPG 1/8/26) by the Institute of Hydrology, Wallingford.

Lloyd, C S, Tasker, M L and Partridge, K, 1991. *The status of seabirds in Britain and Ireland.* Poyser, London.

Lloyd's Register, 1995. *Marine exhaust emissions research programme.* Lloyd's Register Engineering Services, London, pp63.

Lye, C M, Frid, C L J and McCormick, D, 1997. *Abnormalities in the reproductive health of flounder platichthys flesus exposed to effluent from a sewage treatment works.* Marine Pollution Bulletin, 34, pp34-41.

Mann, R H K and Welton, S, 1995. *Eel stock assessment in the UK.* Institute of Freshwater Ecology report, project no. T11063AL to MAFF, 67pp.

Marine Conservation Society, 1997. *Beachwatch '97. Nationwide Beach-Clean and Survey Report.* Marine Conservation Society, Ross On Wye.

Marine Pollution Monitoring Management Group (MPMMG), 1998a. *Survey of the quality of UK coastal waters.* MPMMG, 80pp.

Marine Pollution Monitoring Management Group (MPMMG), 1998b. *The impacts of marine litter.* MPMMG draft report. Unpublished.

Matthiessen, P, Allen, Y T, Allchin, C R, Feist, S W, Kirby, M F, Law, R J, Scott, A P, Thain, J E and Thomas, K V, 1998. *Oestrogenic endocrine disruption in flounder (Platichthys flesus L.) from United Kingdom estuarine and marine waters.* The Centre for Environment, Fisheries and Aquiculture Science (CEFAS), Science Series Technical Report No. 107. CEFAS, Lowestoft, 48pp.

Mettam, C, 1979. *Faunal changes in the Severn Estuary over several decades.* Marine Pollution Bulletin 10.

Midlen, A, 1998. *What future for Europe's fisheries?* CoastNET, the Bulletin of Coastal Network, Vol 3(1), Europe, spring, pp16.

Ministry of Agriculture, Fisheries and Food (MAFF), 1992. *Evidence to House of Commons Committee of Public Accounts, thirteenth report on coastal defences in England.* HMSO, London.

Ministry of Agriculture Fisheries and Food (MAFF), 1993a. *Coastal defence and the environment- a guide to good practice.* PB1191. MAFF, London, 156pp.

Ministry of Agriculture Fisheries and Food (MAFF), 1993b. *Flood and coastal defence project appraisal guidance notes.* PB1214 MAFF, London, 63pp.

Ministry of Agriculture, Fisheries and Food (MAFF), 1994. *Coastal protection survey of England: summary survey report.* MAFF, London, 8pp.

Ministry of Agriculture, Fisheries and Food (MAFF), 1996. *UK sea fisheries statistics 1995.* HMSO, London, 198pp.

Ministry of Agriculture, Fisheries and Food (MAFF), 1997. *Controls over the deposit of materials at sea and approval of oil dispersants, guidance notes.* MAFF, London

Ministry of Agriculture, Fisheries and Food (MAFF), 1998. *The Government's Response to the Agriculture Select Committee on Flood and Coastal Defence.*

Ministry of Agriculture Fisheries and Food (MAFF) and Scottish Environmental Protection Agency (SEPA), 1998. *Radioactivity in food and the environment, 1997.* MAFF, London and SEPA, Stirling, 162pp. ISSN 1365-6414.

Ministry of Agriculture Fisheries and Food (MAFF) and the Welsh Office, 1993. *Strategy for flood and coastal defence in England and Wales.* MAFF and the Welsh Office, London, 38pp.

National Audit Office, 1992. *Coastal defences in England.* Report by the Comptroller and Auditor General. HMSO, London, 44pp. ISBN 0-10-200993-7.

Natural Environment Research Council (NERC), 1996. *Report of the Scientific Group on Decommissioning Offshore Structures.* NERC, Swindon.

National Radiological Protection Board (NRPB), 1993. *Board statement on the 1990 recommendations of the ICRP.* Doc NRPB 4, No. 1. The Stationery Office, London.

National Rivers Authority (NRA), 1992. *Sea defence survey.* NRA, Bristol, 7pp.

National Rivers Authority (NRA), 1993. *Discharges of waste under the EC titanium dioxide Directives.* Water Quality Series No.10. NRA, Bristol, pp70.

National Rivers Authority (NRA), 1995. *The Mersey Estuary: a report on environmental quality.* HMSO, London, 44pp.

National Rivers Authority (NRA), 1996. *The national coastal baseline survey 1993, 1994 and 1995.* Unpublished.

National Trust, 1998. Personal communication. Phone call to Richard Offen, who provided details on lengths of coastline protected and cost of coast protection, 5 October 1998.

NOP Social and Political, 1997. *Environment expenditure.* Prepared for the Environment Agency. Jn 46510. Environment Agency, Bristol, 7pp.

North Atlantic Salmon Conservation Organisation (NASCO), 1998. *Report of the ICES committee on fishery management.* Council Paper CNL (98)12. NASCO, Edinburgh, 37pp.

North Sea Task Force, 1993. *North Sea quality status report 1993.* Oslo and Paris Commissions, London, 132pp.

Northridge, S, 1988. *Marine mammals and fisheries: a study of the conflicts with fishing gear in British waters.* Report to Wildlife Link's Seals Group by International Institute for Environment and Development and Marine Resources Assessment Group of Centre for Environmental Technology, Imperial College of Science and Technology, London, 140pp.

Northridge, S P, Tasker, M L, Webb, A and Williams, J M, 1995. *Distribution and relative abundance of harbour porpoises (Phocoena phocoena L.), white-beaked dolphins (Lagenorhynchus albirostris Gray), and minke whales (Balaenoptera acutorostrata Lacepède) around the British Isles.* ICES Journal of Marine Science 52, pp55-56.

Nunny, R S and Chillingworth, P C H, 1986. *Marine dredging for sand and gravel.* Minerals Planning Research Project No. PECD 7/1/163-99/84. HMSO, London.

Office for National Statistics, 1997. *Social trends.* The Stationery Office, London, 248pp. ISBN 0-11-620838-4.

Office of Water Services (OFWAT), 1994. *Future charges for water and sewerage services: the outcome of the periodic review.* OFWAT, Brimingham, 59pp. ISBN 1-874234-11-6.

Office of Water Services (OFWAT), 1995. *1994-95 report on the financial performance and capital investment of the water companies in England and Wales.* OFWAT, Brimingham, 56pp. ISBN 1-874234-18-3.

Office of Water Services (OFWAT), 1996. *1995-96 report on levels of service for the water industry in England and Wales.* OFWAT, Birmingham, 48pp. ISBN 1-874234-26-4.

Office of Water Services (OFWAT), 1998a. *Setting the quality framework - an analysis of the main quality costings submission 2000-05.* An open letter to the Secretary of State for the Environment, Transport and the Regions and the Secretary of State for Wales. OFWAT, Birmingham, 64pp. ISBN 1-874234-38-8.

Office of Water Services (OFWAT), 1998b. *Collation of water companies July Returns, Table 38.*

Office of Water Services (OFWAT), 1998c. *Representing water customers: the 1997-98 annual report of the OFWAT National Customer Council and the ten regional customer service committees.* OFWAT, Birmingham, 108pp. ISBN 1-87423-440-X.

Organisation for Economic Cooperation and Development (OECD), 1982. *Eutrophication of waters: monitoring, assessment and control.* Report prepared by Vollenweider & Kerekes. OECD, Paris.

O'Riordan, T and Ward, R, 1997. *Building trust in shoreline management: creating participatory consultation in shoreline management plans.* Land Use Policy, Vol. 14, No. 4, pp257-276.

Oslo Commission, 1992. *Dumping and incineration at sea.* Oslo and Paris Commission. London.

Oslo and Paris Commissions (OSPAR), 1997. *Point and diffuse sources.* Report on discharges from refineries (1981to 1993). Report on discharges, waste handling and air emissions from offshore installations for 1984-1995. OSPARCOM, London, pp3-43.

Oslo and Paris Commissions (OSPAR), 1998a. *OSPAR strategy to combat eutrophication.* OSPAR Summary Record 98/14/1, Annex 36. Reference number: 1998-18.

Oslo and Paris Commission (OSPAR), 1998b. *Final statement of the 1998 ministerial meeting of the OSPAR Commission (Sintra Statement).* OSPAR Commission. Point 98/2/Info.1-E. 6pp.

Penning-Rowsell, E C, Green, C H, Thompson, P M, Coker, A M, Tunstall, S M, Richards, C and Parker, D J, 1992. *The economics of coastal management: a manual of benefit assessment techniques.* Belhaven Press, London, 380pp. ISBN 1-85293-161-2.

Pentreath, R J, 1988. *Radionuclides in the aquatic environment.* In: Carter, M W, (Editor), Radionuclides in the food chain. Springer-Verlag, Berlin, pp99-119.

Pentreath, R J, 1994. *Persistent chemicals: controlling their input to marine waters.* Ocean Challenge 1994; 5:26-34.

Pentreath, R J, in press. *Estimating the quantities of persistent chemicals entering coastal waters of England and Wales from land-based sources.* Submitted to Science of the Total Environment. Elsevier Science.

Pethick, J, 1984. *An introduction to coastal geomorphology.* Edward Arnold, London.

Pethick, J, 1993. *Holderness, the Humber and the North Sea.* Paper presented to the KIMO Conference, Hull.

Pickett, G D, Eaton, D R, Cunningham, S, Dunn, M R, Potten, S D and Whitmarsh, D, 1995. *An appraisal of the UK bass fishery and its management.* Laboratory leaflet number 75. MAFF Directorate of Fisheries Research, Lowestoft, 47pp.

Pienkowski, M W, 1983. *Identification of the relative importance of sites by studies of movement and population turnover.* In: Evans, P R, Hafner, H and L'Hermite, P (Editors), Shorebirds and large water birds conservation. European Commission, Brussels.

Posford Duvivier Environment, 1991. *Mablethorpe to Skegness sea defences strategic appraisal study: amenity value of beach recharge option.* Prepared for the National Rivers Authority. Unpublished.

Potts, G W and Swaby, S E, 1993. *Review of the status of estuarine fishes.* Research report no.34. English Nature, Peterborough.

Proudfoot, R, Rogers V, Wilkinson, M, Foster-Smith, R S, Mercer, T, Walton, R and Wormald, C, 1998. *The Durham Coast: an approach to monitoring environmental improvements following the cessation of coal spoil dumping.* A report for the East Durham Task Force.

Pugh, D T and Skinner L M, 1996. *An analysis of marine-related activities in the UK economy and supporting science and technology.* Information Document No 5. Inter-Agency Committee on Marine Science and Technology (IACMST), Southampton.

Pye, K and French, P W, 1993a. *Targets for coastal habitat recreation.* English Nature Science No.13. English Nature, Peterborough, 85pp.

Pye, K and French, P W, 1993b. *Erosion and accretion processes on British saltmarshes.* Volume three, national survey of erosion and accretion status. Final report to MAFF, contract no. CSA 1976.

Report no. ES19B(3). Cambridge Environmental Research Consultants Ltd, Cambridge.

Readman, J W, Mantoura, R F C and Rhead, M M, 1987. *A record of polycyclic aromatic hydrocarbon (PAH) pollution obtained from accreting sediments of the Tamar Estuary, U.K. - evidence for non-equilibrium behaviour of PAH.* The Science of the Total Environment, 66, pp73-94.

Rees, G and Pond K, 1994. *Norwich Union Coastwatch UK survey report 1994.* Farnborough College of Technology, Farnborough.

Rehfisch, M.M. et al., 1997. *Predicting the effect of habitat change on waterfowl communities: a novel empirical approach.* In: Predicting habitat loss. ed. by J. Goss-Custard, R. Rufino & A. Luis, 116 - 126. The Stationery Office, London.

Rendel Geotechnics, 1993. *Coastal planning and management: a review.* Prepared for the Department of the Environment. HMSO, London, 178pp. ISBN 0-11-752817-X.

Rogers, S I and Millner, R S, 1996. *Factors affecting the annual abundance and regional distribution of English inshore demersal fish populations: 1973 to 1995.* ICES Journal of Marine Science 53, pp1094-1112.

Royal Commission on Environmental Pollution, 1981. *Oil pollution of the sea.* Eighth report. HMSO, London, 307pp.

Russell, I C, Ives, M J, Potter, E C E, Buckley, A A and Duckett, L, 1995. *Salmon and migratory trout statistics for England and Wales, 1951-1990.* Fisheries Research Data Report 38, 252pp.

Sea Empress Environmental Evaluation Committee, 1998. *The environmental impact of the Sea Empress oil spill.* Final report of the Sea Empress Environmental Evaluation Committee. The Stationery Office, London, 135pp.

Seaby, R M H and Henderson, P A, 1998. *Fish and crustacean captures at Hinkley Point B nuclear power station, January 1996 to March 1998.* PISCES Conservation Ltd, Lymington.

Sir Alister Hardy Foundation for Ocean Science (SAHFOS), 1995. *Annual Report 1995.* SAFOS, Plymouth, 45pp.

Sneddon, P and Randall R E, 1993. *Coastal vegetated shingle structures of GB: main report.* JNCC, Peterborough.

Social and Community Planning Research (SCPR), 1997. *UK day visits survey.* Summary of the 1996 survey findings. SCPR, London.

Solomon, D J, 1992. *Diversion and entrapment of fish at water intakes and outfalls.* National Rivers Authority, R&D Report 1, Contract 307, July 1992, pp51. ISBN 1-873160-29-1.

Spence, S K, Bryan, G W, Gibbs, P E, Masters, D, Morgan, L and Hawkins, S C, 1990. *Effects of TBT contamination on Nucella populations.* Functional Ecology 4, pp425-439.

Sports Council, 1991. *A digest of sports statistics for the UK.* 3rd Ed. Sports Council. ISBN 1- 872158-25-0.

Stanners, D and Bourdeau, P, (Editors), 1995. *Europe's Environment. The Dobris Assessment.* European Environment Agency, Copenhagen, 676pp. ISBN 92-826-5409-5.

Tasker, M L and Becker, P H, 1992. *Influences of human activities on seabird populations in the North Sea.* Netherlands Journal of Aquatic Ecology, 26(1), pp59-73.

Thompson, K R, Brindley, E and Heubeck, M, 1997. *Seabird numbers and breeding success in Britain and Ireland, 1996.* UK Nature Conservation No. 21, JNCC, RSPB, Shetland Oil Terminal Environmental Advisory Group, JNCC, Peterborough 1997.

Thompson, R and Hoare, K, 1997. *Microscopic plastics in beach sediments.* Proceedings of one-day conference Coastal and Riverine Litter, Developing Effective Solutions, 2 December 1997. Available from Earll, R. Coastal Management for Sustainability, Candle Cottage, Kempley, Gloucestershire.

Tittley, I, 1998. *Littoral and sublittoral chalk reefs.* Draft Biodiversity Action Plan. Unpublished.

Toft, A R, Pethick, J S, Burd, F, Gray, A J, Doody, J P and Penning-Rowsell, E, 1995. *A guide to the understanding and management of saltmarshes.* NRA R&D Note 324, Foundation for Water Research, Marlow, 213pp.

Townend, I, 1997. *Industry: an overview of some of the port issues.* Paper presented at the IEEP workshop on the implementation of the Habitats Directive, Morecambe, UK, June 1997, pp9.

Turner, R K, Adger, N and Doktor, P, 1995. *Assessing the economic costs of sea level rise.* Environment and Planning Vol. 27, pp1777-1796.

Turner, R K, Lorenzoni, I and Beaumont, N, 1997. *Coastal management and environmental economics: analysing environmental and socio-economic changes on the British coast.* Presented at the Royal Geographical Society Conference, Enhancing coastal resilience: planning for an uncertain future, October 1997, London.

Turner, R K, Lorenzoni, I, Beaumont, N, Bateman, I J, Langford, I H, and McDonald, A L, 1998. *Coastal management for sustainable development: analysing environmental and socio-economic changes on the UK coast.* The Geographical Journal, Vol. 164, No. 3, 269-281.

Turner, R K, Adger, W N, Crooks, S, Lorenzoni, I and Ledoux, L, in press. *Sustainable coastal resources management: principles and practice.* Sustainable Coastal Resources Management, Natural Resources Forum.

UK Biodiversity Steering Group, 1995a. *Biodiversity: the UK steering group report.* Volume two: action plans. HMSO, London, 324pp. ISBN 0-11-753228-2.

UK Biodiversity Steering Group, 1995b. *Biodiversity: the UK steering group report.* Volume one: meeting the Rio challenge. HMSO, London, 103pp. ISBN 0-11-753218-5.

UK Biodiversity Group, 1998. *UK biodiversity group: tranche two action plans.* Volume one: vertebrates and vascular plants. English Nature, Peterborough, 267pp. ISBN 1-85716-406-7.

UK Centre for Economic and Environmental Development, 1993. *Environmental impacts of the British marine industry.* November 1993. UKCEED, Cambridge. 311pp.

United Nations Environment Programme (UNEP), 1994. *The impacts of climate on fisheries.* No 13 in the UNEP Environment Library. UNEP, Nairobi 1994. Words and Publications, Oxford, England.

University of Wales, Cardiff, 1997. *Coastal management in Wales: looking to the future.* Prepared for the Countryside Council for Wales. University of Wales, Cardiff, 65pp.

US Commission on Marine Science, Engineering and Resources, 1969. *Our nation and sea.* United States Government printing office, Washington DC.

Vas, P, 1995. *The status and conservation of sharks in Britain.* Aquatic Conservation of Marine and Freshwater Ecosystems 5, pp67-79.

Wade, R J, 1996. *Flow requirements to estuaries.* Water Environment '96, pp223-235.

Warner, A J and Hays, G C, 1994. *Sampling by the continuous plankton recorder survey.* Progress in Oceanography 34, pp237-256.

Water Services Association, 1996. *Waterfacts '96.* Water Services Association, London, pp74. ISBN 0-947886-39-7.

Whitehouse, J W, Khalanski, M, Saroglia M G and Jenner, H A, 1985. *The control of biofouling in marine and estuarine power stations: a collaborative research working group for use by station designers and station managers.* Central Electricity Generating Board, Leatherhead.

Widdows, J, Donlin, P, Brinsley, M D, Evans, S V, Salkeld, P N, Franklin, A, Law, R J and Waldock, M J, 1995. *Scope for growth and contaminant levels in North Sea mussels Mytilus edulis.* Marine Ecology Progress Series, 127, pp131-148.

Woodworth, P L, Tsimplis, M N, and Flather, R A, in press. *A review of the trends observed in British Isles mean sea level data measured by tide gauges.*

Worrall, F and McIntyre, P, 1998. *The Wansbeck Barrage scheme: twenty-one years of environmental impact.* The Journal of the Chartered Institution of Water and Environmental Management, 12, No. 2, pp144-149. ISSN 0951-7359.

WRc, 1998. *Environmental problems from antifouling agents: survey of manufacturers, chandlers (suppliers) and treatment sites.* Prepared for the Environment Agency. R&D Technical Report P215. Environment Agency, Bristol, 58pp.

Glossary

Algae	Simple microscopic (sometimes larger) plants.
Algal bloom	Rapid growth of algae (see above) which when excessive can cause problems to water users and other life.
Ammonia	A substance found in water often as the result of pollution by sewage or livestock effluent. Ammonia affects fish and abstractions for potable water supply.
Anthropogenic	Made or produced by humans.
Attenuation	The process of reduction of intensity or force.
Barrage	An artificial barrier across a river, estuary or bay.
Benthic	Associated with the bed of a waterbody.
Best Available Techniques Not Entailing Excessive Cost (BATNEEC)	The level of pollution control required for sites regulated under the Environmental Protection Act 1990. Includes the technology and management of the site to prevent the release of prescribed substances, or to reduce the release to a minimum and to render harmless any other substances that might cause harm if released.
Best practicable environmental option (BPEO)	The BPEO procedure establishes, for a given set of objectives, the integrated pollution control option that provides the most benefit or least damage to the environment as a whole, at acceptable cost, in the long, as well as the short term.
Billion	One thousand million.
Bioaccumulation	The build-up of toxic substances in living organisms at concentrations often many times those of the surrounding environment.
Bioassay	The assessment of the strength and effect of a substance by testing it on a living organism.
Bioavailability	How available a substance is to living organisms. For example, some potentially toxic substances occur in the environment, but not in forms which can be used readily by animals and plants. These are not bioavailable.
Biochemical oxygen demand (BOD)	The quantity of dissolved oxygen in water (mg/l) consumed under test conditions during a given period (five days) through the microbiological oxidation of biodegradable organic. One of the standard tests used to characterise effluent quality in the presence of allyl thiourea.
Biodiversity	The number of different plant and animal species, including variants within each species, in an ecosystem. The variety of life.
CASI	Compact Airborne Spectrographic Imager system for making colour images of the land and sea surface.
Catchment (of a river)	Area drained by a river or river system.
Cetaceans	Mammals which spend their lives at sea and have a fish-like form, including whales and dolphins.
Chlorophyll	A plant pigment, of which chlorophyll-a is a common measure. Used as a measure of abundance of planktonic algae.
Coastal cell	A stretch of coastline in which the sediment amount is more or less stable and self-contained. The cell is employed in the management of coastline in much the same way as the drainage basin is used in river management.

Coastal defence	The term given to both sea defences and coastal protection works, and sometimes to structures which serve both purposes.
Coastal protection	Works that are to prevent the erosion of land and encroachment by the sea and are predominantly the responsibility of local authorities.
Coastal squeeze	Occurs when sea level rises along a shore protected by a hard barrier such as a sea defence or rocky cliff constraining the shore from moving inland.
Combined sewer overflow (CSO)	Most sewers receive sewage and rainfall runoff from roads and other surfaces. After heavy rainfall, the flows may exceed the capacity of the sewers or the sewage treatment works. CSOs allow the dilute and excess flow to discharge to a receiving water.
Consent	A statutory document issued by the Agency which defines the legal limits and conditions on the discharge of an effluent to a watercourse.
Contamination	The presence of substances not normally present in the environment or at a higher concentration than normal that do not apparently cause ill effects.
Controlled water	Controlled waters include all rivers, canals, streams, brooks, drainage ditches, lakes, reservoirs, estuaries, coastal waters and groundwater to which British pollution control legislation applies. Small ponds and reservoirs which do not themselves feed other rivers or watercourses are not included within the definition of a controlled water unless the Secretary of State defines them as such - which he has done in the case of water supply reservoirs in the Controlled Waters (Lakes and Ponds) Order 1989.
Crustaceans	Group of animals which includes crabs, shrimps and barnacles.
Dangerous Substances	Substances defined by the European Commission as in need of special control because they are toxic, accumulate in plants or animals and are persistent (Dangerous Substances Directive, 76/464/EEC).
Defence element	Most coastal defences are made up of several 'elements', for example, a foreshore with an earth embankment, or groynes in front of a sea wall, and so a length of coastline 100km long may be defended by more than 100km of defence elements.
Diffuse source	A source of pollution which is not an identifiable point discharge but includes field or urban runoff, atmospheric emissions or numerous poorly defined discharges.
Direct Toxicity Assessment (DTA)	A method for testing the quality of effluent or water using the response of standard test organisms which will show the overall toxicity of a mixture of chemicals.
Directive	Legislation issued by the European Community which requires a member state to implement its requirements, for example to achieve specified environmental standards.
Dissolved oxygen (DO)	Oxygen dissolved in a liquid, the solubility depending on temperature, partial pressure and salinity, expressed in milligrams per litre or percentage saturation.
'drins	The family of organochlorine pesticides which includes endrin, aldrin, isodrin and dieldrin.
E.coli (Escherichia coli)	A bacterium used as an indicator of sewage contamination.
Ecosystem	All life and non-living matter within a defined space, such as a river or a lake, and their interactions.
Effluent	Water discharged from a site which may be contaminated, for example with sewage or waste substances from industrial processes.
Endocrine disruption	Any disruption of the normal functioning of the endocrine (hormonal) system by either artificial or naturally occurring chemicals, thereby affecting those physiological processes which are under hormonal control.

Environmental Quality Standard (EQS)	The concentration for example, of a substance in the environment which should not be exceeded in order to protect natural or human uses.
Estuary	A partially enclosed area, open to saline waters from the sea and receiving fresh water from rivers, land runoff or seepage.
Eustatic	Change in sea level due to long-term fluctuations in ocean circulation or ocean volume. These fluctuations can be brought about by warming or cooling of the oceans, or by the addition or subtraction of water previously locked up in other forms, for example ice.
Eutrophic sensitive area	Area designated under the Urban Waste Water Treatment Directive (91/271/EEC) as affected by or at risk from the adverse effects of nutrient enrichment.
Eutrophication	The enrichment of water by nutrients, especially compounds of nitrogen and/or phosphorus, causing an accelerated growth of algae and higher forms of plant life to produce disturbance to the balance of organisms present in the water and to the quality of the water concerned.
Exceedance	The failure of an environmental standard, for example where the rate of deposition of a pollutant is above the critical load or the concentration is above the critical level.
Groundwater	Water occurring in permeable underground strata, for example chalk and sandstone.
Harmonised Monitoring Scheme (HMS)	The DETR programme for monitoring river quality, based on chemical sampling mostly at the tidal limit of rivers or the downstream end of major tributaries.
Heavy metals	A general term for those metals which are toxic when present in elevated concentrations. These include elements such as zinc, copper, lead, nickel, cadmium and mercury, all of which are commonly used by industry.
High load estimates	The calculation of the load whereby concentrations measured below the limit of detection are assumed to be the level of detection itself.
Imposex	The acquisition by the female of male characteristics, which in some animals has prevented reproduction.
Integrated Pollution Control (IPC)	Applied by the Agency under the Environmental Protection Act 1990 to control the most complex and polluting industrial processes. It integrates the control of emissions to air, land and water to seek the best overall option.
Intertidal zone	The area which is covered at high tide and uncovered at low tide.
Invertebrates	Animals without backbones. They include, for example, insects, crustaceans, worms and molluscs living on the river bed.
Isostatic readjustment	The process by which the land rebounds following the removal of the ice sheets that weighed down parts of the earth's crust during the last ice age.
LIDAR	Light Detection and Range system for making digital terrain maps with fine resolution. LIDAR is deployed in light aircraft.
List I	Substances selected under the Dangerous Substances Directive (76/464/EC) mainly on the basis of their toxicity, persistence and bio-accumulation.
List II	Substances selected under the Dangerous Substances Directive (76/464/EC) which have a deleterious effect on the aquatic environment depending on the characteristics and location of the water into which they are discharged.
Load	The quantity or mass of any substance transported in a river or effluent per unit time (the product of concentration of pollutant multiplied by flow)

Local Environment Agency Plan (LEAP)	The process by which the Agency plans to meet all the environmental issues in a catchment. A consultation plan is published followed by an action plan which is reviewed at-five year intervals.
Long sea outfall	Long pipes, built in some locations to move discharges further from the shore into deeper water to gain better initial dilution, or into stronger currents which would disperse effluents more effectively.
Low load estimates	The calculation of the load whereby concentrations measured below the limit of detection are assumed to be zero.
Macroinvertebrate	An invertebrate animal of sufficient size to be retained in a net with a specified mesh size, usually about one millimetre.
Managed realignment/retreat	Defences are breached and the intertidal zone is allowed to move landward to some pre-determined set back line.
National Water Council	A council which sat between 1974 and 1983, and was established when the water industry was nationalised, as a central co-ordinating, consultative and advisory body, having the principal duties of advising Ministers on national policy for water and promoting and assisting the efficient performance of the functions of the water authorities.
Mean	An average value. In precise terms the arithmetic mean.
Median	The middle number of a set of numbers arranged in size order.
Microalgal	Marine plants (algae), of microscopic size which drift with the surrounding water. Number and species composition vary with the season, being more abundant during the warmer months. Where there are a large number an algal bloom is said to occur. Requires the presence of nutrients, solar radiation and elevated temperatures for rapid growth.
Microbiological	Pertaining to microscopic or ultramicroscopic organisms as bacteria, viruses and fungi.
Molluscs	A varied group of unsegmented animals which classically may include some or all of the characteristics of a broad locomotory foot, a protective shell, a tongue-like feeding organ and a special respiratory gill, for example mussels, oysters and whelks.
National Monitoring Programme	A programme initiated to co-ordinate marine monitoring in the UK with a view to establishing a clear overall picture of the spatial distribution of contaminants and their biological effect, upon which decisions as to future monitoring requirements would be based.
Net catches	The number of fish caught by licensed fishermen using nets.
Nitrate Sensitive Area (NSA)	Area designated by the Ministry of Agriculture, Fisheries and Food, with advice from the Environment Agency, where agricultural activities are controlled to reduce nitrate contamination of groundwaters.
Nitrate Vulnerable Zone (NVZ)	Area designated under the EC Nitrate Directive (91/676/EEC) where restrictions on the application and timing of nitrogen fertiliser and organic manures are in place to protect waters vulnerable to nitrate pollution.
Non-compliance	Failure to meet the standards set out in the relevant legislation.
North Sea Conference	Forum in which states surrounding the North Sea established agreements to cut the discharge of certain pollutants to the sea via rivers.
Nutrient	A substance such as nitrogen or phosphorus which provides nourishment to organisms.
Oestrogen(ic)	Oestrogen is the name for a class of hormones produced in ovaries which are important in regulating the reproductive system of female animals. 'Oestrogenic' is the adjective used to describe any chemical compound which mimics oestrogen.

Organic pollution	Substances which consume dissolved oxygen in rivers as they are degraded by bacteria, including sewage, farm and food wastes.
Organochlorines	Organochlorine insecticides are formed by the chlorination of hydrocarbons. They include DDT, aldrin, dieldrin, endrin, chlordane, lindane and hexachlorobenzene.
Oslo and Paris Commissions (OSPAR)	The Oslo Commission was established by the Convention for the Prevention of Marine Pollution by Dumping from Ships and Aircraft. The Convention entered into force in 1974 and has been ratified by 13 European States. The Convention for the Prevention of Marine Pollution from Land-Based Sources (the Paris Convention) entered into force in 1978.
PARCOM	Paris Commission. Contracting parties to the Paris Convention are obliged to report each year to the Secretariat of the Oslo and Paris Commissions data from the previous year.
Pesticide	A chemical used to control biological pests - includes insecticides, herbicides and fungicides.
pH	A measure of acidity based on a logarithmic scale of concentrations of hydrogen ions. Neutral is pH 7, acidic is below pH 7, alkaline is above pH 7; pH 6 is 10 times as acidic as pH 7, and pH 5 is 100 times as acidic as pH 7.
Phytoplankton	The microscopic plants drifting at any depth in the sea or fresh water.
Plankton	Plankton is the collective name for drifting microscopic organisms at any depth in the sea or fresh water.
Point source	A source of pollution which is a discrete identifiable discharge, such as a sewage outfall or industrial discharge.
Pollution	The introduction by man, directly or indirectly, of a substance or energy into the environment resulting in such deleterious effects as hazards to human health, harm to living resources and to ecosystems, damage to amenities or interference with other legitimate uses of the environment.
Pollution incident	Pollution caused by accidents or illegal practices.
Polychlorinated biphenyls (PCBs)	The commercial production of the group of chemicals called PCBs began in 1930. They have been widely used in electrical equipment and as fire-resistant liquids, but they are now banned.
Polycyclic aromatic hydrocarbons (PAHs)	Semi-volatile organic compounds are produced when a material containing hydrogen and carbon is burned incompletely, such as in domestic fires, during refuse burning or in car engines, and some occur naturally. PAHs are among the most significant of these organic compounds because many of them are known to be carcinogenic.
Primary treatment	The physical treatment of sewage effluent, usually settlement, to remove gross solids and reduce suspended solids by about 50 per cent and BOD by about 20 per cent.
Ria	Narrow inlet of the sea formed by partial submergence of an unglaciated river valley.
Riverine inputs	The substances carried by a river collected from the catchment, of natural and human origin, which are deposited in the estuary or sea, such as naturally eroded material or polluting chemicals.
Salmonid	Fish of the family Salmonidae, notably salmon, brown trout and sea trout.
Saltmarsh	Marsh land liable to be flooded periodically with salt water.
Scope for growth	A measure of the energy available to an animal to grow which may be reduced when the animal is stressed. Used as an indicator of pollution.
Sea defence	Defences to protect low-lying areas against sea flooding. These are usually the responsibility of the Agency

Secondary treatment	Biological treatment and secondary settlement of sewage effluent, normally following primary treatment, capable of producing a substantial reduction in BOD and suspended solids.
Sewage treatment works (STW)	A term for the structures, plant and equipment used for collecting and treating sewage, which may have some sewage sludge drying.
Sewerage	System or provision of sewers.
Site of Special Scientific Interest (SSSI)	Site designated by English Nature or the Countryside Council for Wales under the Wildlife and Countryside Act 1981 for its importance to nature conservation.
Special Area for Conservation (SAC)	Site notified under the Habitats Directive (92/43/EEC) for its conservation value.
Special Protection Area (SPA)	Site designated under the Conservation of Wild Birds Directive (79/409/EEC).
Storm sewer overflow	See combined sewer overflow (above). Storm sewers may contain only runoff or also sewage, as in a combined sewer overflow.
Suspended sediment/solids	Particles floating in water, measured as milligrams per litre.
Sustainable development	Development that meets the needs of the present without jeopardising the ability of future generations to meet their own needs.
Taxa, Taxon	Taxa is the plural of taxon, which is the species, family or other group to which an organism belongs.
Tertiary treatment	Any treatment following secondary treatment which produces a high sewage effluent quality by means of, for instance, grass plots, microstrainers, nutrient removal or ultra-violet treatment.
Tidal defence	Defences which protect low-lying areas against tidal flooding such as rivers to the tidal limit and estuaries, usually the responsibility of the Agency.
Turbidity	The opacity of a liquid to light (its cloudiness) due to particles in suspension. May be used as a measure of suspended solids.
Vascular plants	Plants which have vessels for transporting fluids around the plant.
Waders	A bird that wades in search of food, for example the snipe or sandpiper.
Zooplankton	The animals, mostly microscopic, drifting at any depth in the sea or fresh water.

Common and Latin names for main plant and animal species

Common name	Latin name
Allis shad	Alosa alosa
American oyster drill	Urosalpix cinerea
American jack knife clam	Ensis americanus
American hard-shelled clam	Mercenaria mercenaria
Atlantic lejeunea liverwort	Lejeunea mandonii
Bass	Dicentrarchus labrax
Black-backed meadow ant	Formica pratensis
Bladderwrack	Fucus vesiculosus
Blue shark	Prionace glauca
Bright wave moth	Idaea ochrata
Chinese mitten crab	Eriocheir sinensis
Common cord grass	Spartina anglica
Common mussel	Mytilus edulis
Cushion starfish	Asterina phylactica
Dog whelk	Nucella lapillus
Dublin Bay prawn	Nephrops norvegicus
Dunlin	Calidris alpina
Eyebrights	Euphrasia spp
Fen orchid	Liparis loeselii
Green algae	Enteromorpha
Harbour porpoise	Phocoena phocoena
Ivell's sea anemone	Edwardsia ivelli
Japanese weed	Sargassum muticum
King ragworm	Nereis virens
Knot	Calidris canutus
Lampreys	Lampetra fluviatilis, Petromyzon marinus
Leathery sea squirt	Styela clava
Lundy cabbage	Coincya wrightii
Marram grass	Ammophila arenaria
Natterjack toad	Bufo calamita
Pacific oyster	Crassostrea gigas
Peppery furrow shell clam	Scrobicularia plana
Petalwort	Petalophyllum ralfsii
Ragworm	Nereis diversicolor
Sand lizard	Lacerta agilis
Sandbowl snail	Catinella arenaria
Sea grass	Zostera
Shore dock	Rumex rupestris
Slipper limpet	Crepidula fornicata
Smooth snake	Coronella austriaca
Soft-shelled clam	Mya arenaria
Starlet sea anemone	Nematostella vectensis
Swim bladder parasite of eels	Anguillicola crassus
Twaite shad	Alosa fallax

199

Index